Models of Proposal Planning & Writing

Models of
Proposal Planning & Writing

Jeremy T. Miner and Lynn E. Miner

Westport, Connecticut
London

Library of Congress Cataloging-in-Publication Data

Miner, Jeremy T.
    Models of proposal planning and writing / Jeremy T. Miner and Lynn E. Miner
        p. cm.
    Includes bibliographical references and index.
    ISBN 0–275–98696–9 (alk. paper)
    1. Proposal writing for grants—United States.   2. Proposal writing
for grants—United States—Case studies.   I. Miner, Lynn E.   II. Title.
    HG177.5.U6M558 2005
    658.15'244—dc22   2004028101

British Library Cataloguing in Publication Data is available.

Library of Congress Catalog Card Number: 2004028101
ISBN: 0–275–98696–9

First published in 2005

Praeger Publishers, 88 Post Road West, Westport, CT 06881
An imprint of Greenwood Publishing Group, Inc.
www.praeger.com

Printed in the United States of America

The paper used in this book complies with the
Permanent Paper Standard issued by the National
                            ·ion (Z39.48–1984).

Contents

Preface

"Do you have any sample proposals that you'd be willing to share?" is a common request that we have received over the past fifteen years from individuals from all across the country who have participated in our grantwriting workshops. Successful grantseekers know that examining copies of funded proposals is an effective way to begin preparing to write their own proposals.

Inevitably, though, these individuals with whom we have shared sample proposals contact us again later and ask two questions: "How did you know what to write?" and "Why did you write it like that?" In reality, these grantseekers are asking us to put the proposals in context; they want to understand better the processes that led to the final products.

Many grants manuals, including our own *Proposal Planning & Writing* (Greenwood Press), employ a "how-to" or "systems approach" to developing grant proposals. These books tell you *what* to write and *how* to write it. They frequently provide examples from successfully funded proposals. In a few cases, brief summary analyses of the proposals are also included. More often, however, the sample proposals stand on their own as self-explanatory.

While these sample proposals are useful, they leave gaps. Namely, they neglect to explain *why* specific proposal elements are persuasive to a sponsor. As a result, you must figure out independently what made the proposals successful and then determine how to incorporate similar elements into your own grant proposals. In other words, these proposals are samples, not models.

Models of Proposal Planning & Writing attempts to bridge this gap. The purpose of this book is to walk you step by step, from beginning to end, through an integrated process of planning and writing persuasive proposals. You will see the questions that we asked of ourselves and those asked of sponsors *before* we developed a complete grant application. You will read the actual proposals we submitted to private and public sponsors, including paragraph-by-paragraph analyses of the key features that made them persuasive. You will examine the verbatim reviewer comments and award letters we received back from the sponsors. As a whole, these annotated models serve as a springboard from which you can begin to develop your own fundable proposals.

It is fairly easy to secure copies of federally funded proposals—they are public information. Some federal program officers are willing to share them with you directly. You can also obtain copies under the Freedom of Information Act. On the other hand, it is more difficult to secure samples of funded proposals from private foundations. There are two main reasons why: (1) foundations consider proposals they receive to be the proprietary intellectual property of individual applicants, and (2) foundations are not required by law to share them. When you are able to obtain samples of private and public proposals, they seldom include an explanation of the thought processes behind proposal development or an explanation of why they were funded.

The models included in this book provide a solid framework for planning and practical strategies for writing that grantseekers can use to improve the quality—and persuasiveness—of their proposals. This means going beyond explaining the *what* and *how* of a grant project to describing the *why* of the project, using the available means of logical and psychological persuasion.

TARGET AUDIENCES

The people who have attended our grantwriting workshops[1] and who are currently using the ideas presented in this book represent a wide variety of professions and disciplines. Seven major categories stand out.

- *Education*: Day care programs, adult education, public and private schools, special education departments, colleges and universities, English as foreign language programs.
- *Social Services*: Sociolegal, mental health, community development, and rehabilitation agencies.
- *Health Care*: Physicians' offices, hospitals and health systems, nursing homes, public health organizations, Veterans Administration.
- *Religions*: Churches, synagogues, mosques, and other houses of worship; their administration offices, schools, and development offices.
- *Philanthropy*: Foundations, charitable organizations, service clubs.
- *Government*: Local, state, and federal agencies, courts, human services agencies, law enforcement agencies.
- *Economic Development*: City planning, land use, urban revitalization, workforce development, and job creation offices.

Other groups include the fine and performing arts, senior citizens' advocates and agencies, and special interest groups. Because grantseekers are such a diverse group, you must present your ideas clearly to the public and private sponsors that fund worthy recipients. Health care systems, institutions of higher education, and agencies that are involved with the development and submission of numerous grant proposals will find the information in this book useful for strengthening the capacity of their faculty, staff, administrators, and collaborators to secure extramural funding for programs that fulfill their organizational missions.

STRUCTURE AND CONTENT

In this book you will find three model proposals: two sponsored by private foundations and one sponsored by a federal agency. By topic, the proposals represent a community health project, an oral health education project, and a curriculum development project in special education. By applicant, the proposals represent a community-based coalition affiliated with a pediatric hospital, the dental school of a graduate research university, and a private liberal arts college. By type, the proposals represent a planning grant, a demonstration grant, and a special project grant.

Models of Proposal Planning & Writing illustrates, in intimate detail previously unpublished, grants processes *and* products. The first three chapters in the book present a framework for developing persuasive proposals. This includes introducing the "Persuasion Intersection" and identifying the "Roads to the Persuasion Intersection," describing the "RFP Analysis Process," and outlining the "Complete Grant Application." The remaining chapters contain three actual grant applications that were funded along with paragraph-by-paragraph interpretations of:

- Request for Proposal (RFP) guidelines
- Cover letters
- Application forms
- Project summaries
- Letters of intent
- Full proposals
- Budgets and budget narratives
- Reviewer comments
- Grant award notifications

Whether you are a novice, intermediate, or experienced grantseeker, these models are ones that you can follow for planning and writing persuasive proposals of your own.

ACKNOWLEDGMENTS

Nobel Laureate Toni Morrison once proposed, "If there's a book you really want to read, but it hasn't been written yet, then you must write it." And so we did. The RFP guidelines, proposals, and reviewer comments presented in this book are real—so much so, in fact, that we did not correct ex post facto any errors in grammar, spelling, or punctuation. In some cases, the sponsors made minor mistakes; in other instances, we did. We preserved these mistakes in their original forms to demonstrate to you that proposals do not need to be perfect in order to attract funding. Persuasion is the key to successful grantseeking.

Models of Proposal Planning & Writing would not have been possible without the talented and dedicated individuals who were responsible for imple-

---

1. Visit the Miner and Associates, Inc. Web site for a list of grants workshops, workshop calendar dates, grantwriting tips, and clients— http://www.MinerAndAssociates.com

menting the projects described in this book. For their roles in controlling pediatric asthma, we wish to thank Dr. John R. Meurer, associate professor of pediatrics (community care), Medical College of Wisconsin, and Fight Asthma Milwaukee Allies coalition director, Children's Hospital and Health System; Dr. Kevin J. Kelly, professor of pediatrics (allergy/immunology), Medical College of Wisconsin, and medical director of the asthma-allergy program, Children's Hospital of Wisconsin; and Dr. Ramesh C. Sachdeva, associate professor of pediatrics (critical care), Medical College of Wisconsin, and vice president of quality and outcomes, Children's Hospital of Wisconsin. To learn more about current coalition activities visit their FAM Allies Web site at http://www.famallies.org.

We gratefully acknowledge Dr. Anthony Iacopino, professor and associate dean for research and graduate studies, Marquette University School of Dentistry, and Dr. Joseph Best, adjunct assistant professor (clinical), Marquette University School of Dentistry, for their efforts to help shape a national agenda for dental education reform. Additional information about their program efforts, products, and resources is available online at http://www.dental.mu.edu/fipse/fipse.htm.

We recognize Barbara Natelle, administrator, Syble Hopp School, for her insights on enhancing special education pedagogy and commitment to improving the quality of life for children with disabilities, and Scott Menzel, assistive technology lab supervisor, St. Norbert College, for being an exemplar to the community and a constant source of inspiration and hope. For a detailed description of St. Norbert College's graduate and certification programs in adaptive education, visit http://www.snc.edu/adaped.

And finally, for her wisdom, guidance, encouragement, and support for the development of a new companion text to our original grants manual, *Proposal Planning & Writing*, we also extend sincere thanks to Susan Slesinger, executive editor of education, Praeger Publishers, a division of Greenwood Press. Search their online database of grants, education, and reference publications at http://www.greenwood.com.

THE INFAMOUS BOTTOM LINE

Successful grantseekers are often individuals who are so dedicated to their ideas that they will find the means to carry them out with or without extramural support. Sponsors have clear objectives and expectations that they hope to realize by providing financial support to such dedicated persons. A persuasively written grant proposal is the link between them. This book provides detailed models to help you forge that link.

Now let's begin planning your best grant ever!

CHAPTER 1
Introduction to Persuasive Proposal Writing

In today's competitive grants environment, "good" proposals seldom get funded; "excellent" proposals get funded. Excellent proposals *persuade* sponsors to open up their checkbooks to invest in your project. To increase the competitiveness of your grant applications and chances for funding success, this book models a systematic process for identifying and incorporating persuasion throughout your proposals.

Inevitably, sponsors (grantmakers) receive more proposals than they can possibly fund. In a stack of applications, grant reviewers quickly discern between proposals that are responsive to Request for Proposal (RFP) guidelines and those that are not; nonresponsive proposals are rejected immediately. Good proposals provide information to demonstrate that they comply with every requirement in the RFP. Excellent proposals, however, stand out from the competition because they go beyond merely complying with the requirements of the RFP to satisfying the needs of the sponsor. Proposals are persuasive when they connect your project ideas to the values of the sponsor. Connecting with the values of the sponsor means that your proposal must present the right balance of logic, emotion, and relationships.

The Persuasion Intersection

As a grantseeker, your job is to secure extramural funding for projects that are important to your organization. However, sponsors rarely award grant funding just because you support a specific cause or work for a specific organization. You must persuade them to invest in your projects and organization. Providing information about your project is a necessary but not sufficient condition to win grant funding; do not expect sponsors to immediately understand the value of your project. Information is not persuasion. Persuasion is the key to funding success. Persuasion occurs at the intersection of sponsor values, applicant credibility, proposal logics, and proposal psychologics. As illustrated in Figure 1 and defined below, these four elements make up the Persuasion Intersection.

Sponsor Values. Sponsors have a particular view of the world. They are vitally concerned about specific problems, injustices, or inequities. They are so concerned, in fact, that they are willing to commit their own money to address these problems. In essence, they see a gap between a current situation and an improved situation, between "what is" and "what ought to be." Their mission is to close this gap. The gap represents sponsor values—how they view problems of interest to them.

For instance, one private foundation concerned about preventing child abuse describes its values:

> The Prevent Abuse Foundation is committed to ensuring a safe environment for children through support of primary prevention activities throughout the state, advocating support for children and families, as well as educating professionals and communities about the role of prevention in eliminating child abuse. Over the last 20 years, the Prevent Abuse Foundation has become a vital resource to communities across the state by supporting a variety of family support strategies, including parent education, home visitation, family resource centers and public awareness campaigns. The Prevent Abuse Foundation also provides grass roots, community-based groups with technical and professional assistance, sharing the best program practices and evaluation techniques.

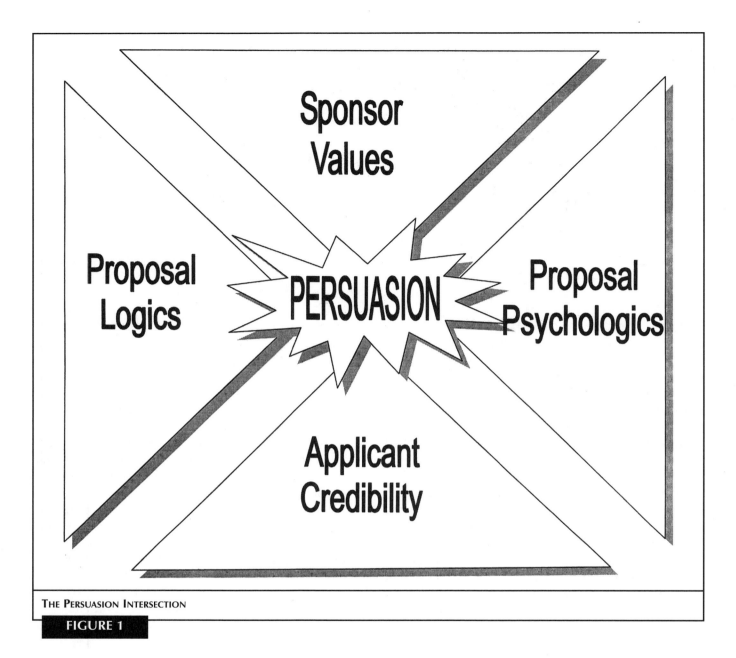

FIGURE 1

Applicant Credibility. As the applicant, your job is to establish three types of credibility: organizational, individual, and project. You have a creditable organization proposing a creditable idea to be directed by a creditable project director. Enhance your credibility by establishing your uniqueness. Differentiate yourself from your potential competition. What makes your organization stand out from others? What can your project director do better than anyone else? What makes your project innovative? Uniqueness is a strength when it relates to your exceptional ability to conduct the proposed project.

The following example illustrates how a university biology department seeking funding for genetics research describes itself:

The biology department at Major State University is uniquely suited to conduct this crucial genetics research. Stemming from the department's solid past of 30 years of doctoral studies in biological science, its faculty includes Drs. Kwasny, Lee, and Dilworth. This distinguished academic core cumulatively represents 117 years of productive research experience at our university. With a special focus on the molecular basis of oncogenesis, our current research uses unique systems to analyze the genetic and hormonal factors responsible for gene regulation. While these systems are not widely studied in established programs of cell biology, they are most suitable for answering the cutting-edge questions of gene expression and regulation—and our department is endowed with the intellectual talent to succeed.

Proposal Logics. Proposal logics include the systematic development of proposal components to show the relationship between an identified gap, an improved situation, and resulting benefits to the target population. Problems represent gaps between what exists today and what could exist tomorrow. Objectives are the specific, measurable activities that will help solve the problem. Benefits represent the good things that will occur by achieving the objectives. These elements must reflect an intimate relationship between the proposed project and the values of the sponsor.

As an illustration, the RFP guidelines from one private foundation that supports medical, cultural, civic, and educational programs benefiting youth under the age of eighteen indicate:

> Please provide a concise description of the need or problem to be addressed. Include the overall goals and purpose of your organization or specific department concerned, the specific purpose of the funds, and how your objectives will be accomplished. Include a project timeline. Please summarize your target population in measurable terms. Indicate how your organization will evaluate the program.

Proposal Psychologics. Sponsors fund projects for psychological as well as for logical reasons. Proposal psychologics respond to the emotional needs of the sponsor. Successful proposals go beyond addressing the minimum performance standards outlined in the application materials; they also display intangible elements: trust, energy, passion, ownership, and commitment. Sponsors' emotions store the lessons of experience. They do not want to take a lot of risks with their money. Sponsors view grants as investments in an improved future. Thus, before they award funding, they need to feel comfortable with you, to trust that you understand their concerns and share their values.

In a proposal to a federal agency, a private college describes its lengthy history of success collaborating with community partners, directing national programs that serve the targeted minority population, and institutionalizing project activities:

> For more than a decade project partners have collaborated on a variety of grant-related initiatives, including a six-year joint teacher education program between the College of Native Americans and Midwestern Regional College. The project director has led several successful national intervention projects for Native American middle school students, including Kids Math Camp, Achievement in Math, and Math and Science Immersion. Each one of these projects has been sustained beyond the conclusion of its granting period through the generosity of individual philanthropy and in-kind contributions from partner institutions.

Successful proposal writers understand the relationship between sponsor values and their own organizational capabilities and between proposal logics and proposal psychologics. Proposals are more persuasive when they reflect the priorities of the sponsor. Novice proposal writers often focus on their own need for funds instead of matching their project's goals with the sponsor's priorities. Proposals are funded when they express the values shared by the sponsor. Projects are rejected when they do not precisely reflect the priorities of the sponsor.

In the following three pairs of examples, contrast how proposals with self-oriented needs were recast to reflect sponsor-oriented values.

Self-Oriented Needs	Sponsor-Oriented Values
The Family Welfare Agency requests a grant of $25,000 to meet its operating expenses.	The Family Welfare Agency invites your investment of $25,000 to sustain the delivery of crucial services to victims of violence and abuse.
Top Flite High School invites you to share in a $100,000 project to buy new computers.	Top Flite High School invites your participation in a $100,000 project to reduce student achievement gaps in science and mathematics.
La Casa de Esperanza requests your support of $50,000 to hire a case manager.	La Casa de Esperanza invites you to share in a $50,000 project to improve the quality of life for Hispanics with chronic health conditions.

In all three examples, the message is clear and simple: Sponsors usually give money to organizations that help other people; sponsors seldom give money to organizations that help only themselves. You should select a sponsor that shares your view of the world and tailor proposals to them.

Roads to the Persuasion Intersection

Persuasion is an interaction of elements. Proposal logics or proposal psychologics alone are not sufficient to persuade a sponsor to fund a project. The sponsor must also be involved, have a vested interest in your project and its outcomes. The Roads to the Persuasion Intersection bring together objective and subjective writing approaches to fine-tune your proposal so that it more closely matches sponsor values. As illustrated in Figure 2, this means navigating among Request for Proposal (RFP) guidelines, evaluation criteria, hot buttons and distinctive features, and strategic thinking and preproposal contacts. Traveling these four roads will deepen your understanding of the values of sponsors and will help you persuade them that you can satisfy their needs.

RFP Guidelines. A Request for Proposal (RFP) is an invitation by a sponsor to submit a grant application. RFP guidelines spell out the details you need to develop a proposal. They generally provide an overview of what the funding announcement is all about, the background or problem that led to this invitation, priority funding areas, sample methodological approaches, timelines, deadlines, evaluation criteria, funds available, and acceptable uses of grant funds. RFP guidelines also supply you with a first look at how sponsors view the world: magnitudes and key dimensions of problems they wish to solve.

Some sponsors, however, do not issue specific RFP guidelines; rather, they may have broad guidelines that they use in all circumstances. Other sponsors, most notably small foundations, may not have any guidelines at all. In these cases, follow the generic structure described in Chapter 3 under "Developing the Proposal." Chapter 4 examines an RFP from a private, special purpose foundation that uses a three-stage application process. Chapter 5 dissects the application guidelines issued by a federal agency that uses a two-stage application process. And finally, Chapter 6 interprets the broad instructions provided by a private, family foundation that uses a single-stage application process.

Evaluation Criteria. Sponsors' evaluation criteria describe technical aspects of the application process and proposal review procedures. RFP evaluation criteria help you understand the logical components that must go into the proposal. These components are the sponsors' minimum performance standards, the yardstick against which your proposal is being measured. Proposals that do not meet these minimum expectations will be rejected. To develop a proposal that meets sponsor expectations, however, you also need to know who is reviewing the proposals and the conditions under which they are being reviewed. You will write differently for general audiences who skim read compared to technical audiences who critical read proposals.

Strategic Thinking and Preproposal Contact. Strategic thinking forces you to understand your strengths and weaknesses in relation to the values of the sponsor. Your credibility and uniqueness—organizational, individual, and project—are strengths only to the extent that they fulfill sponsor needs. Contrary to popular belief, sponsors do not give money away. They contract with organizations offering services and programs that are consistent with their needs and interests. Sponsors award funds to make a difference in the lives of people. Strategic thinking demonstrates to sponsors that a good match exists between their priorities and your capabilities. Preproposal contact is a process for gathering supplemental information about sponsors, their values and priorities. Making contact with program officers, past grantees, and past grant reviewers can help fine-tune your proposal so that it mirrors the sponsor's concern for specific problems, injustices, and inequities.

Hot Buttons and Distinctive Features. Hot buttons and distinctive features help you establish a level of trust and understanding with the sponsor. Hot buttons represent the logical and psychological concerns of the sponsor that have an impact on how the project will be conducted. These primary concerns affect the shape of a project's structure and implementation processes. Hot buttons are emphasized repeatedly in the RFP and preproposal contact and gain force through their repetition. However, hot buttons are not always stated as evaluation criteria; watch for recurring themes such as accountability, collaboration, communication, cost-effectiveness, outcomes, participation, replication, sustainability, and technical training.

Sponsors may also have secondary concerns that influence the design of certain aspects of the project. Because secondary concerns do not appear repeatedly, they are not hot buttons; rather, they are distinctive features. Distinctive features appear as singular instances identified in the RFP and preproposal contact.

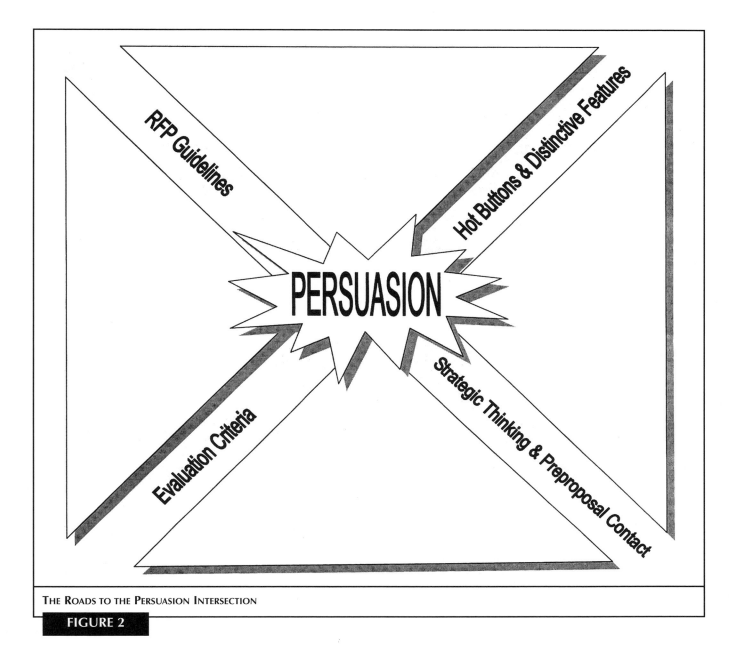

THE ROADS TO THE PERSUASION INTERSECTION

FIGURE 2

They often reflect activities in which you are already engaged, yet the sponsor wants explicit assurance that you will continue to do them, e.g., comply with federal regulations, standardize treatment following national guidelines, be able to recruit and retain quality personnel. Other times, distinctive features are sponsor-imposed activities necessary to meet the terms of the grant, e.g., submit timely progress reports, participate in annual national project meetings, utilize resources provided by the sponsor. Failing to acknowledge distinctive features in your proposal may be viewed by the sponsor as a project weakness. In contrast, addressing hot buttons and distinctive features will make your proposal stand out from the competition.

Sponsors receive numerous requests for a limited pool of funding dollars. During the review process they discern among proposals by looking for weaknesses—faults in logic, facts, approaches, or conclusions. But even when the logic is sound, proposals may be rejected because they fail to establish a "connection" with the sponsor. On the other hand, persuasive proposals present a seamless argument that stands the test of reason, addresses psychological concerns, and connects project ideas to the values of the sponsor. In the next chapter we describe a systematic process for moving down the Roads to the Persuasion Intersection.

CHAPTER 2
Analyzing Request for Proposals

Analyzing Request for Proposal (RFP) guidelines means asking a lot of questions: questions to determine if this program is a good match for your organization and how much work will need to go into developing a competitive application. To effectively analyze an RFP, read it in multiple passes with increasing scrutiny. The three-step RFP Analysis Process described below will help your organization answer questions about relevance, feasibility, and probability:

- Step One: **R**elevance—Do we want to do this?
- Step Two: **F**easibility—Can we do this?
- Step Three: **P**robability—Will we be competitive?

In incremental fashion, this RFP Analysis Process moves you along the Roads to the Persuasion Intersection. Step One navigates through the RFP Guidelines. Step Two proceeds along the paths of Evaluation Criteria and Hot Buttons and Distinctive Features. Step Three examines Strategic Thinking and Preproposal Contact. Together, these steps provide you with the details necessary to develop a persuasive proposal.

Step One: Relevance—Do We Want to Do This?

RFP Guidelines. At this most basic level, read the RFP guidelines and develop a short list of bulleted points that summarizes the main ideas. The purpose of this list is twofold: (1) to help you understand exactly what this program is all about, and (2) to quickly assess its relevance, determining whether or not it is a good match for your organization—answering the question, "Do we want to do this?"

This bulleted list of key points can also form the basis of an internal memorandum designed to secure organizational support from key personnel for developing an application. Design the one-page memorandum to inform potential project partners, supervisors, and other administrators that you are interested in pursuing the funding opportunity. The memorandum, which can be skimmed in thirty seconds or less, may take on the following structure:

[Sponsor's] [program] is designed to [program purpose]. An overview of some of the key points:

- [estimated number of awards]
- [eligibility criteria]
- [funding levels]
- [project timeframes]
- [identified project objectives]
- [specific target population]
- [any known "break points" for your organization, e.g., ability to provide mandatory matching dollars, to meet the percent effort required for project directors, or to sustain activities beyond the granting period]
- [key dates—for letters of intent, full proposals, conference calls, submitting written questions]

For more information about the program, visit this Web address: [http://www.sponsor.org/guidelines]. Let's meet this week [day, date, and time] to discuss further the possibility of developing an application.

Step Two: Feasibility—Can We Do This?

Evaluation Criteria. Assuming that the RFP appears initially to be a good match for your organization and that you intend to develop a proposal, examine the RFP for technical aspects of the application procedure and for stated evaluation criteria. This analysis will begin to answer the question of feasibility—"Can we do this?"—and give you an indication of how much effort will be necessary to develop a proposal. Ask yourself the following types of questions:

- Is a letter of intent required *prior* to the full proposal?
- What specific information should be included in the narrative?
- Can supplemental information be included in an appendix?
- Are letters of support and commitment encouraged?
- Are there budget restrictions on the use of grant funds?
- How many copies of the narrative and budget should be submitted?
- Are there page limitations, type size, and line spacing recommendations for the narrative?
- Does the sponsor have any specific application forms that must be completed and submitted?

Hot Buttons and Distinctive Features. In addition, read between the lines of the RFP for hot buttons and distinctive features that must be addressed. Hot buttons represent the logical and psychological concerns of the sponsor, repeated throughout the RFP, that have an impact on how the project will be conducted. These concerns generally influence the shape of a project's structure and implementation processes. Hot buttons may be stated as evaluation criteria, but often times they are not. Look for recurring themes in the RFP such as *accountability, collaboration, communication, cost-effectiveness, outcomes, participation, replication, sustainability,* and *technical training.* Distinctive features are secondary concerns raised by the sponsor that influence the design of the project but are not repeated throughout the RFP. In short, competitive proposals do more than speak to the minimum performance standards in the stated evaluation criteria; they address sponsors' subjective and objective needs.

Step Three: Probability—Will We Be Competitive?

To develop a highly competitive proposal, this third level of analysis will force you to examine your individual and organizational strengths and weaknesses in relation to the values of the sponsor. As you begin to prepare a proposal, strategic thinking and preproposal contact attempt to answer the question, "Will we be competitive?" or more bluntly, "Is it *really* worth my time and effort to develop an application?" While there are no ironclad guarantees of funding, strategic thinking and preproposal contact will improve your probabilities for success.

Strategic Thinking. Strategic thinking means systematically and objectively assessing internal and external structures, processes, and characteristics associated with the delivery and receipt of project services.

- Evaluate your individual and organizational credibility and uniqueness—are you the *first, only, newest, oldest, largest,* or *best* at what you do?
- Identify areas of improvement—do your competitors have more effective infrastructures, systems and procedures, personnel, or environments?
- Prioritize issues and resources—what are the key problems, obstacles, and constraints that need to be addressed to successfully implement this project?
- Compare alternative possibilities—how else could project goals be achieved? Strategic thinking allows you to build on strengths, minimize weaknesses, and connect with sponsor values.

Although RFP guidelines are intended to answer your questions, they may actually generate more questions for you. You may find yourself getting frustrated as you try to decipher and understand the RFP guidelines. As described in more detail below, three types of challenges include interpreting ambiguities, inconsistencies and discrepancies, and omissions.

Ambiguities

Ambiguities in RFP guidelines are often caused by careless word choices. Terms may be inadequately defined, intentionally vague, or have multiple interpretations. For example, you may ask the sponsor:

- Which aspects of "quality of life" do you consider to be the most important?
- How do you define "community," e.g., by zip codes, census tracts, geographic or ethnic boundaries?
- What do you consider to be a "significant" impact on the target population? How much change has to occur to be "significant"?
- What is your capital threshold for classifying items as "equipment" or "supplies"?
- Is there a *preferred* level of in-kind contributions?

Inconsistencies and Discrepancies

Inconsistencies and discrepancies occur due to hurried final editing and proofreading: Multiple individuals responsible for developing the RFP may use different terminology to describe the same concept; last-minute changes to one section may not be carried throughout the RFP. For instance, you may question:

- The term "project coordinator" is used only once in the RFP whereas the term "project manager" is used throughout. Is the project coordinator the same as the project manager? Or are these two different individuals?
- Why does the Program Description describe the target population as "children under age 18" whereas Appendix B of the RFP says "children ages 5–18"?
- The RFP indicates that grantees must participate in an annual conference in Washington, D.C., yet it also specifies that "grant funds may not be used for travel expenses." Are grantees expected to cover these costs with internal dollars or will other sponsor funds be made available to fund airfare, hotel accommodations, ground transportation, and meals?
- Section Four of the RFP asks for a description of project methods and Section Five requests a detailed workplan. What's the difference between the project methods and workplan?
- Why does the section on goals and objectives describe four project outcomes whereas the section on evaluation identifies five key outcomes?

Omissions

Omissions occur both unintentionally and intentionally. The RFP may intentionally remain silent on some program aspects to avoid inhibiting the creativity of applicants in addressing the problem. On the other hand, sponsors may unintentionally omit information because they did not consider the full implications of their own guidelines. Or, under the crunch of a deadline for releasing the RFP, sponsors may not have all of the final program details worked out. As an illustration, does the RFP answer the following questions:

- Does the sponsor require principal investigators to be U.S. citizens, or are permanent residents equally eligible to apply?
- Who owns data once it is collected—the applicant or the sponsor?
- Are indirect costs allowed as a budget item? At what level?
- Does the due date mean that proposals must be postmarked and mailed by July 19 or received at the sponsor's office by July 19?

- Under what conditions will proposals be reviewed—mail, panel, or electronic reviews?

In addition to questions raised by the RFP, you need to ask probing questions about the capacity of your organization to carry out the project, if awarded. What makes your organization unique? What is your special niche? What do you do better than others? Being good at what you do usually isn't good enough in the highly competitive world of grants; you have to be among the best. Establishing your uniqueness enhances your credibility, both for your organization and for your project. Answering the following types of questions will convey to sponsors that you are capable of doing the things that you say you will do and justifies why they should fund you.

- What data documents the extent of the problem in the community, especially compared to other known areas?
- How can we illustrate that we have ready access to the target population?
- Is our proposed solution to the problem realistic and cost-effective?
- Why did we select this methodology over other possible methodologies?
- Do we have the individual expertise and organizational capability to implement a quality action plan?
- Are adequate infrastructure, systems and procedures, and resources in place to effectively carry out the project?
- Which current programs demonstrate our experience with projects of this size and budget?
- Do we have the organizational and fiscal capabilities to manage and report on the award?
- How will we evaluate the project's impact in the community?
- What will be the specific benefits of this program to the target population?

This iterative analysis process systematically guides you through the types of questions that you will need to address to develop a highly competitive proposal.

Preproposal Contact. To increase your chances of getting funded, engage in preproposal contacts. Preproposal contact can help fine-tune your proposal so that it more closely matches the sponsor's priorities, thereby helping you gain a competitive funding edge. Experienced grantseekers triangulate preproposal contact information from three sources:

1. Call past grant winners to learn their secrets of success.

2. Call past grant reviewers to learn about proposal evaluation policies and procedures.
3. Call program officers to validate information and seek further clarifications.

Beginning grantseekers often wonder, "Will these people really talk to me?" The answer is yes, even more so when you have something of value to offer in return. A remarkable level of collegiality exists among grantseekers. Grant winners are willing to talk freely about their experiences with a sponsor when they see potential for long-term networking, information exchanges, collaborative possibilities, and proposal swaps. Past grant reviewers gladly share their experiences when they know that the sponsor referred you to them. Most public program officers welcome preproposal contact. It saves them—and you—time. Private sponsors vary in their receptivity to preproposal contact, a point they usually make in their RFP guidelines.

The list of preproposal contact questions that you could pose is theoretically endless. Nevertheless, experienced grantseekers know that in order to write a successful proposal they must PREP first. PREP is an acronym by which to remember four basic types of questions to ask:

1. **P**osition: What are the baseline situations, present circumstances, and basic facts?
2. **R**ationale: What are the problems, needs, and injustices that exist today?
3. **E**xpectation: What are the implications for addressing these problems?
4. **P**riority: What approaches are most likely to lead to an improved situation now?

Collectively, PREP questions span a continuum of time, from past action to future intentions. Position questions explore baseline information and relationships with the sponsor and lay the foundation for more probing types of questions. Rationale questions go to the heart of sponsor giving, exploring motivations behind funding projects. Expectation questions identify the sponsor's outlook for changing the problem situa-

tion. Priority questions concentrate on identifying the top activities that will effectively and efficiently improve the conditions surrounding the identified problems, needs, and injustices that exist today. Beginning grantseekers often make the mistake of asking too many Position questions and too few Rationale, Expectation, and Priority questions.

At a minimum, use preproposal contacts to learn more about the proposal review process. Your goal is to understand the actual process followed when your proposal is reviewed. In particular, you will want to know:

• Who will be reviewing proposals?
• How will proposals be reviewed?
• Against what yardstick are proposals measured?

By learning about who will be reviewing proposals and their qualifications (e.g., reviewer ages, background, and formal education; sponsor criteria for selecting and training a specific number of reviewers), you can tailor the language of your proposal to meet their expertise. Knowing how proposals will be reviewed (e.g., type of review—mail, panel, and/or electronic; use of a specific reviewer's evaluation form; time allocated to each proposal) enables you to customize your writing style to meet their needs. Understanding the yardstick against which proposals are measured (e.g., scored independently against the guidelines; ranked against each other; prioritized within sponsor funding categories; ordered to special criteria such as geographic distribution of awards; first come, first funded) allows you to emphasize hot buttons and distinctive features, incorporate counters to your competition, and make timely proposal submissions.

For example, in the following hypothetical scenario, two reviewers each spend a total of fifteen hours reviewing a sample of twenty-page proposals. The first is serving as a reviewer for a federal program. The second is a reviewer for a private foundation. Because their review conditions are very different, proposal writers will need to utilize distinct writing strategies to accommodate critical reading, search reading, and skim reading styles.

	Federal Reviewer	Foundation Reviewer
Review Conditions	The sponsor received 500 proposals for projects designed to address the health of children with special needs. A mail review was utilized to solicit comments about five of the proposals from seven practicing physicians. Each physician spends a total of two hours reviewing each twenty-page proposal and one hour writing a ten-page analysis. Proposals are scored independently against the application guidelines with the help of a reviewer's evaluation form. Reviewers recommend funding levels to the sponsor for "approved" proposals but do not actually award or disperse grant dollars.	The sponsor received sixty proposals for projects designed to address the health of children with special needs. A panel review was utilized to solicit comments from seven parents of children with special needs about all sixty proposals. Three parents have bachelor's degrees, and four have high school diplomas. The panel spends a total of ten minutes reviewing each twenty-page proposal and five minutes discussing its merits before voting to approve or reject the proposal. The "approved" proposals are subsequently ranked against each other and awarded funding until all of the grant dollars are dispersed.
Writing Strategies	Proposal writers should organize their proposals following the structure of the reviewer's evaluation form. Use the same headings and subheadings so reviewers can quickly and easily locate your answers. Because reviewers are educated experts, include pertinent literature citations to demonstrate your familiarity with current research. Make effective use of transitional paragraphs to show logical connections between each section of the proposal; reviewers may use these interim summary statements verbatim in their written analysis of your proposal.	Proposal writers should organize their proposals to be highly skimable. Given ten minutes to read a twenty-page proposal, reviewers will spend approximately thirty seconds per page on your proposal. Begin the narrative with a one-sentence summary of the entire proposal. Write in short and simple sentences, no more than twenty words per sentence. Include boldface headings to identify major sections of the proposal. Use bulleted lists to highlight key points. Make judicious use of white space to visually break up long copy. Because reviewers are educated nonexperts, avoid professional jargon. Balance the logical presentation of statistics with the emotional significance of the numbers.

Preproposal contact has two main benefits. First, you can get additional information that will help sharpen the focus of your proposal so that it matches closely with the sponsor's priorities and application guidelines. Second, it gives you an opportunity to establish your credibility, which is particularly important if your organization is unknown to the sponsor.

By using the RFP Analysis Process we are able to answer questions about relevance, feasibility, and probability for funding success. In the next chapter we describe the steps for preparing a complete grant application.

CHAPTER 3

The Complete Grant Application

A complete grant application generally includes six basic components. The following table lists these components in the sequence in which proposal reviewers typically read them, as well as the sequence in which proposal writers usually write them; they are not the same.

Proposal Reviewer Sequence
• Cover Letter
• Application Forms
• Project Summary
• Proposal
• Budget and Budget Narrative
• Appendixes

Proposal Writer Sequence
• Proposal
• Budget and Budget Narrative
• Appendixes
• Project Summary
• Application Forms
• Cover Letter

The reviewer column shows the way in which most grant applications are assembled for submission; the writer column shows the progression followed when preparing a complete grant application. Each section is described below.

DEVELOPING THE PROPOSAL

Analyzing the Request for Proposal (RFP) guidelines was the first step in developing a proposal. Through this iterative analysis process, you quickly determined whether the program is a good match for your organization. And once you secured organizational support for pursuing the grant opportunity, you examined RFP evaluation criteria and identified hot buttons. Evaluation criteria and hot buttons dictate the form and structure of your proposal. Strategic thinking and pre-proposal contact supply additional information so that you can fill in the details of the proposal, fine-tuning it to closely match the sponsor's priorities. In their generic structure, proposals include six categories of information.

- *Problems.* Problems represent gaps between what exists today and what could exist tomorrow. This section of the proposal justifies *why* your project is needed.
- *Objectives.* Objectives are the specific, measurable activities that will help solve the problems. They describe *what* the project will do.
- *Methods.* Methods are the steps necessary to implement the objectives. The methodology section explains *how* the project will be conducted.
- *Qualifications.* Qualifications describes individual and organizational resources required to carry out the methods. This section identifies *who* will implement the project and their capabilities to do so.
- *Budgets.* Budgets identify the cost to fulfill the objectives with the identified methods and qualifications. Budgets explain *how much* the project will cost.

- *Benefits*. Benefits represent the good things that will occur by achieving the objectives. This section of the proposal describes the intended *outcomes* of the project.

As you develop the proposal, your job is to anticipate and answer the major questions that sponsors will be asking as they read your narrative. Your proposal must convince the sponsor, both logically and psychologically, that you can solve the identified problems and produce specific benefits. Addressing evaluation criteria and hot buttons enables you to communicate this message in one seamless argument.

Just as analyzing the RFP guidelines was an iterative process, so too is the process for developing the proposal. In fact, this iterative process works for letters of intent as well as full proposals. Some sponsors require a short letter of intent prior to proposal submission. Letters of intent are used on a competing and noncompeting basis. On a competitive basis, sponsors use letters of intent as a screening device before inviting a select number of applicants to submit full proposals. In this case, letters of intent represent a conceptual shell of your proposed project. On a noncompetitive basis, sponsors use letters of intent to get an estimate of how many proposals they will receive in which topic areas. These letters help sponsors to better prepare for the review process, e.g., allow enough time to identify a sufficient number of qualified reviewers.

As you develop your proposal, or letter of intent, do so in passes. The beginning admonition from experienced writers is this: "The first draft is for getting down, not for getting good." Rewriting is easier than original writing. On each pass, address a different feature.

1. *Content and Organization*. Does your proposal respond to evaluation criteria? Does it have enough substance? Are your ideas complete? Is your organization logical? Are hot buttons addressed repeatedly throughout the proposal?
2. *Clarity*. Have you expressed your ideas clearly? Are there smooth transitions between proposal sections? Are all acronyms defined?
3. *Mechanics*. Are words spelled correctly, especially proper names? Are all numbers and computations accurate? Are sentences grammatically correct? Are sentences punctuated properly?
4. *Design*. Is the proposal design visually appealing? Did you include ample white space? Are headings specific to your project?

Proposal Design

While you will obviously spend much time working on the content of your proposal, you should also pay attention to its appearance or design. A well-designed proposal makes even complex information look accessible and simplifies the reviewers' jobs. That is, a good proposal design highlights the proposal's structure, hierarchy, and order, helping reviewers find the information they need. Some RFP guidelines, more so at the public than private level, stipulate proposal design formats that you must use. If so, follow them! On the other hand, if the RFP does not specify formatting details, follow these practical tips, which are used by experienced proposal writers.

Charts and Tables. Include charts and tables in the narrative only if they are absolutely necessary to the central body of the proposal. Keep charts and tables simple; complicated displays disrupt the reader's fluency.

Headings. Headings act like a table of contents placed directly in your proposal text; at a glance, they reveal the organization of your proposal to the reader. Use headings specific to the RFP. Effective use of white space sets off headings and enhances readability.

Lists. Lists help get the message to the reader with a sense of immediacy, without being wordy. Lists help to visually break up long blocks of text. They are easy for reviewers to skim because they convey chunks of information quickly. Use numbered lists when items need to be examined in a specific sequence. Use bulleted lists, rather than writing in long prose, to summarize clearly a series of facts or conclusions.

Margins. A proposal with ragged right margins is easier to read than one that is fully justified, because the proportional spacing in justified type slows down readability. Unless guidelines indicate otherwise, use standard one-inch margins all around.

Page Numbers. Place page numbers in the top right or bottom center of the proposal. In addition, in the left-hand corner of the page include the name of the project director and applicant organization. In a stack of proposals, this added detail facilitates reassembly if proposal pages become separated.

Type Style. Unless RFP guidelines recommend a particular type style, consider using a serif typeface, like Times Roman, for the text of your proposal and a sans serif typeface, like Arial, for headings. This contrast in type styles makes headings stand off from the body of the text. For the proposal narrative use 12 point type size.

White Space. Use white space to break up long copy. Ample white space makes your proposal appear inviting and user-friendly. White space gives readers a visual clue to the structure of your proposal. In a page full of print, a block of unprinted lines, or white space, stands out immediately, often indicating that one section is ending and another is beginning. When text is single spaced, double space between minor paragraphs and triple space between major proposal sections. When text is double spaced, indent five spaces at the beginning of minor paragraphs and insert a full line of white space between major proposal sections.

DEVELOPING THE BUDGET AND BUDGET NARRATIVE

A project budget is more than a statement of proposed expenditures. It is an alternate way to express your project, establish its credibility, and communicate your project's value. Reviewers will scrutinize your budget to see how well it fits your proposed activities. Incomplete budgets are examples of sloppy preparation. Inflated budgets are signals of waste. Low budgets cast doubt on your planning ability. In essence, your budget is as much a credibility statement as your project narrative.

In addition to preparing a budget, you should develop a budget narrative. The budget narrative serves as a bridge between the proposal and the budget. It explains the basis of budget calculations and is meant to persuade reviewers that sufficient funds are requested to achieve project goals and objectives in a cost-effective manner. The budget narrative should include an explanation for every budget line item that describes: (1) the specific item, (2) the item's relevance to the project, and (3) the basis of cost calculations for the item. Reviewers are subject to eliminating or supporting only a percentage of line items that are not well justified.

Three broad categories of information that should go into your budget narrative include:

- *Personnel.* Personnel costs include items such as salaries, wages, consultant fees, and fringe benefits. Whether you are using internal staff or external consultants, describe their roles, responsibilities, and levels of effort as related to the project's objectives and activities. Indicate the rate and elements of your institution's fringe benefit package. For contractual agreements, identify key dates, dollars, and deliverables for services to be provided.

- *Nonpersonnel.* Nonpersonnel costs include such items as equipment, supplies, and travel. For equipment and supplies, describe how items will be used to fulfill project goals and how estimates for each item were determined. For any travel by internal staff and external consultants, outline who is traveling, the purpose, the destination, the duration, and rates for airfare, ground transportation, per diem, and lodging.

- *Indirect Costs.* Indirect costs are expenses that are necessary to conduct the grant but are not easily identified, e.g., utilities, space, library usage, payroll processing, and general project administration. Organizations regularly receiving government grants have an approved federal indirect cost rate that is included in the budget and budget narrative of federal proposals. Foundations vary considerably in their policies regarding indirect costs. Some allow indirect costs. Others allow only a fixed percentage. Some do not fund indirect costs. Check with your program officers to determine their stance.

Prepare a line item budget and budget narrative for each year of funding support requested. In addition, prepare a consolidated line item budget for the entire proposed granting period. If you are cost sharing a portion of the project budget, be sure to explain the amount and source of matching support. Include a budget narrative with your proposal immediately following your budget to explain or justify any unusual expenditure items, even if it is not specifically requested in the RFP guidelines.

DEVELOPING THE APPENDIXES

Proposal appendixes contain supportive secondary information that will further strengthen your proposal narrative. They can demonstrate that you have logically and systematically documented and addressed all of the essential elements that will contribute to project success. As a writer, you may need to include appendix items such as:

- Agency publications
- Annual reports
- Certifications
- Consortia agreements
- Definitions of terms
- IRS tax exemption determination
- Letters of support and commitment
- Lists of board officials

- Maps of service areas
- Organizational charts
- Organizational fiscal reports
- Organizational policies and procedures
- Past success stories
- Publicity material
- Reprints of articles
- Resumes
- Significant case histories
- Subcontractor data
- Tabular data
- Vendor quotes

Some sponsors do not circulate copies of appendixes when transmitting proposals to reviewers, a practice you should clarify with your program officer. As a consequence, essential proposal information should go in the narrative. Nevertheless, the use of appendixes is recommended, especially when sponsor page limits are constraining.

DEVELOPING THE PROJECT SUMMARY

The project summary, or abstract, serves as a condensed substitute for the entire proposal. It should be carefully written, providing a cogent synopsis of your proposed project. It should provide a quick overview of what you propose to do and a rapid understanding of the project's significance, generalizability, and potential contribution. Project end-products should also be clearly identified. Unless otherwise indicated, limit your summary to between 250 and 500 words. Addressing the project's main points in such a limited space is not easy. Project summaries require exceptional conciseness and clarity of expression.

To ensure consistency of presentation, write the project summary *after* you have completed the proposal. The project summary should adhere to the order of the proposal, maintaining the same overall style and tone. Use major section headings in the project summary and include at least one sentence each on problems, objectives, methods, and benefits (outcomes). Although brevity is of the utmost concern, write in complete sentences, include necessary transitional expressions, and spell out all acronyms.

Often, proposal reviewers must write up a summary of your project for presentation to a larger review panel. If you do a thorough job on your project summary, program officers may use it as a basis for their proposal review. A quality abstract simplifies the job of your reviewers. Poorly written summaries make reviewers' jobs more difficult and diminish your funding chances.

COMPLETING THE APPLICATION FORMS

Some sponsors require you to submit an application form along with your proposal. The elements and formats of application forms vary widely within and among public and private sponsors. Nevertheless, sponsor application forms often request a few precise details from five categories of information: You must describe your organization, project director, project, and budget and provide assurances that you will comply with the terms and conditions of grant awards.

At first blush, completing application forms may seem to be a relatively unimportant step in a bureaucratic paperwork process. The reality is that application forms establish and present your credibility in a condensed format. They reveal to sponsors both logical and psychological dimensions of your organization, key individuals, and the project. For instance, if you do not follow basic instructions when filling out an application form, the sponsor may wonder if you will also be as inattentive when implementing project activities and filing progress reports. Inaccuracies or inconsistencies in budget calculations may suggest to the sponsor that your project is apt to have significant over- or under-expenditures, signs of waste. On the other hand, a neat, clear, and concise application form can indicate that you are careful, efficient, and passionate about your project. Hence, it is essential that you take the time necessary to complete the application forms thoroughly and accurately.

Organization. When you provide sponsors with the following types of information, at a glance they can assess the legal status of your organization to receive funding and identify any existing networking relationships with your organization. In the case where top administrators at your institution have a prior history with a sponsor, your organizational reputation may precede your current project request.

- Organization name
- Address
- Chairperson of governing body
- Institutional chief executive official
- Institutional chief financial officer
- Institutional authorized representative
- Employer Identification Number (EIN)
- Taxpayer Identification Number (TIN)
- Data Universal Numbering System (DUNS #)
- Organization type (state, county, municipal, township, interstate, intermunicipal, special district, independent school district, state controlled institution

of higher learning, private university, Indian tribe, individual, profit organization, hospital, private non-profit)

- Date of establishment
- Number of full time and volunteer employees
- Congressional district

Project Director. In addition to providing basic contact information, sponsors may wish for you to supply a few pieces of confidential demographic information, which will facilitate their efforts to ensure that traditionally under-represented groups have equitable access to and involvement in grant programs.

- Name
- Title
- Address
- Contact information (telephone, fax, e-mail)
- Gender
- Race/Ethnicity
- Disability status (hearing impairment, visual impairment, mobility/orthopedic impairment, other)
- Citizenship (U.S., Permanent Resident, other non-U.S. Citizen)
- Social security number
- Highest degree and year obtained
- Grant experience (no previous support, prior support only, current support only, current and prior support)

Project. With the following types of summary details, sponsors can quickly understand what your project is all about: *what* you will be doing, *when* it will take place, and *who* will benefit.

- Title
- Purpose
- Summary
- Principal geographic area served
- Type of grant (construction, non-construction, capital, project, operating)
- Type of application (new, renewal, continuation)
- Catalog of Federal Domestic Assistance number
- Date submitted
- Duration
- Starting and ending dates

Budget. Before sponsors will invest in your project, they must trust that you will be a good steward of their funds. The following types of details illustrate that your project budget is realistic within sponsor-defined grant award limits, and that your organization has the capacity and experience to successfully administer a grant award of this size.

- Organizational budget (past and current year)
- Dates of organizational fiscal year
- Project direct costs
- Project indirect costs
- Total project cost
- Amount requested from sponsor
- Estimated funding from other sources (federal, state, local, applicant, other, program income)

Assurance and Compliance. Sponsors may want to know that your organization has policies and procedures in place to ensure that project activities, and individuals involved in them, meet ethical standards and comply with all applicable laws and regulations. For instance:

- Drug-free workplace requirements
- Environmental tobacco smoke
- Civil Rights Act of 1964
- Fair use of human subjects (Institutional Review Board approval date and assurance of compliance number)
- Fair use of animal subjects (Institutional Animal Care and Use Committee approval date and animal welfare assurance number)
- Assurances for construction programs
- Assurances for non-construction programs
- Debarment and suspension
- Disclosure of lobbying
- Proprietary and privileged information
- Inventions and patents
- Executive Order 12372 (Intergovernmental review of federal programs)
- Program fraud civil remedies act
- Signature of institutional authorized representative

DEVELOPING THE COVER LETTER

The cover letter is usually the first read and one of the last written sections of your grant application. Although cover letters are generally short in length—one to two pages—they should be written carefully because they must highlight a lot of information in a brief space. They should:

- identify the program to which the proposal is being submitted;
- overview the proposal;
- provide an understanding of the project's significance;

- highlight organizational and individual uniqueness, qualifications, and capabilities to conduct the project;
- reflect the project's consistency with sponsor values, funding priorities, evaluation criteria, and hot buttons;
- name a key individual who can be contacted for more information.

Some public and private sponsors have rather restrictive application forms and guidelines; that is, their forms do not always let you include all of the information that you regard as critical. In such instances, use the cover letter as a transmittal letter for their completed application forms and include the details that you weren't able to include in the proposal. This allows you to build a stronger case for securing funding support.

The following is an example of the operative opening paragraph in a transmittal letter. Notice how the first two sentences set the stage for transmitting the required application materials and the last two sentences slip in information that was not requested by the RFP guidelines.

> The Care for Children Hospital (CCH) is pleased to submit an application to the Lotsa BigDollars Foundation for an "Health Intervention for Inner-City Children." As required by the guidelines, enclosed are an original and five copies of our completed application forms. Of particular note, the goal of this project is to reduce health disparities among urban and minority children. Given a 62% prevalence rate of moderate-to-severe chronic health conditions among targeted children in our community, our proposal emphasizes a multidisciplinary approach to intervention activities.

PUTTING IT ALL TOGETHER

After analyzing the Request for Proposal and developing the cover letter, application forms, project summary, proposal, budget narrative, and appendixes, your application is now ready to be assembled and submitted. The entire grant application may range from 5 to 250 pages. In certain respects, a short proposal is more challenging to write than a long proposal. Each sentence must carry a heavy information load. Furthermore, there is very little relation between proposal length and the amount of money requested. You may write 100 pages of detail for a $10,000 grant from one

sponsor and five pages of detail for a $1 million grant from another sponsor.

Whether you are a novice or experienced grantseeker, it is often helpful to study samples of winning proposals. Examining previously funded applications shows you how experienced grantees have responded to specific sponsors and RFPs. They help you see how a persuasive argument is developed and what levels of detail sponsors require. Samples may even provide inspiration to overcome writer's block. Models of successful proposals illustrate what constitutes compelling content, effective organization, and forceful style.

The remaining chapters contain three complete, successful models of proposal planning and writing. Chapter 4 analyzes a community health project funded by a special purpose foundation. Chapter 5 examines an oral health education project funded by a federal agency. Chapter 6 dissects an education project funded by a family foundation. Chapters are designed so that the right-hand (odd numbered) pages of this book present the actual RFP, complete grant application (except for appendixes), and correspondence with the sponsor. Meanwhile, the left-hand (even numbered) pages of this book interpret and explain subtle nuances of the RFP, complete grant application, and correspondence with the sponsor. In other words, you can read this book in three ways:

- Read only the odd numbered pages to see the finished written products.
- Read only the even numbered pages to understand the planning process.
- Read the pages sequentially to detail the planning and writing process step by step.

From RFP to full proposal to grant award notification, these examples provide a paragraph-by-paragraph analysis of salient features that help connect project ideas to the values of the sponsor. They identify the location and interaction of key elements—logic, emotion, and relationships—that make the proposal persuasive. These examples are models that you can follow for planning and writing persuasive proposals of your own.

In sum, while there are no guarantees of winning a grant award, this iterative process for analyzing the RFP and developing the proposal will move you toward the Persuasion Intersection, thus increasing your likelihood for funding success.

Now, go write your best proposal ever!

CHAPTER 4
The Robert Wood Johnson Foundation

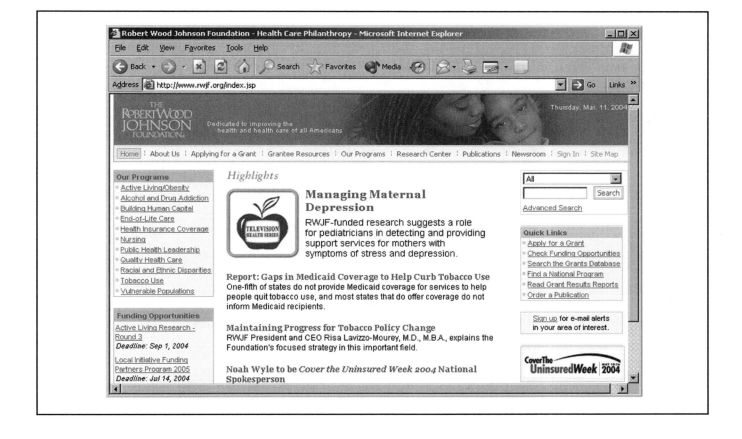

Perhaps the best known special purpose foundation in the United States is The Robert Wood Johnson Foundation. The Foundation specializes in funding health and health care issues. Approximately three-quarters of their $360 million in annual grantmaking (2002 figure) takes the form of national programs—organized, multisite efforts to implement a proven strategy or develop new approaches to a problem. The remaining one-quarter of grants are awarded to a single site in response to an unsolicited proposal or at the Foundation's initiative.

The Robert Wood Johnson Foundation supports research, training, and service demonstrations. They like to field-test promising ideas and evaluate the results; take proven ideas and approaches to scale; give heightened visibility to an issue, idea, or intervention; cause coalitions of like-minded or disparate individuals and groups to form and act around a problem or issue; and research and engage organizations and institutions that would not otherwise seek philanthropic support. They provide a wealth of information about their history, mission, grantmaking priorities, and application processes online at http://www.rwjf.org.

In this chapter we will take an in-depth look at a successful application to The Robert Wood Johnson Foundation's "Allies Against Asthma" initiative, a national demonstration program to support coalition-based efforts to improve asthma care for children and adolescents. Coalitions can apply for a one-year planning grant to develop an overall framework and strategy for addressing pediatric asthma in their communities. Upon successful completion of the planning period, coalitions may apply for a three-year implementation grant to support the coalition, targeted activities, and program evaluation.

For this national demonstration program, The Robert Wood Johnson Foundation uses a three-stage application process. In the first stage, applicants submit a five-page letter of intent that responds to the Foundation's Request for Proposal (RFP). In the second stage, the Foundation invites select applicants to submit a 15-page full proposal. In the third stage, the Foundation conducts site visits with select applicants. Accordingly, this chapter is divided into three sections, one for each stage of the application process.

Stage One: Letter of Intent

- The Request for Proposal
- The Cover Letter
- The Letter of Intent

Stage Two: Full Proposal

- The Request for Proposal
- The Cover Letter
- The Application Form
- The Cross-Walk
- The Project Summary
- The Full Proposal
- The Budget and Budget Narrative

Stage Three: Site Visit

- The Site Visit
- The Grant Award Notification

The chapter is designed so that the right-hand (odd numbered) pages present the actual RFPs, complete grant applications, and correspondence with the sponsor. The left-hand (even numbered) pages interpret and explain subtle nuances of the RFPs, applications, and correspondence. In other words, you can read this chapter in three ways:

- Read only the odd numbered pages to see the finished written products.
- Read only the even numbered pages to understand the planning process.
- Read the pages sequentially to detail the planning and writing process step by step.

This application is a model of persuasive proposal writing; it presents the right balance of logic, emotion, and relationships to connect with the values of the sponsor.

ANALYZING THE REQUEST FOR PROPOSAL

Analyzing Request for Proposal (RFP) guidelines means asking a lot of questions. We ask questions to determine if this program is a good match for our organization and how much work will need to go into developing a competitive application. To effectively analyze the RFP, we read it in multiple passes with increasing scrutiny. In this first section of the chapter we follow our three-step RFP Analysis Process to begin answering questions about *relevance, feasibility,* and *probability.*

Step One: Relevance—Do We Want to Do This?

Children's Health System's Fight Asthma Milwaukee coalition engages in a variety of education, intervention, and research initiatives designed to improve pediatric asthma care. Through activities such as asthma community forums, an annual asthma wellness day, in-service education programs, speakers bureaus, and parent advocacy group meetings, coalition members work to connect children and their families to caring individuals, thereby reducing hospital stays and supporting healthy lives. As the only community-based asthma coalition in Wisconsin, we face the challenge of sustaining a unified, specific purpose with large numbers of activities and diverse backgrounds and interests of members. As a result, we must look for partners and sponsors who understand that the combined effects of cooperating agents working toward a common cause can be greater than the sum of their individual effects.

In step one of our RFP Analysis Process, we made a cursory read of the RFP guidelines and developed a one-page summary of the main points. We distributed this summary as a memorandum to key personnel to assess their interest in pursuing this grant opportunity further. In 30 seconds or less, potential project partners, supervisors, and other administrators can skim read the following memorandum and answer the question, "Do we want to do this?"

RFP Guidelines. The Robert Wood Johnson Foundation's "Allies Against Asthma" program is designed to improve efforts to control pediatric asthma. Some key points in the RFP include:

- Eight community-based coalitions will be awarded funding over a four-year period.

- $150,000 is available for one year for organization and planning.
- $450,000 is available per year for three years for project implementation.
- $150,000 in matching funds is required per year during project implementation.
- The program's primary aims are: to reduce hospital admissions, emergency room visits, and missed school days; to enhance the quality of life of children with asthma; and, to develop a sustainable strategy for asthma management in the community.
- The target population is children under the age of 18, especially inner-city children.
- Only one application per community will be accepted.
- A five-page letter of intent is due January 14, 2000.
- A full proposal from those invited to apply is due June 2, 2000.

For more information about the program, visit: www.sph.umich.edu/aaa. This appears to be a good match for us. Let's meet this week Thursday at noon in the conference room to discuss further the possibility of developing an application.

Step Two: Feasibility—Can We Do This?

After securing institutional support for pursuing this funding opportunity, in step two we examined the RFP guidelines for evaluation criteria, hot buttons, and distinctive features. This second level of analysis begins to answer the question, "Can we do this?"

Evaluation Criteria. The Robert Wood Johnson Foundation will use the following stated evaluation criteria in their selection process.

- A five-page letter of intent should describe the:
  Project's principal objectives
  Target population
  Expertise, experience, and commitment to asthma control and coalition approaches
  Diverse and broad-based support and commitment of coalition members
  Proposed framework for planning and developing targeted activities for asthma control
  Evaluation approach, including quality and availability of data to be used
  Potential for sustaining the coalition efforts over time
  Task and timetable, and budget for the planning grant
  Primary contact person's name, address, and telephone number

ALLIES AGAINST ASTHMA

The Robert Wood Johnson Foundation

Purpose

Allies Against Asthma is designed to improve efforts to control pediatric asthma. This national program will provide support to community-based coalitions to develop and implement comprehensive asthma management programs that include improved access to and quality of medical services, education, family and community support, and environmental and policy initiatives. The primary aims of the program are to reduce hospital admissions, emergency room visits, and missed school days, to enhance the quality of life of children with asthma and to develop a sustainable strategy for asthma management in the community.

Under this program, $12.5 million was authorized in 1999 to be awarded over a four-year period for up to eight community-based coalitions. Grants will be awarded in two stages. One-year organization and planning grants of up to $150,000 will be awarded to up to eight communities. Sites that successfully complete the planning process will be eligible to apply for the implementation grants of up to $450,000 a year for up to three years to support the coalition, targeted activities, and evaluation.

Background

Asthma is a chronic inflammatory disease of the airways. It affects some 15 million Americans and is the most common chronic disease of childhood, affecting an estimated 5 million children. The total number of new cases of children and adults with asthma has more than doubled in the past two decades increasing from 7 million to 15 million today. Asthma prevalence rates have been increasing for all age groups. However, rates remain the highest for children, increasing by 92% over the past decade. Asthma occurs in all social classes, racial and ethnic groups, yet the greatest burden is among children from poor, urban, and minority communities. The economic costs associated with asthma are substantial. Annually the disease accounts for about 15 million outpatient visits, over 445,000 hospitalizations, 1.2 million emergency room visits, and 10 million missed school days. The estimated health care costs of asthma in 1996 were $14 billion.

In the past decade there have been significant advances in asthma management, so that most people with asthma can live active and healthy lives. Recommendations for diagnosing and treating asthma have been translated by the National Asthma Education and Prevention Program (NAEPP) of the National Heart, Lung and Blood Institute (NHLBI) into guidelines for patient care and have been distributed widely. Health care providers, caregivers, patients and their families need to work together to manage the disease. Quality

- Restrictions on the use of funds include:
    Allowable items: project staff salaries, consultant fees, data processing, supplies, a limited amount of equipment, and other direct expenses essential to the proposed project.
    Unallowable items: paying for patient care, clinical trials, approved drugs or devices, personnel providing patient service, or the construction or renovation of facilities.
- Use 12 point font
- Submit ten copies of the letter of intent
- No specific application forms need to be completed
- Due date: January 14, 2000

Hot Buttons and Distinctive Features. By reading between the lines of the RFP guidelines, we identified three hot buttons and three distinctive features that influenced the design, shape, and direction of the proposed project. Hot buttons repeated throughout the RFP gain force over other criteria and include:

- community-based collaborative efforts;
- evaluation and outcomes;
- matching funds and sustainability.

Distinctive features raised in the RFP guidelines include:

- subscribing to national asthma guidelines;
- support from government officials;
- collaboration with the National Program Office.

Responding to distinctive features in the letter of intent will not guarantee funding success; however, failing to acknowledge them may be viewed as a project weakness. In other words, to increase the competitiveness of the letter of intent, these hot buttons and distinctive features—logical and psychological needs—must be strategically addressed in the narrative.

Hot Button: Community-Based Collaborative Efforts

The RFP guidelines use over two dozen different words and phrases to emphasize the importance of project efforts being "community-based" and "collaborative." Broad descriptive words for this hot button include: *community, community-based, coalitions, broad-based efforts, families, linkages, partnerships,* and *joining forces.* Specific examples of community partners are also articulated in the RFP:

schools, childcare providers, parents and caregivers of children with asthma, medical providers, public health and environmental agencies, housing professionals, community organizations, state and local government officials, grassroots advocacy groups, safety net providers, academic institutions, businesses, religious organizations, voluntary health agencies, community residents, and children with asthma.

This emphasis on community-based collaborative efforts is punctuated further by the sponsor's stated preference that this initiative "seeks a single application per community."

Hot Button: Evaluation and Outcomes

Five key words appear approximately twenty times throughout the RFP guidelines emphasizing The Robert Wood Johnson Foundation's hot button concern for systematic evaluation and measurable outcomes: *evaluation, outcomes, impacts, assessing* and *monitoring.* As grant dollars become increasingly competitive, comprehensive program evaluations ensure a measure of accountability—that project funds are being spent wisely, that the project is making a difference, and that project benefits are being distributed across the target population or community.

In fact, the RFP guidelines explicitly point out, "The following selection criteria will be used in evaluating proposals: strength of the proposed evaluation plan." That is, proposal reviewers will assess how applicants plan to evaluate the project. The significance of evaluation is emphasized further in the RFP by the fact that "all grantees, as a condition of accepting grant funds, will be required to participate in such an [independent] evaluation."

Hot Button: Matching Funds and Sustainability

The RFP guidelines outline the expectation that applicants will contribute to the costs of implementing the project and continue to fund it even after grant dollars expire. Hot button phrases repeated over a dozen times throughout the application include: *matching funds, direct and in-kind contributions, innovative funding mechanisms, sustain and institutionalize, sustainable strategy,* and *coalition will continue.* More significantly, rather than inviting applicants to cost share voluntarily, matching funds are mandatory. The RFP spells out the expected level of matching funds: "A commitment of matching funds totaling one-third of the annual budget (both direct and in-kind contributions) each year for three years is required."

Matching funds also encourage project sustainability. Executive administrators who buy into a proj-

medical care, self-management of symptoms, and a reduction in exposure to allergens such as house dust-mites, cockroaches, animal dander, tobacco smoke, and mold can reduce the frequency and severity of asthma attacks.

Yet, many children continue to suffer with asthma due to a complex set of factors. Despite the use of practice guidelines, there are still large variations in recommendations and practices of many health care providers and in treatment adherence by patients and their families. Furthermore, often children living in poverty lack access to quality health services and are exposed to high levels of environmental allergens and irritants. Schools and childcare providers may limit access to medications, and families may lack resources to purchase medications and necessary equipment for effective self-monitoring of symptoms, or social support to manage the disease on a long-term basis.

Communities are mobilizing to address asthma among children and adolescents. Schools, parents and caregivers of children with asthma, medical providers, public health and environmental agencies, housing professionals, community organizations, local officials, and grassroots advocacy groups are joining forces to develop innovative approaches to manage asthma. If these coalitions are successful in improving asthma management, this approach can be replicated and potentially serve as a model for other conditions.

The program

The Allies Against Asthma program seeks to support community-based coalitions working to control asthma, which are organized to achieve specific outcomes for children such as fewer episodes of wheezing, decreases in emergency department and hospital admissions, fewer missed days of school for children, and greater quality of life for child and family. The coalition is expected to be a broad-based effort designed to:

- Improve the quality of or provide new access to asthma-related medical services in clinic, school, or community sites;
- Develop and implement provider education and other strategies based on existing national guidelines to ensure standard and appropriate treatment of children;
- Develop or improve tracking systems to identify and follow patients and families;
- Develop and implement targeted communication strategies to build awareness, support, and involvement of professionals, patients, families, and community;
- Provide community-based health education to improve identification and self-management of asthma and involvement in coalition activities; undertake prevention efforts to reduce exposure to environmental precipitants (e.g. tobacco smoke, allergens, etc.);
- Establish policies to support self-management, enhance services, and provide resources to foster self-management and control asthma (e.g.

ect conceptually and financially are more likely to provide future funding support after the initial granting period ends. The RFP guidelines do not ask for an absolute guarantee of future project funding; rather, proposal reviewers are looking for evidence of a sustainability plan.

Distinctive Feature: Subscribing to National Asthma Guidelines

A distinctive feature noted in the RFP guidelines is that the sponsor endorses the national asthma guidelines established by the National Asthma Education and Prevention Program. Implied in this endorsement is that successful applicants will also subscribe to these guidelines. In the "Background" section of the RFP guidelines, the sponsor foreshadows its belief that universal and consistent application of the national asthma guidelines would help solve the problem: Guidelines for patient care have been distributed widely, yet "despite the use of practice guidelines, there are still large variations in recommendations and practices of many health care providers and in treatment adherence by patients and their families."

"The Program" section of the RFP guidelines, in fact, goes so far as to articulate that coalitions are expected to "develop and implement provider education and other strategies based on existing national guidelines to ensure standard and appropriate treatment of children." And yet, interestingly, this expectation is not part of the RFP "Eligibility and Selection Criteria." Applicants should not reinvent the wheel by designing new implementation strategies; rather, they should educate health care providers to follow the current national asthma guidelines. Failing to embrace these national guidelines may be perceived as a project weakness.

Distinctive Feature: Support from Government Officials

While community-based collaborative efforts is a hot button, coalition support from government officials is a distinctive feature. The sponsor does not include government officials in the RFP guidelines list of "Constituents of the Coalition" but does include them as a specific bulleted item in the "Eligibility and Selection Criteria" section: "evidence of government commitment to the effort including support from key state and local government officials." Coalitions with representation from government officials may be perceived as being more competitive than those who do not. Although not explicitly stated, the sponsor may view state and local government participation as a crucial factor for shaping public policy and securing long-term funding support.

Distinctive Feature: Collaboration with the National Program Office

In addition to community-based collaborative efforts, the sponsor expects coalitions to collaborate with the National Program Office. This distinctive feature appears in the "Direction and Technical Assistance" section of the RFP guidelines: "Direction and technical assistance for the program *will be provided* by a National Program Office" (emphasis added). Applicants who reassure the sponsor that they will actively collaborate with the National Program Office may be received more favorably than those who remain silent on this point. Active collaboration means sharing "lessons learned" and contributing to the development of best practice standards that can be replicated in other communities.

Step Three: Probability—Will We Be Competitive?

In step three, we ask probing questions about our organizational strengths and weaknesses in relation to the values of the sponsor, and we pose questions raised by ambiguities, inconsistencies, discrepancies, and omissions in the RFP guidelines. Strategic thinking helps define institutional uniqueness. Preproposal contact allows an opportunity to build credibility with the sponsor. This third level of analysis answers the question, "Will we be competitive?"

Strategic Thinking. As we read each major section of RFP guidelines, we generated a list of strategic thinking questions that needed to be addressed internally to assess our competitiveness before engaging in preproposal contacts with the sponsor.

Purpose

- Can our community-based coalition compete in a national program?
- Which other local and regional community-based coalitions might apply?
- How can we make our proposal stand out from the competition?
- Can we provide a comprehensive array of asthma management programs and services?
- Do we have access to hospital, emergency room, and school data?
- How will we measure children's quality of life?

coverage of appropriate equipment; access to medication in schools and childcare settings);

- Establish linkages with existing asthma or other relevant surveillance systems; and
- Conduct an evaluation to assess the coalition activities including the extent to which they strengthen the coalition's capacity to be effective and achieve asthma control outcomes.

Target Populations: The intent of the coalition is to reach children under the age of 18, especially those seen under publicly financed systems of care; those targeted by safety net providers (e.g. WIC, Early Intervention, Immunization Services, Community and School-Based Health Centers); and by other systems designed to serve inner city or other populations that experience difficulties in securing care.

Constituents of the Coalition: It is expected that there will be active engagement and participation of core representatives on the coalition, including such groups as: community-based organizations, schools, medical service providers, public health and environmental agencies, managed care organizations, housing organizations, academic institutions, childcare providers, businesses, religious organizations, media, voluntary health agencies, grassroots groups, children with asthma, parents of children with asthma, and other community residents.

Organization and Planning Phase: Coalitions awarded the one-year planning grants of up to $150,000 will be expected to develop an overall framework and strategy for addressing pediatric asthma in their communities. The steps would include: developing a structure to ensure an inclusive but manageable planning process; assessing the scope of the asthma problem to identify opportunities for intervention and resources available; and developing a plan with strategic and targeted interventions with specific outcomes and articulated coalition member roles and responsibilities. The plan should identify specific initial outcomes and long-term impacts and efforts to sustain and institutionalize the changes. Successful applicants also must secure a commitment for matching funds totaling one-third of each year's budget (for three years) to qualify for funding for the implementation phase of the project. Planning grant applicants who have secured a commitment for matching funds for the implementation phase, will be considered to be more competitive.

Implementation Phase: Implementation grants of up to $450,000 a year for up to three years will support the coalition, targeted activities, and evaluation. Communities completing the organization and planning phase will be eligible to apply for the implementation grants. Types of strategies that would be of interest include: community-based health worker/liaison approaches to asthma management; asthma management systems in schools; safe home and housing initiatives; clinical care in non-traditional settings; organized clinician referral systems to assist families in obtaining medical care; innovative means to identify children with undiagnosed and/or undertreated asthma; ways to ensure that patients receive adequate therapeutic recommendations from clinicians

- Do we have evaluation results from current coalition activities?
- What strategies do we have for sustaining community efforts?
- Are our odds of getting funded good enough to merit submitting a proposal?

Background

- How many children are affected by asthma locally, statewide, and regionally?
- Do we have local, statewide, and regional asthma prevalence and severity data by age groups and socioeconomic status?
- Do we have local hospital data for outpatient visits, hospitalizations, and emergency room visits?
- Do we have local data about missed school days due to asthma?
- Do we have recent total estimated health care costs for asthma locally, statewide, and regionally?
- Do we know and subscribe to National Asthma Education and Prevention Program (NAEPP) and National Heart, Lung and Blood Institute (NHLBI) guidelines for asthma management?
- Are physicians trained in NAEPP and NHLBI guidelines?
- Do current coalition activities address reducing exposure to allergens such as house dustmites, cockroaches, animal dander, tobacco smoke, and mold? What data do we have to document the effectiveness of these activities?
- What local and statewide data do we have about children's access to health care services?
- Does the coalition have linkages to schools, parents, and caregivers of children with asthma, medical providers, public health and environmental agencies, housing professionals, community organizations, local officials, and grassroots advocacy groups? Which groups are missing?
- Are we prepared to help set the national standard for improving asthma management?
- Do we have experience designing models of care for other chronic health conditions that could apply to improving asthma management?
- Do we have experience designing models of care that have been replicated by others?

The Program

- Can we realistically accomplish all eight of the stated program objectives—provide community-based health education, develop and implement provider education, develop and implement targeted communication strategies, provide access to asthma-related medical services in community sites, establish linkages with surveillance systems, establish policies to support self-management, reduce exposure to environmental precipitants, and assess coalition activities?
- Do we have current efforts in all eight objective areas upon which we can build?
- Do we have data to document the effectiveness of current activities in these eight areas?
- Are there barriers that might prevent the coalition from addressing these eight objectives effectively?

Target Populations:

- How many inner-city children are in the various publicly financed systems?
- How many inner-city children can we realistically serve?
- What is the race/ethnicity, age, and gender status and the geographic disbursement of targeted children?

Constituents of the Coalition:

- Which types of organizations are currently involved in the coalition?
- Which missing groups can easily be recruited to the coalition?
- Have any organizations been approached and declined to participate in the coalition?
- Does the coalition have diverse representation, including an appropriate mix of race/ethnicity and gender?
- Who else needs to be included in the coalition to make it more inclusive?

Organization and Planning Phase:

- Are there existing frameworks for addressing chronic health conditions that can be adapted to pediatric asthma?
- What is the current structure of the coalition?
- Is the coalition's structure flexible enough to accommodate new partners?
- What strategies are in place for effectively managing the coalition?
- What structure and process changes might be necessary to maintain the manageability of a larger, more inclusive coalition?
- Have we done a community needs assessment?
- Do we have recent needs assessment data to document the problem in our community?

combined with strategies to enhance compliance of patients with therapeutic plans, including avoidance of asthma triggers; ways to improve provider and patient communication and interaction; and adaptation of evaluated effective models for provider, patient, school, family, and community education, and/or comprehensive service delivery. A commitment of matching funds totaling one-third of the annual budget (both direct and in-kind contributions) each year for three years is required. It is anticipated that implementation grant proposals will be due nine months subsequent to the award of the planning grant.

Eligibility and selection criteria

The initiative seeks a single application per community. Both public and private organizations are eligible to apply on behalf of the coalition under this program. Preference will be given to applicants that are public agencies or are tax exempt under Section 501(c)(3) of the Internal Revenue Code. Private foundations, as defined under Section 509(a), are ineligible. Public-private partnerships are encouraged. The following selection criteria will be used in evaluating proposals:

- Potential for substantially changing systems for asthma control;
- The use of innovative funding mechanisms to ensure that the coalition is sustainable;
- Evidence of a strong, broad-based coalition that is poised to develop and implement multi-component approaches;
- Evidence of participation by community-based organizations in the coalition and involvement in planning and implementation of coalition plans;
- Representation and involvement of the target population in the coalition;
- Salience of the coalition and its activities;
- Applicant's experience and qualifications for providing leadership, mobilizing key constituents and facilitating the planning process;
- Commitment of the coalition collaborators including their acceptance of significant roles, the amount of their direct financial support and in-kind contributions, and evidence of their institutional capacity to contribute to coalition success;
- Strength of the planning process and proposed activities grounded in science and field experience;
- Evidence of government commitment to the effort including support from key state and local government officials;
- Evidence of knowledge of the clinical aspects of asthma and science base for asthma control;
- The technical and political feasibility of the project;
- Likelihood that the coalition will continue after the grant period and that lasting changes will be made in community capacity to control asthma;
- Commitment of matching funds, including both direct and in-kind contributions; and
- Strength of the proposed evaluation plan, including the quality and availability of data to be used.

- Have we identified initial opportunities for interventions?
- What resources are currently serving or could be tapped to serve the community?
- Do we have experience developing community-wide plans to address chronic health conditions?
- Who will pay for all of this?
- What cash and in-kind resources can our organization contribute to this project?
- What levels of cash and in-kind support can we realistically expect from our partners?

Implementation Phase:

- Does the coalition have experience with any of the identified implementation strategies? Do we have data to show their effectiveness?
- What does the current literature say about the effectiveness of each of these strategies?
- Will these strategies apply equally in our community?
- What resources are currently being used to serve the target population?
- Can we secure verbal or written commitments from collaborative partners for the required matching funds?

Eligibility and Selection Criteria

- Who in our community might apply?
- Who in our community is best suited to apply?
- Who else might apply statewide and regionally?
- Where else might we face competition?
- How strong are our current public-private partnerships?
- How can we strengthen and broaden our public-private partnerships?
- Does the coalition have support from state and local government officials?
- What innovative funding methods might be used to sustain the project: coalition membership fees, product sales, phone-a-thons, special events, sponsorships?
- Is there another profitable service or activity that could be expanded to cover the costs of running this new project?
- Can our organization or partner agencies absorb future funding responsibilities within general operating budgets once grant funds end?
- Will the project generate any revenue that can be used for sustainability?
- Do we have examples of other programs that have made lasting changes and have been sustained beyond an initial granting period?

Program Evaluation and Monitoring

- Should evaluations be conducted internally, externally, or both?
- Do internal evaluators have the expertise, experience, capability, and resources to objectively assess the coalition and its activities?
- Are internal evaluators willing to participate in national program assessments across all eight award sites?
- What types of evaluations are most appropriate for this project—structure, process, outcome, cost-effectiveness, return-on-investment analyses?

Use of Funds

- Are all of our costs allowable under the terms and conditions of the grant program?
- Will we be able to meet the sponsor's requirements for submitting annual and final progress and financial reports?
- Will this project cost us money beyond the matching requirement?

Direction and Technical Assistance

- Do coalition members know any of the individuals identified at the National Program Office and at The Robert Wood Johnson Foundation?
- Have any of these individuals published books, journals, or online resources that might be used as reference materials?

How to Apply

- How can we recast the eight objectives identified by the sponsor to be SIMPLE—specific, immediate, measurable, practical, logical, and evaluable?
- How do we reconcile the fact that two of the objectives identified by the sponsor are to "develop and implement" activities, yet the purpose of the first year of funding is for "organization and planning"?
- Should we foreshadow potential implementation activities before we actually conduct the organization and planning phase? Will that require us to conduct those activities even if at the conclusion of the organization and planning phase the coalition determines a different course of action is more appropriate?
- Should the evaluation approach assess the organization and planning period, the proposed implementation activities, or both?

Program evaluation and monitoring

The Foundation may undertake an overall evaluation of this program. Such an evaluation would be conducted by an independent research group and would focus on key questions about the program's impact on improving care for children with asthma. All grantees, as a condition of accepting grant funds, will be required to participate in such an evaluation.

Use of funds

Grant funds may be used for project staff salaries, consultant fees, data processing, supplies, a limited amount of equipment, and other direct expenses essential to the proposed project. Funds may not be used to pay for patient care, support clinical trials or approved drugs or devices, for personnel providing patient service, or for the construction or renovation of facilities.

Grantees will be expected to meet Foundation requirements for the submission of annual and final progress and financial reports. Project directors will be expected to provide a written report on the project and its findings, suitable for wide dissemination.

Direction and technical assistance

Direction and technical assistance for the program will be provided by a National Program Office headed by Noreen M. Clark, PhD, program director, and Linda Jo Doctor, deputy director from the University of Michigan, School of Public Health. At the Robert Wood Johnson Foundation, responsible staff are Seth Emont, PhD, senior program officer; Doriane Miller, MD, vice president; Phyllis Kane, program assistant; and Liisa Rand, financial analyst.

A National Advisory Committee will assist in the evaluation of proposals, participate in site visits, and make recommendations to Foundation staff regarding funding.

How to apply

Those wishing to apply for funds under this program should first submit ten copies of a letter of intent (an original and nine copies), rather than a fully developed proposal, not to exceed five pages. They should be provided in 12 point or larger font per single line of text. Letters of intent more than five pages will not be accepted. The letter of intent should include the following:

- Brief statement of the proposed project's principal objectives;
- Its target population;

Timetable

- If we are selected to submit a full proposal, will we be able to do so during the sponsor's scheduled timeframe?
- Is the sponsor's projected timetable consistent with our strategic plan for coalition and program development?

About RWJF

- Have any coalition members ever received funding from The Robert Wood Johnson Foundation?
- What else can we learn from The Robert Wood Johnson Foundation and Allies Against Asthma Web sites?
- Do we know others who might have received funding from the sponsor?

Preproposal Contact. When talking with the sponsor, we explained that we analyzed their RFP guidelines carefully but still have some unanswered questions that we would like to raise to ensure that our proposal would be of value to them. We briefly described our project and then asked the following types of PREP (Position-Rationale-Expectation-Priority) questions. Our opening conversation went like this.

> Hi, Ms. Doctor. I'm John Meurer, Assistant Professor of Pediatrics at the Medical College of Wisconsin and Children's Health System. Our Fight Asthma Milwaukee coalition is very interested in submitting an application to your "Allies Against Asthma" program. While we've studied the guidelines carefully, we still have some unanswered questions that we'd like to raise to ensure that our proposal would be of value to you. If your schedule allows, I'd like to ask a few questions not addressed in the guidelines.

Position: The Baseline Situation

- What can you tell us about the review process?
- Who are the National Advisory Committee members that will assist in the evaluation of proposals?
- Under what conditions are proposals reviewed?
- How much time will reviewers have to read the proposals?
- Will awards be made on the basis of any special criteria, e.g., geography, size of target population, size of the coalition?
- Is there a specific reviewer's evaluation form that we can see?
- What is the anticipated application-to-award ratio?

- Can supplemental information be included in an appendix?
- Would it be of value to include letters of support and commitment from collaborating agencies? How many would be appropriate?
- Do you anticipate any modifications to the timetable of when proposals will be due, reviewed, and announced?
- For budget development purposes, should we estimate an October 1, 2000, start date?
- What level of detail should go into the budget? Should a line item budget with budget narrative be attached to the five-page narrative?
- Are "supplies" considered to be office supplies, or do they include medical supplies such as spacers and allergy screenings?
- Are these items allowable direct costs: incentives for community participants, meetings, postage, telephone, and travel?
- Are indirect costs allowable? At what level?

Rationale: Problems Existing Today

- Although it is not requested in the RFP guidelines, should we describe the magnitude and severity of the asthma problem in our community compared to the national asthma data provided?
- What are the major variables in this larger problem?
- What are the biggest hurdles in this area now?
- What are the biggest sources of dissatisfaction with current approaches?
- Which dimensions of this problem need to be addressed next?

Expectation: Basic Implications for Addressing Problems

- Are applicants expected to fulfill all eight of the stated program objectives? Or is it more realistic to prioritize the objectives and address only some of them? If so, how many would be appropriate?
- One selection criterion used in evaluating proposals is the "Potential for substantially changing systems for asthma control." What is considered "substantial" change? How much change has to occur for the project to be a success?
- Which measures of children's quality of life do you prefer to evaluate?
- Who owns the evaluation data once it is collected?
- What would you like to see addressed in a proposal that other applicants may have overlooked?

- Expertise, experience, and demonstrated commitment to asthma control and coalition approaches;
- Indication of diverse and broad-based support and commitment of coalition members;
- Proposed framework(s) for planning and developing targeted activities for asthma control;
- Evaluation approach, including quality and availability of data to be used;
- Potential for sustaining the coalition efforts over time;
- An estimated task and timetable, and budget for the planning grant; and
- The name, address, and telephone number of the individual who is to act as the primary contact during the application process.

Full proposals will be requested only from applicants whose letters of intent best meet the program's criteria. Full proposals will be reviewed by the National Advisory Committee, and site visits will be made as needed. The Foundation does not provide individual critiques of letters of intent or proposals submitted.

Letters of intent and all inquiries should be addressed to:

Linda Jo Doctor, Deputy Director
Allies Against Asthma
University of Michigan, School of Public Health
109 South Observatory Street
Ann Arbor, Michigan 48109
Phone: 734-615-3312
Fax: 734-763-7379
Email: asthma@umich.edu

Please Note: All letters of intent must be received at the above address by January 14, 2000. Faxed or emailed letters of intent will NOT be accepted or reviewed.

For more information about the program, consult the Allies Against Asthma Web site: www.sph.umich.edu/aaa

Timetable

Letters of intent and applications will be reviewed according to the following timetable:

January 14, 2000 Deadline for receipt of letters of intent.
March 15, 2000 Notification of applicants selected to submit full proposals.
June 2, 2000 Deadline for receipt of full proposals from those invited to apply.
Fall, 2000 Grant Recipients announced.
July, 2001 Estimated deadline for implementation grant proposals.

Priority: Approaches for an Improved Situation

- What is essential that is not happening now?
- What is needed to close the gap?
- Would this approach produce what is needed?
- What outcomes do you expect from grantees?

Using this iterative, three-step RFP Analysis Process, we move along the Roads to the Persuasion Intersection, gathering the details necessary to develop a persuasive letter of intent. Next, we examine how we arrive at the Persuasion Intersection—connecting our project idea to the values of the sponsor through the right balance of logic, emotion, and relationships—in the cover letter and letter of intent.

About RWJF

The Robert Wood Johnson Foundation® was established as a national philanthropy in 1972 and today is the largest U.S. foundation devoted to health care. The Foundation concentrates its grantmaking toward three goal areas:

- To assure that all Americans have access to basic health care at reasonable cost;
- To improve the care and support for people with chronic health conditions; and
- To promote health and reduce the personal, social, and economic harm caused by substance abuse—tobacco, alcohol, and illicit drugs.

This document, as well as many other Foundation publications and resources, is available on the Foundation's World Wide Web site: www.rwjf.org

The Robert Wood Johnson Foundation
Route 1 and College Road East
Post Office Box 2316
Princeton, New Jersey 08543-2316

THE REQUEST FOR PROPOSAL

STAGE ONE: LETTER OF INTENT

DEVELOPING THE COVER LETTER

The cover letter is the first section of our complete grant application to be read, yet is the last one to be written. Developing the cover letter *after* completing the letter of intent ensures consistency in the presentation of our main ideas. In one page we:

- identify the program to which the letter of intent is being submitted;
- overview the proposal;
- provide an understanding of the project's significance;
- highlight organizational uniqueness, qualifications, and capabilities to conduct the project;
- reflect the project's consistency with sponsor values, funding priorities, evaluation criteria, and hot buttons;
- name the project director who can be contacted for more information.

Elements of the Cover Letter

Heading. The boldface heading centered at the top of the page identifies that this is a cover letter and *not* the first page of the letter of intent. It also names the applicant organization and gives the title of the project. This information will help an administrative assistant opening the mail know quickly what the letter is about and how to process it.

Paragraph #1. This first paragraph is an overview of the entire grant application. It names the applicant organization, relates to the sponsor eligibility criteria for supporting community-based coalitions, names the specific program to which the letter of intent is being submitted, and reiterates the goal of the program. In generic form, the first sentence takes the form: [self-identification] is pleased to submit [letter of intent/proposal] to [sponsor] to [project benefit]. Note that the project benefit is expressed in terms of sponsor-oriented values rather than self-oriented needs. The second sentence indicates that we followed the RFP guidelines and submitted the required number of copies of the letter of intent.

Paragraph #2. The second paragraph begins to establish our organizational uniqueness and credibility—the only community-based asthma coalition in the state and one of the first established in the country. This paragraph also foreshadows our approach to one of the sponsor's hot buttons: community-based collaborative efforts. Namely, partnerships are essential to addressing community health problems. In the last sentence of the paragraph we attempt to align ourselves with the sponsor, reiterating a quote that was presented in a journal article about community, practice, and academic partnerships written by the director of the sponsor's National Program Office.

Paragraph #3. In the third paragraph we articulate the extent of the asthma problem, identify the primary aims of the project, and appeal to two more sponsor hot buttons: (1) matching funds and sustainability, and (2) evaluation and outcomes. The first part of the first sentence conveys that the coalition existed long before this grant opportunity appeared and will continue to serve the community until their needs are met. Said differently, we are not simply chasing grant dollars because they are available. The second part of the sentence quantifies the needs of the community—our rate of pediatric asthma is ten times the federally established Healthy People standard. The last sentence of the paragraph articulates the significance of the project and relates to improved health outcomes.

Paragraph #4. The last paragraph provides telephone and e-mail contact information for the project director and ends on a positive note reflecting our mutual interest for improving pediatric health in the community.

Signature Line. The highest ranking organizational official signs the letter of intent to show that this application has full institutional support.

■ Cover Letter ■
Children's Health System:
Milwaukee *Allies Against Asthma*

Linda Jo Doctor   January 10, 2000
Deputy Director
Allies Against Asthma
University of Michigan, School of Public Health
109 South Observatory Street
Ann Arbor, MI 48109

Dear Ms. Doctor:

Children's Health System (CHS), on behalf of our Fight Asthma Milwaukee coalition, is pleased to submit a letter of intent to the Robert Wood Johnson Foundation's "Allies Against Asthma" program to improve efforts to control pediatric asthma. As your guidelines request, we've enclosed ten total copies of our letter of intent.

As you read our letter of intent, you'll note that CHS' Fight Asthma Milwaukee is the only community-based asthma coalition in Wisconsin, and was one of the first established in the country. Partnerships between community-based organizations, public health practice, and academia are an invaluable means to enhancing our community's capacity to address health problems. After all, as we learned from an Ashanti folk tale, "No one person has all the world's wisdom. People everywhere share small pieces of it whenever they exchange ideas."

Fight Asthma Milwaukee was formed in 1994 in response to state health department data showing that parts of Milwaukee's inner city had the highest asthma hospitalization rates in the state: 20 per 1000 residents—ten times the federal Healthy People 2000 goal! Accordingly, this project aims to reduce hospital admissions and emergency department visits, reduce missed school days, enhance quality of life of asthmatic children, and develop a sustainable strategy for asthma management in the community.

Thank you for your consideration of our letter of intent. Please contact John R. Meurer, MD, MBA, to answer questions or provide further information—phone: (414) 456-4116 or email: jmeurer@mcw.edu. We look forward to submitting a full proposal to the Robert Wood Johnson Foundation for this important health initiative.

Sincerely,

Jon E. Vice
President

THE COVER LETTER

STAGE ONE: LETTER OF INTENT

DEVELOPING THE LETTER OF INTENT

Analyzing the Request for Proposal (RFP) guidelines was the first step in developing a letter of intent. We quickly determined that the program was a good match for our organization. And once we secured institutional support to pursue this grant opportunity, we examined the RFP for evaluation criteria, hot buttons, and distinctive features. Together, these elements dictated the form and structure of our application. Strategic thinking and preproposal contact supplied us with additional information to fill in the details of the proposal, fine-tuning it to closely match the sponsor's priorities. This iterative analysis process moved us down the Roads to the Persuasion Intersection.

Elements of the Letter of Intent

Title. The boldface heading at the top of the page identifies the applicant and the project title. The project title, "Milwaukee Allies Against Asthma," reflects that of the sponsor's grant program yet it is customized to our community. It is descriptive without being cutesy or a tricky acronym. Equally important, the title will still be appropriate even after sponsor grant funding ends.

Overview. The opening paragraph summarizes the entire letter of intent and carries a heavy information load. The first sentence identifies the applicant organization and uniqueness and sets up a shared desire for achieving the overall project goal. The second sentence briefly quantifies the extent of the problem in our community and begins to create a sense of urgency for addressing the problem now. Subsequent sentences spell out how we meet sponsor eligibility criteria.

This paragraph also foreshadows the three hot buttons that will be reiterated throughout the letter of intent: (1) community-based collaborative efforts; (2) evaluation and outcomes; and (3) matching funds and sustainability. For instance, the fourth sentence conveys that coalition efforts aim to improve health outcomes and promote healthy lifestyles; the fifth sentence demonstrates that the coalition has diverse community representation from parents and professionals; and the sixth sentence expresses the idea that with the help of the sponsor, the coalition can develop a strategy to sustain project efforts long-term. Notice that the paragraph ends by articulating the benefit of the project to the target population; this positioning strategically reflects our understanding of the values of the sponsor.

Statement of the Problem. Although the evaluation criteria in the RFP guidelines do not specifically request data that describes the extent of the problem, research suggests that the statement of the problem is the single most important proposal component that influences funding success. The statement of the problem justifies to the sponsor *why* this project is needed. Accordingly, we document the extent of the asthma problem, substantiating that the need is greater in our community than in the rest of the state.

Furthermore, because one of the stated project aims in "The Program" section of the RFP guidelines is to reduce missed school days, we selected pertinent research conducted by our project director to illustrate the vulnerability of children in local public schools. Simultaneously, this published research begins to establish the credibility of our project director. The final sentences of the paragraph discuss the adverse consequences of not addressing the asthma problem and emphasize the coalition's ability to reduce the impact of pediatric asthma in the community. Note that this paragraph addresses the hot button of community-based collaborative efforts: The project director is already collaborating with local schools to educate children about asthma and assess its prevalence and impact.

Project Aims & Objectives. From this point forward, the letter of intent follows the format and structure established by the evaluation criteria described in the RFP guidelines on "How to Apply." Boldface headings reflect key words from each of the nine bulleted points. "Project Aims & Objectives" tell the sponsor exactly *what* we are going to do to solve the identified problem. The primary aims of the project—taken directly from the RFP—are detailed here as the "big picture" approach to solving the problem.

To achieve these primary aims, the coalition will need to take specific measurable steps. Thus, the coalition customized and prioritized the eight project objectives identified in the RFP guidelines and presented them as bulleted points in decreasing order of emphasis. Equally important for the sponsor, our coalition subscribes to the national asthma guidelines established by the National Asthma Education and Prevention Program, a distinctive feature raised in the RFP. As a whole, this section touches on all three sponsor hot buttons. Note the use of key words, such as *coalition*, *community*, *community-based*, *evaluation*, *assess*, *outcomes*, and *sustainable strategy*.

Target Population. This section of the letter of intent tells the sponsor *where* the project is taking place and *who will benefit* from targeted activities. These paragraphs on "Target Population" serve two

Children's Health System: Milwaukee *Allies Against Asthma*

Children's Health System (CHS), Wisconsin's only independent nonprofit health care system dedicated solely to the health and well-being of children, is deeply concerned about controlling pediatric asthma. Asthma is the number one reason for hospitalization at CHS—nearly 1,000 admissions per year. But our concern for children extends beyond the walls of our hospital. Our Fight Asthma Milwaukee coalition provides quality asthma education, outreach, and referral services that enable children, families, and the community to maintain healthy lifestyles. Coalition constituents include medical service and managed care providers, schools, academic institutions, community-based organizations, childcare providers, and parents and children with asthma. The "Allies Against Asthma" grant opportunity will help to develop a sustainable strategy for asthma management that will improve the health status of vulnerable urban youth.

Asthma is the most common chronic illnesses of childhood, affecting an estimated 100,000 of the state's children under age 18, a majority of whom live in southeastern Wisconsin. Asthma is the leading cause of health-related school absenteeism in Milwaukee; preliminary research suggests that asthma affects 10% of urban school-age children. Between 1997–1999, CHS' Health Education Center, through their "Awesome Asthma School Days" program, surveyed more than 2,000 children with asthma from Milwaukee Public Schools. Most recent survey results illustrate the vulnerability of inner city school children:

- 72% lack spacers for inhalers at school
- 69% do not have a written asthma self-care plan
- 66% with persistent symptoms do not use an anti-inflammatory control medicine
- 59% report smoke exposure in their home (JR Meurer, J School Health, 1999).

More significantly, children who do not receive adequate asthma care have poorer development of lung function and more rapid decline in adult lung function than children who received appropriate primary medical and specialty care. CHS' Fight Asthma Milwaukee coalition can help address these needs to reduce the adverse impact of pediatric asthma in the community.

Project Aims & Objectives. Education, early diagnosis and treatment hold the promise for children with asthma to lead full, active lives. Aggressive identification of children who are at risk can prevent irreversible injury to lungs, improve school performance, and promote healthy lifestyles. The primary aims of this Milwaukee project are to reduce hospital admissions, reduce emergency department visits, reduce missed school days, enhance quality of life of children with asthma, and develop a sustainable strategy for asthma management in the community.

To achieve these aims, our coalition identified eight objectives that cover asthma education, referral, outreach, and reflect the goals of the National Asthma Education & Prevention Program:

- Provide community-based health education to improve identification and self-management of asthma and involvement in coalition activities.
- Develop and implement provider education and other strategies based on existing national guidelines to ensure appropriate treatment of children.
- Develop and implement targeted communication strategies to build asthma awareness, support, and involvement of professionals, children, families, and community.
- Improve the quality of and provide new access to asthma-related medical services in clinic, school, and community sites.
- Establish linkages with existing asthma or other relevant surveillance systems.
- Establish policies to support self-management, enhance services, provide resources, and build capacity of families and communities to control asthma.
- Undertake prevention efforts to reduce exposure to environmental precipitants.
- Conduct evaluations to assess coalition activities including the extent to which they strengthen the coalition's capacity to be effective and achieve asthma control outcomes.

John Meurer, MD, MBA, Project Director   1

roles. First, they describe the racial/ethnic and socioeconomic status of inner-city children. Second, they document further the extent of the asthma problem in the community.

These paragraphs appeal to details presented in the "Background" and "Target Populations" portions of the RFP guidelines: disparities of asthma prevalence among children and minorities, hospitalizations and emergency department visits, national goals and guidelines, economic costs, uninsured, publicly financed systems of care, and safety net providers. For instance, the second sentence quantifies the needs of the community and relates them to a federally established Healthy People standard. The third sentence emphasizes our organizational credibility and uniqueness and describes our access to the target population; in essence, this answers the question, "Why should the sponsor fund you?" *Because we are already treating the vast majority of the community's children who seek emergency care or are hospitalized for asthma.*

The data table included in the narrative illustrates complex information in a simple manner. Proposal reviewers can easily determine the size of the potential target population and the magnitude of the health disparities among urban and minority children. The final paragraph reemphasizes that the project will serve the children targeted by the RFP, but more importantly, it goes a step further in bulleted list fashion to describe prevention efforts for specific age groups. These prevention efforts relate to the project objectives described in the previous section, and echo the sponsor's hot button for evaluation and outcomes: Assorted evaluation strategies will be necessary to measure the effectiveness of activities serving different age groups.

Expertise & Experience. This section on "Expertise & Experience" and the subsequent section on "Broad-Based Support" let the sponsor know *who* is responsible for and *who* is participating in the project. In three paragraphs we establish the credibility of the organization, the coalition, and the project director. These paragraphs also address all three hot buttons: community-based collaborative efforts, evaluation and outcomes, and matching funds and sustainability.

In addition to describing a century's worth of organizational history and experience, the first paragraph emphasizes collaborative relationships with local and state organizations, a distinctive feature raised in the RFP. The second paragraph conveys that our community-based coalition existed long before this grant opportunity appeared and will continue to serve the community until their needs are met. In other words, we are not simply chasing grant dollars

because they are available. Participating in two federally sponsored statewide grant initiatives demonstrates the coalition's credibility to the sponsor, saying, in essence, "We have a history of good stewardship and affecting change in the community. We can do it again."

The final paragraph describes the qualifications of the project director to lead this initiative. His credentials include dual academic degrees (M.D. and M.B.A.), which address the medical and administrative aspects of project managment. Moreover, he has a history of extensive collaborative relationships with community-based agencies and myriad academic publications stemming from federally grant-funded asthma outcomes research. Collectively these paragraphs express the idea that this project is a systematic continuation of prior community efforts where we have turned vision into success.

Broad-Based Support. These two paragraphs give concrete examples of broad-based member support and of intervention activities, thus enhancing the coalition's overall credibility. The names of key coalition constituents from a variety of local and state agencies, education, and service providers are presented in bulleted list fashion.

Representative coalition constituents were selected carefully so that their organization names were self-explanatory relative to the type of service they provided, e.g., community health center, or to the population they served, e.g., African-Americans, or to their geographic emphasis, e.g., state department of health and family services. Moreover, two coalition members also reflect an RFP distinctive feature: support from local and state government officials.

The samples of intervention activities in the second paragraph illustrate coalition successes in collaborating with diverse organizations serving quantified numbers of children, families, and professionals. In fact, the second example demonstrates that individual coalition members have the ability to secure federal grant funding for asthma-related projects. A history of successful grantseeking reinforces the hot button concept of project sustainability and shows a long-term commitment to serving the needs of the community. More broadly, the first paragraph builds on the credibility established in the previous section, and the second paragraph provides a smooth transition to the subsequent methodology section.

Project Framework. Whereas project objectives tell the sponsor exactly *what* we plan to do, the "Project Framework" describes *how* we plan to accomplish those objectives. In particular, this section: (1) iden-

Target Population. Asthma disproportionately affects children and minorities. The asthma hospitalization rate for children in Milwaukee County is 4.9 per 1000, nearly five times the draft federal Healthy People 2010 goal of 1.0 per 1000. In 1997, there were 1,312 asthma inpatient hospitalizations for children in Milwaukee County, 56% of whom had Medicaid as their primary payer. CHS is uniquely suited to lead this project because we treat greater than 90% of children in Milwaukee seeking emergency care or hospitalization for asthma. The table below compares the ethnic composition of children ages 0–17 in Milwaukee County and CHS asthma emergency department visits in 1998. Although African Americans make up less than one-third of the County's population, they account for over half of emergency department visits for asthma!

Ethnicity of:	Milwaukee County Children		CHS Asthma Emergency Visits	
Race	Number	Percent of Total	Number	Percent of Total
African American	78,680	31%	1,896	56%
White	141,390	57%	1,156	34%
Hispanic	19,120	8%	274	8%
Asian	5,830	3%	29	1%
Native American	2,220	1%	5	1%
Totals	247,240	100%	3,400	100%

This project targets children under age 18, especially those residing in the inner city, uninsured or eligible for publicly financed systems, and receiving care from safety net providers. More concretely, project activities will reach four age-specific groups with tailored prevention foci:
- Under age 2: early detection and diagnosis
- Age 2–5: preventing emergency department visits for asthma
- Age 6–12: asthma screening, education, and treatment in school settings
- Age 13–18: preventing ongoing asthma-related problems, including tobacco use

These activities will help reduce health disparities among urban and minority children.

Expertise & Experience. Children's Health System, as lead applicant in a multidisciplinary collaboration of local and state organizations, has the experience and expertise to develop and implement comprehensive asthma management programs that improve access to and quality of medical services, education, family and community support, and environmental initiatives. For over a century, CHS and affiliates have supplied comprehensive medical treatment to children throughout the state and region; in 1998 alone, CHS admitted more than 18,000 children.

CHS' Fight Asthma Milwaukee (FAM) is the only community-based asthma coalition in Wisconsin, and was one of the first established in the country. For half a decade, project partners have worked together on a variety of asthma education, intervention, and research initiatives in the state, including participating in two Centers for Disease Control & Prevention cooperative agreements—Wisconsin's Community-Based Asthma Intervention Project and Wisconsin's Asthma Education Program for Welfare-to-Work Families. These programs demonstrate that the FAM coalition is a powerful and effective mechanism for realizing change at the local level. Quite simply, the best way to reinforce health education is to involve the community so they can advocate for themselves. FAM's parent advisory group ensures appropriate representation and involvement of the target population in the coalition. Creating a sense of community ownership facilitates FAM's vision to be a leading resource for asthma education, outreach, and referrals.

John R. Meurer, MD, MBA, Project Director, has the expertise to make this project succeed. Dr. Meurer is Assistant Professor of Community Pediatrics in the Center for the Advancement of Urban Children at CHS and

tifies the theoretical model that will guide planning and implementation activities; (2) describes key ingredients for a successful planning phase; (3) describes a multifactorial approach to the project's implementation phase; and (4) justifies this methodological approach to controlling pediatric asthma. These paragraphs also appeal to each of the sponsor's three hot buttons—community-based collaborative efforts, evaluation and outcomes, and matching funds and sustainability. Notice the strategic repetition of terms, such as: *coalition, community, inclusive plan, measurable outcomes, evaluation, outcomes-based framework, long-term changes, matching funds,* and *sustainable structure.*

In the first paragraph, the second sentence identifies the conceptual framework underpinning the project's design. More importantly, it also justifies this selection: This framework is the dominant health education planning and community health promotion model in the field. The fourth and fifth sentences further justify this methodology in terms of sponsor hot buttons: "this model focuses on improving health *outcomes* for individuals, families, and the *community* as a whole . . . are more likely to see positive, *long-term changes.*" In other words, rather than reinventing the wheel, the coalition will draw on nationally recognized best practices to affect sustainable change in the community.

The second and third paragraphs detail the activities that will occur in the organization and planning phase and the implementation phase. These paragraphs were tailored to reflect the language and ideas presented in the RFP guidelines "Organization and Planning Phase" and "Implementation Phase" sections. For instance, we categorized the RFP listing of potential implementation strategies into four types: coalition policy initiatives, community education, parent and child education, and provider education. The four types emphasize a multifactorial and multidisciplinary approach to accomplishing project aims and objectives.

Further, a review of the literature over the past fifteen years revealed that the asthma intervention strategies identified are the currently accepted best practices in the field; we particularly noted that individuals from The Robert Wood Johnson Foundation and the National Program Office have published articles about some of these specific strategies. More broadly, customizing details from the RFP guidelines demonstrates to the sponsor that we are not simply repeating their words back to them; rather, we are systematically analyzing and synthesizing all pertinent

information to design a project that will meet the needs of the community.

The fourth paragraph justifies the coalition's methodological approach, relating to sponsor hot buttons. Namely, all of the critical elements are in place: a broad-based asthma coalition, a resource-rich environment with verbally committed matching funds, and an outcomes-based theoretical framework to guide activities. The last sentence of this section takes the next step, looking at the long-term significance of this project framework and echoing the last sentence of the "Background" section of the RFP guidelines: "this approach can be replicated and potentially serve as a model for other conditions." Replicable models create a win-win situation: Our organizational credibility goes up, and the sponsor receives credit for contributing to nationally recognized best practices.

Evaluation. The "Evaluation" section, similar to "Project Framework," answers *how*—how project effectiveness will be determined. The RFP guidelines make immediately and repeatedly clear that evaluation and outcomes are a hot button for the sponsor. Specifically, the RFP states that proposal reviewers will assess the "strength of the proposed evaluation plan" and that "all grantees, as a condition of accepting grant funds, will be required to participate in an evaluation." Thus, this evaluation section was designed purposefully to address the logical and psychological concerns of the sponsor. Logically, evaluation means assessing whether project funds are being spent wisely, that the project is making a difference, and that project benefits are being distributed across the target population and community. Psychologically, evaluation contributes to enhanced organizational credibility, recognition, and prestige.

Because this entire section is a hot button, it is essential that we provide more persuasive detail than the RFP guidelines minimum expectation of describing the "evaluation approach, including quality and availability of data to be used." This means: (1) identifying and justifying the theoretical model that will guide evaluation activities; (2) describing the types of evaluations that will be conducted and sources of data; (3) establishing the credibility and capabilities of internal evaluators; and (4) indicating the coalition's willingness to participate in a national cross-site evaluation.

In the first paragraph, the second and third sentences identify the nationally recognized models that will be used to systematically evaluate the coalition and its activities. Evaluation is an iterative process that is integrated into the project framework. The

the Medical College of Wisconsin. He has received federal funding for research on childhood asthma, and has published findings about school-based asthma education, costs of inpatient services for pediatric asthma, trends in the severity of childhood asthma, and risk factors for pediatric emergency visits. Dr. Meurer has collaborated extensively with FAM, coalition members, and the Community Collaboration for Healthcare Quality.

Broad-Based Support. Fight Asthma Milwaukee has broad-based support from community agencies, education and service providers, and concerned parents who have access to children with asthma in our four targeted age groups. FAM will provide leadership, facilitate the planning process, and mobilize key constituents to address pediatric asthma in Milwaukee:

- Medical College of Wisconsin
- The Health Education Center
- American Lung Association-Wisconsin
- Black Health Coalition
- La Causa Inc.
- 16th Street Community Health Center
- Childcare Advisory Committee
- Community Collaboration for Healthcare Quality

- City of Milwaukee Health Department
- WI Dept. of Health and Family Services
- Children's Health Alliance of Wisconsin
- PrimeCare, CompCare, Humana, and Managed Health Services health plans
- Children's, Aurora, Covenant, and Horizon health systems
- Milwaukee Public Schools and their School-Based Health Centers

A sample of coalition strengths: the American Lung Association-Wisconsin developed award-winning asthma management training curricula for childcare providers and school teachers; 16th Street Community Health Center, with US Environmental Protection Agency funding, distributed 15,000 asthma self-care plans in English and Spanish to children in Milwaukee Public Schools through the Child Health Champion Campaign; the Community Collaboration for Healthcare Quality, a coalition of health care systems, health plans, and public health agencies distributed asthma practice guidelines to more than 2,000 physicians in Milwaukee County.

Project Framework. The project design will take a multifactorial approach to accomplishing aims and objectives. Specifically, the FAM coalition will adapt a conceptual framework from the dominant health education planning and community health promotion model, *PRECEDE/ PROCEDE*. This framework will facilitate assessing administrative, educational, behavioral, epidemiologic, and social "diagnoses." Equally important, this model focuses on improving health outcomes for individuals, families, and the community as a whole. Research suggests that by addressing the individual within this larger context, programs are more likely to see positive, long-term changes in the populations they serve.

The key factors in community change are a clear vision and mission, an action plan, quality leadership, resources for community mobilizers, documentation and feedback on changes, technical assistance, and measurable outcomes. Accordingly, during the organization and planning phase, coalition members will produce an inclusive plan that will direct asthma prevention and intervention activities. In particular, the coalition will review the specific needs of the community, define members' roles and responsibilities, identify measurable objectives, assess organizational and administrative capacities, plan systematic and sustainable change in the community, and assess risk and cost factors. In the implementation phase, education and service delivery activities will target four areas:

John Meurer, MD, MBA, Project Director   3

fourth and fifth sentences describe the types of evaluations that will be conducted: *process evaluations* look internally to assess the effectiveness of organizational systems and procedures established to make sure that the project is on track to achieve stated objectives; *outcome evaluations* look externally to assess whether project objectives were achieved and the impact that the project had on the target population and community. Both types of evaluation are essential to project success.

The subsequent bulleted list verifies that evaluation is also an inclusive process: parents, community members, and professionals from local and state, traditional and nontraditional settings will provide access to primary and secondary data that will demonstrate the effectiveness of the coalition and asthma intervention activities. Moreover, the first bulleted point addresses a distinctive feature: support from government officials.

The first two sentences of the final paragraph identify personnel responsible for conducting the evaluation, establish their credibility through their individual and organizational uniqueness, and describe their contributions to the project, e.g., maintain objectivity, rigorous standards of research, and cultural sensitivity. The third sentence addresses a distinctive feature raised in the RFP guidelines: collaboration with the National Program Office. The third and fourth sentences together reassure the sponsor that the coalition will receive direction and actively participate in the national program evaluation. National evaluation is particularly important to the sponsor because if coalitions are successful in implementing asthma management strategies, these approaches can be replicated and serve as models for other chronic health care conditions.

Sustaining Efforts. Although this section is considerably shorter than previous sections, its significance and information load are quite high; after all, this entire section is a hot button. The first part of the first sentence identifies high personnel turnover as a widespread problem for many community-based organizations; the second part of this sentence serves to differentiate our coalition from other potential applicants: our "coalition is engrained in an organizational structure that offers long-term stability and sustainability."

The second sentence explicitly answers the RFP's question about our potential for sustaining the coalition efforts over time: We can do it. The final two sentences of the paragraph justify our belief that project efforts can be sustained beyond the initial granting period by giving a concrete example of another local community coalition that was started with federal funding and continued after grant dollars ended. This history of successful grantseeking and coalition sustainability strengthens the argument that we can do it again. Recall, the RFP guidelines are not looking for an absolute guarantee of future project funding; rather, proposal reviewers are looking for evidence of a sustainability plan—or in this case, access to a proven model for coalition sustainability.

Task & Timetable & Budget. This section of the letter of intent describes to the sponsor *when* project activities will occur and *how much* the project will cost. The first paragraph overviews the time frames for key tasks to be accomplished during the project period. In essence, this paragraph is a synthesis of the main ideas presented in the "Timetable," "Organization and Planning Phase," and "Implementation Phase" sections of the RFP guidelines. Once again, we appeal to sponsor hot buttons using key words such as: *coalition member roles, inclusive, specific outcomes, long-term impacts, sustain and institutionalize changes, available resources,* and *matching funds totaling $150,000 annually.*

In this paragraph we repeat our commitment to securing matching funds and take it to the next level: In the "Project Framework" section we have *verbal* commitments for matching funds; in this section we state that by Spring we will obtain *written* commitments for annual matching funds. These institutionally authorized written commitments demonstrate to the sponsor that organizational executives buy into the project conceptually and financially—a critical step toward project sustainability.

The second paragraph briefly sketches out our budget request. The first sentence requests the full amount for the organization and planning grant; subsequent sentences give a breakdown of how funds will be spent within the given "Use of Funds" parameters outlined in the RFP guidelines. Note in particular that full-time equivalencies (FTEs) were identified with project personnel salaries and fringe benefits. Listing FTEs helps the sponsor to understand the basis of calculations and shows the level of commitment to the project. Budget line items also reflect that funding will go to support all parts of the coalition: community leaders, families, and local agencies. Distributing grant dollars across the coalition demonstrates to the sponsor that this truly is a collaborative project with inclusive participation.

Contact Person. This final paragraph provides the requested contact information for the project director,

Coalition Policy Initiatives

- Asthma management systems in schools and childcare settings, including access to medication and equipment
- Safe housing initiatives to protect children from allergens
- Payer coverage of appropriate equipment

Community Education

- Open communication among professionals, children, families, and community
- Community-based health education and case management
- Access to medical services in clinic, school, and community sites

Parent & Child Education

- Enhance patients' adherence to therapeutic plans and avoidance of triggers, especially tobacco
- Adapt asthma education curriculums for school and childcare settings
- Identify children with undiagnosed and undertreated asthma

Provider Education

- Improve provider/patient communication
- Ensure clinician compliance with asthma guidelines based on self-regulation theory
- Implement guidelines for clinician referral systems to asthma specialists
- Provide effective clinical care in non-traditional settings

Recognized and respected asthma specialists Kevin J. Kelly, MD, and John Clare, MD, will lend their expertise to project design and evaluation. Further, coalition members have verbally committed matching funds totaling one-third of each year's budget for three years—$150,000 per year. In short, our methodology has all the critical elements for a successful planning year: a broad-based asthma coalition, a resource-rich environment, highly trained professionals, and a theoretical model to guide activities. This outcomes-based framework represents a clinically effective and fiscally responsible way to establish a sustainable structure that addresses pediatric asthma, one that can be replicated and potentially serve as a model for other health conditions.

Evaluation. Performance monitoring, evaluation, and dissemination are essential components for achieving objectives. FAM will use the Institute of Medicine's *Community Health Improvement Process* to develop a pediatric asthma community health profile based on socio-demographic characteristics, health and functional status, risk factors, resource consumption, and quality of life. The iterative process of problem identification, prioritization, analysis, and implementation will be integrated with the *PRECEDE* framework to meet community needs. Assessing the effectiveness of FAM coalition efforts and activities means conducting process and outcome evaluations. Process evaluations improve project efficacy during the granting period, and outcome evaluations document the extent to which project objectives were achieved:

- Establish linkages with relevant surveillance systems and access valid and reliable data available from the Wisconsin Bureau of Health Information as well as from members of the Community Collaboration for Healthcare Quality, specifically the Milwaukee Health Department, four major health delivery systems, and four major health plans.
- Improve tracking systems to identify and follow patients and families in both clinical and non-traditional settings.
- Assess coalition activities, overall effectiveness, and capacity to achieve asthma control outcomes by engaging stakeholders, describing the program, focusing the evaluation design, justifying our conclusions, ensuring useful information, and sharing lessons learned.

To make certain that the evaluation of community interventions is objective, meets rigorous standards of research, and is sensitive to ethnic and cultural difference, the FAM coalition will team up with CHS' Center for Outcomes Research and Quality Management, one of only a few centers of its kind in the country. Ramesh

John Meurer, MD, MBA, Project Director   4

who is serving as the primary contact during the application process. Given the prevalence of Internet users, and the speed and efficiency of e-mail communications, we included the project director's e-mail address even though it was not specifically requested by the sponsor.

Although space did not permit, ideally we would have included a concluding paragraph to this letter of intent that tied together our main points and hot buttons, maintaining a focus on the impact that this project will have on the target population and community: "In short, CHS' Fight Asthma Milwaukee coalition has the expertise and experience to successfully develop and implement a sustainable strategy for asthma management that will help to reduce health disparities among urban and minority children, enhance the quality of life of children with asthma and their families, and ultimately control pediatric asthma."

Letter of Intent Design

A well-designed letter of intent makes even complex information look accessible and simplifies the reviewers' jobs. The following design features highlight the structure, hierarchy, and order of the letter of intent, helping reviewers find the information that they need.

Bulleted Lists. Bulleted lists help to get the message to the reader with a sense of immediacy without being wordy. They also help to visually break up long blocks of text. For example, the bulleted list of coalition education and service delivery activities is sandwiched between several long paragraphs describing the project framework.

Charts and Tables. In order to stay within strict page limitations, we include only one table that is absolutely necessary to the central body of the proposal.

The table is simple, comparing the ethnic composition of children in our community and emergency department visits; data in this table is too complex to present clearly in paragraph form.

Headings. Headings act like a table of contents placed directly in the proposal text; at a glance they reveal the organization of our proposal to reviewers. Boldface headings reflect key words taken from each of the nine bulleted points from the RFP section on "How to Apply." Effective use of white space sets off headings and enhances readability.

Margins. A proposal with ragged right margins is easier to read than one that is fully justified because the proportional spacing in justified type slows down readability. We used standard one-inch margins all around.

Page Numbers. Page numbers are placed in the bottom center of the proposal, and in the bottom left-hand corner of the page, we included the name of the project director.

Type Style. The text of the proposal is written in Times Roman, a serif typeface, and headings are in Arial, a sans serif typeface. This contrast in type styles makes headings stand out from the body of the text. Following RFP guidelines, we used 12 point type size.

White Space. Ample white space gives reviewers a visual clue to the structure of the proposal, often indicating that one section is ending and another is beginning. The text is single spaced, with a double space between minor paragraphs, and a triple space between major proposal sections. By design, most paragraphs are less than ten lines long, preceded and followed by a line of white space. In a page full of print, a block of unprinted lines, or white space, stands out immediately, making the proposal appear inviting and user-friendly.

Sachdeva, MD, PhD, MBA, Center Director will ensure that studies are high quality and statistically valid. Further, FAM will benefit from the direction and technical assistance of the National Program Office and Advisory Committee, and will participate in the overall evaluation of the program. Coalition members will contribute to and use tools developed by the "Allies Against Asthma" program for planning, implementing, and evaluating pediatric asthma management programs and systems of care.

Sustaining Efforts. While many community-based organizations have high personnel turnover, CHS' FAM coalition is engrained in an organizational structure that offers long-term stability and sustainability. Accordingly, FAM has the potential for substantially changing systems for pediatric asthma control beyond the granting period. With initial CDC grant support, Milwaukee has sustained an effective environmental lead prevention coalition. We anticipate that generous RWJF support will have a similar impact on asthma in our community.

Task & Timetable & Budget. With respect to the "Allies Against Asthma" initiative, in October 2000, the FAM coalition will develop a structure to ensure an inclusive but manageable planning process. In Fall 2000, we will assess the scope of the asthma problem and identify available resources. In Winter 2000–01, we will develop a plan with strategic and targeted interventions, specific outcomes and long-term impacts, and articulated coalition member roles and responsibilities. In Spring 2001, we will identify efforts to sustain and institutionalize changes and will secure a written commitment for matching funds totaling $150,000 annually for three years. By July 2001, we will submit an implementation grant proposal to RWJF.

With the demonstrated concern that you have shown for addressing pediatric asthma, we request an organization and planning grant of $150,000. Funds will support: salaries and fringe benefits for the .25 FTE project director ($22,900) and 1.0 FTE project coordinator ($37,200); consultant fees for community leaders and mobilizers ($20,000); incentives for asthmatic children and their families to participate in planning activities ($25,000); data processing by delivery systems, health plans, and public health agencies ($20,000); data analysis by the CHS Outcomes Research Center ($20,000); office supplies ($900); and spirometers for screening children in the community and school-based health centers ($4,000).

Contact Person. To answer questions or provide further information, please contact:
Dr. John R. Meurer, Center for the Advancement of Urban Children, Medical College of Wisconsin, 8701 Watertown Plank Road, Milwaukee, WI 53226. Phone: (414) 456-4116; Fax: (414) 456-6539; Email: jmeurer@mcw.edu

John Meurer, MD, MBA, Project Director   5

ANALYZING THE REQUEST FOR PROPOSAL

Our letter of intent to The Robert Wood Johnson Foundation's "Allies Against Asthma" program received a favorable review, and we were invited to submit a full proposal. In this second section of the chapter, we again follow our three-step RFP Analysis Process to determine how much work will need to go into developing a competitive application. To begin to answer questions about *relevance*, *feasibility*, and *probability*, in iterative fashion we read through three documents provided by the sponsor: the invitation to submit a full proposal, the "Issues to be Addressed by Applicant in Full Proposal," and the RFP guidelines.

Step One: Relevance—Do We Want to Do This?

Before we submitted our letter of intent, we determined that this program was indeed relevant to our organization. Thus, this time in step one of our RFP Analysis Process we did not need to assess the level of interest among key personnel and administrators for pursuing this grant opportunity. Instead, we developed a one-page memorandum summarizing the main points of the invitation to submit a full proposal and the RFP guidelines as a way to generate enthusiasm for our initial success and to reaffirm our decision to proceed with developing a complete grant application.

RFP Guidelines. You'll be pleased to know that our initial hard work has been recognized. The Robert Wood Johnson Foundation invited our coalition as 1 of 26 applicants to submit a full proposal to their "Allies Against Asthma" program. Some key points in the RFP guidelines for the full proposal include:

- 26 of 253 applicants (10%) were selected to submit a full proposal.
- 8 of 26 applicants (30%) will be awarded funding over a four-year period.
- $150,000 is available for one year for organization and planning.
- $450,000 is available per year for three years for project implementation.
- $150,000 in matching funds are required per year during project implementation.
- A full fifteen-page proposal is due June 2, 2000.
- Proposals must address specific questions raised during the letter of intent review process.

- Site visits will occur in July through September 2000.
- Funding decisions will be made in November 2000.

Let's meet this week Thursday at noon in the conference room to discuss timeframes and responsibilities for developing the full proposal. And again, congratulations on advancing to this stage of a highly competitive grant process.

Step Two: Feasibility—Can We Do This?

In step two of the RFP Analysis Process, we examined the "Issues to be Addressed by Applicant in Full Proposal" and RFP guidelines for evaluation criteria, hot buttons, and distinctive features. The expanded guidelines in this stage of the application procedure require us to describe our project in considerable detail. We recognize that we will need to invest a significant amount of time and effort into proposal planning and writing, and we remain confident that we can do it.

Evaluation Criteria. The Robert Wood Johnson Foundation will use the following stated evaluation criteria in their selection process. Proposals should include:

- A one-page cover letter
- A table of contents
- An application form
- A one-page project summary
- A fifteen-page proposal narrative that describes:
    Vision and principal objectives
    Target population and level of need
    Expertise and experience in asthma control
    Coalition membership, infrastructure, and capacity
    Planning approach and timeline
    Preliminary implementation approach
    Evaluation approach
    Sustaining coalition efforts over time
- A budget and budget narrative
- Attachments:
    Resumes of key project personnel
    Description of the application process
    Letters of support
- Issues to be Addressed by Applicant in Full Proposal:
    Plans for evaluation and outcomes
    Coalition leaders and staff
    Potential for sustaining coalition efforts
    Efforts to address health system weaknesses and challenges
    Potential approaches for system-wide change

The University of Michigan

School of Public Health
Allies Against Asthma
109 S. Observatory Street
Ann Arbor, Michigan 48109-2029

March 14, 2000

Dr. John Meurer
Children's Health System
9000 W. Wisconsin Avenue
P.O. Box 1997
Milwaukee, WI 53201

Dear Dr. Meurer:

We are pleased to inform you that the Letter of Intent submitted on behalf of your coalition for the Robert Wood Johnson Foundation program, "Allies Against Asthma" has been reviewed and we are interested in receiving a full proposal from you.

We received 253 Letters of Intent, reflecting enormous energy and creativity that is percolating throughout the country as communities mobilize to improve pediatric asthma management. We have invited 26 applicants to submit full proposals and anticipate funding 8 coalitions.

The enclosed application packet provides information and forms necessary to complete this phase of the grant process. This packet includes information to guide you in developing the narrative and budget components of your proposal. It also provides the forms necessary to complete the application process. The application kit also contains questions/considerations specific to your coalition, if any were raised during the review of your Letter of Intent. Concise and complete responses to these issues are integral to the review of the proposal.

Your completed application must be received by 5 PM on June 2, 2000 to be eligible for consideration for funding. All applications will be reviewed by the Allies Against Asthma National Advisory Committee, as well as by staff from the Foundation and the National Program Office. You will be notified in July 2000 if your coalition has been selected for a site visit, and should be informed by Fall, 2000 of the funding decision.

Should you have any questions or concerns, please do not hesitate to contact Linda Jo Doctor, Deputy Director, by telephone at 734-647-3179 or email (lindoc@umich.edu).

Congratulations on advancing to this next round of the grant process.

Best wishes,

Noreen M. Clark, Ph.D.
Director

*   *   *

Issues to be Addressed by Applicant in Full Grant Application

ID Number: 36

Coalition: Fight Asthma Milwaukee Coalition

Please include responses to the following issues in your application narrative:

    1. Describe plans for evaluation and specify particular outcomes of interest.

THE REQUEST FOR PROPOSAL

STAGE TWO: FULL PROPOSAL

- Use 12 point font
- Submit ten copies of the full proposal
- Due date: June 2, 2000

Hot Buttons and Distinctive Features. Reading between the lines of the "Issues to be Addressed by Applicant in Full Grant Application" and the RFP guidelines reveals three hot buttons and three distinctive features. In particular, the three hot buttons identified during development of the letter of intent are once again repeated throughout the application materials:

- community-based collaborative efforts;
- evaluation and outcomes;
- matching funds and sustainability.

All five of the "Issues to be Addressed" relate to these hot buttons. The first three issues—evaluation plans, coalition leadership and management, and sustainability plans—match up explicitly with hot buttons. The fourth and fifth issues are more subtle versions of these hot buttons. Specifically, the issue of organizational "weaknesses and challenges" relates to community-based collaborative efforts and outcomes. And the issue of "potential approaches for system-wide change" relates to project sustainability. In other words, the question we must be able to answer is, "When a diverse mix of organizations come together around a single topic, can they agree to implement and institutionalize changes that will impact systems of care over the long-term?"

Distinctive features appear as singular occurrences in the RFP, yet they represent real sponsor concerns. While they are not repeated throughout the application materials like hot buttons, they command attention nevertheless because they affect a project's technical approach. Three distinctive features raised in the RFP guidelines include:

- research-based approach to asthma control;
- racial/ethnic composition of the coalition;
- collaboration with the National Program Office.

While responding to distinctive features in the full proposal will not guarantee funding success, failing to acknowledge them may be viewed as a project weakness. To increase the competitiveness of our full proposal, these hot buttons and distinctive features—logical and psychological needs of the sponsor—must be systematically addressed in the narrative.

Hot Button: Community-Based Collaborative Efforts

The RFP guidelines use over two dozen different words and phrases to emphasize the importance of project efforts being "community-based" and "collaborative." Broad descriptive hot button words include: *community, community-based, coalitions, coalition-based, families, linkages, meaningful involvement,* and *sufficiently inclusive.*

Specific examples of community partners are also articulated in the "Coalition Membership" section of the RFP:

> parents and other family members of children with asthma, children with asthma, medical and clinical providers, health care delivery system entities, schools and childcare providers, public health and environmental agencies, state and local government, housing organizations, payers or insurers and managed care organizations, voluntary health organizations, community-based organizations, churches and other religious organizations, grassroots groups, academic institutions, media, business and industry.

The RFP guidelines stress that coalitions should have comprehensive membership and inclusive participation. Applicants must provide a complete list of coalition members, their organizational affiliations, and the sector that they represent. The RFP even states, "Reviewers will look for evidence that the planning process was comprehensive, that it included meaningful level of involvement from key stakeholder groups."

Hot Button: Evaluation and Outcomes

Ten key words and phrases appear approximately thirty-five times throughout the RFP guidelines emphasizing The Robert Wood Johnson Foundation's hot button concern for systematic evaluation and measurable outcomes: *evaluation, cross-site evaluation, evaluation efforts, outcomes, asthma control, assess, data, baseline data, data collection* and *analysis.*

And for the first time, the RFP identified specific examples of outcome measures to be collected, including: *pediatric asthma morbidity, including measures of health care use, symptom/disease status, mortality, and the quality of life of children with asthma.* Projects must also include outcome measures that relate to system-level change and to the composition and strength of coalition and planning efforts.

Furthermore, the "Evaluation Approach" section of the RFP guidelines also has an emphasis on evaluation data—availability of baseline data, access to primary and secondary data sources, and timing of data collection and analysis. In other words, the sponsor is

2. Describe the staff and personnel who will lead/oversee the Coalition and manage Coalition efforts over time.

3. Discuss the potential for sustaining Coalition efforts following the end of the grant period.

4. What component or efforts of the Coalition will address health system weaknesses and challenges?

5. What potential approaches hold most promising for system-wide change?

$$* \quad * \quad *$$

PROPOSAL FORMAT

A. REQUIRED CONTENTS OF THE APPLICATION

A checklist for use in preparing your proposal is included in Appendix I. Each proposal should include the following items:

1. Cover Letter

Include a one-page cover letter that provides the following information:

- Name of the coalition
- Identification of the lead organization submitting the application (name, address, phone, fax, and name of director or senior executive);
- The amount of grant funds requested and the time period
- Statement about the current legal and organizational status of the lead organization (see instructions for The Robert Wood Johnson Foundation "Request for Project Support and Conditions of Grant" Form)
- Signature of the individual authorized to legally bind and negotiate on behalf of the coalition

A sample cover letter is included in Appendix II.

2. Table of Contents

Include a Table of Contents that lists all the information contained in the proposal.

3. The Robert Wood Johnson Foundation "Request for Project Support and Conditions of Grant" Form

Include a completed "Request for Project Support and Conditions of Grant" Form with original signatures from the applicant. This document contains information regarding the legal, financial, communications, and program responsibilities of a Foundation grantee, and becomes binding upon the grantee if the application results in a grant award. The Robert Wood Johnson Foundation "Request for Project Support and Conditions of Grant" Form is included as Appendix III of this document, along with a summary of applicant tax documentation submission requirements prepared by the General Counsel of the Foundation.

4. One-page Project Summary

Provide a short description of the community and the geographic area for which the application is being submitted, the target population of children with asthma, the coalition, and the proposed approach during the planning phase.

5. Proposal Narrative (Section B provides detailed guidance)

This section is the heart of the proposal. It should describe the vision for the project and the proposed approach. Taken as a whole, information in this section should convey to the reader a clear sense that (1) there is a need for improving systems of care for children with asthma, (2) the proposed approach is comprehensive, feasible, and likely to improve the health and quality of life of a significant number of children with asthma; and (3) the outcomes specified are reasonable and the applicant has the capability to measure the effects of coalition efforts on these outcomes.

THE REQUEST FOR PROPOSAL

STAGE TWO: FULL PROPOSAL

looking for a considerable amount of detail: *Who* will be collecting and evaluating *what* data, *when*, and *how*. The significance of evaluation is emphasized further by the stipulation, "projects will be expected to participate in periodic meetings with other projects and the National Program Office designed to coordinate, streamline and enhance the value of local evaluation efforts."

Hot Button: Matching Funds and Sustainability

The RFP guidelines outline the expectation that applicants contribute to the costs of implementing this project and continue to fund it even after grant dollars expire. Hot button phrases repeated a dozen times throughout the application include: *matching contributions*, *direct and in-kind support*, *resources*, *sustain coalition efforts*, *institutionalize effective strategies*, and *continue beyond the time period funded*.

The RFP spells out the required level of matching funds: "applicants must secure matching contributions for the implementation phase that total at least one-third of the applicant's total annual budget (or roughly $150,000)." Quite simply, matching funds encourage project sustainability. Supervisors and administrators who buy into a project conceptually and financially are more likely to provide future funding support and institutionalize effective strategies after the initial granting period ends. The RFP guidelines are looking for evidence of a sustainability plan, not an absolute guarantee of future project funding.

Distinctive Feature: Research-Based Approach to Asthma Control

A research-based approach to asthma control is a modified version of the distinctive feature noted in the first stage of the application procedure: subscribing to national asthma guidelines. In the first stage, the sponsor specifically endorses the recommendations for diagnosing and treating asthma translated by the National Asthma Education and Prevention Program (NAEPP). In the second stage, the RFP does not mention the NAEPP guidelines; rather, the "Preliminary Implementation Approach" section states that intervention strategies should be "grounded in sound and relevant research and practice."

In reality, the two versions of this distinctive feature are complementary. That is, the national asthma guidelines are based on the most recent scientific literature and treatment methods. The NAEPP even has a Web site that serves as a focal point through which lo-

cal asthma coalitions can learn about each other's activities and exchange information (www.nhlbi.nih.gov/about/naepp). Applicants can draw on these resources to justify their selection of methodological approaches. Said differently, rather than inventing new strategies for asthma control, the sponsor values approaches that have already been researched and demonstrated to be effective.

Distinctive Feature: Racial/Ethnic Composition of the Coalition

In both the first and second stage of the application procedure, the RFP guidelines articulate a distinctive feature that relates to the hot button of community-based collaborative efforts. Support from government officials caught our attention as a distinctive feature because of an inconsistency in the guidelines for the letter of intent. Namely, government officials were not required constituents of the coalition, yet evidence of their participation was essential to satisfy the sponsor's eligibility and selection criteria.

The RFP guidelines for the full proposal clarify this inconsistency, specifically listing state and local government among required coalition constituents, and include a new distinctive feature: racial/ethnic composition of the coalition. In the "Coalition Membership" section, the guidelines request a table that provides a complete list of member representatives and, almost in passing, state, "Applicants should also describe the extent to which the coalition as proposed reflects the racial and ethnic composition of the target community." Because asthma disproportionately affects minority groups, the sponsor recognizes that their participation in the organization and planning phase will improve the likelihood of success during the project's implementation phase.

Distinctive Feature: Collaboration with the National Program Office

Collaboration with the National Program Office is a distinctive feature that is consistent in both the first and second stages of the application procedure. For the full proposal, this distinctive feature appears twice in the "Evaluation Approach" section of the RFP guidelines: "Projects will be expected to participate in periodic meetings with other projects and the NPO designed to coordinate, streamline, and enhance the value of local evaluation efforts" and "Projects will also collaborate in and contribute to a cross-site evaluation of the Allies Against Asthma Initiative that will be directed out of the National Program Office."

The narrative should address the following 8 areas (described further in Section B, which begins on page 12):

    a. Vision and principal objectives
    b. Target population and level of need
    c. Expertise and experience in asthma control
    d. Coalition membership, infrastructure, and capacity
    e. Planning approach and timeline
    f. Preliminary implementation approach
    g. Evaluation approach
    h. Sustaining coalition efforts over time;

It is recognized that specifics in some of these areas will be refined during the planning process. Applicants should, however, at least demonstrate a grasp of the issues involved and options that should be considered. In general, it is better to be explicit about areas of uncertainty and speak to how this will be dealt with rather than making definitive statements based on weak information.

Applicants are encouraged to limit the narrative section to 15 pages. Reviewers will consider favorably proposals that are organized well and that address each area completely and concisely.

6. Proposed Budget and Budget Narrative

Applications must include a detailed budget and accompanying budget narrative for the one-year planning phase. The budget documents will allow reviewers to cross-walk budget items with the proposed approach to ensure consistency and compatibility. The budget submitted should project accurately the expenses anticipated and delineate how Foundation funds would be used. It must also specify other sources of direct and in-kind support for coalition efforts.

Applicants are strongly encouraged to pay close attention to the Foundation's guidelines for allowable uses of grant funds when preparing their budgets. Applicants are also reminded that the maximum award for the planning period is $150,000; the Foundation's contribution can be lower than but cannot exceed this maximum amount.

A copy of The Robert Wood Johnson Foundation "National Program Site Budget Preparation Guidelines" is included in Appendix IV. To be eligible for an award, applications must include budgets that comply with Foundation policies and guidelines. The proposed budget will be reviewed carefully, and negotiations may be held with the applicant lead agency to identify areas requiring change or clarification to comply with Foundation policies.

7. Key Staff and Leadership

In an attachment to the proposal, provide a resume or a summary of experience for key project staff (hired directly or through a subcontract) and individuals who will serve in a leadership/governance capacity. Include individuals responsible for managing the daily operations of the coalition and planning efforts, and individuals responsible for evaluation activities.

In addition, for each key staff position provide the following:

    A description of the position (duties and qualifications)

    A description of the hiring process and the individuals or organizations responsible for making hiring decisions

8. Description of the Application Process

Provide a description of the process involved in preparing the planning grant application, and provide documentation to characterize the effort involved (meetings, individuals involved, etc.).

B. DETAILED INSTRUCTIONS FOR NARRATIVE SECTION

The narrative section of the proposal should be organized into the following areas, and applicants should follow the guidelines outlined below in preparing each section. This portion of the proposal will receive the greatest attention by the review committee, and applicants are encouraged to pay close attention to the content and organization of each section. ***In preparing***

Clearly, the sponsor views this grant initiative as a shared partnership. That is, in addition to providing financial support, the sponsor is participating in the design and conduct of the program. Applicants may be received more favorably when they explicitly acknowledge and assure the sponsor that they will actively collaborate with the National Program Office. In particular, this means submitting timely progress and final reports, sharing "lessons learned," and contributing to the development of best practice standards that can be replicated in other communities.

Step Three: Probability—Will We Be Competitive?

In step three of the RFP Analysis Process, we ask probing questions about our organizational strengths and weaknesses in relation to the values of the sponsor, and we pose questions raised by ambiguities, inconsistencies, discrepancies, and omissions in the RFP guidelines. Strategic thinking helps to define institutional uniqueness, while preproposal contact allows an opportunity to build credibility with the sponsor. This step ensures that our proposal will be competitive.

Strategic Thinking. As we read each major section of the RFP guidelines, we generated the following list of strategic thinking questions that needed to be addressed internally to assess our competitiveness before engaging in preproposal contacts with the sponsor. Here are some questions generated from the "Detailed Instructions for Narrative Section" of the RFP guidelines.

Vision and Principal Objectives

- What theoretical model will guide project efforts?
- What types of problems justify the need for this project?
- Which factors pose the greatest challenges to asthma control?
- Which factors hold the greatest potential for immediate success and long-term improvement?
- Which subsystems are the most important for influencing community change?
- Which changes will promote stronger systems of care?
- Are objectives realistic, expressed in terms that are SIMPLE—specific, immediate, measurable, practical, logical, and evaluable?
- Why does the sponsor ask for goals and objectives for the implementation phase when the purpose of the planning phase is to prepare for an effective implementation phase?

Target Population and Level of Need

- What specific geographic areas will be served—county, city, inner city, census tracts, zip codes, neighborhood strategic planning areas?
- What are the greatest quantifiable risks and barriers to care in the community?
- What research have National Advisory Committee members published about the pediatric asthma problem and potential solutions?
- What gaps in data exist about the prevalence of pediatric asthma in the community?
- How will the project address these gaps in data?

Asthma Control Expertise and Experience

- Are there any key members who need to be added to the coalition?
- Have we identified the core individuals, their degrees, areas of expertise, and organizations?

Coalition Membership, Infrastructure, and Capacity

- Are all of the groups identified in the RFP guidelines represented in the coalition?
- Which groups need to be added?
- How will new members be recruited and retained?
- Who has contacts with individuals in these groups to be added?
- Is representation balanced across the various types of groups?
- Does the coalition have diverse representation and an appropriate racial/ethnic mix?
- Do we have existing memoranda of understanding to show commitment to the coalition?
- How long have memoranda of understanding been in effect?
- Do we have sample letters of support and commitment?
- What strategies are in place to effectively manage the coalition?
- What structure and process changes might be necessary to maintain the manageability of a larger, more inclusive coalition?
- How will committees be organized to accommodate inclusive participation?
- Will committees follow a hierarchical structure?
- How many committees are realistic?

these sections, applicants should also ensure that any specific areas or items noted in the letter from the National Program Office (items identified during the letter of intent review process) are addressed completely.

1. Vision and Principal Objectives

This section should begin by describing the overall vision for the proposed effort, including: why the effort is needed and the types of changes envisioned. Applicants may provide a diagram or a flow chart if it will help in conveying this vision clearly.

Proposals should also include a brief and specific statement of the project's overall goals and objectives. Include and differentiate as relevant goals and objectives for the (1) organization and planning phase, and the (2) implementation phase. Discuss why the community is applying for the grant, and what is hoped that the project will accomplish. Ensure that stated goals and objectives are realistic, give the time frame and magnitude of project efforts.

Applicants should demonstrate an understanding of the various factors and sub-systems (i.e., families, health care settings, schools, housing) that influence asthma control and quality of life for children with asthma within a community. Consideration should be given to changes at the organizational and sub-system levels and their relationships that are needed to promote stronger community-wide systems of care.

2. Target Population and Level of Need

As outlined earlier, the intent of the Allies Against Asthma program is to improve systems of care for children with asthma, especially those facing greater risks and barriers to care because of their socioeconomic status. Applicants must provide a clear description of the geographic area(s) and population(s) targeted by the proposed project. The description must include information sufficient to characterize the number of children with asthma likely to be affected (estimates are acceptable), where they are located, and the level of need within their families and communities. In addition, information contained in this section should demonstrate the applicant's working knowledge of populations targeted by the project.

It is recognized that many communities lack complete data on pediatric asthma prevalence. Applicants are expected to make the best use of available data, and to outline clearly important gaps and how these will be addressed by the project.

3. Asthma Control Expertise and Experience

It is essential that the coalition have within its membership sufficient expertise in the clinical aspects of pediatric asthma and in the scientific foundation for asthma control. This section should identify the individuals and organizations that will contribute this type of expertise, describe their background/nature of their expertise in pediatric asthma and its control, and discuss how this expertise will be tapped during the planning process.

4. Coalition Membership, Infrastructure, and Capacity

The purpose of the coalition is to ensure that efforts during the planning and implementation phase will be shaped and guided by representatives from the various sub-systems influencing asthma control and quality of care for children with asthma. This section of the proposal must describe the coalition membership, the staff and infrastructure for supporting coalition activities, and the applicant's expertise and experience with coalition approaches.

Coalition membership. Applicants are strongly encouraged to include in the coalition representatives from the following sectors:

> a. Parents and other family members of children with asthma
> b. Children with asthma
> c. Medical/clinical providers (physicians, nurses, other health care professionals)
> d. Health care delivery system entities (hospitals, school-based health clinics, safety net clinics, other)
> e. Schools and childcare providers
> f. Public health and environmental agencies
> g. State and local government
> h. Housing organizations
> i. Payers or insurers and managed care organizations for low-income and uninsured populations
> j. Voluntary health organizations
> k. Community-based organizations such as churches and other religious organizations, grassroots groups, and others representing the proposed target population

- How many individuals will participate on each committee?
- How will we handle committee appointments, reappointments, and term-limits?
- How do committees communicate with each other?
- Do we have documented effectiveness of prior coalition activities?
- Will the coalition follow a theoretical model for managing the coalition and its committees?
- How will committee conflicts be addressed and resolved?
- How frequently should committee meetings be held?
- How long will committee meetings run?
- When is the best time of day to hold committee meetings to ensure inclusive participation?
- Who will be responsible for promoting community awareness of the initiative?
- How do constituents want to receive information?
- What dissemination strategies are broad-reaching and cost-effective—press releases, newsletters, newspapers, radio, television, billboards, Web pages, e-mail, pamphlets, presentations, displays?
- How will we ensure that communications are culturally sensitive?

Planning Approach and Timetable

- What are the key factors in planning community change?
- What conceptual model will drive the planning approach?
- How does the planning approach fit into the project's overarching theoretical model?
- How do we ensure that the coalition structure is inclusive?
- How do we ensure that project planning activities are manageable?
- How do we ensure that coalition planning outcomes are specific?
- How do specific planning activities relate to the overall project vision?
- How should we illustrate a timetable of planning activities, timeframes, and personnel responsible?

Preliminary Implementation Approach

- What conceptual model will guide the implementation approach?
- How does the implementation approach fit into the project's overarching theoretical model?
- What research documents the most effective asthma control implementation strategies?

- Have the National Advisory Committee members published research about potential implementation strategies?
- Do implementation strategies address environmental issues as well as the needs of children, parents, families, providers, health professionals, and the community as a whole?

Evaluation Approach

- What conceptual model will guide the evaluation approach?
- How does the evaluation approach fit into the project's overarching theoretical model?
- What types of evaluations are most appropriate for this project—structure, process, outcome, cost-effectiveness, return-on-investment analyses?
- How will evaluation feedback be used?
- Does the coalition have community baseline data from prior asthma intervention activities?
- Does the coalition have access to a variety of sources for primary and secondary data collection?
- Do internal evaluators have the capacity to manage and share data with collaborative partners?
- Are tracking systems at partner agencies compatible for sharing data?
- How will the coalition secure informed consent, ensure the integrity and confidentiality of data, and protect the rights of human subjects?
- How much change has to occur in which specific outcomes for the project to be a success?
- What contributions can internal evaluators make to the national cross-site evaluation—expertise, experience, resources?

Sustaining and Institutionalizing Coalition Efforts

- What resources are currently being used to serve the target population?
- What cash and in-kind resources can our organization contribute to this project?
- What levels of cash and in-kind support can we realistically expect from our partners?
- How will we secure financial support from partners?
- How will we track cash and in-kind contributions from collaborators?
- Can our organization or partner agencies absorb future funding responsibilities within general operating budgets once grant funds end?
- Will the project generate any revenue that can be used for sustainability?
- What innovative funding methods might be used to

l. Academic institutions and individuals with expertise in evaluation
m. Media
n. Business and industry

In table format, applicants should provide a complete list of coalition members that indicates:

(1) the name of each individual involved
(2) their organizational affiliation (if applicable)
(3) the sector they represent (defined using categories a through n outlined above)
(4) whether they are already committed, or their involvement needs to be secured
(5) a brief description of their role

Applicants should also describe the extent to which the coalition as proposed reflects the racial and ethnic composition of the target community(ies).

If new members will be added to the coalition, applicants should discuss how these individuals will be identified and recruited.

In an attachment to the proposal, the applicant should include memoranda of understanding and letters of support for those members/groups already committed to the coalition.

Coalition Infrastructure. Applicants must describe how the coalition will be structured and supported. Descriptions should address the following areas:

Leadership/governance: organization(s) and individuals who will play leadership roles in the coalition and a discussion of their expertise in this capacity. Description of governance or leadership committees, if any, for the proposed or existing coalition;

Committee structure, including a description of key committees and subcommittees already identified, and how important committee positions will be filled;

In cases where the proposed coalition builds on one or more existing coalition(s), applicants must clarify whether or not these other coalitions will continue to function and, if so, how the proposed coalition will differ from and/or relate to these other groups.

Coalition Capacity. Provide evidence of the capacity of the proposed coalition to function successfully to improve asthma control outcomes. Focus on the following two areas when describing the capacity of the proposed coalition:

- Past experience with coalition-based approaches to improving health outcomes
- Approach for managing and supporting the coalition

Administrative support: the person(s) responsible for organizing meetings and handling administrative functions such as preparing agendas, arranging for meeting times and locations, and facilitating meeting activities;

Management approach: the process of coordinating and facilitating consensus-building, establishing and maintaining linkages among relevant organizations and individuals, and ensuring that the role played by the coalition is appropriate and reflects the changing needs of the project over time. Clarify the role of the coalition and membership in the planning process, and the role envisioned for the implementation phase.

Communication strategy: the methods the coalition will use to promote community awareness of the initiative, secure involvement of a wide group of people, and disseminate findings of its accomplishments.

5. Planning Approach and Timetable

The purpose of the planning phase is to prepare for an effective implementation phase and to strengthen local capacity for sustaining over time a coalition-based approach to asthma control. To that end, the proposed planning process should demonstrate the following:

sustain the project: coalition membership fees, product sales, phone-a-thons, special events, sponsorships?

- Is there another profitable service or activity that could be expanded to cover the costs of running this new project?
- Why does the sponsor ask for a plan to secure sources of support to sustain coalition activities before the planning phase has even identified which strategies will be most appropriate for our community?

Preproposal Contact. When talking with the sponsor, we explained that we analyzed their RFP guidelines carefully but still have some unanswered questions that we would like to raise to ensure that our proposal would be of value to them. We briefly described our project and then asked the following types of PREP questions. Notice that at this second stage of the application process we ask fewer introductory "Position" and "Rationale" questions in favor of more higher order "Expectation" and "Priority" questions. Our opening conversation went like this.

> Hi, Ms. Doctor. This is John Meurer calling on behalf of the Fight Asthma Milwaukee coalition. Thank you for sharing the packet of application materials so that we may submit a full proposal to the "Allies Against Asthma" program. We've had a chance to read the RFP guidelines and the specific "issues to be addressed," and if I've caught you at a good time, I'd welcome your answers to a few specific questions.

Position: The Baseline Situation

- What can you tell us about the review process?
- Is there a specific reviewer's evaluation form that we can see?
- Who are the National Advisory Committee members that will assist in the evaluation of proposals?
- Will awards be made on the basis of any special criteria, e.g., geography, size of target population, size of the coalition?
- How many letters of support and commitment from collaborating agencies would be appropriate to include?
- Do you anticipate any modifications to the timetable of when proposals will be due, reviewed, and announced?

Rationale: Problems Existing Today

- What do you consider to be the major variables of this problem of pediatric asthma?

- What are the biggest hurdles applicants face in reaching their grant objectives?
- What are the biggest sources of dissatisfaction with current approaches?
- Which dimensions of this problem need to be addressed next?

Expectation: Basic Implications for Addressing Problems

- Why does the RFP ask applicants to "include and differentiate as relevant goals and objectives for the (1) organization and planning phase, and the (2) implementation phase" when the purpose of the planning phase is to prepare for an effective implementation phase?
- One selection criteria used in evaluating proposals is the "potential for substantially changing systems for asthma control." What is considered "substantial" change? How much change has to occur for the project to be a success?
- What's the desired local impact you'd like to see, while maintaining a balance across project breadth, depth, and financial resources available?
- Which measures of children's quality of life do you prefer to evaluate?
- Which quality of life survey tools do you recommend that coalitions use?
- Which types of evaluations do you consider to be most appropriate for this project so that results can also be used in the national cross-site evaluation?
- Who owns the evaluation data once it is collected?
- The RFP guidelines indicate that model programs must be sustainable. Does that mean activities must be institutionalized, or are there other strategies for supporting project continuation that applicants typically include in their proposals?
- What are the most common mistakes in proposals you receive?
- What would you like to see addressed in a proposal that other applicants may have overlooked?

Priority: Approaches for an Improved Situation

- What do you see as essential to improving systems of care for children with asthma that isn't happening now?
- What's needed to close the gap?
- What would be the key features of an ideal solution?
- Would this approach produce what is needed?

- A logical and feasible process for assessing asthma-related needs and resources, identifying gaps, and developing goals and objectives for improving community-wide systems of care

- Adequate focus on building assessment and planning capacity at the community level

- Meaningful involvement of the many individuals and organizations with a role in asthma control (health systems and health care professionals, payers and policy leaders, school administrators and teachers, parents and patients, etc.)

- Consideration of the full gamut of potential strategies and settings for asthma control

- Evidence that the approach will gain the acceptance of families and other community members targeted by the proposed interventions

- A resulting plan that specifies strategies and interventions, coalition member roles and responsibilities, and measurable intermediate and longer-term outcomes

- Integration with existing community health improvement efforts.

It is expected that this section of the proposal will be very concrete. Specific activities and tasks should be described clearly, along with how these activities relate to each other and to an overall strategy or vision. Applicants should include a timeline that depicts that order, frequency and duration of specific activities during the planning phase.

Some communities and coalitions will be starting the planning process from scratch while others will be further along. In cases where the coalition will build on previous efforts (for example, to assess needs and resources and/or to identify strategies and interventions), applicants must describe the planning process that was involved. Reviewers will look for evidence that the planning process was comprehensive, that it included a meaningful level of involvement from key stakeholder groups, and that the resulting goals and strategies have been shaped and understood by those groups most affected within the community. To the extent that the planning approach was not comprehensive or sufficiently inclusive, applicants should take steps during the planning phase to expand on and refine previous planning efforts.

6. Preliminary Implementation Approach

Although we expect the planning process to influence coalition decisions about specific strategies and interventions during the implementation phase, applicants should provide a preliminary sketch or vision of the types of interventions the coalition would consider employing during the implementation phase. In addition to identifying the types of strategies and interventions the coalition may employ, discuss the relationship or linkages among the different interventions and strategies. This discussion should complement yet go one step further than the discussion in the section on "Vision and Objectives."

Reviewers will consider the extent to which the proposed approach: is innovative, comprehensive and oriented toward systems change; is grounded in sound and relevant research and practice; and reflects an understanding of the interplay among various approaches, settings and systems. Even more important than the specific interventions and strategies is the way in which the proposal makes clear the relationships between the different pieces, and how together they are likely to result in meaningful improvements in systems of care for children with asthma.

7. Evaluation Approach

Each project is expected to conduct an evaluation to assess the effectiveness of coalition efforts during both the planning phase and the implementation phase. Projects will also collaborate in and contribute to a cross-site evaluation of the Allies Against Asthma Initiative that will be directed out of the National Program Office. The Foundation may also undertake an evaluation of its multi-pronged Pediatric Asthma Initiative, which would be conducted by an independent research group, and grantees would also be expected to participate in such an evaluation as well. The evaluation section of the proposal should address project-specific evaluation activities, and include the following:

- Identification of specific outcomes relevant to both the planning and implementation phases (recognizing that these will be refined further during the planning phase). Outcomes must adequately capture the impact of coalition efforts on pediatric asthma morbidity, including measures of health care use, symptom/disease status, mortality, and the quality of life of children with asthma. In addition, it is expected that projects will include outcome measures that relate to system-level change and to the composition and strength of coalition and planning efforts.

- What outcomes do you expect from grantees?
- Conducting a comprehensive evaluation of the planning and implementation phases of the project can mean examining a variety of humanistic, economic, and functional status outcome indicators; are there any specific outcome indicators that you prefer to see evaluated?
- What are the preferred strategies for disseminating project results?

This iterative, three-step RFP Analysis Process moves us along the Roads to the Persuasion Intersection. Next, we examine how we connect our project idea to the values of the sponsor through the right balance of logic, emotion, and relationships in the complete grant application.

- Discussion of available data sources, including sources of baseline data and limitations or gaps in available data sources and how these will be addressed.

- Discussion of how the coalition will secure access to data from secondary sources, such as hospitals and schools, including any issues related to confidentiality.

- Discussion of methods for measuring changes in outcomes due to coalition efforts.

- Discussion of how the coalition plans to obtain and use input from a broad range of coalition members in the design and implementation of the evaluation.

- A brief outline of the timing of design, data collection and analysis activities.

- Identification of the individual(s) with primary responsibility for evaluation activities.

Projects will be expected to participate in periodic meetings with other projects and the NPO designed to coordinate, streamline and enhance the value of local evaluation efforts. In addition, projects will be expected to submit periodic program updates that include information about the evaluation, and to prepare a final evaluation report, suitable for wide dissemination.

8. Sustaining and Institutionalizing Coalition Efforts

It is expected that coalition efforts will continue beyond the time period funded by the Foundation, and to this end applicants must secure matching contributions for the implementation phase that total at least one-third of the applicant's total annual budget (or roughly $150,000). Beyond this support, sustaining coalition efforts will require changes at the provider, policy and system level to institutionalize effective strategies and approaches. This section of the application should discuss how the coalition plans to secure other sources of in-kind and financial support to sustain coalition efforts, and other ways in which the coalition will ensure that effective strategies become institutionalized within the community.

C. PROPOSAL SUBMISSION DETAILS

Applicants should submit one (1) original signed proposal and nine (9) copies. Applications must be received by the Allies Against Asthma National Program Office before 5:00 p.m. (Eastern Time) on Friday, June 2, 2000. Applications should be mailed to the following address:

Linda Jo Doctor, Deputy Director
Allies Against Asthma
University of Michigan, School of Public Health
109 South Observatory Street
Ann Arbor, Michigan 48109

Please note that FAX copies will not be accepted. The application should be prepared with a font size of at least 12 point and with one-inch margins.

D. PROPOSAL REVIEW

After an initial review of the applications, communities may be asked to respond to questions or to provide further clarification on some aspect(s) of their proposal. Site visits will be conducted to selected applicants during the months of June through September. The Foundation expects to announce grant awards in November, 2000.

E. APPENDIXES

Appendix I: Proposal Preparation Checklist
Appendix II: Sample Cover Letter
Appendix III: The Robert Wood Johnson Foundation "Request for Project Support and Conditions of Grant" Form and Tax Documentation Submission Requirements
Appendix IV: The Robert Wood Johnson Foundation National Program Site Budget Preparation Guidelines

THE REQUEST FOR PROPOSAL

STAGE TWO: FULL PROPOSAL

DEVELOPING THE COVER LETTER

Developing the cover letter for our full proposal was quite easy because we followed the model established by the sponsor in Appendix II of the RFP guidelines. Although the cover letter is short in length, it carries a heavy information load. The first paragraph:

- identifies the coalition;
- specifies the lead organization submitting the application;
- names the program to which the proposal is being submitted;
- highlights the coalition's uniqueness and credibility;
- stipulates the amount of grant funds requested and the time period.

The remainder of the cover letter

- includes a statement about the current legal and organizational status of the lead organization;
- identifies the name and address of the president of our organization;
- provides contact information for the project director—telephone, fax, and e-mail;
- includes the signature of the project director, the individual authorized to legally bind and negotiate on behalf of the coalition.

This model cover letter, however, does not allow us to present an overview of the proposal, describe the project's significance, or reflect the project's consistency with sponsor values, funding priorities, evaluation criteria, and hot buttons. Thus, it is essential that we incorporate these ideas into the project summary and the first paragraph of the full proposal.

Because we do not want our proposal to be rejected on a technicality, we adhere to the format of sponsor's sample cover letter. Working within the RFP guidelines can sometimes be a challenge, yet we find creative ways to tell the sponsor both what they want to know and what we want them to know. Addressing logical and psychological needs in one seamless argument throughout our complete grant application will increase our chances for funding success.

Linda Jo Doctor, MPH   May 31, 2000
Deputy Director
Allies Against Asthma National Program Office
At The University of Michigan
School of Public Health
109 S. Observatory, Room M5318 SPH II
Ann Arbor, MI 48109-2029

Reference: Fight Asthma Milwaukee Coalition (ID #36)

Dear Ms. Doctor:

On behalf of the Fight Asthma Milwaukee coalition, Children's Health System is
submitting a proposal under the *Allies Against Asthma* initiative. Fight Asthma
Milwaukee is the only community-based asthma coalition in Wisconsin, and was one of
the first established in the country. We are requesting $150,000 to fund the planning
phase of this effort between November 1, 2000, and October 31, 2001.

The attached copies of our tax documentation are true and current copies of the
originals are on file with Children's Health System and they remain in full force and
effect.

The President of our organization is:
        Jon E. Vice, President
        Children's Health System
        9000 W. Wisconsin Avenue
        P.O. Box 1997
        Milwaukee, WI 53201

To answer questions or provide further information, please contact me directly by—
phone: (414) 456-4116; fax: (414) 456-6539; or, email: jmeurer@mcw.edu

Sincerely,

John R. Meurer, MD, MBA, Project Director
Assistant Professor of Community Pediatrics and Health Policy,
Center for the Advancement of Urban Children,
Medical College of Wisconsin and Children's Health System

THE COVER LETTER

STAGE TWO: FULL PROPOSAL

DEVELOPING THE APPLICATION FORM

The Robert Wood Johnson Foundation requires a completed "Request for Project Support" application form to be submitted with the full proposal. This form helps establish our credibility in a condensed format. In ten line item elements, we present information about our organization, institutional officials, project director, project, and budget. Each element is described below.

Elements of the Application Form

Item 1: Title of Project. Our project title is short and descriptive, "Milwaukee Allies Against Asthma." This title reflects the collaborative nature of our project and connects us to the priorities and values of the sponsor.

Item 2: Purpose of Project. The application form limits us to a one-sentence statement of purpose for our project. In a telegraphic phrase (thirteen words), we describe both our overarching goal, i.e., "to improve efforts to control pediatric asthma," and methodological approach, i.e, "through a community-based coalition." These two concepts were taken directly from the first two sentences of the Request for Proposal (RFP) guidelines.

Item 3: Applicant Institution. Grant awards are made to institutions, not individuals. Thus, Children's Health System, Inc., is the legal applicant for this project. Our asthma coalition is a subsidiary under this parent entity. As required, we provide a complete mailing address.

Item 4: Amount of Support Requested. In this line item we enter the amount of project funding requested from the sponsor. At a glance, reviewers can determine that our request adheres to the imposed limit of $150,000 for a one-year planning grant.

Item 5: Period for Which Support is Requested. Following the RFP guidelines, we enter the starting date for the project as November 1, 2000. This means that our twelve-month project is estimated to end on October 31, 2001.

Item 6: Project Director. The Project Director serves as the key point of contact between The Robert Wood Johnson Foundation and our institution and is the individual ultimately responsible for all programmatic aspects of this initiative. Although not specifically requested, we provide a fax number along with the telephone number. More significantly, reviewers will recognize that our project director is well-qualified to lead this project. He has advanced degrees that address both the medical side (M.D.) and the administrative side (M.B.A.) of this initiative. This is an important credibility statement for the proposal.

Item 7: Check to be Made Payable to. As the fiscal agent (and legal applicant) for the project, grant funds will be made payable to Children's Health System, Inc. The sponsor includes this line item in case the applicant institution and fiscal agent are not one in the same.

Item 8: Institutional Financial Officer. We enter the name and title of the official who has responsibility for all financial matters for the institution, including management, reporting, and audits.

Item 9: Applicant Institutional Approval. We enter the name and title of the official who has the authority to accept grant funding and commit the institution to executing the proposed project.

Item 10: Evidence of Tax-Exempt Status. Under federal law, most grant awards made by private foundations are to tax-exempt nonprofit organizations. Children's Health System, Inc., is such an organization under Section 501(c)(3) of the Internal Revenue Code.

The Robert Wood Johnson Foundation
Route 1 and College Road East
Princeton, NJ 08543-2316

Request for Project Support

Title of Project:
Milwaukee Allies Against Asthma

Purpose of Project:
To improve efforts to control pediatric asthma in Milwaukee through a community-based coalition

Applicant Institution (name and address):	**Check to be Made Payable to:**
Children's Health System, Inc. 9000 W. Wisconsin Avenue Milwaukee, WI 53201	Children's Health System, Inc.

Amount of Support Requested:	**Institutional Financial Officer (name, title, telephone):**
$150,000	Timothy L. Birkenstock
Period for Which Support is Requested:	Treasurer/CFO
from 11/01/2000 through 10/31/2001	Children's Health System, Inc. (414) 266-6220; (414) 266-6409 FAX

*Project Director (name, title, telephone):	**Applicant Institutional Approval:**
John R. Meurer, MD, MBA Assistant Professor of Pediatrics Medical College of Wisconsin (414) 456-4116; (414) 456-6539 FAX	Jon E. Vice President Children's Health System, Inc.

Please provide the following evidence of your institution's tax status:

If your institution is a tax-exempt organization described in Section 501(c)3 of the Internal Revenue Code. (i) a copy of the letter of your institution received from the Internal Revenue Service stating that your institution is exempt form taxation by virtue of being described in Section 501(c)3; (ii) a copy of the letter your institution received from the Internal Revenue Service stating that your institution is not a private foundation described in Section 509(a) or stating that your institution is an exempt operating foundation described in Section 4940(d)2; and (iii) a copy of Form 4653 or Form 1023 and other data, if any, your institution has filed with or received from the Internal Revenue Service concerning your tax status.

In your institution is an organization described in Section 170(c)1 or Section 511(a)2B of the Internal Revenue Code. (i) a copy of the correspondence, if any, from the Internal Revenue Service stating that fact; or (ii) a copy of the legislation establishing your institution.

These documents must be accompanied by a letter signed by a responsible officer of your institution certifying that the copies so provided are true and correct copies of the originals on file with your institution and that they remain in full force and effect.

Any questions you may have about your tax-exempt status should be directed to the Office of the Vice President, General Counsel and Secretary (609) 243-5908.

* The project director is the individual directly responsible for developing the proposed activity, its implementation, and day-to-day direct supervision of the project should funds be made available.

THE APPLICATION FORM

STAGE TWO: FULL PROPOSAL

DEVELOPING THE CROSS-WALK

Although the Request for Proposal (RFP) guidelines did not specifically ask for it, we included a one-page "cross-walk" to the location of responses to specific reviewer questions. The cross-walk restates each of the five questions presented in the "Issues to be Addressed by Applicant in Full Grant Application" and presents in bulleted list fashion the page number, proposal section, and an overview of the answers. Because all five of the "Issues to be Addressed" relate to hot buttons, the answers to these questions are emphasized throughout the proposal.

The cross-walk, similar to the project summary, previews the proposal and is a useful tool for reviewers when writing up an analysis of our project. Although the proposal answers all five specific "Issues to be Addressed," it was a challenge to provide succinct answers within the context of the prescriptive structure and page limits of the proposal narrative. The cross-walk is a surreptitious way to circumvent space restrictions yet do so in a way that simplifies the jobs of reviewers. The stimulus idea for including a cross-walk came from the "Proposed Budget and Budget Narrative" section of the RFP, which suggested "the budget documents will allow reviewers to cross-walk budget items with the proposed approach to ensure consistency and compatibility."

The first three "Issues to be Addressed" match up directly with hot buttons and relate to specific sections of the RFP, e.g., "Evaluation Approach," "Expertise and Experience in Asthma Control," and "Sustaining Coalition Efforts over Time." The fourth and fifth issues are more subtle versions of hot buttons and relate to multiple sections of the RFP.

The fourth issue, "health system weaknesses and challenges," relates to the hot buttons of community-based collaborative efforts and outcomes. That is, one challenge for our coalition is to broaden its community-based membership. The RFP guidelines "strongly encourage" coalitions to include representatives from 14 different public and private sectors, and at the same time, membership should reflect the racial and ethnic diversity of the community. A second challenge for our coalition will be to effectively implement research-based strategies that improve asthma control outcomes. Although coalition members know and subscribe to national asthma guidelines, large variations still exist in the recommendations and practices of some health care providers. In short, addressing challenges at the system level is necessary to affect long-term outcomes.

The fifth issue, "potential approaches for system-wide change," relates to the hot button of project sustainability. The RFP guidelines are clear that to sustain over time a coalition-based approach to asthma control, we must: have meaningful involvement of the many individuals and organizations with a role in asthma control; consider the full gamut of potential strategies and settings for asthma control; and develop a plan that specifies strategies and interventions, coalition member roles and responsibilities, and measurable intermediate and longer-term outcomes. Said differently, when diverse organizations plan, implement, and institutionalize effective strategies for asthma control, they will be able to produce system-wide change.

As a whole, the cross-walk illustrates how these issues, which are also sponsor hot buttons, are addressed throughout the proposal. Further, it foreshadows how our project design will satisfy the logical and psychological needs of the sponsor.

Cross-Walk to Specific Reviewer Questions

1. Describe plans for evaluation and specify particular outcomes of interest.
- Pages 13–15, "Evaluation Approach" describe relevant outcomes, sources of primary and secondary data, methodology for measuring change, and key evaluation personnel.

2. Describe the staff and personnel who will lead/oversee the Coalition and manage Coalition efforts over time.
- Page 5, "Asthma Control Expertise & Experience" provides detail about the Project Director and Committee Chairs and Coordinators.

- The Attachment, "Key Staff & Leadership" contains curriculum vitae for key individuals who will serve in a leadership/governance capacity.

3. Discuss the potential for sustaining Coalition efforts following the end of the grant period.
- Page 15, "Sustaining & Institutionalizing Coalition Efforts" describes coalition contributions during planning and implementation years, and strategies for long-term sustainability.

- The Attachment, "Description of the Application Process" includes a coalition-generated list of potential sources of support beyond the granting period.

4. What component or efforts of the Coalition will address health system weaknesses and challenges?
- Pages 5–10, "Coalition Membership, Infrastructure, & Capacity" describe how MAAA will become more inclusive by broadening the mission of member agencies, developing more comprehensive strategies, and recruiting new members annually; will have a multi-disciplinary committee structure to address family, community, provider, environmental, surveillance, and evaluation issues through multiple communication mechanisms. The Budget Narrative contains a table illustrating MAAA Coalition expanded roles.

- Pages 10–11, "Planning Approach & Timetable" articulate how strategic plans will be based on psychosocial theory and scientific evidence and have an on-going evaluation of processes and outcomes of asthma care from primary and secondary sources.

- Pages 12–13, "Preliminary Implementation Approach" describe effective interventions to promote physician adoption of national asthma practice guidelines.

5. What potential approaches hold most promising for system-wide change?
- Pages 10–12, "Planning Approach & Timetable" outlines a planning process that is inclusive, manageable, and has specific outcomes; contains a coalition-generated list of problems facing children with asthma and potential approaches for implementing change.

- Pages 12–13, "Preliminary Implementation Approach" details a mixture of strategies to produce system-wide change: family & community advocacy, provider quality improvement, and environmental risk reduction.

THE CROSS-WALK

STAGE TWO: FULL PROPOSAL

DEVELOPING THE PROJECT SUMMARY

The project summary serves as a condensed 500-word substitute for our entire proposal. It provides a quick overview of what we propose to do and a rapid understanding of the project's significance, generalizability, and potential contribution. To ensure consistency of presentation, the project summary was written *after* the proposal was completed. The project summary also adheres to the order of the proposal, uses major section headings, and maintains the same overall style and tone.

Elements of the Project Summary

Heading. The boldface heading at the top center of the page identifies that this is the project summary and *not* the first page of the proposal.

Paragraph #1. This first paragraph identifies the applicant organization, describes our organizational uniqueness, establishes coalition credibility, and defines the significance of the project in terms of *what* we will accomplish—developing a sustainable strategy for asthma management that will improve health outcomes for the target population. This paragraph is quite similar to the first paragraph of the full proposal. The first and last sentences, in fact, are identical.

Key acronyms for our organization, coalition, and project are spelled out in full. This paragraph also introduces the three hot buttons that will be reiterated throughout the proposal: community-based collaborative efforts, evaluation and outcomes, and matching funds and sustainability. Notice the use of key phrases such as *coalition, improved health status,* and *sustainable strategy.* Finally, articulating the benefit of the project to the target population in the last sentence provides a smooth transition to the next paragraph.

Paragraph #2. "Target Community & Population" quantifies the extent of the asthma problem among targeted community members. That is, this paragraph identifies *where* the project is taking place, *who will benefit* from targeted activities, and *why* the project is needed. The first sentence recognizes that the asthma problem disproportionately affects children and minorities. The second sentence justifies why the need is greater in our community than in other parts of the state: Nearly half of the state's total inpatient hospitalizations occur here. The third sentence compares our community's asthma hospitalization rate against the federal standard. The final sentence states our credibility to lead this project and effectively segues to the next section.

Paragraph #3. This "MAAA Coalition" paragraph describes the value of community-based coalitions and identifies exactly *who* is responsible for leading project efforts. In bulleted list fashion we overview three unique features of our coalition that relate to sponsor hot buttons: inclusive participation, expert leadership, and shared vision. These features demonstrate to the sponsor that we've put in a considerable amount of thought into developing a manageable project that will have a significant long-term impact in the community.

Paragraph #4. The "Planning Approach" describes our project methodology—*how* the project will be conducted in order to achieve the desired results. Taken as a whole, this paragraph conveys to the sponsor that our approach is comprehensive, feasible, measurable, based in sound theory and relevant practice, and is likely to improve health outcomes for children with asthma. Notice how the fourth sentence justifies our methodological selections to guide planning and implementation phases; namely, we are using the dominant health education and community health promotion models in the field. The final sentence describes how enacting this combination of approaches will enable us to achieve project goals including affecting system-wide change, which is detailed further in the next paragraph.

Paragraph #5. This concluding paragraph on "System-Wide Change" ties the whole proposal together. It succinctly summarizes our credibility and capacity to carry out this project, and it highlights the main points and hot buttons repeated throughout the proposal. We have all of the critical elements in place to implement a successful project: highly trained professionals, broad-based support, a resource-rich environment, and a sound approach to realizing lasting change in the community. The summary ends on a humanistic note, articulating the benefit of the project to the target population.

Project Summary

Children's Health System (CHS), Wisconsin's only independent nonprofit health system dedicated solely to the well-being of children, is deeply concerned about controlling pediatric asthma. Our Fight Asthma Milwaukee (FAM) coalition is the only community-based asthma coalition in the state, and was one of the first established in the country. Building on the strengths of FAM, this project will create a new, more inclusive *Milwaukee Allies Against Asthma (MAAA)* coalition. MAAA will develop a sustainable strategy for asthma management that will improve the health status of vulnerable urban youth.

Target Community & Population. Although asthma affects people of all ages, races, and ethnic groups, low-income and minority populations experience substantially higher rates of fatalities, hospital admissions, and emergency department visits due to asthma. Nearly half of Wisconsin's total asthma inpatient hospitalizations of children ages 0–17 occur in Milwaukee County. The asthma hospitalization rate for children in Milwaukee County is 4.49 per 1000, over four times the Healthy People 2010 goal of 1.0 per 1000. Although African Americans make up less than one-third of the County's population, they account for over two-thirds of asthma hospitalizations. Children's Health System is uniquely suited to lead this project because we treat greater than 95% of children admitted for asthma care in Milwaukee.

MAAA Coalition. Coalitions are powerful and effective mechanisms for realizing change at the local level. Dr. John Meurer, Project Director, has the expertise and collaborative history with coalition partners to make this project succeed. MAAA is driven by three key principles:

- *Inclusive Participation*—the coalition includes diverse health-related agencies, community-based organizations, educational institutions, and concerned parents of children with asthma.
- *Expert Leadership*—a core group of respected asthma specialists and dedicated parents lend their expertise to designing effective community projects and maintaining the coalition.
- *Shared Vision*—coalition participants accept the shared responsibility and decision-making for improving the quality of life for children with asthma and their families.

Planning Approach. MAAA's planning approach is driven by and directly responsive to community needs. Programs and evaluations will reflect a theoretical understanding of behavior change. Our application of social learning theory will address both the psychosocial dynamics underlying health behavior and the methods of promoting behavior change, while emphasizing cognitive processes and their effect on behavior. MAAA will promote stronger community-wide systems of care by integrating two conceptual models into planning and implementation: *PRECEDE/PROCEED*, the dominant health education and community health promotion model, and the Institute of Medicine's Community Health Improvement Process, a planned approach for improving health. MAAA will take a multifactorial approach to achieving goals and objectives, enacting a mixture of strategies broadly targeting families, providers, and environmental risks.

System-Wide Change. MAAA is uniquely positioned to harness and focus collective talents, expertise, and asthma resources to effect lasting change in the community. When properly nurtured, coalitions have tremendous potential to shape public policy, to reach asthma patients with programs and services, and to educate health care providers. Collectively, these approaches hold the most promise for long-term, system-wide change that will enhance the quality of life of children with asthma and their families.

DEVELOPING THE FULL PROPOSAL

The invitation to submit a full proposal came as a direct result of our letter of intent. We want to build on this initial success. The first step in developing the full proposal was to analyze the invitation to submit a full proposal, the "Issues to be Addressed by Applicant in Full Grant Application," and Request for Proposal (RFP) guidelines. This analysis revealed evaluation criteria, hot buttons, and distinctive features that influence the form and structure of the proposal. Strategic thinking and preproposal contact gives us additional information so that the details of our proposal match the values of the sponsor. These steps increase the persuasiveness of our proposal because we present the right balance of logical, emotional, and relational elements.

Because the full proposal recaps and expands the letter of intent, there will be some overlap in the information presented. In this case, select redundancy is a proposal strength. It shows the sponsor a level of consistency in project development, and more importantly, ideas gain strength through repetition. The same three hot buttons that we identified for the letter of intent are once again addressed repeatedly throughout the full proposal. Distinctive features in the full proposal are similar, but not identical, to those in the letter of intent. Each distinctive feature is addressed twice in the full proposal, thus ensuring that reviewers who skim read do not miss them.

Elements of the Full Proposal

Title. The boldface heading at the top of the page, identical to the letter of intent, identifies the applicant and the project title. The project title, "Milwaukee Allies Against Asthma," reflects that of the sponsor's grant program yet is customized to our community. It is descriptive without being cutesy or a tricky acronym. Equally important, the title will still be appropriate even after sponsor funding ends.

Overview. The opening paragraph summarizes the entire proposal, identifying the applicant organization, the extent of the problem in the community, and the overall project goal. For the purposes of consistency, the opening is quite similar to that used in the letter of intent—the first four sentences, in fact, are identical. These sentences describe our organization's uniqueness, quantify the asthma problem, and overview current coalition asthma control activities.

Subsequent sentences in this opening paragraph establish coalition credibility and uniqueness and foreshadow the three hot buttons that will be reiterated throughout the full proposal: (1) community-based collaborative efforts; (2) evaluation and outcomes; and (3) matching funds and sustainability. Specifically, the coalition will expand to be more inclusive; coalition efforts aim to improve the health status of vulnerable urban youth; and, the coalition will develop a sustainable strategy for asthma management. The paragraph ends on a humanistic note, articulating the benefit of the project to the target population.

Vision & Principal Objectives. The "Vision & Principal Objectives" section establishes the tone for the entire project. It summarizes the asthma problem, describes the project's vision, goals, and objectives based on a theoretical model, and illustrates the project's framework. And when considered in combination with the next section, "Target Population & Need," approximately 25 percent of the narrative is dedicated to explaining *why* we are applying for grant funding and *what* we hope to accomplish in our community.

Our vision statement paints, in broad brush strokes, the "big picture" or the lay of the land. It shows the sponsor that we know where we are at and where we are going; we have identified the problem, a solution, and the potential benefits to the target population. Principal objectives describe to the sponsor exactly *what* we are going to do to solve the identified problem. When sponsors fund projects, they are literally "buying" project objectives. That is why objectives must be SIMPLE—specific, immediate, measurable, practical, logical, and evaluable.

The first paragraph summarizes the extent of the asthma problem. The first three sentences describe the problem at national, state, and local levels. The fourth sentence articulates the consequences of pediatric asthma: poorer development of lung function. The paragraph ends on a positive note, asserting that our coalition can reduce the adverse impact of asthma in the community, measuring ourselves against the federally established Healthy People standards.

The next paragraphs present our solution to the asthma problem. The project design is based on a nationally recognized theoretical model for addressing structure, process, and outcomes. Following this model, "Project Aims & Objectives" presented in the letter of intent are recast as project goals and objectives to be accomplished in the organization and planning phase and the implementation phase. The need for these objectives is addressed in the next section of the proposal, "Target Population & Need."

Following the suggestion in the RFP guidelines, to

Children's Health System: *Milwaukee Allies Against Asthma*

Children's Health System (CHS), Wisconsin's only independent nonprofit health system dedicated solely to the well-being of children, is deeply concerned about controlling pediatric asthma. Asthma is the number one reason for hospitalization at CHS—nearly 1,000 admissions per year. But our concern for children extends beyond the walls of our hospital. Our Fight Asthma Milwaukee (FAM) coalition provides quality asthma education, outreach, and referral services that enable children, families, and the community to maintain healthy lifestyles. FAM is the only community-based asthma coalition in Wisconsin, and was one of the first established in the country. Building on the strengths of FAM, this project will create a new, more inclusive *Milwaukee Allies Against Asthma (MAAA)* coalition. MAAA will develop a sustainable strategy for asthma management that will improve the health status of vulnerable urban youth.

1. Vision & Principal Objectives. An epidemic is underway in the US. The number of people with asthma has more than doubled in the past 15 years. Asthma is the most common chronic childhood illness, affecting nearly 100,000 of Wisconsin's children under age 18, a majority of whom live in southeastern Wisconsin. Children who do not receive adequate asthma care have poorer development of lung function and more rapid decline in adult lung function than children who received appropriate primary medical and specialty care (Pappas 1997). The Milwaukee Allies Against Asthma coalition, using national Healthy People 2010 goals for asthma as targets, aims to reduce the adverse impact of pediatric asthma in the community.

MAAA's vision for the overall project effort is based on Lu Ann Aday's "Framework for Classifying Topics and Issues in Health Services Research" (1998). Project goals and objectives reflect Aday's model for addressing structure, process, and outcomes. More specifically, addressing **structure** goals during the Organization & Planning Phase will allow us to accomplish **process** and **outcomes** goals during the Implementation Phase.

Structure Goal: Develop a sustainable strategy for asthma management in the community
  Health Policy Objective: Develop approaches to address barriers to asthma care financing and treatment: establish policies to support self-management, enhance services, provide resources, and build capacity of families and communities to control asthma.

  Delivery System Objectives: Develop and implement provider education based on existing national guidelines to ensure standard and appropriate treatment of children. Establish linkages with existing asthma and other relevant surveillance systems.

  Population at Risk Objectives: Develop a pediatric community health profile. Decrease racial/ethnic disparities in asthma care. Provide community-based health education to improve asthma identification/self-management and involvement in coalition activities.

  Environment Objective: Assess the prevalence of environmental allergens and tobacco smoke. Use *PRECEDE/PROCEED* and *Community Health Improvement Process* models to evaluate physical, social, and economic environments.

Process Goal: Develop and implement targeted communication strategies to build asthma awareness, support, and involvement of professionals, children, families, and community
  Realized Access Objectives: Improve the quality of and provide new access to asthma-related medical services in clinic, school, child care, and community sites. Improve access to resources to obtain appropriate asthma medications and asthma equipment.

  Health Risks Objective: Undertake prevention efforts to reduce exposure to environmental precipitants, e.g., tobacco smoke, household dust mites, and cockroaches.

Intermediate Outcome Goal: Reduce hospital admissions, emergency department visits, missed school days, and wheezing episodes
  Effectiveness, Equity, & Efficiency Objective: Conduct evaluations to assess coalition activities including the extent to which they strengthen the coalition's capacity to be effective and achieve asthma control outcomes.

Ultimate Outcome Goal: Control pediatric asthma
  Health Objective: Enhance the quality of life of children with asthma and their families.

Framework for *Milwaukee Allies Against Asthma.* The following diagram depicts our adaptation of Aday's model to address pediatric asthma, and illustrates the complex relationship between factors and sub-systems that influence asthma control within the community.

2. Target Population & Need. Although asthma affects people of all ages, races, and ethnic groups, low-income and minority populations experience substantially higher rates of fatalities, hospital admissions, and emergency department visits due to asthma (DHHS 2000). The asthma hospitalization rate for children in Milwaukee County is 4.49 per 1000, over four times the Healthy People 2010 goal of 1.0 per 1000. The Wisconsin Office of Health Care Information reports that nearly half of the state's total asthma inpatient hospitalizations of children ages 0–17 occur in Milwaukee County. Children's Health System is uniquely suited to lead this project because we treat greater than 95% of children admitted for asthma care in Milwaukee.

Hospitalization Rates. The table below, "Child Asthma Hospitalization Rates in Milwaukee County, 1998," illustrates asthma rates per thousand. Table cells also show the number of children admitted for asthma divided by the population of children. Of the 638 central city children and the 439 non-central city children, 74% and 48% respectively were enrolled in Medicaid; total Medicaid charges exceeded $1.3 million. And although Blacks make up less than one-third of Milwaukee County's population, they accounted for 68% of asthma hospitalizations.

Description	Central City Milwaukee Rates	Non-central City Milw. County Rates	Healthy People Goals
AGE: 0–4 years	337/31,418 = **10.73**	187/41,908 = **4.46**	2.50
AGE: 5–17 years	301/70,050 = **4.30**	252/96,646 = **2.61**	.80
RACE: Black	539/66,272 = **8.13**	185/10,807 = **17.12**	2.65
RACE: White	49/23,564 = **2.08**	201/122,028 = **1.65**	NA
RACE: Hispanic	37/10,934 = **3.38**	46/7,176 = **6.41**	2.65

John Meurer, MD, MBA, Project Director   1

THE FULL PROPOSAL

help convey our project vision we provided a diagram illustrating the complex relationship between factors and systems that influence asthma control within the community. The added value of a diagram is that it depicts patterns and associations that may otherwise have gone unnoticed in the narrative alone. Our project framework quickly reveals our conceptual approach to addressing structure, process, and outcome goals. This framework also guides our division of organization and planning and implementation activities into structure, process, and outcomes. In other words, "Vision & Principal Objectives" overviews the project in relation to the community, while "Planning Approach & Timetable" and "Preliminary Implementation Approach" detail specific activities that will make the project a success.

Equally significant, this section introduces the three sponsor hot buttons that will be repeatedly addressed throughout the proposal: community-based collaborative efforts, evaluation and outcomes, and matching funds and sustainability. Note the use of key words and phrases, such as: *coalition, community, professionals, children, families, linkages, assess, outcomes, evaluate, quality of life, resources,* and *sustainable strategy.* Strategic repetition of ideas that speaks to a sponsor's subjective and objective needs increases the competitiveness of our proposal.

Target Population & Need. This "Target Population & Need" section of the proposal tells the sponsor *where* the project is taking place, *who will benefit* from targeted activities, and *why* the project is needed. Although the sponsor did not request details about the statement of the problem—or level of need—in the letter of intent, we included it as a means to make our application stand out from the competition. Documentation of the need is a crucial factor for reviewers because it provides the rationale for our project.

In this full proposal we supplement the letter of intent's presentation of four types of needs: hospitalization rates, poverty, school absenteeism, and smoke exposure. These categories of problems came from analyzing the RFP guidelines for the letter of intent, most notably in the "Background" and "The Program" sections. These different types of needs also reflect gaps in the system, e.g., treatment does not follow national guidelines, and gaps in status, e.g., health disparities exist between minority and nonminority children.

We subsequently expand our discussion of the statement of the problem to include two additional needs: morbidity and mortality, and gaps in data. The issue of "gaps in data" is specifically identified in the RFP. Gaps in knowledge and supporting data may actually contribute to the pediatric asthma problem. "Morbidity and mortality," on the other hand, is an unfortunate consequence of the asthma problem, an extension of hospitalization rates. Collectively these problems are the reason for implementing project objectives. More broadly, repetition of key topics maintains the continuity between our letter of intent and full proposal. Introducing new issues and details shows our comprehensive knowledge and understanding of the needs of the community.

The first paragraph, similar to our presentation in the letter of intent, recognizes that the asthma problem disproportionately affects children and minorities. The second sentence quantifies the need in our community: a hospitalization rate that is over four times the federal standard. This sentence also foreshadows the subsequent table, which illustrates hospitalization rates inside and outside of the central city by age and race, and compares them with the Healthy People goals. The third sentence justifies why the need is greater in our community than in other parts of the state: Nearly half of the state's total pediatric inpatient hospitalizations occur here. The final sentence emphasizes our credibility and uniqueness to lead this project; namely, we treat more than 95 percent of children admitted for asthma care in our community.

Hospitalization Rates

In this subheading on "Hospitalization Rates," we include two paragraphs and a table that provide concrete details about the number of children affected by asthma and hospitalized in our community. The second sentence of the first paragraph explains the basis of the numbers and calculations included in the hospitalization rates table; for ease of reading, hospitalization rates are listed in the table in boldface type. The third and fourth sentences translate those numbers of children into dollars spent on asthma care. The last sentence before the table reiterates the idea that disparities exist among low-income and minority populations.

In the short paragraph after the table, the first sentence emphasizes that hospitalization rates are highest in areas with high poverty rates and hints at the problem described in the next paragraph. As a whole, this final paragraph reinforces the hot button of community-based collaborative efforts. Together, coalition partners have direct access to significant numbers of children in the target population.

Structure Goal: develop a sustainable strategy for asthma management

Process Goal: Implement targeted communication strategies to build asthma awareness

Intermediate Outcome Goal: Reduce hospital admissions, emergency department visits, missed school days, and wheezing episodes

Ultimate Outcome Goal: Control pediatric asthma

Health Policy
—facilitate asthma financing & treatment
—support self-management, enhance services, and build capacity of families

Delivery System
—implement provider education
—link with other asthma systems

Population at Risk
—develop community health profile
—decrease racial/ethnic disparities
—provide community education

Environment
—assess allergens & tobacco smoke
—evaluate physical, social, & economic environments

Realized Access
—improve access to asthma services, resources, medications, & equipment

Health Risks
—reduce exposure to environmental precipitants

Effectiveness
—evaluate and improve effective clinical and population programs

Equity
—evaluate and improve equitable access to asthma services for urban children

Efficiency
—evaluate and improve efficient delivery of asthma services for urban children

Health
—enhance the quality of life of children with asthma and their families

Between 1992–1994, hospitalization rates were highest (> 15/1000 population) in Milwaukee zip codes with high poverty rates (53205-6, 12, 10) (WI OHCI 1996). In 1999, clinics representing four health systems in the Milwaukee Allies Against Asthma coalition—Children's, Aurora, Covenant, and Horizon—collectively served nearly 5,000 children with asthma. And two health plans in MAAA—United Healthcare and Humana—served 2,000 pediatric asthma members.

Poverty. Milwaukee County children, particularly those in the central city, experience compromised access to health services due to economic, structural, and environmental barriers. University of Wisconsin-Milwaukee data (1998) reveal that many families in the County do not earn enough to adequately support their children: 113,000 children were in employed families with income below 185% Federal Poverty Level. Further, research attests that children of low socioeconomic status are subjected to inadequate medical management of their asthma (Togias 1997). Asthma management for children in the central city is characterized by reliance on episodic and emergency care, non-conformance to asthma medication management guidelines, and prevalent school absences and workdays lost due to asthma symptoms (Rand 2000).

Morbidity & Mortality. Asthma morbidity and mortality are disproportionately high in urban centers, and minority children are especially vulnerable. The age-adjusted asthma mortality rate in Milwaukee is 2.3 per 100,000 residents (NHLBI 1999). African American children are over four times as likely to die from asthma than white children (DHHS 2000). Factors that contribute to this disparity include inadequate preventive care for asthma management, inadequate asthma knowledge and management skills among children and their families, psychosocial factors, and environmental exposure to allergens or irritants (Malveaux 1995). Although effective therapy is available, many African Americans and Latino children receive episodic treatment for asthma that does not follow current guidelines for care (Evans 1997). Further, increased asthma morbidity and mortality may be associated with a combination of social, structural, and physical factors in the environment, e.g., inadequate housing, exposure to toxins, unemployment, and the lack of supportive interpersonal relationships (Israel 1994).

School Absenteeism. Asthma is the leading cause of health-related school absenteeism. Nationwide, children with asthma miss an average 7.2 school days per year compared to 3.4 days per year for children without asthma. Locally, preliminary research from clinics and schools suggests that asthma affects 10–16% of Milwaukee's urban school-age children. Among 369 children with asthma served by 12 clinics in metropolitan Milwaukee, risk factors significantly associated with emergency department visits for asthma were age 0–3 years, persistent asthma symptoms, African-American race, and parents without high school diplomas (Meurer, in press). Between 1997–2000, CHS' Health Education Center, through their "Awesome Asthma School Days" program, surveyed 1,579 children with asthma from Milwaukee Public Schools. Most recent survey results illustrate the vulnerability of inner city school children:

- 73% do not have a written asthma self-care plan
- 66% with persistent symptoms do not use an anti-inflammatory control medicine
- 57% report smoke exposure in their home (Meurer 1999, and unpublished).

Smoke Exposure. Wisconsin's incidence of smoking increased from 32% in 1993 to 38% in 1999 (WI Youth Behavior Survey 2000). Nearly 20,000 of 215,000 smokers in Milwaukee County are children ages 14–17; the Wisconsin Department of Health & Family Services determined the direct health care costs of smoking in Milwaukee County to exceed $207 million annually! Exposure to tobacco smoke contributes to onset of asthma earlier in life and is a risk factor for asthma morbidity. Since disparity of asthma mortality and morbidity among minority children in urban centers is closely linked to socioeconomic status and poverty, measures to reduce exposure to environmental allergens/irritants and to eliminate barriers to access to health care are likely to have a major positive impact. Interventions for children in urban Milwaukee must focus on prevention of asthma symptoms and promotion of wellness (Malveaux 1995).

THE FULL PROPOSAL

STAGE TWO: FULL PROPOSAL

Poverty

This "Poverty" subheading confirms that many children in the central city face greater risks and barriers to care because of their socioeconomic status. Current research documents the number of children in the community who are below the federal poverty level and articulates the consequences of poverty, e.g., inadequate medical management, reliance on emergency care, and missed school days. These examples foreshadow the asthma-related problems in subsequent paragraphs.

Morbidity & Mortality

Morbidity and mortality is an extension of hospitalization. This subheading provides the asthma morbidity and mortality rate in our community, articulates the extent of disparities between minority and nonminority children, describes factors that contribute to this disparity, and foreshadows additional asthma-related problems, e.g., gaps between the theory and practice of asthma guidelines. The literature cited in this paragraph reflects asthma best practices in the field, including articles published by National Advisory Committee members.

School Absenteeism

Asthma-related school absenteeism was introduced as a serious problem in the letter of intent and is supplemented here. For comparison purposes, national and local data are provided about school absenteeism. The literature cited illustrates the vulnerability of local central city school children. Simultaneously, this published literature begins to establish the credibility of our project director, whose expertise and experience are detailed more fully in the next proposal section. This paragraph also touches on sponsor hot buttons of community-based collaborative efforts and evaluation and outcomes. That is, the project director has already joined forces with local schools to educate children about asthma and assess its prevalence and impact. The last bulleted point, "57% of children report smoke exposure in their home," effectively transitions to the next paragraph on smoke exposure.

Smoke Exposure

This subheading on "Smoke Exposure" documents the statewide increase in smoking, estimates the number of smokers in our community, quantifies the direct health care costs of smoking, articulates the consequences of youth smoking, and ties smoke exposure to two other asthma-related problems: morbidity and mortality, and poverty. The final sentence of the paragraph begins to hint at a solution to these problems—focus on prevention and wellness.

Gaps in Data

The final subheading in this section reemphasizes that the project will serve the children targeted by the RFP with tailored prevention foci for specific age groups, as described initially in the letter of intent. The RFP guidelines also set up the expectation that many communities lack complete data on pediatric asthma prevalence. By acknowledging this "weaknesses" in the proposal, in effect we turn it into a strength. That is, we know what we do not know. Accordingly, we can address weaknesses in the organization and planning phase. Our community faces two specific gaps: (1) a shortage of data on the number of children under age two with asthma, and (2) a disparity between recommended and actual asthma management practices at both the provider and family levels. The paragraph and section end on a positive note: our coalition can overcome these barriers to improve the quality of life for children.

Asthma Control Expertise & Experience. This section of the proposal establishes our credibility to successfully carry out this project, describing the asthma control expertise and experience of our organization, coalition, and key personnel. These paragraphs let the sponsor know exactly *who* is responsible for and *who* is participating in the coalition efforts. Although this is one of the shortest sections of the proposal (only 6 percent of the total), we compensate by including supplemental information in the appendixes, e.g., biosketches and letters of support and commitment. Each paragraph in this section also contributes to the development of sponsor hot buttons: community-based collaborative efforts, evaluation and outcomes, and matching funds and sustainability.

Similar to the letter of intent, the first paragraph describes a century's worth of organizational history and experience and emphasizes collaborative relationships with local and state organizations, a distinctive feature raised in the original RFP guidelines. The second paragraph draws on research published by individuals at the National Program Office to support the coalition's multidisciplinary project approach. In other words, we recognize the sponsor's expertise in research-based approaches to asthma control—a distinctive feature raised in the RFP guidelines for this

Gaps in Data. This project targets children under age 18, especially those residing in the inner city, uninsured or eligible for publicly financed systems, and receiving care from safety net providers. We will reach four age-specific groups: (1) Under age 2: early detection and diagnosis; (2) Age 2–5: prevent emergency department visits; (3) Age 6–12: educate/screen in schools; (4) Age 13–18: reduce tobacco use. MAAA understands the community's asthma needs; however, a shortage of data exists on the number of children under age two with asthma. And despite the existence of national asthma diagnosis and management guidelines, a substantial gap remains between their recommendations and actual practices (DHHS 2000). According to Cabana (1999), barriers to physician adherence to clinical practice guidelines are related to *knowledge* (lack of awareness or familiarity), *attitudes* (lack of agreement with guidelines, lack of self-efficacy or outcome expectancy, or inertia of previous practice), and *behavior* (external barriers related to guideline, patient, or environmental factors). Likewise, parents may not recognize early signs of asthma or fail to avoid environmental factors that trigger their child's asthma. MAAA activities will help reduce health disparities among urban and minority children.

3. Asthma Control Expertise & Experience. Children's Health System, as lead applicant in a multidisciplinary collaboration of local and state organizations, has the clinical expertise and research experience to develop and implement comprehensive asthma management programs in Milwaukee. For over a century, CHS has supplied comprehensive medical treatment to children throughout the state and region; in 1999 alone, CHS admitted more than 19,000 children.

Combating increases in asthma morbidity and mortality necessitates an understanding of social and behavioral aspects of the disease. Education for patients, professionals, and the public based on the most current scientific information is required (Clark 1993). Accordingly, MAAA asthma control activities are designed to improve access to and quality of medical services, education, family and community support, and environmental initiatives. MAAA coalition leaders include:

John R. Meurer, MD, MBA, Project Director, has the expertise and collaborative history with coalition partners to make this project succeed. Dr. Meurer is Assistant Professor of Community Pediatrics in the Center for Advancement of Urban Children at CHS and the Medical College of Wisconsin. He has received federal funding for research on childhood asthma, and has published findings about school-based asthma education, costs of inpatient services for pediatric asthma, trends in the severity of childhood asthma, and risk factors for pediatric emergency visits.

Kevin J. Kelly, MD, MAAA Steering Committee Chair, is the Director of CHS' Asthma and Allergy Center and Professor of Pediatrics at Medical College of Wisconsin. A Board Certified allergist and pediatrician with 20 years experience, Dr. Kelly's expertise in allergy is recognized nationally and was instrumental in the State of Wisconsin's asthma surveillance and intervention program funded by the Centers for Disease Control and Prevention from 1996–1999.

Ramesh Sachdeva, MD, PhD, MBA, MAAA Surveillance & Evaluation Committee Chair, is the Director of CHS' Center for Outcomes Research and Quality Management, one of only a handful of centers of its kind in the country. Dr. Sachdeva's PhD in epidemiology focuses on Health Policy/Management and Biometry emphasizing study and survey design, health economics, decision analysis, and statistical modeling. Dr. Sachdeva will ensure that outcome measures and studies are high quality, meet standards of research, and are sensitive to cultural differences.

Additional MAAA experts who contribute to project planning as Committee Chairs and Coordinators: **Family & Community Advocacy—** *Wayne Gresky,* American Lung Association-Wisconsin and *Cameron Nicholaus,* Fight Asthma Milwaukee; **Provider Quality Improvement —** *Brychan William, MPH,* Community Collaboration for Healthcare Quality and *John Calder,* Children's Hospital Respiratory Therapist; **Environmental Risk Reduction—** *Jerry Curry, MPH,* Milwaukee Health Department and *Samantha Ayla, MPA,* Medical College of Wisconsin; and Advisory consultants to the **Surveillance & Evaluation Committee—** *Patrick Ignatius, PhD, RN,* Black Health Coalition, and *Karen Tilly, MD, MPH,* Director of the Center for Advancement of Urban Children at Medical College of Wisconsin.

4. Coalition Membership, Infrastructure & Capacity. MAAA members represent mixed organizations and parents working together to achieve a common goal: control pediatric asthma. Researchers are still investigating factors that influence the success of coalitions, yet preliminary findings indicate that the maturation of coalitions requires time, effort, and resources (Institute of Medicine 1997). Accordingly, this Milwaukee Allies Against Asthma coalition expands prior Fight Asthma Milwaukee coalition efforts, and is driven by three underlying principles:

- **Inclusive Participation**—the coalition includes diverse health-related agencies, community-based organizations, educational institutions, and concerned parents of children with asthma.
- **Expert Leadership**—a core group of respected asthma specialists and dedicated parents lend their expertise to designing effective community projects and maintaining the coalition.
- **Shared Vision**—coalition participants accept the shared responsibility and decision-making for improving the quality of life for children with asthma and their families.

Indeed, multiple stakeholders *must* be involved in designing, implementing, and evaluating health education programs (Israel 1995). State of the art community-based health promotion requires explicitly acknowledging the diverse interests of the parties at the earliest stages of program planning; making concerted efforts to bridge cultural gaps; structuring funding to allow lead time for partnerships to develop or using social reconnaissance to identify strong existing partnerships; and integrating evaluation more closely into program development (Cheadle 1997).

Coalition Membership. The following table is a complete list of current coalition members, approximately 20% of whom represent key minority groups. Letters of support from core organizations are attached. During planning and implementation phases, coalition committee members will be required to identify and recruit new members annually. In year one, we will reach out to businesses, housing organizations, media, and elected offices. By participating in the coalition, businesses, for example, may benefit from a more productive workforce if community efforts can improve asthma control among dependents of employees. Demonstrated benefits to target groups will ensure that new members stay active in project activities.

Coalition Infrastructure. MAAA has the necessary infrastructure, systems and procedures to effectively govern and operate coalition activities. As illustrated in an Organization Chart in the attachments, a Steering Committee will assume full authority, oversight, and responsibility for the coalition, and four standing committees ensure that educational, advocacy, environmental, and evaluation activities are consonant with the coalition's overall mission. MAAA's inclusive nature and family-centeredness make it unique, and importantly, responsive to community needs.

John Meurer, MD, MBA, Project Director   3

second stage of the application procedure—and demonstrate that we share their values.

The third, fourth, and fifth paragraphs establish the expertise and experience of the project director, the coalition steering committee chair, and the coalition surveillance and evaluation committee chair. These paragraphs in particular appeal to the sponsor's hot buttons: Key personnel have a history of participating in collaborative community-based efforts, are recognized nationally as skilled researchers and evaluators, and have successfully secured federal grant dollars to implement and support a variety of asthma-related projects.

The final paragraph illustrates that the coalition has inclusive participation from myriad individuals and organizations, and it suggests that the project will be sustainable beyond the granting period. That is, the sheer diversity of organizations committed to project efforts increases the likelihood that intervention activities will be institutionalized by coalition members. Because approaches are community-centered and community-driven, each organization takes responsibility for contributing to a project that is greater than any one partner could manage. The overview of steering committee leadership and the four core project planning committees also provides a smooth transition to the following section on coalition membership, infrastructure, and capacity.

Coalition Membership, Infrastructure, & Capacity. To ensure that the project planning and implementation phases will be shaped by representatives from the various subsystems influencing asthma control, the RFP guidelines ask for considerable detail about coalition membership, infrastructure, and capacity. Consequently, this is the longest section of narrative, approximately 30 percent of the proposal's length. The first two paragraphs provide the overview of this entire section, accentuating that project efforts are collaborative and community-based, a sponsor hot button. They reiterate the overall project goal, i.e., to control pediatric asthma, that we defined in the first section of the proposal; document the elements of a successful coalition; identify the three underlying concepts that drive our coalition; and draw on current research to justify our approach to coalition membership and infrastructure.

To increase the readability and manageability of this lengthy section, we introduced three unifying concepts that relate to hot buttons: inclusive participation, expert leadership, and shared vision. Each paragraph in this section contributes to at least one of these concepts and serves to establish the overall cred-

ibility of the coalition and its members to make this project a success. This level of detail also shows the sponsor that we are *not* simply chasing grant dollars because they are available; rather, we have put a considerable amount of time, effort, and energy into developing a project that will truly make a difference in the community.

Coalition Membership

The RFP guidelines want to know who is and is not represented in the coalition. Accordingly, we provide a table that illustrates a complete list of coalition members by names, organizational affiliation, sector, and major roles. This "Coalition Membership" subheading also begins to describe the extent to which the coalition reflects the racial and ethnic composition of the community, a distinctive feature raised in the RFP. To further emphasize our inclusiveness and shared vision, we strategically make a cross-reference to the proposal attachments, which contain letters of support and commitment from coalition members.

While a majority of the constituents recommended by the RFP guidelines already participate in our coalition, not all are represented. We acknowledge this "weakness" and identify four specific groups that will be added to the coalition during the planning and implementation phases. Syntactically, however, we have minimized the effect of this weakness by burying it in the middle of the paragraph. And in the last two sentences we turn this weakness into a relative strength by explaining the benefits of recruiting new constituents to the coalition. Page limitations prohibited an expanded discussion of exactly how individuals will be recruited into the coalition.

Coalition Infrastructure

In this subheading on "Coalition Infrastructure," three paragraphs describe the coalition's structure, leadership, and responsiveness to community needs. A steering committee provides oversight for the coalition, and four standing committees ensure that the educational, advocacy, environmental, and evaluation activities are consonant with the coalition's overall mission. We identify the number of individuals who will participate on each committee, the frequency of committee meetings, and a summary of committee roles and responsibilities.

In case reviewers want more detail, these paragraphs make explicit references to two documents in the proposal attachments: an "Organization Chart" and a "List of Committees, Representation, and Key

Milwaukee Allies Against Asthma Coalition Partners

Sector	Individuals Involved	Organization Affiliation	Major Roles
Parents of Children with Asthma and Adolescents with Asthma	• Cody Austin, Alejandro Fernandez, Julie Mitchell, Nicole Jordan, Charles Taylor, Lauren Walker, Steve Schneider, Emily Simpson, Sandy Williams, Chelly Matthews, Hannah Stevens • Wayne Allen (16 yrs), Kevin James (14 yrs)	None	Representation on all committees Collect primary survey data from other parents and children with asthma and recruit them to join the coalition Develop a family-focused plan and interventions
Clinical Providers	• Brychan William, John Clare • Michelle Berg, Ron Nextall • Sara Recchi	• Community Collaboration for Healthcare Quality • Downtown Health Center • Children's Medical Group School-Based Health Center	Representation on Provider Quality Improvement Committee. Collect primary survey data from providers Develop provider-focused plan and interventions
Health Care Delivery Systems	• Ron Blake, Erica Jardins, Martha Sorley, Luke Robidall, Chris Panger, Adrianna Foote • Amy Ryan • Sean Kyle, Jacqueline Bradley • John Calder, Stacey Douglas, Todd Russell, Jon Vice	• Aurora HealthCare • Horizon • Covenant • Children's Hospital of Wisconsin	Representation on all committees Collect primary data from providers and patients Collect secondary data from hospitals, emergency departments, and clinics Develop a community-focused plan and interventions
Schools and Childcare Providers	• Maria Lemieux • Paula Karina • Brett Hall, Mary Proud	• Milwaukee Public Schools • Planning Council • Milw. County Human Services Dept. Child Care Advisory Cmt.	Represent Family & Environ.Cmt. Collect primary survey data Develop a community-focused plan and interventions
Public Health and Environment Agencies	• Jerry Curry, Earl Tucker, Lisa Marcell • Justin Heatley, Wendy Rogers, Megan Roy, Kris Tselios, Tyrone Harris, Grace Barry, Gloria Cesar, Charles Manning • Elizabeth Marie	• Milwaukee Health Department • Wisconsin Division of Public Health • Wisconsin Division of Health Care Financing	Lead Environmental Cmt. or representation on all committees Provide secondary data from hospital, Medicaid, and environmental data bases Develop a community-focused plan and interventions
State/Local Govt.	• Leonard Tyson	• WI Dept. of Health & Family Services- Southeast Region	Provide access to necessary personnel for coalition development
Payers, Insurers, and Managed Care Organizations	• Alexis Mogly, Jarome Jagger, Terrell Reed, Jamal Demarcus • Orlando Nelson • Hillary Colby, Deb Abrahams • Katrina Nellis	• UnitedHealthcare of WI • Humana • Innovative Resource Group (CompcareBlue) • United Wisconsin Services	Represent Family & Provider Cmts. Provide primary survey data from members and secondary data about pediatric asthma utilization including medications Develop family- and provider-focused plan and interventions
Voluntary Health Agencies	• Wayne Gresky, Javier Sainz, Lindy Ross • Jessica Kwasny	• American Lung Association of Wisconsin • Children's Health Education Center	Lead Family Cmt. And representation on Steering and Evaluation Cmts. Collect primary survey data Develop a family-focused plan and interventions
Community-Based Organizations	• Cameron Nicholaus • Ray Bork, Katy Bourland, Esther Rodriguez, Pilar Witt • Jonathan Christopher • Patrick Ignatius • Margarita Rodriguez • Alfred Morgan	• Fight Asthma Milwaukee • 16th St. Community Health Center • Children's Health Alliance of WI • Black Health Coalition of WI • Bilingual Communications and Consulting • Interfaith Conference of Greater Milwaukee	Representation on all committees Collect primary survey data Develop culturally and linguistically appropriate education, prevention, and intervention strategies Coordinate and integrate asthma activities with existing community health efforts Support coalition's community awareness campaign
Academic Institution	• Kevin Kelly, Ramesh Sachdeva, Karen Tilly, John Meurer, Samantha Ayla, Griffin Boyes	• Medical College of Wisconsin	Lead Steering and Evaluation Cmts. Communicate to link all Cmts. Develop an integrated plan and sustainable strategy

John Meurer, MD, MBA, Project Director

4

THE FULL PROPOSAL

STAGE TWO: FULL PROPOSAL

Tasks." The RFP guidelines did not specifically request these types of attachments; rather, we took the liberty to include them with the requested resumes, letters of support, and description of the application process. Attachments are a good way to overcome constraints on page limits. However, because some sponsors instruct reviewers not to spend much time reading attachments, we included the most vital information in the proposal narrative.

These paragraphs also answer the RFP's question about how this project will build on an existing coalition. Namely, the steering committee chair conceptualized, developed, and secured funding for the first coalition; now he is steering efforts to expand the coalition to make it larger and more inclusive. In other words, these three paragraphs illustrate inclusive participation, expert leadership, and a shared vision.

Coalition Capacity

In this subheading we demonstrate "Coalition Capacity" by providing evidence of our past experience with coalition-based approaches to improving health outcomes and outlining our planned approach to managing and supporting the coalition. The first paragraph and subsequent four bulleted points reiterate key ideas from our letter of intent, describing coalition uniqueness, federal funding history, and concrete examples of coalition efforts to improve asthma outcomes: educate 1,500 children, develop award-winning training curricula, distribute 15,000 asthma care plans, and distribute 2,000 asthma management guidelines. Recapping these main points provides a basis for understanding our vision and approach to expanding the coalition to be more inclusive.

The second paragraph draws on current research to support our emphasis on a community-based collaborative approach to asthma control. Six bulleted points, shown in a two-column format, present specific examples of expanded coalition functions and do so in a manner that conserves space. The third and fourth paragraphs identify the particular individuals who will assume administrative and managerial responsibilities. More importantly, the fifth paragraph justifies this managerial approach in terms of published research. Effectively managing a coalition also means recognizing the intangibles: trust, energy, respect, passion, and commitment. With sponsor support, our coalition can systematically build on prior efforts to affect greater change in the community.

The sixth paragraph describes the importance of promoting community awareness of the initiative and disseminating key findings—to affect the knowledge, attitudes, and behaviors of children, parents and providers relative to asthma principles and practices. This justification of dissemination goes well beyond providing a laundry list of potential strategies. It moves from providing information to persuading the sponsor that we are doing the right things for the right reasons.

Because coalition activities target general and professional audiences, we included a variety of dissemination strategies. Notice the level of detail: Newsletters are distributed quarterly; press kits include newspaper, radio, and television announcements; our Web site address is listed. Unfortunately, page limitations prohibited us from including the names of professional journals, tentative titles, and submission dates of manuscripts to be published. The section ends on a confident note, echoing a sponsor hot button and focusing on the target population: Our coalition has the capacity to develop sustainable systems of change that will improve community health.

Planning Approach & Timetable. This "Planning Approach & Timetable" section comprises 15 percent of the narrative and serves to translate theory into practice: Specific activities in the planning approach fulfill the vision and principal objectives described in the first section of the proposal. The project methodology, derived directly from our theoretical model, describes *how* we will set up appropriate systems and procedures that will produce desired results. Literature citations support our methodological selections. Furthermore, the bulleted points in the first paragraph build on the unifying concepts presented in the previous section and set the stage for illustrating our planning approach in the timetable. The timetable depicts the order, frequency, and duration of specific planning phase activities.

The RFP guidelines explicitly state, "It is expected that this section of the proposal will be very concrete." Accordingly, the third paragraph starts with the transition, "More concretely, we will . . ." The rest of the paragraph, similar to the letter of intent, identifies and justifies our selection of conceptual models to guide planning and implementation phases; namely, these are the dominant models in the field. Similar to the project's theoretical model, the timetable is divided into three categories: inclusive structure, manageable process, and specific outcomes.

The timetable reveals which coalition committees will be responsible for ensuring that specific activities occur at key points during the planning year. Activities are presented in bulleted point fashion; key phrases start with descriptive verbs. Reviewers can

Leadership/Governance. The coalition will be governed by a 12 member *Steering Committee,* who have a cumulative 100 years of experience in pediatric care, management, health education programming, and community leadership. The Steering Committee will convene every two months and integrate coalition activities into existing community health improvement efforts. Steering Committee Chair, Dr. Kevin Kelly, was instrumental to conceptualizing, developing, and securing funding for the Fight Asthma Milwaukee coalition. MAAA member agencies will identify and mobilize parents of children with asthma to participate on the committees and in quarterly Coalition Conferences. Parents will reflect Milwaukee's racial and ethnic diversity, and bring a range of personal expertise to the coalition.

Committee Structure. The Steering Committee will appoint and oversee *Family & Community Advocacy, Provider Quality Improvement, and Environmental Risk Reduction Committees*. These committees will meet eight times a year, and consist of 12–15 members, including parents of children with asthma, and health and education experts. These committees will make recommendations to the Steering Committee regarding MAAA's strategic direction and policy such as identifying asthma programming and outreach opportunities; identifying appropriate cultural and linguistic mediums; evaluating asthma education activities; and, adapting to the needs of the community. In addition, a *Surveillance & Evaluation Committee*, comprised of 12 researchers, academicians, and parents will meet every two months, alternating with the Steering Committee. A list of committees, representation, and key tasks is attached.

Coalition Capacity. Fight Asthma Milwaukee is the only community-based asthma coalition in Wisconsin, and was one of the first established in the country. For half a decade, partners have collaborated on education, intervention, and research initiatives, including participating in two Centers for Disease Control cooperative agreements—Wisconsin's Community-Based Asthma Intervention Project and Wisconsin's Asthma Education Program for Welfare-to-Work Families. Further examples of Milwaukee coalition-based approaches to improving asthma outcomes:

- *CHS' Health Education Center* provided asthma education to more than 1,500 Milwaukee Public School children through their "Awesome Asthma School Days" program.
- *American Lung Association-Wisconsin* developed award-winning asthma management training curricula for childcare providers and school teachers and coaches.
- *16th St. Community Health Center* distributed 15,000 asthma self-care plans in English and Spanish to children in Milwaukee Public Schools through Child Health Champion Campaign.
- *Community Collaboration for Healthcare Quality* distributed the National Asthma Education and Prevention Program guidelines to more than 2,000 physicians in Milwaukee.

These programs demonstrate that coalitions are powerful and effective mechanisms for realizing change at the local level. To make our coalition work, enlightened community leaders will intensify existing dialogues accentuating the benefits of collaboration and disadvantages of division, learning from one another, affirming and respecting each other's unique ethnic and cultural differences, increasing trust, and struggling to remove barriers which impact negatively on participating groups (Torres 2000). With RWJF support, the new MAAA coalition will build on FAM successes and systematically expand its functions (Braithwaite 2000):

- Broaden the mission of member agencies
- Develop more comprehensive strategies
- Develop wider public support for issues
- Increase participation from diverse sectors
- Increase accountability
- Improve capacity to plan and evaluate

Administrative Support. Samantha Ayla, MPA, Research Coordinator in the Center for the Advancement of Urban Children, will serve as MAAA Project Coordinator. She will be responsible for organizing and attending all committee meetings and handling administrative functions such as preparing agendas, arranging for meeting times and locations, and facilitating meeting activities. She will report directly to Dr. John Meurer, Project Director.

Management Approach. Dr. Kelly, Steering Committee Chair, and Dr. Meurer will oversee the process of coordinating and facilitating consensus-building, establishing and maintaining linkages to relevant organizations and individuals, and ensuring that the role played by the coalition is appropriate and reflects the changing needs of the project over time. Steering Committee members will convene every two months to identify asthma problems in the community, prioritize potential approaches that hold the most promise for system-wide change, and identify readily available community resources. Coalition members respect Drs. Kelly and Meurer for their asthma experience, expertise, and enthusiasm to make this coalition succeed.

Drs. Kelly and Meurer will foster a participative management style nurturing the valuable contributions of every coalition member. To optimize collaboration, they will constructively apply basic principles of assertive problem solving and conflict resolution. They will separate people from problems; focus on needs and interests, not positions; invent options for mutual gain; and insist on using objective criteria (Fisher 1983). Further, they will use memorandums of understanding, orient new members, recruit continually, recognize member achievements, conduct training and technical assistance, and plan strategically (Braithwaite 2000).

Communication Strategy. The intended outcomes of dissemination strategies are to affect the knowledge, attitudes, and behaviors of children, parents, and providers relative to asthma principles and practices. Accordingly, MAAA will use a combination of strategies to promote community awareness, secure wide involvement, and disseminate findings, including: (1) newsletters distributed quarterly to providers and parents; (2) press kits for public reporting—newspapers, radio, and television public service announcements; (3) a Web page through CHS: http://www.chw.org; (4) professional forums and manuscripts; (5) annual reports submitted to RWJF and other state and local groups. In sum, MAAA has the membership, infrastructure, and capacity to develop sustainable systems of change that will improve community health.

5. Planning Approach & Timetable. MAAA's planning approach is driven by and directly responsive to community needs. The key factors in community change are a clear vision and mission, an action plan, quality leadership, resources for community mobilizers, feedback on changes, technical assistance, and measurable outcomes. Our methodology for the planning phase follows directly from Aday's model of addressing structure, process, and outcomes:

John Meurer, MD, MBA, Project Director   5

quickly skim read the table and understand the entire planning approach. Bulleted organization and planning activities address sponsor hot buttons, e.g., recruit new coalition members annually, evaluate and assess coalition activities, and secure commitment for annual matching funds.

The paragraph after the timetable describes the planning process that went into developing this grant application. The first sentence provides evidence of meaningful involvement, i.e., inclusive participation in the process: A series of community meetings brought together 20 agencies representing the major local and state asthma stakeholders. We cross-reference reviewers to the attachments for a more full description of the application process. During the planning process, the major stakeholders began to identify problems facing children with asthma and prioritize potential solutions.

The table of "Problems & Solutions" demonstrates stakeholders' consideration of the full gamut of potential strategies and settings for asthma control that reflect the needs of the community. It also shows coalition members' commitment to controlling pediatric asthma: Although the organization and planning phase has not even started yet, coalition members are already evaluating approaches that hold the most promise for system-wide change. The subsequent paragraph, in bulleted point fashion, addresses another concern raised in the RFP: demonstrating community acceptance of project efforts. Survey results quantify the concerns of parents of children with asthma and suggests their willingness to participate in interventions that focus on these areas.

The final paragraph summarizes the critical elements that will make our coalition successful, strategically hinting at all three sponsor hot buttons. The second sentence provides a smooth transition to the next section of the proposal, "planning efforts will produce an implementation plan." The last sentence reflects our shared values with the sponsor—our model for planning is based in sound theory, rigorous research, relevant practice, and can be replicated for other health conditions.

Collectively, these paragraphs appeal to each of the three hot buttons. Notice the strategic repetition of words and phrases, such as *community*, *inclusive*, *meaningful involvement*, *coalition*, *outcomes*, *quality of life*, *baseline data*, *evaluate and assess*, *resources*, *matching funds*, and *system-wide change*.

Preliminary Implementation Approach. The "Preliminary Implementation Approach" tells the sponsor *how* the project plan will be accomplished. Although

the purpose of the planning process is to develop an implementation plan, the RFP guidelines put the cart before the horse, asking for a description of the types of interventions that might be employed. Because some of the implementation approaches are yet to be determined, this section is a bit shorter than the previous section on "Planning Approach & Timetable." In total, we dedicate one page of narrative to this section, nearly 8 percent of the proposal's total length.

Planning grants, in general, support the development of new partnerships to explore a specific issue. In this case, an underlying assumption in the RFP guidelines is that the partnerships already exist and community members have engaged in preliminary discussions about the pediatric asthma problem. Thus, planning funds can be used to take the coalition to the next level of development, expanding partners and creating action plans for community-driven interventions. Moreover, the next two proposal sections ask for a description of how these potential strategies will be evaluated and sustained.

Our preliminary planning indicated that several categories of problems exist. Accordingly, the first paragraph of this section describes a multidimensional approach to project implementation. Strategic use of journal citations shows our coalition's sensitivity to a distinctive feature raised in the RFP; namely, approaches to asthma control must be research-based and reflect an interplay among the various settings and systems.

Paragraphs two, three, and four include specific examples of our comprehensive approach to systems change, targeting family and community advocacy, provider quality improvement, and environmental risk reduction. These three categories represent a refinement of the broad implementation areas originally identified in the letter of intent. Note that each paragraph contains at least two citations of published research, which justify our methodological selections to address these particular problems. The asthma intervention strategies identified also represent the currently accepted best practices in the field, many of which have been written about by individuals at The Robert Wood Johnson Foundation, the National Program Office, and the National Advisory Committee. These citations reflect our shared values with the sponsor.

The final paragraph summarizes and clarifies the relationships among the different strategies: "because asthma is triggered and exacerbated by a complex mix of medical and social factors, the coalition will triangulate educational, advocacy, and environmental out-

- **Coalition structure is inclusive**, enjoying meaningful involvement from major private and public community stakeholders and concerned parents with a role in asthma control.
- **Coalition process activities are manageable**, logical, and integrate into existing community health improvement efforts. Theoretical models systematically identify community needs.
- **Coalition outcomes are specific**, thus establishing the groundwork for an effective Implementation Phase. Collectively, structure, process, and outcomes strengthen the coalition's capacity to sustain over time a community-driven approach to asthma control.

MAAA will design both programs and evaluations that reflect a theoretical understanding of behavior change (Clark 1994), and project design will take a multifactorial approach to accomplishing goals and objectives. That is, our application of social learning theory will address both the psychosocial dynamics underlying health behavior and the methods of promoting behavior change, while emphasizing cognitive processes and their effect on behavior. An individual's behavior is uniquely determined by a combination of social and environmental factors; thus, these factors become the elements for intervention strategies (Kelder 1996).

More concretely, we will promote stronger community-wide systems of care by integrating two conceptual models into planning and implementation. *PRECEDE/PROCEED,* the dominant health education and community health promotion model, uses an interdisciplinary framework that draws on the fields of epidemiology, social and behavioral science, administration, and education, and emphasizes two core propositions: health and health risks are caused by multiple factors, and efforts to effect change must affect both behavior and environment (Green 1999; Kreuter 1998). The *Community Health Improvement Process* supports the development and implementation of a planned approach for improving health. This means developing a pediatric community health profile based on socio-demographic characteristics, risk factors, health and functional status, resource consumption, and quality of life (Institute of Medicine 1997). The table below illustrates iterative planning activities that will improve community health outcomes.

Organization & Planning Phase Activities	Begin	End Date	Personnel
Inclusive Structure			
• Host quarterly Coalition Conferences	Nov. 2000	Sept. 2001	Entire Coalition
• Recruit parents of children with asthma to participate on the coalition committees	Nov. 2000	Oct. 2001	Entire Coalition
• Establish and convene alternating bimonthly Steering and Evaluation committees; monthly Family, Provider, & Environmental committee	Nov. 2000	Oct. 2001	All Committees
• Recruit new coalition members annually	Nov. 2000	Oct. 2001	Entire Coalition
Manageable Process			
• Evaluate local asthma problems, physical, social, economic environments; develop a community health profile from baseline data	Nov. 2000	Mar. 2001	All Committees
• Conduct a retrospective analysis of community health improvement efforts	Nov. 2000	Mar. 2001	Evaluation, et al, Committees
• Identify opportunities for intervention and assess the quality of available resources	Jan. 2001	Oct. 2001	All Committees
• Link with other asthma systems	Jan. 2001	Oct. 2001	Steering Cmt.
• Coordinate and integrate asthma education activities with current community efforts	Jan. 2001	Oct. 2001	All Committees
• Gather program development information from diverse community stakeholders and families	Jan. 2001	Oct. 2001	Family Committee
• Evaluate and assess coalition activities	Jan. 2001	Oct. 2001	Evaluation Cmt.
Specific Outcomes			
• Develop an implementation plan with: (1) strategic goals and objectives, (2) targeted interventions, (3) specific outcomes, and (4) articulated coalition roles and responsibilities	Feb. 2001	June 2001	Steering and all Committees
• Secure commitment for annual matching funds	Apr. 2001	June 2001	Steering Cmt.
• Initiate community awareness campaign	May 2001	Oct. 2001	All Committees
• Provide community-based asthma education	July 2001	Oct. 2001	Fam/Env. Cmt.
• Enhance asthma education for providers	July 2001	Oct. 2001	Provider Cmt.
• Develop culturally and linguistically appropriate education and publicity materials	July 2001	Oct. 2001	Family Cmt.
• Submit Implementation grant proposal	July 2001	July 2001	Steering Cmt.

To ensure inclusive participation in coalition planning efforts, Dr. Meurer organized a series of community meetings that brought together major asthma stakeholders, over 30 individuals from 20 different local and state agencies. At these meetings, participants began to identify the key problems facing children with asthma in the community and prioritize potential approaches that hold the most promise for system-wide change. (c.f., Description of the Application Process).

Problems	Solutions
• Asthma management is not coordinated among children, families, schools, day cares, and health care providers.	• Establish comprehensive asthma case management based on the local prenatal care coordination model.
• Health care providers vary widely in their use of asthma practice; parents need more family-centered approaches to education.	• Establish organizational linkages to integrate medical services, provider and family education, & environmental control.
• Families face multiple socioeconomic issues and critical survival needs perceived as more important than asthma.	• Implement media communication strategies uniquely targeting families/professionals, and to build awareness of the coalition.
• Many children are exposed to high levels of irritants and environmental allergens.	• Reduce exposure to environmental triggers through safe housing initiatives.

John Meurer, MD, MBA, Project Director   6

STAGE TWO: FULL PROPOSAL

reach strategies to promote wider use of current knowledge to diagnose and manage asthma." The last sentence of this section goes the next step to describe the significance of this multifaceted approach; namely, it facilitates achieving project goals and objectives, e.g., reduce the use of emergency services and improve quality of life.

Evaluation Approach. The "Evaluation Approach" answers *how* project effectiveness will be assessed. Because this entire section is a sponsor hot button, we provide substantial detail to establish our credibility to conduct and participate in local and national evaluations using a variety of tools that are based on recognized scientific models for assessment. In all, this section makes up approximately 10 percent of the total length of the proposal.

The first paragraph defines the characteristics of a quality evaluation approach. By defining the characteristics first, in effect, we create the yardstick against which to measure ourselves and others. Not surprisingly, we measure up. The "Evaluation Approach" goes beyond describing how the project will be evaluated and explains how evaluation feedback will be used to improve the likelihood of achieving the overall project goal. This added detail makes our proposal stand out from other applicants.

The remaining seven paragraphs address each of the bulleted points in the RFP guidelines; due to page limitations, the bulleted points on soliciting broad coalition input and outlining a brief timeline were combined into one paragraph. The second paragraph in this section describes who will be surveyed by whom to assess relevant outcomes according to national asthma guidelines. At the same time, we strategically appeal to a distinctive feature raised in the RFP—research-based approaches to asthma control.

The third paragraph provides examples of existing protocols that will be adapted to gather baseline and primary data. The fourth paragraph lists collaborative partners who have volunteered access to pediatric asthma data. Equally significant, we describe measures to ensure the confidential and ethical use of data; although the RFP guidelines do not address issues of confidentiality, including this persuasive detail shows the sponsor that we have put considerable thought into developing our project.

The fifth paragraph describes types of evaluation and sample methodologies that will be used to assess the coalition, its processes, and resulting outcomes. Building on the ideas presented in the proposal sections on "Asthma Control Expertise & Experience" and "Coalition Membership, Infrastructure & Capac-

ity," the sixth paragraph emphasizes that a broad range of research experts and coalition members are involved in evaluation planning and implementation, and that they will follow a specific timeline for evaluation design, data collection, and analysis.

Paragraph seven reaffirms that the coalition will coordinate evaluation activities with the National Program Office and other funded project sites, a distinctive feature raised in the RFP. The purpose of evaluation, as articulated in the last sentence of the paragraph, is to contribute to best practices standards that can be disseminated and replicated.

The final paragraph identifies personnel responsible for conducting the evaluation, establishes their credibility and capabilities, and relates their methodological approaches to the project's overarching theoretical framework. We also engage a distinctive feature raised in the RFP guidelines. Specifically, the section ends by affirming the coalition's willingness to collaborate with and take direction and technical assistance from the sponsor; grant dollars represent a shared investment in an improved future.

Sustaining & Institutionalizing Coalition Efforts. While "Sustaining & Institutionalizing Coalition Efforts" is a relatively short section (5 percent of the proposal's total length), it is an important one because it addresses a sponsor hot button. In the first paragraph, the first sentence reintroduces two unifying concepts from the "Coalition Membership, Infrastructure, and Capacity" section—inclusive participation and shared vision—and describes how they form the basis of long-term coalition sustainability. The second sentence borrows from the letter of intent to emphasize that because the coalition is engrained in an organizational structure that offers stability, coalition initiatives are more likely to be institutionalized by member agencies. The third sentence stresses the significance of sustainability and institutionalization of coalition efforts; namely, they allow communities to substantially change systems of care for pediatric asthma beyond the granting period.

The second paragraph provides explicit detail about matching contributions and plans to secure other sources of financial support to support coalition efforts. The first sentence describes both mandatory and voluntary cost sharing. As one of the eligibility requirements, the sponsor requires matching dollars totaling at least one-third of the total annual budget, roughly $150,000 per year during the project's implementation years. Coalition partners exceeded this mandatory amount, committing a total of $250,000 per year. As an additional incentive to the sponsor to

A separate survey revealed similar concerns: during FAM's Asthma Wellness Day, 41 parents answered the question "What are the biggest problems in trying to care for your child's asthma?"

- 68% Too many asthma triggers at home (smoke, dust, cockroaches, mold).
- 41% We don't have enough useful asthma education materials.
- 32% Doctors and nurses aren't sensitive to my culture.

MAAA has all the critical elements for a successful planning year: a broad-based and inclusive coalition, a resource-rich environment, highly trained professionals, dedicated parents, and a theoretical model to guide activities. Planning efforts will produce an implementation plan with strategic goals and objectives, targeted interventions, specific outcomes, and articulated coalition member roles and responsibilities. Our approach can be replicated and serve as a model for other conditions because it is based in sound theory, rigorous research, and relevant practice.

6. Preliminary Implementation Approach. In the Implementation Phase, we will enact a mixture of strategies to enhance the quality of life of children. MAAA has already identified innovative approaches that are technically, politically, and economically feasible. Initiatives will broadly target families, providers, and environmental risks. Dominant theoretical models used in health education today are based in social psychology, and seek to explain causes of health problems, whereas principles of practice assist intervenors to achieve objectives. By elucidating the relationships between theory and practice, we can develop more effective interventions (Freudenberg 1995). Educational efforts to change policy and behavior of individuals and communities currently constitute our best chance to promote health. Thus, health education programs will be theory-based, multidisciplinary, and outcome-oriented (Clark 1995).

Family & Community Advocacy. Family education programs for asthma self-management will be based on social cognitive theory, targeted behavior capability, self-efficacy, and outcome expectations as integral parts of clinical care (Bartholomew 1997). People are predisposed to take action to manage asthma by virtue of internal (knowledge, attitudes, beliefs) and external (models of behavior, technical advice, money) factors. Through processes of self-regulation, i.e., the ability to observe, make judgments, and react to their own behavior, people learn which management strategies—prevention, symptom management, negotiation, communication—work for them (Clark 1994). Self-regulation behaviors are associated with more frequent use of asthma management strategies by patients; counseling by providers can encourage self-regulation and better at-home management of asthma (Clark 1994 JA). Examples of effective preventive interventions include small-group discussions, outreach to high-risk populations, and training peers and volunteers (Janz 1996).

Provider Quality Improvement. Potentially effective interventions to promote physician adoption of practice guidelines include reminder systems, restructured medical records, academic detailing and educational outreach by educationally influential clinicians, multiple interventions, concurrent audit and feedback targeted to specific providers. Interventions will be delivered by peers or opinion leaders (Davis 1997), physicians (Greco 1993), patient involvement (Grimshaw 1994), interactive seminars based on self-regulation (Clark 1998 P), and interactive educational meetings (Bero 1998). Training will be based on NAEPP guidelines, including screening to identify new cases, health education to improve family management, promotion of written asthma management plans and anti-inflammatory medications for persistent asthma, and strong administrative support to promote provider behavior change (Evans 1997).

Environmental Risk Reduction. Urban minority families with children with asthma often live in homes with high allergen and irritant levels. Decreasing asthma severity in this population means preventing and controlling known risk factors in the home. We will emphasize smoking cessation programs, covering mattresses, and dust and animal dander control (Huss 1994). The Fresno California Asthma Project will serve as a model intervention to control asthma in a low-income, multiethnic, inner city community. In the last few months of the planning phase, we will initiate innovative education for pediatric asthma providers in the central city. Small group education will be provided in age- and culturally-appropriate formats to children and families in convenient settings for them. General and ethnic media and a speaker's bureau will be used to raise public awareness of asthma as a serious but controllable health problem (Wilson 1998).

Because asthma is triggered and exacerbated by a complex mix of medical and social factors, MAAA will triangulate educational, advocacy, and environmental outreach strategies to promote wider use of current knowledge to diagnose and manage asthma. This multifaceted approach reflects a comprehensive understanding of the interplay among multiple audiences, settings, and systems. Most importantly, research shows that effective medical management and patient education reduces the use of emergency services and improves quality of life (DHHS 2000).

7. Evaluation Approach. Evaluation is integral to ensuring long-term project success. Sound evaluations should have utility, feasibility, propriety, and accuracy. That is, MAAA's evaluation will serve the information needs of intended users; be realistic, prudent, and frugal; be conducted legally, ethically, and with due regard for the welfare of those involved, as well as those affected by its results; and determine the merit of the program being evaluated (Joint Cmt. On Standards for Educational Evaluation 1994). Based on evaluation feedback, the coalition can better allocate resources, improve services, and strengthen overall project performance, thus improving the likelihood of accomplishing ultimate outcome goals—control pediatric asthma.

Relevant Outcomes. Through primary surveys of patients, families, and providers by partner organizations, MAAA will monitor activity limitations and school days missed due to asthma. Further, we will monitor the proportion of children with asthma and their families who receive formal patient education, including information about community and self-help resources as an essential part of the management of their condition. We also will assess the proportion of children who receive appropriate care according to NAEPP guidelines. Finally, we will establish a surveillance system for tracking asthma death, illness, disability, impact of environmental factors on asthma, access to medical care, and asthma management (DHHS 2000).

THE FULL PROPOSAL

STAGE TWO: FULL PROPOSAL

select our project for grant funding, coalition members volunteered matching funds totaling $250,000 during the planning year. We refer reviewers to the attached budget and letters of support for documentation and levels of matching support from collaborative partners.

The bulleted list in the second paragraph demonstrates that coalition members are committed to sustaining project efforts and have given extensive thought to securing future sources of financial support. These concrete examples of future funding mechanisms inspire more confidence than a general statement, "we will continue to look for alternative sources of support for this project." More samples are included in the attachment "Description of the Application Process." In short, this combination of mandatory and voluntary cost sharing, and an articulated albeit tentative plan for future project funding, was strategically designed to increase our chances of funding success.

The concluding paragraph ties the whole proposal together. It succinctly summarizes our credibility, uniqueness, and capability to carry out this project, and it highlights the main points and hot buttons repeated throughout the proposal. The final sentence ends on a positive note, maintaining a focus on the impact that this project will have on the target population and touching on all three hot buttons: "Collectively, these strategies will provide *long-term*, continuous support to our *community-based asthma coalition* and enhance the *quality of life* of children with asthma and their families."

Proposal Design

For the purpose of consistency, we incorporated many of the same proposal design features that we used in the letter of intent. A familiar looking document is a friendly document. Effective proposal design responds to the helpful hint in the RFP guidelines that "reviewers will consider favorably proposals that are organized well and that address each area completely and concisely." The following design features highlight our proposal's structure, hierarchy, and order, helping reviewers find the information that they need.

Bulleted Lists. Bulleted lists convey chunks of information quickly without being wordy. For instance, reviewers can skim read the bulleted organization and planning phase activities and know what the entire "Planning Approach & Timetable" section is all about. Bulleted lists also help to visually break up long blocks of text. In the section on "Target Population & Need," the bulleted points about school absenteeism stand out from the other paragraphs of text.

Charts and Tables. This full proposal contains four charts and tables within the narrative: hospitalization rates, coalition membership, organization and planning phase activities, and problems and solutions. Table headings use an inverse (white on black) Arial type style to stand out from the table elements, which are Times Roman type style. These charts and tables present complex information in a manner that is easy to read and understand. Only charts and tables considered absolutely necessary were included in the text of the proposal; additional charts and tables, e.g., a description of the planning process, are included in the attachments.

Headings and Subheadings. Headings and subheadings act like a table of contents placed directly in the proposal text; at a glance they reveal the organization of the proposal to the reader. Headings and subheadings reflect key words taken from the "Detailed Instructions for Narrative Section" of the RFP guidelines.

Our proposal uses three main levels of organization. Level one headings for major proposal sections use boldface Arial type style, e.g., "Vision & Principal Objectives." Level two headings within a proposal section use boldface Times Roman type style, e.g., "Structure Goal." Level three headings use boldface Times Roman type style, italics, and are indented, e.g., "Health Policy Objective." Effective use of horizontal and vertical white space sets off the various levels of headings and enhances overall proposal readability.

Margins. Ragged right margins are easier to read than fully justified margins. We used standard one-inch margins all around.

Page Numbers. Identical to the letter of intent, page numbers are placed in the bottom center of the proposal, and the bottom left-hand corner of the page includes the name of the project director.

Type Style. The text of the proposal is Times Roman, a serif typeface, and level one headings are Arial, a sans serif typeface. This contrast in type styles makes headings stand off from the body of the text. Following the RFP guidelines, we used 12 point type size.

White Space. White space breaks up long copy, making the proposal appear inviting and user-friendly. White space gives reviewers a visual clue to the structure of the proposal. In a page full of print, a block of unprinted lines, or white space, stands out immediately, often indicating that one section is ending and another is beginning. The narrative is single spaced, with a double space between minor paragraphs, and a triple space between major proposal sections.

Data Sources. Elements of the design and methods of the National Cooperative Inner City Asthma Study may be adapted for epidemiological investigation of a cross-sectional sample of accessible children with asthma. The protocol will include an eligibility assessment and a baseline visit, during which symptom data, e.g., wheezing, lost sleep, changes in activities of daily living, inpatient admissions, and emergency department and clinic visits will be collected. Asthma knowledge and attitudes will be assessed. Currently mailed surveys to more than 700 parents of children with asthma at six Medical College of Wisconsin clinics will begin the process of surveillance (Helstad 1999). In addition, access and barriers to the medical system will be addressed by a series of questions including the location, availability, and consistency of treatment for asthma attacks, follow-up care, and primary care. Prior Milwaukee studies will be reviewed of in-home dust sample allergen collection and documentation of home environments.

Secondary Data Sources. Partnering hospital systems, health plans, school-based health centers, and the State have volunteered access to asthma data including deaths, hospitalizations and total charges, emergency department visits, clinic visits, and asthma medication prescriptions by patient age group, race/ethnicity, payer, and zip code of residence. Computer-based prediction models can identify children at high risk for adverse asthma outcomes, and will be used in our population-based efforts to improve asthma management (Lieu 1998). MAAA will apply the ethical standards set forth in the US Department of Health and Human Services policy for the protection of human research subjects. To protect confidentiality, MAAA will not use nor permit others to use data in any way except for research, analysis, and aggregate statistical reporting. MAAA also intends to participate in NAEPP's Asthma Coalition Exchange.

Measuring Change. Formative, process, and summative evaluations will be conducted to assess coalition effectiveness. Formative evaluations will assess coalition formation through a meeting effectiveness inventory, surveys on committee functioning and member satisfaction, and community needs assessments (Butterfoss 1996). Process evaluations will assess project plan implementation, i.e., correlation between activities and plans. Summative evaluations will assess the impact of interventions on key process, intermediate outcome, and ultimate outcome measures (Goodman 1996). Randomized controlled trials or prospective cohort studies will be designed to study the effectiveness of proposed interventions on accessible samples of children.

Coalition Input & Timing. Clearly, for this evaluation to be successful, MAAA must obtain and use input from a broad range of coalition members in project design and implementation. Accordingly, community-based research experts and parents are integral members of the Surveillance & Evaluation Committee chaired by Dr. Ramesh Sachdeva. In November 2000, this committee will begin to design the evaluation; by January 2001 they will begin to collect data, and in March 2001 they will begin data analysis and interpretation.

Drs. Meurer and Sachdeva will also participate in periodic meetings with other projects and the National Program Office to coordinate, streamline, and enhance the value of local evaluation efforts. And, of course, they will submit annual program updates that include information about progress to date, planned action items, project strengths/weaknesses, and process evaluations of the coalition and activities. In Winter 2004–5, a final evaluation suitable for wide dissemination will be prepared and contain a comprehensive analysis of the Milwaukee Allies Against Asthma coalition, including lessons learned and best practices for community-based asthma coalitions.

Key Individuals. To make certain that evaluations of community interventions are objective, meet rigorous standards of research, and are sensitive to ethnic and cultural differences, MAAA will team up with CHS' Center for Outcomes Research and Quality Management. Dr. Sachdeva, Center Director will help design epidemiological and outcome studies, ensure quality control of data and statistical validity of findings, and supervise statistical analysis. Following Aday's research model, Dr. Sachdeva will set up appropriate systems to capture and analyze data that illustrates effectiveness, equity, and efficiency. MAAA will also benefit from the direction and technical assistance of the National Program Office and Advisory Committee, and will participate in and can contribute to the overall cross-site evaluation of the program.

8. Sustaining & Institutionalizing Coalition Efforts. MAAA is built on inclusive participation and a shared vision, principles that form the cornerstone of long-term coalition sustainability. MAAA is engrained in an organizational structure that offers stability, and based on expected education, environmental, and community outcomes, provides the basis for many initiatives to be institutionalized by member agencies and the community. In short, MAAA has the potential for changing systems for pediatric asthma control beyond the granting period.

MAAA coalition members have already demonstrated their commitment to success, providing matching funds of $250,000 during the planning year and funds exceeding one-third of each year's budget for three implementation years—$250,000 per year. (c.f., Budget and Letters of Support). Additionally, during community meetings, major asthma stakeholders brainstormed a list of innovative mechanisms to support coalition efforts after RWJF funding is complete:

- Obtain support from pharmaceutical firms, e.g., through the Prescription Assistance Program, and from other Milwaukee businesses whose employees are affected by childhood asthma.
- Expand Medicaid coverage and reimbursement and use Title V funds for comprehensive asthma services including multidisciplinary team care, case management, individual and group patient education, and multiple medications/holding chambers for home and school.
- Collaborate with elected State officials to appropriate general purpose revenue for the coalition for the public health agency involvement.
- Apply to the Tobacco Control Board, state and federal government, local and national private foundations for support (c.f., Description of the Application Process).

Milwaukee Allies Against Asthma is uniquely positioned to harness and focus collective talents, expertise, and asthma resources to effect lasting change in the community. When properly nurtured, coalitions have tremendous potential to shape public policy, to reach asthma patients with programs and services, and to educate health care providers (Schmidt 1999). Collectively, these strategies will provide long-term, continuous support to Milwaukee's community-based asthma coalition and enhance the quality of life of children with asthma and their families.

THE FULL PROPOSAL

STAGE TWO: FULL PROPOSAL

DEVELOPING THE BUDGET AND BUDGET NARRATIVE

A detailed budget and budget narrative allow the sponsor to examine the relationship between a proposed project approach and associated cost items. Although the budget and budget narrative are frequently developed after the proposal narrative is nearly completed, they should be planned and constructed with the same care that went into writing the narrative. Reviewers scrutinize the budget and budget narrative to see whether expenses are:

- realistic projections to accomplish project goals and objectives;
- consistent with the degree, breadth, and depth of activities described in the narrative;
- necessary and sufficient to fulfill individual project activities;
- accurately calculated;
- compatible with the sponsor's vision, priorities, and program purpose;
- within sponsor-defined grant award limits;
- allowable under sponsor's policy guidelines and budgeting practices.

Expenses listed in the budget must be incurred during the proposed project period and should relate directly to activities described in the proposal narrative or appendixes. With few exceptions, the costs of developing a grant application may not be included in the project budget because the work was completed prior to the start of the granting period.

In the budget and budget narrative, line item costs must be clearly identified and explained. Any combination of ambiguities, inconsistencies, discrepancies, and omissions between the proposal narrative and the budget and budget narrative may provide reviewers with enough justification to reduce a funding request or reject the grant application. The budget and budget narrative should demonstrate to reviewers that sufficient funds are requested to achieve project goals and objectives in a cost-effective manner.

Elements of the Budget

The budget should be independent of the proposal narrative, and unless sponsor regulations indicate otherwise, it can include every reasonable expense associated with the project, such as:

- Accounting
- Advertising
- Legal services
- Maintenance
- Animals
- Audiovisual instruction
- Auditing
- Binding
- Books
- Computer time
- Consultants
- Dues
- Equipment
- Fringe benefits
- Indirect costs
- Instruments
- Insurance
- Periodicals
- Postage
- Publication
- Recruitment
- Rent
- Repairs
- Salaries and wages
- Security
- Subcontracts
- Supplies
- Telephone
- Travel
- Tuition

In this case, The Robert Wood Johnson Foundation "National Program Site Budget Preparation Guidelines" indicate that they preclude support for:

- Ongoing general operating expenses or existing deficits.
- Items for which third-party reimbursement is available.
- Endowment or capital costs, including construction, renovation, or equipment.
- Basic biomedical research.
- Conferences or symposia, publications or media projects—unless they are integrally related to the Foundation's program objectives or an outgrowth of one of its grant programs.
- Research on unapproved drug therapies or devices.
- International programs or institutions.
- Direct support to individuals.

As we developed our budget, we modeled it after the sponsor's sample line item budget, which shows the format for identifying costs associated with the proposed project. Although the budget preparation guidelines offer that we may present the budget using our institution's format instead of the sample line item budget, for the sake of convenience and familiarity for reviewers, we use the style that they are expecting to see—their own. The budget preparation guidelines also caution that some line items may not be applicable to our specific proposal and that we should not include items entitled "Miscellaneous."

The budget is divided into five line item categories:

1. Personnel
2. Other Direct Costs
3. Indirect Costs
4. Equipment
5. Consultant/Contractual Agreements

Milwaukee Allies Against Asthma
Detailed Line Item Project Budget
Grant Period: from 11/1/00 to 10/31/01
Budget Period: from 11/1/00 to 10/31/01
Project Year One (Planning Phase)

I. PERSONNEL (employed by Children's Health System)

Name	Position	Base Salary	% Time	Total	RWJF Support	Other Support	Source of Other
Cameron Nicholaus	Family Advocacy Cmt. Coordinator	40,000	60%	24,000	16,000	8,000	CHEC
Jessica Kwasny	Steering Cmt. Member	55,500	10%	5,500	2,775	2,775	CHEC
TBA Biostats	Evaluation Cmt. Coordinator	47,500	58%	27,500	7,500	20,000	CHW
John Calder	Provider QI Coordinator	47,000	10%	4,700	0	4,700	CHW
Jonathan Christopher	Steering Cmt. Member	85,000	10%	8,500	0	8,500	CHAW
TBA Manager	Family Advocacy Cmt. Member	34,000	10%	3,400	0	3,400	CHAW
Fringe Benefits (28%)			158%	19,670	7,357	12,313	CHS
SUBTOTAL PERSONNEL				93,320	33,632	59,688	

II. OTHER DIRECT COSTS

Description	Total	RWJF	Other	Source
OFFICE OPERATIONS				
Supplies	1,431	1,431	0	
Duplicating	1,300	1,300	0	
Telephone	600	600	0	
Postage	1,500	1,500	0	
Equipment Rental	0	0	0	
Service Agreements	5,000	0	5,000	WI BEH
Training & Tech Support	4,000	4,000	0	
COMMUNICATE/MARKET	4,000	4,000	0	
SOFTWARE	0	0	0	
COMPUTER TIME	0	0	0	
MEETING COSTS	0	0	0	
TRAVEL	5,060	2,780	2,280	MCW
SUBTOTAL OTHER DIRECT	22,891	15,611	7,280	

III. INDIRECT COSTS (9%)

Description	Total	RWJF	Other	Source
Indirect Costs	4,432	4,432		

IV. EQUIPMENT

Description	Total	RWJF	Other	Source
None	0	0	0	

Within these line item categories, to illustrate the basis of budget calculations and to delineate between requested support and matching funds, budget columns identify:

- Name of Personnel
- Position
- Base Salary
- Percent Time
- Total
- RWJF Support
- Other Support
- Source of Other Support

In this format, for the line item categories of Personnel and Consultant/Contractual Agreements, reviewers can quickly see that "Base Salary" times "Percent Time" equals the "Total" cost. In all categories, reviewers will examine the extent to which project costs ("Total") are distributed among the sponsor ("RWJF Support") and the applicant ("Other Support").

The "Other Support" column illustrates which items are partially funded by the sponsor and partially funded by another source. The fact that we contributed matching dollars to the project, especially when they were not required in this planning phase, is more noteworthy than the actual distribution of the cost sharing. In some cases either we or the sponsor picked up the full item cost, and in others we cofunded items. Due to space limitations, the "Source of Other Support" column simply lists the acronym of the organization providing financial support; the budget narrative explains the source of this nonsponsor support in full detail.

The budget is divided into 12-month project periods. For multiyear requests, a line item budget and budget narrative should be prepared for each year of sponsor support, and a consolidated line item budget should be prepared for the entire proposed grant period. For example, a four-year project would require five budgets: one for each of the four individual project years and one that summarizes the entire four-year project.

Multiyear budgets should also plan for standard cost of living increases for key personnel. Cost of living raises often range from 3 to 5 percent per year and should be explained in the budget narrative. Recognize that these annual adjustments for inflation will have a corresponding impact on the amount of grant funding required for salary-related fringe benefits. Annual budget adjustments for nonpersonnel categories, such as equipment, travel, and materials and supplies, are not based on a fixed percentage; rather, they are realistic estimates based on predicted usage and projected price increases.

As we developed the budget, we kept in mind that The Robert Wood Johnson Foundation "Financial Reporting/Budgeting Practices and Grant Budget Revision Guidelines" allow for any budget category (Personnel, Other Direct Costs, Equipment, Consultant/Contractual Agreements) to be overspent by 5 percent provided that the approved budget total is not exceeded. In other words, the sponsor allows some flexibility to move grant dollars among budget categories in case project expenses are moderately over- or underestimated.

Further, budget revision guidelines also state that unexpended grant funds remain in the grant account and are not automatically carried forward to the next budget year. Grantees may request that funds unexpended from the previous budget periods be used in subsequent budget periods. A revised budget and budget narrative must be submitted that outlines the use of these funds.

Elements of the Budget Narrative

The budget narrative must include an explanation for every line item, which describes in as much detail as possible:

- the specific item;
- the item's relevance to the project;
- the basis of cost calculations for the item.

This level of detail explains *what* items are needed, *why* they are needed, *how much* they will cost. In a few cases, to strengthen the budget narrative we make cross-references to information contained on specific pages in our proposal narrative.

Following the sample budget narrative provided in The Robert Wood Johnson Foundation "National Program Site Budget Preparation Guidelines," we use Roman numerals corresponding to the line item budget to organize each category description. In each description we specify the level of funding requested from the sponsor and the level, type (cash or in-kind), and source of matching funds.

I. PERSONNEL. Similar to the information required on the sample line item budget form, we include a detailed description of the key personnel's title, name, professional education degree, role in the project, and full-time equivalency (FTE). Specific activities performed by key personnel touch on all three

V. CONSULTANT/CONTRACTUAL AGREEMENT

Name	Positon	Salary	Time	Total	RWJF	Other	Source
Subcontract with MCW							
John Meurer	Project Director	110,000	40%	44,000	22,000	22,000	MCW
Samantha Ayla	Steering Cmt. Coordinator	45,000	40%	18,000	9,000	9,000	MCW
Ramesh Sachdeva	Evaluation Cmt. Chair	195,000	10%	19,500	9,750	9,750	MCW
Kevin Kelly	Steering Cmt. Chair	205,000	5%	10,250	5,125	5,125	MCW
Karen Tilly	Family Advocacy Cmt. Member	165,000	5%	8,250	4,125	4,125	MCW
Fringe Benefits (25%)				25,000	12,500	12,500	MCW
Subtotal MCW			100%	125,000	62,500	62,500	
Subcontracts with Other Organizations or Individuals							
10 TBA Parents	Family Advocacy (6); Provider QI (2); Environ (2)			10,560	10,560	0	
3 TBA Parents	Co-Chairs of Family, Provider, Environ Cmt.			3,265	3,265	0	
Wayne Gresky	Family Advocacy Cmt. Co-Chair			15,500	4,000	11,500	ALA
Brychan William	Provider QI Cmt. Co-Chair			4,000	4,000	0	MSMC
Patrick Ignatius	Evaluation Cmt. Consultant			4,000	4,000	0	BHC
Maria Lemieux	Family Advocacy Cmt. Member			2,000	2,000	0	MPS
Paula Karina	Family Advocacy Cmt. Member			2,000	2,000	0	PC
Margarita Rodriguez	Provider QI Cmt. Member			2,000	2,000	0	BCC
Ray Bork	Environment Cmt. Member			2,000	2,000	0	SSCHC
Subtotal Other Organizations				45,325	33,825	11,500	
Organizations Providing In-Kind But Not Requiring Subcontracts							
Justin Heatley	Environment Cmt. Member		30%	29,300	0	29,300	WI BEH
Kris Tselios	Family Advocacy Cmt. Member		10%	10,000	0	10,000	WI BFCH
Peter Berg	Provider QI Cmt. Member		5%	5,000	0	5,000	WI BCD
TBA WI DPH staff	Regional Public Health Coordinator		1%	700	0	700	WI DHFS
TBA Child Care staff	Family Advocacy, Environment Cmt			30,000	0	30,000	MC DHS
Jerry Curry	Environment Cmt. Co-Chair				0		MHD
Ron Blake	Provider QI Cmt. Member			10,000	0	10,000	Aurora
Erica Jardins	Family Advocacy Cmt. Member			6,376	0	6,376	Aurora
Martha Sorley	Provider QI Cmt. Member			14,976	0	14,976	Aurora
TBA Parish Nurse	Environment Cmt. Member			1,115	0	1,115	Aurora
TBA Resp. Therapist	Environment Cmt. Member			6,000	0	6,000	Aurora
Alexis Mogly	Family Advocacy Cmt. Member			3,800	0	3,800	UHC
Jarome Jagger	Evaluation Cmt. Member			3,000	0	3,000	UHC
Subtotal In-kind Support				120,297	0	120,297	
SUBTOTAL AGREEMENTS				290,622	96,325	194,297	
TOTAL				411,265	150,000	261,265	

sponsor hot buttons: community-based collaborative efforts, evaluation and outcomes, and matching funds and sustainability. Note the use of phrases such as, "identifies, recruits, and retains families, children with asthma, representatives of schools, child care centers, churches, public health agencies, health plan asthma managers, and others"; "supervises collection of secondary data from data managers at hospitals, health plans, and public health agencies"; and "develops a sustainable coalition and an integrated strategic plan and targeted interventions."

Paragraphs are strategically designed to facilitate the skim-reading process. In each case, the first sentence identifies the key personnel by title and the last sentence indicates the amount of funding requested from the sponsor and the amount contributed by other sources. This presentation allows reviewers who are programmatically oriented to glance at topic sentences to find relevant information and it allows reviewers who are financially oriented to scan concluding sentences to find specific budget details.

Although this is only a one-year grant, it poses a common budgeting challenge: The award period crosses over two fiscal years. That is to say, during a twelve-month timeframe, key personnel will receive their present base salary for only a portion of the institution's current fiscal year before they are given a cost of living increase that will raise their base salary during the institution's next fiscal year.

For example, a committee coordinator with a base salary of $39,604 who dedicates 60 percent effort to the program for a full year, at first blush, would require $23,762 in grant support: ($39,604/yr * .60 FTE * 1 yr) = $23,762. In reality, however, the committee coordinator will work only nine months at a base salary of $39,604 before receiving a 4 percent cost of living raise and then work the remaining three months at a base salary of $41,188. This means that the committee coordinator would require $24,000 in grant support: [($39,604/yr * .60 FTE * .75 yr) + ($41,188/yr * .60 FTE * .25 yr)] = $24,000. While the difference between these two amounts, a total of $238, is a rather modest sum, it represents a real cost borne by grant funds.

More broadly, from the beginning, personnel costs must be planned carefully. Otherwise grant funds will need to be re-budgeted later from other categories (e.g., direct costs for Office Operations) to cover any shortfalls. The simple solution is to start the budget planning process by prorating the base salaries of key personnel to match the award period, as illustrated in the example above. This will help ensure that sufficient funds are requested to cover staffing costs. In addition, in the budget narrative, include a parenthetical explanation of these salary modifications. For instance, "the committee coordinator has an annual base salary of $40,000 (adjusted for the granting period) and will dedicate 60 percent effort to the program for one year, thus the requested budget is $24,000."

Fringe Benefits

We list the fringe benefits that will be provided and how the amount was calculated. When different benefit rates are used for different individuals, the budget narrative should contain a table that summarizes the calculation for each individual.

In this case, the fringe benefit rate for personnel at Children's Health System is 28 percent and for subcontracted partners at the Medical College of Wisconsin is 25 percent. Depending on the type of individual position or appointment held, specific fringe benefits may include vacation, holidays, sick leave, short-term and long-term disability, Family Medical Leave Act, leave of absence, life insurance, health insurance, dental insurance, retirement contribution, dependent care reimbursement plan, education, child care, professional liability, and unemployment compensation.

II. OTHER DIRECT COSTS. In addition to salaries and fringe benefits, other direct cost items include Office Operations, Communications/Marketing, Software, Computer Time, Meeting Costs, and Travel.

Office Operations

The projected expenditures for supplies, duplicating, telephone, postage, equipment rental, and service agreements are listed separately along with a description of how estimates for each were determined. Elements such as duplicating, telephone, and postage can be treated as direct or indirect cost items depending on their usage. For the purpose of this project we include them as direct costs because we will exceed their "normal" use, i.e., making long-distance phone calls to the National Program Office and other coalition sites, photocopying materials to distribute at coalition meetings, and mailing surveys to parents of children with asthma. Budget elements such as training and technical support for parents are also classified under this line item category of Office Operations. We identify who will be providing the training and technical

Milwaukee Allies Against Asthma
Budget Narrative

I. PERSONNEL

The Family & Community Advocacy Committee Coordinator, Cameron Nicholaus, is Project Coordinator of Fight Asthma Milwaukee. He identifies, recruits, and retains families, children with asthma, representatives of schools, child care centers, churches, public health agencies, health plan asthma managers, and others for Committee meetings and activities. Specific responsibilities include scheduling and recording minutes and communicating information for the Family Committee. He facilitates collection of primary survey data from parents and children with asthma through Committee members and coalition partners. With the Project Director and Family Committee Chair, he establishes the agenda of meetings to develop a family- and community-focused strategic plan and targeted interventions. He also contributes to quarterly conferences. For Mr. Nicholaus' total 60% effort, the requested budget is $16,000 plus an additonal $8,000 will be supported in-kind by Children's Health Education Center.

The Surveillance & Coalition Evaluation Committee Coordinator will be professional staff with masters level training in epidemiology and biostatistics in the Center for Outcomes Research and Quality Management at Children's Hospital of Wisconsin. The Coordinator assists the Evaluation Committee Chair in the following specific responsibilities: supervises collection of secondary data from data managers at hospitals, health plans, and public health agencies; controls the quality of primary and secondary data; analyzes primary and secondary data; and schedules meetings, records minutes, and communicates information for the Evaluation Committee. For the Evaluation Coordinator's total 58% effort, the requested budget is $7,500 plus an additional $20,000 will be supported in-kind by Children's Hospital of Wisconsin.

The Provider Quality Improvement Committee Coordinator, John Calder, RRT, is Asthma Program Coordinator for Children's Hospital of Wisconsin. He identifies, recruits, and retains parents, physicians, nurses, pharmacists, and others for Committee meetings and activities. Specific responsibilities include scheduling and recording minutes and communicating information for the Provider QI Committee. He facilitates collection of primary survey data from providers through Committee members and coalition partners. With the Project Director and Family Committee Coordinator, he establishes the agenda of meetings to develop a provider-focused strategic plan and targeted interventions. He also contributes to quarterly conferences. For Mr. Calder's total 10% effort, the requested budget is $0 with $4,700 supported in-kind by Children's Hospital of Wisconsin.

Steering Committee Members who are Children's Health System personnel include **Jessica Kwasny, MS,** Education Director of Children's Health Education Center, and **Jonathan Christopher, MBA,** Executive Director of Children's Health Alliance of Wisconsin (CHAW). They will communicate with their constituencies to foster linkages with the coalition. They will contribute to the development of a sustainable coalition and an integrated strategic plan and targeted interventions. They will also contribute to quarterly coalition conferences. Ms. Kwasny directly supervises the Family Committee Coordinator and Mr. Christopher directly supervises the CHAW Project Manager serving on the Family Committee. For Ms. Kwasny's total 10% effort, the requested budget is $2,775 plus and additional $2,775 will be supported in-kind by Children's Health Education Center. For Mr. Christopher's total 10% effort, the requested budget is $0 with $8,500 supported in-kind by Children's Health Alliance of Wisconsin through a sub-contract with the Wisconsin Department of Health and Family Services.

Fringe Benefits: Fringe benefits may include vacation, holidays, sick leave, short-term and long-term disability, Family Medical Leave Act, leave of absence, life insurance, health insurance, dental insurance, retirement plan, dependent care reimbursement plan, education, child care, and professional liability, depending upon the type of individual position or appointment held. The fringe benefit rate is 28% for personnel at Children's Health System.

II. TOTAL DIRECT COSTS

Office Operations:

Supplies: The requested supply budget is $1,431. This includes office supplies such as paper, pens, staples, paper clips, diskettes, ink cartridges, overhead paper, and slide film. Additional supply expenses will be supported in-kind at no cost by partner organizations in the coalition.

Duplicating: The requested duplicating budget is $1,300. This includes photocopying project correspondence and reference material for all committee meetings, conferences, and reports.

Telephone: The requested telephone budget is $600. This includes local calls by Children's Health System personnel and Medical College of Wisconsin sub-contracted partners. It also includes long-distance calls and faxes from the Project Director and Project Coordinator to the National Program Office and other coalition sites. Additional telephone and fax expenses will be supported in-kind at no cost by partner organizations in the coalition.

Postage: The requested postage budget is $1,500. This includes mailing routine correspondence as well as mailing and self-addressed return postage paid envelopes for a limited number of primary surveys of parents, providers, and coalition partners. Most surveys will be administered and collected by coalition partners at meetings, in their organizations, or in their community sites. Additional postage expenses will be supported in-kind at no cost by partner organizations in the coalition.

Equipment Rental: None.

Service Agreement: The requested service agreement budget is $0. However, the Wisconsin Bureau of Environmental Health will provide $5,000 of in-kind support for laboratory analysis of molds and other allergens found in specimens from selected homes, schools, and child care centers.

Training & Technical Support for Parents: The requested training and technical support for parents budget is $4,000. This includes $400 per parent for continuing education regarding effective participation in coalition efforts and infomation on asthma diagnosis and management from the NAEPP guidelines. Training and technical support primarily will be provided by Black Health Coalition of Wisconsin with assistance from Children's Health System, the Medical College of Wisconsin, and the American Lung Association of Wisconsin, among other coalition partners.

Communications/Marketing: The requested communications/marketing budget is $4,000 with additional contributions supported in-kind at no cost from partner organizations in the coalition. Funds will be allocated to increase awareness and visibility as well as to promote our project. This includes billboard advertising and public service announcements on local radio and television stations, brochures, newsletters, press releases,

support and explain its significance in fulfilling project objectives.

Communications/Marketing

Funds allocated to increasing awareness and visibility as well as promoting our project include billboard advertising, public service announcements, and printing of brochures, newsletters, press kits. Along with a brief description here, we make a strategic cross-reference to the "Communication Strategy" section of the proposal narrative for more detail. We also confirm that we will comply with the sponsor's public reporting expectations.

Software and Computer Time

We did not request any sponsor funds for software and computer time; nevertheless, we justify to the sponsor why we do not need funding for this category. Namely, all partner organizations have personal computers with relevant software for written and electronic communications. If we would have required special technology or computer processing, we would have identified the software or service necessary and explained how it related to achieving project objectives.

Meeting Costs

After much discussion among coalition members, meeting space and supplies were offered as in-kind costs supported by partner organizations. This includes such expenses as meeting room rental, audiovisual equipment rental, slide presentation costs, child care, and meals. Because some coalition partners had never calculated the costs of hosting an individual meeting, we did not attempt to quantify the value of this matching support. We do, however, make a strategic cross-reference to the "Coalition Infrastructure" section of the proposal narrative for more detail about the purpose of various meetings.

Travel

Projected travel expenditures for Project Staff and Consultant/Contractual Agreements outline the destination, purpose, and the basis of calculations. Estimates for local travel are consistent with our institution's current policies, e.g., $0.345/mile. In order to maximize the impact of sponsor funds, and to ensure that transportation is not a barrier to inclusive participation, we opted to request local travel funds only for parent representatives to the coalition.

Following the application guidelines, we budgeted

a two-night stay for two project staff to attend the National Program's annual meeting each year. Budget figures include airfare, lodging, meals, and ground transportation. Because we did not use any consultants, we did not need to budget any additional local or nonlocal travel costs.

III. INDIRECT COSTS. According to budget preparation guidelines, indirect costs may be calculated up to 9 percent on budget categories I and II, Personnel and Other Direct Costs. Indirect costs are not calculated on the amounts budgeted for categories IV and V, Equipment and Consultant/Contractual Agreements. This indirect costs line item is intended to cover grant-related expenses that are not easily identified but are necessary to conduct the grant, i.e., reporting costs, payroll processing, utilities, space rental costs, and legal counsel for subcontract development.

Interestingly, the sponsor did not ask for evidence of our actual indirect cost rate. Organizations regularly receiving federal grants often have an approved federal indirect cost rate that they use in calculating budgets and include as an appendix item in their complete grant application. In the budget narrative, a summary statement such as the following is frequently used to indicate the basis of the indirect cost rate, the cognizant agency who approved the rate, and the rate's effective period: "Indirect costs are calculated on the basis of 26 percent of modified total direct costs, a rate approved by the Department of Health and Human Services, effective January 1, 2000 to December 31, 2002." This sentence tells the sponsor that the indirect cost rate being used is an actual and verifiable figure.

IV. EQUIPMENT. The purpose of this one-year grant is to develop an overall plan and strategy for addressing pediatric asthma in the community. We do not require any specific equipment to achieve project goals and objectives. In fact, nearly 87 percent of funds are dedicated to supporting the salaries, wages, and benefits of many individuals participating in the coalition's planning process. During this planning phase, we will need to consider interventions carefully because the sponsor will not support large amounts of equipment in the budget requests for the implementation years.

During the implementation phase, the sponsor will allow a limited amount of equipment if appropriate for the accomplishment of program objectives. We will itemize the equipment requested and include a statement outlining how the equipment will be used to fulfill project goals. We follow our organization's

annual reports, and other media communications noted in the Proposal (see "Communication Strategy"). We will comply with public reporting expectations as identified in Section 7 of the Conditions of the Grant.

Software and Computer Time: The requested software and computer time budget is $0 with additional contributions supported in-kind at no cost from partner organizations in the coalition. All partner organizations have personal computers with Microsoft Office, printers, electronic mail, and Internet access. For parents and older children with asthma who lack personal computers, written information will be mailed and urgent communications will be telephoned.

Meeting Costs: The requested meeting costs budget is $0 with additional contributions supported in-kind at no cost from partner organizations in the coalition. This includes meeting room and audiovisual equipment rental. Meals and child care will be provided by volunteers with the coalition. The purpose of meetings is noted in the Proposal (see "Coalition Infrastructure") and in the table of Committees at the end of the Budget Narrative. Committee meetings may be held at any partner organization with adequate space, parking, and audiovisual equipment. Conferences will be held at the Children's Health Education Center, Children's Hospital of Wisconsin, or the Medical College of Wisconsin.

Travel:

Project Staff Travel:

    Local Travel – The requested travel budget is $2,880 for local travel by parents = (10 parents x $20/meeting x one meeting or conference/month x 12 months) + (3 Co-Chair parents on Steering and Evaluation Committees too x $20/meeting x 2meetings/month x 8 months). The $20 is the estimated average cost of taxi fare plus tip round trip from homes to the meeting or conference location.

    Non-Local Travel – None.

Annual Meeting Travel: The Medical College of Wisconsin Department of Pediatrics Academic Development Funds for Dr. Meurer and Ms. Ayla will be used to provide in-kind support for a two-night stay ($1,140) for the Project Director and Project Coordinator to attend the National Allies Against Asthma Program's annual meeting involving all grantees, Foundation representatives, and the National Program Office, to exchange information and provide mutual assistance (total $2,280).

Consultant Travel: None.

III. INDIRECT COSTS:

The requested indirect cost budget of $4,432 is 9% of Children's Health System personnel and other direct costs only. Indirect costs cover grant-related costs that are not easily identified but are necessary to conduct the grant, i.e., accounting and reporting costs, payroll processing, space rental costs, legal counsel for sub-contract development, etc.

IV. EQUIPMENT: None.

V. CONSULTANT/CONTRACTUAL AGREEMENTS:

Consultants: None.

Contractual Agreements:
A separate contract outlining the contractor, dates, dollars, and specific tasks/deliverables will be made and entered between Children's Health System and the Subcontractor. The Robert Wood Johnson Foundation will not be party to the contract. Children's Health System will maintain fiscal responsibility for its contracts including reporting expenses to the Foundation. We will include accounting and right to audit provisions and record retention and report expectations in the contracts identified in Sections 4 and 5 of the Conditions of Grant. We also will include public reporting expectations in the contracts as identified in Section 7 of the Conditions of the Grant.

The Project Director, John Meurer, MD, MBA, is Assistant Professor of Community Pediatrics and Health Services Research in the Center for the Advancement of Urban Children at the Medical College of Wisconsin and Children's Health System. He is directly responsible for developing the proposed activity, its implementation, and day-to-day direct supervision of the project. He is accountable for planning, organizing, and directing the implementation and operations of this project. Specific responsibilities include directing staff, orientation, training, counseling, evaluation, and discipline in accordance with institutional standards. He directs the implementation and operations, distributes work, directs and personally handles public relations, estimates costs of programs, develops the budget, oversees and negotiates contracts with subcontractors, monitors and assesses project performance and performs other related coalition duties. He develops the agenda for meetings with all Committee Chairs. He contributes to and facilitates as many of the Committee meetings as possible. With the Project Coordinator, he also plans the quarterly conferences. He plans manageable processes based on theoretical models and focused on objectives and outcomes. He builds social relations and communicates to foster linkages, including collaboration with the National Program Office and other Coalitions. He ensures all five Committees remain accountable to one another. The Project Director directly supervises the Project Coordinator. For Dr. Meurer's total 40% effort, the requested budget is $22,000 plus an additional $22,000 will be supported in-kind by the Medical College of Wisconsin.

The Project Coordinator, Samantha Ayla, MPA, is Research Coordinator in the Center for the Advancement of Urban Children at the Medical College of Wisconsin and Children's Health System. She assists the Project Director in all of the above activities. Specific responsibilities include scheduling and recording minutes and communicating information for the Steering, Surveillance and Coalition Evaluation, and Environmental Risk Reduction Committees. She schedules and plans the quarterly conferences. She helps develop the agenda for meetings with all Committee Coordinators. She also serves as the Project Coordinator for the Environmental Risk Reduction Committee and assists the Chair with planning and facilitating meetings and communicating information. She directly supervises optical scanning of primary survey data in the Center for the Advancement of Urban Children. For Ms. Ayla's total 40% effort, the requested budget is $9,000 plus an additional $9,000 will be supported in-kind by the Medical College of Wisconsin.

The Surveillance & Coalition Evaluation Committee Chair, Ramesh Sachdeva, MD, PhD, MBA, is Associate Professor of Critical Care Pediatrics and Epidemiology at the Medical College of Wisconsin and Director of the Center for Outcomes Research and Quality Management at Children's Hospital of Wisconsin. He designs observational and experimental studies with the assistance of academic and community-based researchers. He supervises collection of secondary data from data managers at hospitals, health plans, and public health agencies. He controls the quality of primary and secondary data. In his data management, he respects the confidentiality of individuals and organizations. He

THE BUDGET AND BUDGET NARRATIVE

equipment capitalization threshold policy to determine whether an item is classified under equipment or supplies. Moreover, we will examine the option of purchasing versus leasing or renting and explain our choice. If we decide to purchase, because many manufacturers routinely offer educational or institutional discounts, we will identify in the detailed budget narrative both the list price and the discounted price used to compute the total cost of the project, a copy of the vendor quote will be included as an appendix item in the complete grant application.

V. CONSULTANT/CONTRACTUAL AGREEMENTS.

Consultants are individuals who are brought into grant projects to add expertise in specific areas of professional activity. When these individuals are employed by and represent other organizations, contractual agreements are used to describe the collaborative arrangements between multiple organizations. Whether serving as individuals or part of a consortium, consultants often have great intuitive knowledge of problems and issues and can communicate that information in an immediately usable form. They can act as strong advocates for planned and systematic change.

Consultants

We did not require any individual consultants for this project; all of our outside expertise essential to fulfilling project objectives comes in the form of contractual agreements. When individual consultants are required, we outline the need for each consultant, provide a workplan for each one, and detail tasks to be accomplished. Also note that the budget preparation guidelines limit the sponsor's portion of compensation paid to consultants to $500/day for a full day of work.

Contractual Agreements

For each proposed contract we provide an explanatory paragraph that outlines:

- the contractor
- key dates
- dollar amounts
- specific tasks and deliverables

Following the budget preparation guidelines, The Robert Wood Johnson Foundation will not be listed as a party to the contracts. We will maintain fiscal responsibility for our contracts, which includes reporting expenses associated with the contract to the sponsor. We also include right to audit provisions and record retention expectations when negotiating contracts.

appropriately designs and directs analysis of primary and secondary data. He clearly reports findings to coalition partners. He also contributes to the Steering Committee and quarterly coalition conferences. He directs and supervises the Evaluation Committee Coordinator. For Dr. Sachdeva's total 10% effort, the requested budget is $9,750 plus an additional $9,750 will be supported in-kind by the Medical College of Wisconsin.

The Steering Committee Chair, Kevin Kelly, MD, is Professor of Pediatrics at the Medical College of Wisconsin and Director of the Asthma and Allergy Center at Children's Hospital of Wisconsin. He provides vision and leadership to the coalition, builds social relationships, recognizes achievements, and communicates to foster linkages. Through his efforts, he develops a sustainable coalition and an integrated strategic plan and targeted interventions. Specifically, he develops Steering Committee meeting agendas with the Project Director. He identifies, recruits, and retains Steering Committee and coalition members through respectful, participatory management approaches. He also contributes to Surveillance and Evaluation Committee Meetings and quarterly coalition conferences. For Dr. Kelly's total 5% effort, the requested budget is $5,125 plus an additional $5,125 will be supported in-kind by the Medical College of Wisconsin.

The Family Advocacy Committee Member and Surveillance & Evaluation Committee Member, Karen Tilly, MD, MPH, is Associate Professor of Community Pediatrics and Director of the Center for the Advancement of Urban Children at MCW and CHS. She helps design studies, select survey instruments, and collect primary survey data. For Dr. Tilly's total 5% effort, the requested budget is $4,125 plus an additional $4,125 will be supported in-kind by the Medical College of Wisconsin.

Fringe Benefits for Sub-Contracts with the Medical College of Wisconsin: Fringe benefits for sub-contracted partners at the Medical College of Wisconsin may include vacation, holidays, sick leave, short-term and long-term disability, Family Medical Leave Act, leave of absence, life insurance, health insurance, dental insurance, retirement plan, dependent care reimbursement plan, education, child care, and professional liability, depending upon the type of individual position or appointment held. The fringe benefit rate is 25% at the Medical College of Wisconsin.

Contractual agreements will be established to compensate individuals serving as co-chairs and members of various committees. The Co-Chair of the Family Advocacy Committee, the Co-Chair of the Provider Quality Improvement Committee, and the Evaluation Committee consultant will receive stipends of $4,000 each. Two members of the Family Advocacy Committee, a Provider Quality Improvement member, and Environment Committee member will each receive stipends of $2,000 for their efforts.

A variety of other organizations in the coalition will not require subcontracts for their contributions to committees, but are providing $120,297 in in-kind support.

In total, Milwaukee Allies Against Asthma requests $150,000 in planning funds from The Robert Wood Johnson Foundation and coalition partners will contribute in-kind an additional $261,265.

THE BUDGET AND BUDGET NARRATIVE

STAGE TWO: FULL PROPOSAL

PREPARING FOR THE SITE VISIT

Our full proposal to The Robert Wood Johnson Foundation's "Allies Against Asthma" program received a favorable review and we were selected for a site visit. That is, as part of the evaluation process, the sponsor wanted to see firsthand our operation—its environment and people. Information gathered in a single day by a team of reviewers can decide the fate of an application that has taken us months to prepare. In essence, a site visit represents a "quality control" measure for the sponsor, a way for them to verify our credibility and establish a level of trust with us before awarding project funding.

In this third section of the chapter, we begin to prepare for the site visit by reading through and analyzing three documents provided by the sponsor: the site visit announcement, the site visit sample agenda, and the site visit questions. Then, as requested, we develop written responses to the site visit questions and submit them to the National Program Office five business days in advance of the site visit. Our answers to the "proposal specific" and "general" site visit questions will form the basis of our oral presentation to the site visit team and set the stage for further interview questions.

Site Visit Announcement

Site visits are held when sponsors feel they need information available only at the proposed project site. They are a way for the sponsor to see whether we can accomplish all that we promised in the application narrative. Our job is to show them firsthand that our idea, personnel, and organization are indeed credible. In this case, the sponsor decided to conduct site visits with thirteen of the remaining twenty-six applicants (50 percent); eight sites will be awarded project funding.

Like all good journalistic writing, the site visit announcement answers six major questions about this next stage of the review process: who, what, when, where, why, and how.

- **Who**—a three-member site visit team will include individuals representing The Robert Wood Johnson Foundation, the National Program Office, and the National Advisory Committee.
- **What**—the National Program Office is coordinating site visits for those coalitions that have been selected to move forward to the next stage of the proposal review process.

- **When**—site visits will be conducted in one full day, from 8:30 A.M. to 3:30 P.M., with specific amounts of time budgeted for targeted constituencies within the coalition.
- **Where**—the site visit will occur in the office of the host agency or one of its key partners.
- **Why**—the site visit team will address questions raised during the review of the full proposal and learn more about the coalition and key individuals working to improve pediatric asthma care in the community.
- **How**—the site visit team will meet individually with coalition leadership, key staff of the fiscal agent, and representatives of key partners and will attend a general coalition session with the full membership.

Site Visit Team. The site visit announcement advises, "A copy of any handouts . . . should be made for each member of the team." In the interest of thoroughness, we go one step further. We provide the site visit team with a "take away" folder that includes:

- the agenda
- the project summary
- a copy of our PowerPoint presentation slides
- a copy of our written responses to the "proposal specific" and "general" site visit questions
- a list of other related projects
- contact information for all key participants

Although these additional items were not specifically requested, we include them as a subtle way to reinforce our three hot buttons. For example, contact information illustrates that our project is a community-based collaborative effort and a list of related projects reinforces our concern for evaluation and sustainability.

Logistics. Understandably, the site visit team requested directions from their hotel to the meeting site. But to be good hosts—and to help save on overall site visit costs—coalition leaders volunteered to drive the site visit team to and from the airport, their hotels, and the meeting sites. More importantly, this act of goodwill provided coalition leaders with some additional time to get acquainted with site visitors, including an opportunity to drive through the targeted geographic area and an extra chance to discuss key aspects of the project, e.g., the population to be served.

Agenda. Developing the agenda is the most difficult task. The site visit announcement indicates, "Your responses should also be discussed during the

The University of Michigan

School of Public Health

Allies Against Asthma

109 S. Observatory Street

Ann Arbor, Michigan 48109-2029

August 23, 2000

Dr. John Meurer

Fight Asthma Milwaukee Coalition

Children's Health System

9000 W. Wisconsin Avenue

P.O. Box 1997

Milwaukee, WI 53201

Dear Dr. Meurer:

The Allies Against Asthma National Program Office is currently coordinating site visits for those coalitions that have been selected to move forward to the next stage of the proposal review process. This letter contains information which we hope will assist you as we work together to coordinate the visit.

Site Visit Team

The site visit team will include 3–4 people representing the National Advisory Committee, the Robert Wood Johnson Foundation, and the National Program Office (NPO). We will provide you with a resume of each site visitor prior to the visit. A

site visit, being sure that all questions are addressed by the end of the day." With six site specific and eleven general questions, it would be nearly impossible to discuss all questions in any detail. Consider: The sample site visit agenda allocates a total of two hours with coalition leadership to address these seventeen questions—this averages out to seven minutes per question with no time for a break!

As described below in "Site Visit Questions," rather than trying to answer each question individually during our presentation, we cluster them into groups according to the three hot buttons that we identified and addressed throughout the grant application process. While a detailed agenda gives us an idea of how much time is available to present key information, we remain flexible in case we need to address any unexpected situations or accommodate the wishes of the site visit team.

Site Visit Sample Agenda

Before the sponsor will award project funding, they need to feel comfortable with us, to trust that our coalition understands their concerns and shares their values. The site visit sample agenda is designed so that the site visit team can observe our coalition in action, as much as possible, in a natural environment. During the visit, they will be looking at intangible characteristics among coalition leaders and other members, such as:

- Passion—Do we exhibit enthusiasm for this project?
- Energy—Do we demonstrate the drive to make this project a success?
- Trust—Do we act as a team working together to achieve a common goal?
- Commitment—Do we display a sense of dedication toward each other and for completing the project?
- Ownership—Do we claim responsibility for our successes and challenges?

Especially for collaborative projects, the site visit team may take a "divide-and-conquer" approach to assessing programmatic features such as project leadership, community involvement, communication, accountability, and sustainability. By meeting with key partners individually, the site visit team can quickly determine whether the project is a real or a "phantom" collaboration. Phantom collaborations—relationships that exist only on paper—don't get funded. In real collaborations, project partners' roles are well-defined in themselves and in relation to overall project goals. Collaborators can explain how they plan to cooperate administratively, fiscally, and programmatically in order to make the project a success.

While the site visit team will spend time interviewing the coalition leadership and fiscal agent, the site visit sample agenda also requests that the team should "meet individually with 'key players' whose commitment is needed to implement the initiative, including state and local policy makers." Participation from government officials was a distinctive feature that we identified in the RFP guidelines for the letter of intent, and has taken on an increasing level of importance as we advance through the grant application process.

In addition to state and local officials, we include key players from the community, such as parents and members of community based organizations, and representatives from health care delivery systems and health plans. We select individuals from these groups because, as necessary, they can answer the "proposal specific" (S) and "general" (G) site visit questions about their:

- roles in coalition leadership: S3, S4, and G1
- access to data and data collection systems: G6, G7, G8, G9, G10

The site visit team may also ask collaborative partners the following types of questions:

- Why is this program important to you?
- How long have you been involved with the program?
- What was your involvement in developing the grant application?
- What are your connections to the community?
- If your program is selected for funding, what do you see as your role?
- How do your contributions fit into the "big picture"?

In essence, our task is to form three small groups who will meet individually with the site visit team. Each group will have five to seven members who are knowledgeable about past, present, and future coalition activities, and who reflect the racial/ethnic and gender composition of the coalition. This strategy exposes the site visitors to a diverse cross-section of coalition partners and also keeps the number of participants small enough to allow for productive conversations.

copy of any handouts or other written information you provide throughout the day should be made for each member of the team.

Logistics

Most site visits will be conducted during one day, between approximately 8:30 am and 3:30 pm. We expect the host coalition to make arrangements for a meeting site, preferably in the office of its host agency or one of its key partners, and to communicate with all local participants.

The NPO will arrange accommodations for the team. Recommendations for hotels and restaurants convenient to the meeting site would be appreciated. Once we have made these arrangements we will contact you to get directions from the hotel to the meeting site.

Agenda

The development of the agenda is a joint process between your coalition and the NPO. We would like you to draft a preliminary schedule based on the information provided in this letter. A member of our staff will be assigned to work with you to be sure the agenda meets our mutual needs. We view the site visit as an opportunity to learn more about your coalition, and are interested in meeting the individuals you identify as important to the coalition's development and its efforts to improve pediatric asthma care in your community. At the same time, there are some specific people we would like to meet and specific issues we would like for you to address during the visit.

Attached is a list of questions that arose during the proposal review process. *We would like for you to provide a written response to the National Program Office at least five business days prior to the site visit.* This will give the site visit team time to review your comments before the discussions. Your responses should also be discussed during the site visit, being sure that all questions are addressed by the end of the day.

Site Visit Questions

The sponsor attached a list of seventeen questions that needed to be answered in writing prior to the site visit. Of these questions, six were specific to our coalition and eleven were general questions for all coalition sites. In the RFP guidelines for the letter of intent and full proposal, the sponsor limited the number of pages they would accept. This time, they did not. Intuitively, this makes sense: Coalitions with a greater number of proposal specific questions would require more space to explain their answers than coalitions with fewer site specific questions.

Although we were not constrained by sponsor-imposed page limitations, even conservative estimates of one-half to a full page written answer per question would mean that our responses are 8.5 to 17 pages long. This is approximately the length of another full proposal! Accordingly, we aim to find a balance between length and completeness. Abbreviated answers may cast doubt on our understanding of the planning process. Verbose answers may frustrate reviewers, especially when they have many pages to read in a very short time; written responses are due a mere five business days prior to the site visit. Thus, we must answer the sponsor's questions thoroughly yet concisely. We began by looking for hot buttons around which to organize our responses.

Not surprisingly, the three hot buttons that we identified in our letter of intent and full proposal are once again repeated throughout the "proposal specific" (S) and "general" (G) site visit questions. In particular, hot buttons relate to the following questions.

- Community-based collaborative efforts: G1, G2, G3, G4, and S3, S4
- Evaluation and outcomes: G5, G6, G7, G8, G9, G10, and S1, S2, S5
- Matching funds and sustainability: G11 and S6

Over half of all the site visit questions relate to The Robert Wood Johnson Foundation's concern for systematic evaluation and measurable outcomes. Foremost among all of these is the first specific question: "S1. Please clarify the target population. What is the geographic focus? Is this a city or countywide focus? How many and which children will be targeted?" That is to say, we need to know exactly *which* and *how many* children we are targeting for services before we can assess whether or not we are achieving our goal of controlling pediatric asthma.

More than one-third of the site visit questions focus on determining the extent to which project efforts are community-based and collaborative. The third specific question (S3) and the first general question (G1) both call for examples of how community representatives participate in the leadership and decision-making processes of the coalition. This concern for inclusive participation is reinforced through the design of the site visit sample agenda, which allocates an hour and a half for the site visit team to meet with community members individually. During this time, site visitors will assess whether this project is a real or phantom collaboration.

While only two site visit questions (S6 and G11) focus on the hot button of matching funds and sustainability, during the site visit interview, all coalition members should be prepared to answer a potentially loaded question: "What will happen to this project if it is not selected for funding?" That is, without sponsor support, will the project:

- continue as planned?
- continue on a reduced scale?
- cease to exist?

In either of the two extreme cases, where the project continues as planned or ceases to exist, the site visit team may conclude that grant funding would be better spent somewhere else because it is not necessary to carry out the project or because the project is not sustainable over the long term. The middle option, continuing the project on a reduced scale, demonstrates the coalition's genuine commitment to improving the problem situation and at the same time justifies the need for sponsor support in order to produce large-scale, sustainable change.

Next we elaborate on how to survive the site visit. By tuning into the verbal and nonverbal behaviors of site visitors during the presentation and interview process, we can better connect our project idea to the values of the sponsor.

SURVIVING THE SITE VISIT

Successfully managing the site visit is, in large part, a matter of paying attention to many details. Proper preparation will increase the likelihood that the site visit will go smoothly. The "3 R's" to surviving a site visit include:

- **Reviewing.** Bring together all project personnel and collaborators, have everyone reread the proposal, and review in detail the components of the project.
- **Rehearsing.** Ask outside colleagues to come in and

The visit should be structured so that the individuals most involved in the project's decision-making, planning, implementation, and evaluation are able to participate in all or part of the day. The goal is to include key people, while keeping the number of participants small enough to allow for productive conversation.

In most cases, site visit activities should start at 8:30 am and be completed by 3:30 pm. Given the brief time in which the site visit team will be with you, we have developed a number of recommended site visit components that we feel are important. How you schedule the specific components is up to you. Attached is a sample agenda to give you an idea of how these components might be put together. Be sure to schedule adequate time throughout the day for site visitors to ask questions as they arise.

At some point during the day, the site visit team would like to meet with the following individuals:

➢ Coalition leadership
➢ Key staff of the host agency/fiscal agent
➢ General coalition membership: If at all possible, we would like to attend a general coalition meeting with the full coalition membership. We recognize that this schedule may be difficult for many coalitions, especially those that normally meet outside of business hours. If this is the case, we will work with sites individually to arrange for all or part of the site visit team to arrive early or stay late in order to accommodate this schedule. Other than a brief introduction of the coalition members, we do not require any special agenda for this meeting. As much as possible, we would like to observe the coalition conducting its normal activities and discussions.
➢ Representatives of key partners whose commitment is needed to implement the initiative, including policy makers from the state and local level, hospital and health

conduct a practice site visit. The most common mistake in a site visit is for project personnel to be unfamiliar with proposal details. Rehearsing the site visit will help key participants to learn their roles in the interview process and to stay on schedule during the main event. Presenters should note their own verbal and nonverbal behaviors to ensure that they appear friendly, positive, and engaged.

- **Responding.** Ask sponsors if they have a particular agenda they wish to follow or if they want to see any special background documents. Arrange a private room for them to meet in and conduct interviews. Allow plenty of time for reviewers' questions. Do not bombard reviewers with a lot of new information that was not in the application. Do not unnecessarily repeat material already presented in the application.

Broadly, the site visit consists of two parts: the presentation and the interview. Following the "3 R's" will help us to survive the site visit, and more importantly, to persuade the site visit team that our project merits funding.

The Presentation

The content of our presentation, in this case, is driven by the 17 site visit questions provided by The Robert Wood Johnson Foundation. Because our time is limited, we cluster and prioritize the questions into groups according to the three hot buttons that we identified in our letter of intent and full proposal. Taking a cue from the site visit announcement, we decide to give our presentation in a semistructured style. That is, we develop an outline of our presentation using PowerPoint visual aids, yet we are prepared to deviate from this framework as necessary to accommodate questions and feedback from the site visitors.

To ensure that we have a strong start and finish to our presentation, we memorize the first few minutes of the opening and closing of our speech. In the body of our presentation we may periodically refer to our notes and visual aids. More importantly, during our presentation we practice the characteristics modeled by all good public speakers. We:

- wear confident and natural smiles.
- maintain eye contact with the interviewers.
- position ourselves at an appropriate distance from site visitors when talking.
- are prepared to listen.
- state our points clearly and provide concrete examples.
- use a firm and positive tone.

- use gestures in a natural way.
- interact with visual aids and the site visit team.
- end our presentation on a positive note.

After listening to our presentation, the site visit team may wish to ask other questions about our project, staff, and organization. This interview process provides us with a vital opportunity to clarify any "fuzzy" aspects of our project, to reinforce our key points, and to establish rapport with the site visitors.

The Interview

Site visit interviews can range in format from highly structured to unstructured. In structured interviews, the site visit team asks the same questions of all candidates, thus ensuring a level of consistency in their data collection process. This format, however, may not allow enough spontaneity to fully explore candidates' intangible characteristics. In unstructured interviews, candidates have the flexibility to address the issues that are of greatest concern to them. This format effectively prevents the site visit team from biasing the interview with preconceived notions about the proposed project, yet it may also produce a considerable amount of information not directly related to the site visit purpose. Most site visit interviews compromise and follow a moderately structured format.

The tone of our site visit announcement suggested that a semistructured interview format would be used. Semistructured interviews balance the need for consistency and flexibility. Meaning, the site visit team can use a structured list of questions with all candidates to establish a basis for comparing responses and then use varied follow-up questions to probe for additional details. Interview questions may span a continuum of time, from past actions to future intentions. This combination format of fixed and flexible questioning is an effective way for the site visit team to obtain interview results that are valid and reliable.

Types of Interview Questions. We anticipated that the site visit team would begin the semistructured interview with some open-ended questions from a preestablished list and then follow-up with a combination of open-ended and closed-ended questions. Open-ended questions are broad in nature and require us to explain certain aspects of our project in detail. Closed-ended questions are a way for the site visit team to get specific facts about our project and to verify information from our proposal narrative. In reality, the site visit team has a dual task: ask targeted questions about our project and listen closely to the an-

plan representatives, representatives of the school or public housing systems, and others who may or may not be members of the coalition. When applicable, include representatives of organizations referenced in the attached questions.

All local participants do not need to be present for the entire meeting. The project leader should determine what is feasible and what works best for the project and the day's discussions.

The agenda is designed to allow us to make the most of our time by working through lunch. While we appreciate your arranging the lunch for the site visitors, we are happy to pay for them. It should not be an expense for you to have us visit! Feel free to provide us with a bill for the meal.

A member of our staff will contact you shortly to discuss specific dates for your site visit and your proposed agenda. If you have any questions in the meantime, feel free to contact me (734-647-3179, lindoc@umich.edu) or Hayley Warshaw (734-615-3312, hwarshaw@umich.edu). We look forward to working with and meeting you soon.

Sincerely,

Linda Jo Doctor, MPH
Deputy Director

*　*　*

swers. By maintaining an 80:20 listening to talking ratio they can guide the interview and gather all the information they need to make a funding decision.

From the site visit sample agenda, we knew that our initial presentation would be based on the structured "proposal specific" and "general" site visit questions. During the interview, we will pay particular attention to the style of follow-up questions asked by the site visit team. Follow-up questions may be open-ended or closed-ended and probe for clarification, solicit new information, or refocus responses in more productive directions. Said differently, we can take verbal cues from the site visit team depending on whether they pose follow-up questions in a neutral or leading style.

Consider the following pairs of open-ended questions; one is asked in a neutral style, and the other is asked in a leading style. Neutral questions do not provide any indication of the values of the site visit team. Leading questions provide brief glimpses into the preferences of the site visitors and allow us to shape our answers to match their priorities.

Neutral Questions	Leading Questions
• What did you mean when you said . . . ? • What would you do next? • Why hasn't this been done before? • What results would that produce? • What long-term impacts do you anticipate this would have on children, families, providers, and the community? • What is necessary to secure provider involvement in this project? • What is the current status of pediatric asthma in the community? • Tell me about the target group of children that you have selected. • Why did you select this approach to pediatric asthma management? • Describe the value of this communication process. • Give me an example of a project that you have been able to sustain beyond initial grand funding.	• When you said . . . did you mean . . . ? • And as your next step, would you consider doing . . . ? • This is such a unique approach, why hasn't it been done before? • Would this produce results such as . . . ? • This would have a long term, beneficial impacts on children, families, providers, and the community, right? • With all due respect, don't you think it's a bit excessive to . . . ? • Why is it imperative that this pediatric asthma problem be addressed now? • Wouldn't you agree that children from urban, suburban, and rural communities should be included in the target group? • What do you like best about a community-driven approach to pediatric asthma management? • Why does this communication process work so well? • What do you think is the potential for sustaining this project beyond the granting period?

Similarly, compare the following pairs of closed-ended questions, where one is asked in a neutral style and the other is asked in a leading style. Whereas open-ended questions encourage in-depth responses, closed-ended questions typically require brief "yes/no" answers. For this reason, the site visit team is likely to ask more open- than closed-ended questions.

Allies Against Asthma

Site Visit Sample Agenda

The following is a *sample* agenda. We understand the need to revise the agenda based on availability, and will work with each site individually to develop a final schedule.

8:30–10:30   **Participants**: Coalition leadership

Agenda: The site visit team will provide a short introduction to its members and the purpose of the visit. The coalition leadership should provide a *brief* overview of the proposal and begin to address the questions attached. Time should be included for the site visit team to ask questions based on the discussion.

10:30–11:30   **Participants**: Key staff of the host agency/fiscal agent

Agenda: Clarify relationships between host agency/fiscal agent and coalition. Discuss any of the attached questions related to this relationship.

11:30–1:00   **Participants**: Coalition leadership and key coalition partners

Agenda: The team should meet individually with "key players" whose commitment is needed to implement the initiative, including state and local policy makers. A working lunch is probably necessary to provide sufficient time for such meetings.

1:00–1:30   **Participants**: Site Visit Team

Neutral Questions	Leading Questions
<ul><li>Are you going to . . . ?</li><li>Do you plan to . . . ?</li><li>Do you know much about measuring pediatric quality of life outcomes?</li><li>How long have you been an active member of the coalition?</li><li>Can you tell me how many individuals are members of the Steering Committee?</li><li>What types of intervention strategies do you intend to use in your overall implementation plan?</li><li>Is this approach feasible?</li><li>Have you collaborated with these groups before?</li><li>How often will nurses communicate with parents of children with asthma?</li><li>Who will be responsible for scheduling follow-up visits?</li><li>Would you be willing to participate in the national cross-site evaluation?</li></ul>	<ul><li>So, what you're saying is . . . , right?</li><li>If I'm hearing you correctly, you plan to . . . ?</li><li>Have you published other journal articles in addition to the three listed in the "Works Cited" on measuring pediatric quality of life outcomes?</li><li>Is it true that your coalition was one of the first established in the country?</li><li>With the unique contributions that they can make, do you intend to have parents of children with asthma serve on the Steering Committee?</li><li>One-time interventions have limited effectiveness and pose challenges for measuring outcomes. Do you plan to use them as part of your overall implementation strategy?</li><li>Wouldn't you agree that this approach tries to take on too much at once?</li><li>Will your history of collaboration with those groups influence the success of this project?</li><li>Will nurses communicate with parents of children with asthma at least twice per month?</li><li>Will the asthma counselor be responsible for scheduling follow-up visits?</li><li>As part of your participation in the national cross-site evaluation, do you prefer video conferences or face-to-face meetings?</li></ul>

Whether we are asked neutral or leading questions, when answering we use effective lead-ins to facilitate site visitors' note taking. We use expressions such as, "be sure to note that . . .", "three key points include . . .", "one feature that distinguishes us from everyone else is . . .", and "in summary, the three main characteristics that will make us successful are . . ." Moreover, we avoid using tentative words and phrases that will make us sound more "hopeful" than confident: "might," "maybe," "perhaps," "it could be possible," "it's conceivable that," and "under the right conditions . . ."

In the case when we do not know how to answer a question, or when a question seems irrelevant to our situation, we ask for clarification. For example, we ask, "By that, do you mean . . . ?", "Could you please expand upon your question?", "If I understand you correctly, you want to know more about . . .", "I don't know the answer to that question off the top of my head, but I can have Bob look up that data while we

continue with your other questions." When a question is unclear, we do not try to guess at what the site visit team might mean. A wrong guess could make our answer sound evasive, ill-considered, boastful, or moot. Our task is to make the best use of the time available to convince the site visit team that we merit project funding.

In short, the site visit team may—intentionally or unintentionally—provide verbal prompts indicating the shape and direction they believe that the project should take. They may ask leading questions. They may express approval or disapproval of an answer. They may summarize and paraphrase answers to fit what they want to hear. They may begin to talk too much. They may interrupt and finish an answer, assuming they know exactly what we are going to say. By listening closely to their questions, we can better target our answers to match their values.

Types of Interview Behaviors. In addition to the

Agenda: The Site Visit Team should meet privately in order to discuss the morning's activities.

1:30–3:00   **Participants**: Full coalition membership

Agenda: Provide a brief introduction of coalition members and their affiliation. Conduct general coalition business.

3:00–3:30   **Participants**: Coalition leadership

Agenda: Final opportunity to address remaining questions, outstanding issues.

*   *   *

Allies Against Asthma

Site Visit Questions

Proposal Specific Questions: Fight Asthma Milwaukee Coalition

S1. Please clarify the target population. What is the geographic focus? Is this a city or countywide focus? How many and which children will be targeted?

S2. The proposal states that the project will target children, especially those residing in the inner-city. However, the data provided suggests hospitalization rates for African Americans outside of the city are significantly higher. Why exclude this group?

S3. The leadership role of parents is clear, however the role of grassroots community-based organizations in leadership and decision-making is not clear. Please clarify.

THE SITE VISIT

STAGE THREE: SITE VISIT

verbal hints given by site visit team members, we monitor their nonverbal behaviors for clues indicating that we are on the right track. During everyday conversations, people typically coordinate their verbal and nonverbal behaviors. Facial expressions, body language, and vocalization cues can complement, emphasize, or even contradict what is being said. In many instances, nonverbal behaviors are more important—and more revealing—than verbal communications. Said differently, when the site visit team feels good about their interactions with us, they will feel good about us: They will perceive us to be a credible and competent coalition who will be a good steward of their grant funds.

As we answer the questions posed by the site visit team, we pay attention to their nonverbal behaviors. Although site visitors may try to control their behaviors so as to avoid influencing our responses, we continuously monitor their facial expressions, body language, and vocalization cues to assess

Engaging Behaviors	Disengaging Behaviors
Facial Expressions • Maintaining strong eye contact • Smiling • Giving an encouraging look • Nodding slightly in agreement	• Staring into space • Letting eyes wander • Rolling the eyes • Closing eyes • Frowning • False smiling • Clenching one's teeth • Biting one's tongue • Grimacing • Wrinkling one's forehead • Furrowing one's eyebrows • Shaking one's head
Body Language • Facing the speaker • Leaning forward attentively • Tilting one's head slightly to one side, listening intently • Taking notes • Using touching gestures—patting one on the back, grasping one's shoulder, and touching one's arm	• Leaning back in a chair • Using a hand to cover parts of the face • Holding one's head in one's hands • Folding arms over one's chest • Leaning forward in a challenging stance • Raising one's hand to interrupt • Rubbing the back of one's neck • Massaging one's temples • Clenching fists • Twisting or flipping hair • Picking or biting fingernails • Fidgeting • Shifting weight • Tapping fingers and feet • Crossing legs and locking ankles

S4. Who is on the steering committee?

S5. The objectives listed on pages 1 and 2 include a combination of both objectives and action steps. Please clarify your key objectives.

S6. What portion of the matching funds is cash vs. in-kind contributions?

General Questions for All Sites

G1. Please provide some examples of how community representatives are involved in the leadership and decision-making process of the coalition. How will you ensure this level of involvement continues during the planning and implementation phases?

G 2. Are there any constituencies who are missing from the coalition membership? If yes, who and how and when will you secure their participation?

G 3. A mission of Allies Against Asthma is to develop "connectivity" among intervention strategies in the home, clinical practice, school, health care delivery system, and other community systems. How will the planning process you propose ensure links across the various domains? Which links will you consider as most critical?

G 4. What is the coalition's approach to cultural competency during the planning and implementation phases and evaluation of the project?

G 5. The national evaluation effort is a partnership of the local coalitions and the National Program Office. In addition to the local evaluations, the National Program Office will look across sites to assess the role of coalitions in improving systems of care

Engaging Behaviors	Disengaging Behaviors
Body Language continued	• Fiddling with pens, pencils, cell phones, pagers, and personal digital assistants • Doodling • Glancing at a watch • Adjusting one's clothing • Playing with eye glasses or jewelry—rings, bracelets, earrings, necklaces
Vocalization Cues • Speaking in a warm, upbeat tone of voice • Using vocal variety • Using positive reinforcers—"yes," "right," "absolutely," "uh huh" • Using humor	• Speaking in a monotone voice • Speaking in a harsh tone of voice • Using negative reinforcers—"no," "I don't think so," "tsk, tsk" • Whispering off to the side to other colleagues • Becoming quiet • Becoming loud • Sighing • Yawning • Clearing one's throat • Using sarcasm

whether they are engaged or disengaged with our presentation. Examples of each type of behavior are shown above.

By tuning into to the nonverbal behaviors of the site visit team, we can make adjustments to our presentation style to keep them engaged. For instance, if they look puzzled, we can expand on a point or explain our answer in another way. Or in the extreme case, if we feel that we are "losing" our audience during the presentation, we can revive their interest by involving them in the action in one of the following ways:

- **Referring to Visual Aids.** "If you will please turn to page four of your handouts, you will see a detailed breakdown of our project activity over the past five years."
- **Soliciting Questions.** "Let me pause here for a minute. Are there any questions so far?"
- **Acknowledging Their Behavior.** "I'm getting blank stares from several people right now. Would it be helpful if I went over that point again?"

- **Taking a Break.** "We've been at this for an hour already. Let's take a short ten-minute break so that everyone can stretch their legs and refresh their beverages."
- **Changing Speakers.** "I'm just about finished explaining the first part of this question. In a minute I'm going to ask my colleague, Dennis, to answer the second part."

Using any one or a combination of these simple strategies can help us to reconnect with the site visit team members. It sends the message that we are serious about this proposed project and that we are genuinely concerned about establishing appropriate levels of trust with the sponsor.

In sum, sponsors will invest in our project because we have systematically addressed their logical and psychological concerns, and at the same time, we have clearly expressed the relationship between our organizational capabilities and their values. Our attention to detail pays off. Together, we have reached the Persuasion Intersection; this project was funded.

and pediatric asthma outcomes. For this evaluation each coalition may be asked to identify a number of priority components for their implementation action plan.

Your coalition has done a significant amount of research and planning related to community concerns about asthma care. Thinking to the future and based on your current information, what would you now consider as your top three priority activities?

G 6. What data at the target population level would be available to evaluate the activities listed above?

G 7. What kind of data is accessible from the state/county/local and/or facility based (e.g., hospital, health plan) surveillance systems to track asthma outcomes related to the activities? How will you gain access to these data? Who will manage the data for you?

G 8. Would the coalition be able to identify a population of children who will be exposed to the prioritized activities who could be followed over time in order to evaluate the initiative's impact on health status, health care use, and quality of life?

G 9. Do you have the capacity, e.g., data systems, collaborative arrangements, that would enable you to compare outcomes for a population of children exposed to the coalition activities with outcomes for a population of children not exposed? If so, please describe.

G 10. What data will illustrate that efforts of the coalition were essential to the activities and outcomes? How will your coalition assess and manage these data?

G 11. If new systems of care are shown to be effective, how will they be institutionalized?

RECEIVING THE GRANT AWARD NOTIFICATION

The time between reading the Request for Proposal (RFP) for the "Allies Against Asthma" program and receiving the grant award notification from The Robert Wood Johnson Foundation was more than fourteen months. In particular, three months passed from the submission of our letter of intent to the arrival of the invitation to submit a full proposal; three months passed after we submitted our full proposal until we learned that we were selected for a site visit; and an additional two months passed between the site visit and the arrival of the grant award notification. The application process was long (and rigorous) yet rewarding.

The grant award notice is symbolic of our ability to make a "connection" with the sponsor. Through a balanced presentation of logical, emotional, and relational elements we made a compelling case for project support, one that demonstrated to the sponsor the correlation between our project idea and their funding priorities. In essence, we are a means to fulfilling an end that they value. Namely, funding our coalition will help develop a sustainable strategy for asthma management that will improve the health status of vulnerable urban youth.

Figure 3 summarizes the key elements that we brought together to reach the Persuasion Intersection.

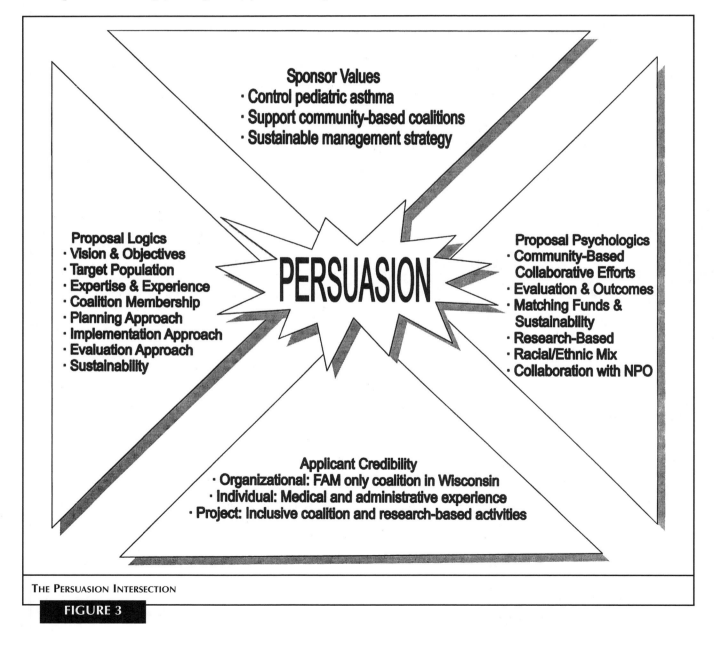

Sponsor Values
· Control pediatric asthma
· Support community-based coalitions
· Sustainable management strategy

PERSUASION

Proposal Logics
· Vision & Objectives
· Target Population
· Expertise & Experience
· Coalition Membership
· Planning Approach
· Implementation Approach
· Evaluation Approach
· Sustainability

Proposal Psychologics
· Community-Based Collaborative Efforts
· Evaluation & Outcomes
· Matching Funds & Sustainability
· Research-Based
· Racial/Ethnic Mix
· Collaboration with NPO

Applicant Credibility
· Organizational: FAM only coalition in Wisconsin
· Individual: Medical and administrative experience
· Project: Inclusive coalition and research-based activities

THE PERSUASION INTERSECTION

FIGURE 3

THE ROBERT WOOD JOHNSON FOUNDATION

December 1, 2000

Dr. John Meurer
Children's Health System
9000 W. Wisconsin Avenue
P.O. Box 1997
Milwaukee, WI 53201

Dear Dr. Meurer:

It is a pleasure to inform you that The Robert Wood Johnson Foundation has approved a grant of $150,000 to Children's Health System, Inc., in 12 month support of its participation in the Foundation's program, Allies Against Asthma.

The funds are to be used in accordance with the proposal to the Foundation and the terms and conditions outline in the Request for Project Support. They are also to be used in accordance with the final budget and are to be applied over the period January 1, 2001, through December 31, 2001. Our Treasurer's Office will be in touch concerning payment of this grant and reporting requirements.

If your organization wishes to issue a news release on this grant, please feel free to do so. We ask that a copy of the draft text be sent to us for our review and information in advance of dissemination. Please allow three days for this process. Address the copy to the Foundation to the attention of Maureen Cozine in our Communications Department.

All of us at The Robert Wood Johnson Foundation wish you success in carrying out this important undertaking.

Sincerely,

Steven A. Schroeder, M.D.
President and CEO

THE GRANT AWARD NOTIFICATION

STAGE THREE: SITE VISIT

CHAPTER 5

U.S. Department of Education, Fund for the Improvement of Postsecondary Education

The Education Amendments Act of 1972 authorized the Secretary of Health, Education, and Welfare to improve postsecondary educational opportunities by providing assistance to educational institutions and agencies for a broad range of reforms and innovations. Now, the U.S. Department of Education holds an annual grant competition through its Fund for the Improvement of Postsecondary Education, or better known in the alphabet soup of the federal government as FIPSE. Their "Comprehensive Program" competition supports innovative educational improvement projects that respond to problems of national significance.

FIPSE is one of the most broadly designed of the thousands of federal grant programs in existence. So much so, in fact, that nearly any reasonable idea with a postsecondary education bent would qualify. The breadth of FIPSE's eligibility criteria is its main advantage. It is also a disadvantage. Why? So many people submit FIPSE proposals that the competition level is very high. In recent years, FIPSE competitions have received 1,200–1,600 Stage One "preliminary proposals," of which 200–300 were invited to submit Stage Two "final proposals." Usually, 50–75 proposals are funded at roughly $75,000 per year for three years. In the period 2000–2003, total FIPSE funding for the "Comprehensive Program" ranged from $25 million to $27 million annually. A wealth of information about FIPSE's grantmaking priorities, application processes, and funding history is available online at http://www.ed.gov/FIPSE.

Although FIPSE's emphasis seems to be on postsecondary education, eligibility is not limited to colleges and universities. A wide range of nonprofit providers of educational services can benefit from FIPSE funding as well. Proposals that involve community partnerships, parent training, economic development, service learning—to name a few among many—can and have received FIPSE support. Although academic institutions are typically the lead applicants, consortium and collaborative partnerships involving nonprofit organizations can be funded. Nonprofits should contact the grants office at a nearby college or university if interested in partnering on a FIPSE proposal.

In this chapter we will take an in-depth look at a successful application to FIPSE's "Comprehensive Program" submitted by the Marquette University School of Dentistry seeking funding for a major curriculum reform project. For this national competition, FIPSE uses a two-stage application process. In the first stage, applicants must submit a five-page, double spaced "preliminary proposal." Applicants receiving a favorable review are invited, in the second stage, to submit a "final proposal," usually 25 double spaced pages, and a detailed budget. Accordingly, this chapter is divided into two sections, one for each stage of the application process. The elements of each stage are as follows.

Stage One: Preliminary Proposal

- The Request for Proposal
- The Title Page Application Form
- The Preliminary Proposal
- The Budget Summary
- The Invitation to Submit a Final Proposal and Reviewer Comments

Stage Two: Final Proposal

- The Request for Proposal
- The Title Page Application Form
- The Abstract
- The Final Proposal
- The Budget Summary and Budget Narrative
- The Grant Award Notification

The chapter is designed so that the right-hand (odd numbered) pages present the actual RFPs, the complete grant applications, and correspondence with the sponsor. The left-hand (even numbered) pages interpret and explain subtle nuances of the RFPs, applications, and correspondence. In other words, you can read this chapter in three ways:

- Read only the odd numbered pages to see the finished written products.
- Read only the even numbered pages to understand the planning process.
- Read the pages sequentially to detail the planning and writing process step by step.

This application is a model of proposal planning and writing; it presents the right balance of logic, emotion, and relationships to connect with the values of the sponsor.

ANALYZING THE REQUEST FOR PROPOSAL

Analyzing the Request for Proposal (RFP) means asking a series of iterative questions: questions about the *relevance* of our project idea to the sponsor's guidelines, the *feasibility* of developing a proposal, and the *probability* of achieving funding success. In this first section of the chapter, we follow our three-step process to analyze the RFP guidelines for the "Comprehensive Program" of the U.S. Department of Education, Fund for the Improvement of Postsecondary Education (FIPSE).

Step One: Relevance—Do We Want to Do This?

For more than a century, the Marquette University School of Dentistry (MUSoD) has been recognized as a leader in clinical education. In 1998 MUSoD made a significant departure from past history when it founded the Office of Research and Graduate Studies as a means of adding a nationally/internationally recognized academic and scholarly component to its profile. This commitment to being a national leader in dental education is rather remarkable for it came at a time when some dental schools were terminating their programs and closing. The commitment—and context for this proposal—manifests itself in its faculty, curriculum, and physical facilities.

Recent faculty hires concentrated on younger, highly trained junior faculty, often ones with both a dental degree (D.D.S. or D.M.D.) and a research degree (Ph.D.). This perspective was crucial because it fostered an integration of basic science and clinical practice offerings, a viewpoint that gradually replaced the preoccupation of training practitioners that existed among many of the senior faculty. At the same time, a new $30 million state-of-the-art dental facility was in the final stages of planning, and construction was ready to commence. In essence, a cultural change was beginning to take place. Since FIPSE's "Comprehensive Program" offered an opportunity to strengthen, reinforce, and implement a new cultural/pedagogical shift, it was relevant to the dental school.

In step one of our RFP Analysis Process, we made a cursory read of the RFP guidelines and developed a one-page memo that the Associate Dean for Research and Graduate Studies sent to all dental school faculty, inviting their "buy-in" to the idea of submitting a proposal. The purpose of this memo, presented below, was to answer the question, "Do we want to do this?"

RFP Guidelines. The U.S. Department of Education, Fund for the Improvement of Postsecondary Education (FIPSE) has just issued a call for innovative proposals as part of their "Comprehensive Program." It seems like a perfect fit with our curricular reform initiatives. Some key points in their RFP guidelines include the following:

- 130 new awards will be made.
- The typical award will range from $150,000 to $600,000 over three years.
- Graduate and professional schools are eligible.
- A top funding priority is educational reform that benefits postsecondary students throughout the country.
- They are looking for approaches that depart from traditional educational practice.
- They encourage faculty to rethink curricular organization and content to better prepare students for the workplace.
- They welcome proposals that creatively integrate technology into the curriculum.
- They invite proposals that refocus critical resources on teaching and learning.
- Stage One of FIPSE's two-stage application process calls for a five-page double spaced proposal to be submitted by January 26, 2001.
- 15–20% of Stage One applicants will be invited to submit a Stage Two proposal.
- Stage Two of FIPSE's application process calls for a full 25-page double spaced proposal to be submitted by April 27, 2001.
- 25–33% of Stage Two proposals will be awarded grant funding.

This appears to fit well with our strategic plan. More details are available online at www.ed.gov/FIPSE. Let's meet this Friday noon in Room 149 to discuss further the possibility of submitting an application. Lunch will be provided.

Step Two: Feasibility—Can We Do This?

The initial luncheon meeting proved successful. Faculty members came from the following dental specialty areas: pediatrics, orthodontics, geriatrics, prosthodontics, community health, surgery, and basic sciences.

The Fund for the Improvement of Postsecondary Education
The Comprehensive Program
Fiscal Year 2001

Deadline for Submission: January 26, 2001

Program Information and Application Materials

Introduction

The Comprehensive Program is the central grant competition of the Fund for the Improvement of Postsecondary Education (FIPSE). The competition is designed to support innovative reform projects that hold promise as models for the resolution of important issues and problems in postsecondary education.

Several characteristics of the Comprehensive Program make it unique among Federal programs.

It is *inclusive*. All nonprofit institutions and organizations offering postsecondary education programs are eligible to receive FIPSE grants. Those grants may be in support of any academic discipline, program, or student support service.

It is *action-oriented*. Although FIPSE will consider proposals to assess existing reforms, or to study the feasibility of reforms in the development stage, it does not ordinarily support basic research. The Comprehensive Program supports a wide range of practical reform initiatives and assists grantees in assessing their results and disseminating what is learned to other institutions and agencies.

It encourages *bold thinking and innovative projects*. The resources of the Comprehensive Program are devoted to new ideas and practices and to the dissemination of proven innovations to others. FIPSE will support controversial or unconventional projects, as long as they are well justified, carefully designed, and responsibly managed.

It is *responsive to practitioners*. In its Agenda for Improvement (see following pages), FIPSE identifies common issues and problems affecting postsecondary education and invites applicants to address these or other problems imaginatively. The Comprehensive Program welcomes proposals addressing any and all topics of postsecondary improvement and reform.

Awards: FIPSE estimates that 130 new awards will be made in FY 2001. Grants may provide one, two, or three years of funding. Since Comprehensive Program grants may support improvement projects of varying scope and complexity, there is no minimum or maximum grant award. FIPSE expects to award grants ranging from $150,000 to $600,000 or more over a typical three-year period. Grant budgets will be considered in the context of the proposed project's significance and promise as a model for the reform of American postsecondary education. Fiscal year 2001 projects may begin as early as October 1, 2001 and no later than January 1, 2002. These figures are only estimates and do not bind the Department of Education to a specific number of grants, or to the amount of any grant, unless that amount is otherwise specified by statute or regulations.

Eligibility: The improvement of postsecondary education requires the participation and cooperation of many types of institutions, organizations, and agencies. FIPSE supports a wide range of non-profit providers of educational services. Proposals may be submitted by two- and four-year colleges and universities, both public and private, accredited or non-accredited; graduate and professional schools; community organizations; libraries; museums; trade and technical schools; unions; consortia; student groups; state and local government agencies; non-profit corporations; and associations. Proposals may be submitted by newly formed as well as

THE REQUEST FOR PROPOSAL

STAGE ONE: PRELIMINARY PROPOSAL

The dental faculty were particularly interested in reviewing the technical aspects of the RFP guidelines to see how much work would be necessary to develop a proposal. Because the Associate Dean for Research and Graduate Studies was the one who convened the meeting, we knew that sufficient institutional support existed for pursuing this funding opportunity. As a result, much time was spent examining the RFP guidelines for evaluation criteria, hot buttons, and distinctive features. This second level of analysis begins to answer the question, "Can we do this?"

Evaluation Criteria. FIPSE's "Comprehensive Program" will use the following stated evaluation criteria in their selection process.

- A completed Title Page application form (ED 40-514).
- A five-page, double spaced narrative should describe the:
  Need for the project
  Significance of the project
  Quality of project design
  Quality of project evaluation
- A budget summary
- A limited number of appendices (no resumes or letters of support)
- Restrictions on the use of funds include:
  Requests for equipment funds, student financial assistance monies, and high indirect costs are rarely competitive
  Construction costs and funds to purchase facilities are not allowed
- Use 11 point font or larger
- Submit one original and two copies
- Due date: January 26, 2001

Stage One proposals will be critiqued by two different reviewers, with all narrative elements being weighted equally. It is important to note that the reviewers may or may not be specialists in the subject matter area. For instance, any given proposal might be read by an assistant professor of Spanish, an associate professor of biomedical engineering, or a full professor of theology. As a result, the proposal must be written at a level that could be understood by an educated professional who may have minimal subject matter knowledge of the topic.

Hot Buttons and Distinctive Features. The dental faculty decided to form a Proposal Development Committee and take a "divide and conquer" approach to proposal development. By carefully reading the key ideas and concepts in the RFP, as well as reading between the lines, three hot buttons and two distinctive

features became apparent. Hot buttons are primary concerns of the sponsor that gain force over other evaluation criteria because they are repeated throughout the RFP guidelines. In this case, hot buttons include:

- innovation and reform;
- national impact;
- evaluation and assessment.

All three hot button concepts are introduced in the opening paragraph of the "Introduction" section of the guidelines: "The competition is designed to support *innovative reform* projects that hold promise as *models* for the *resolution of important issues and problems* in postsecondary education."

The RFP guidelines also raise two distinctive features, secondary concerns of the sponsor, that influence the design of certain aspects of projects. Distinctive features appear as singular occurrences, yet they still command attention over other information in the guidelines because they affect a project's technical approach. In this instance, distinctive features include:

- cost-effectiveness;
- student diversity.

To increase the competitiveness of our Stage One proposal, these hot buttons and distinctive features—logical and psychological needs—must be addressed strategically in the narrative.

Hot Button: Innovation and Reform

In addition to using more than forty different words and phrases—conceptual synonyms—to emphasize the importance of innovation and reform, the RFP guidelines dedicate an entire section to the "Importance of Innovation." Indeed, the opening sentence of the second paragraph in this section touches on all three hot buttons: "FIPSE's goal is to support implementation of *innovative reform* ideas, to *evaluate* how well they work, and to *share the lessons learned with the larger postsecondary education community*." Broad descriptive phrases in the RFP guidelines for the hot button of innovation and reform include:

> innovative reform, reforms, new ideas and practices, innovations, support controversial or unconventional projects, address these or other problems imaginatively, reforms and innovations, creative ideas, experiments in educational reform, effective new way of responding, revolutionary or paradigm-shifting reform, lasting transformations, rethinking curricular orga-

established organizations, but not by individuals or for-profit schools or organizations. Other organizations may be eligible; the list here is not exhaustive.

Authority: The Education Amendments Act of 1972 authorized the Secretary of Health, Education, and Welfare to improve postsecondary educational opportunities by providing assistance to educational institutions and agencies for a broad range of reforms and innovations. The specific authority is now contained in Title VII, Part B of the Higher Education Act as amended in 1998 (Public Law 105-244). Regulations are contained in the Code of Federal Regulations, Title 34 Part 75. In addition, the Education Department General Administrative Regulations (EDGAR) in 34 CFR Parts 74, 77, 79, 80, 81, 82, and 85 apply.

Application Notice: The official Application Notice is published in the *Federal Register*. The information in the Agenda for Improvement and the rest of this application package is intended to aid in preparing applications for this competition. Nothing in this application package supersedes the priorities listed in the Federal Register.

FIPSE Address: (For information only; do not use this address for mailing applications.)
FIPSE
8th Floor
1990 K Street, NW
Washington, DC 20006-8544

Telephone: (202) 502-7500
Email: fipse@ed.gov

FIPSE World Wide Web Site: For information on past and current projects, successfully evaluated projects from previous years, information, evaluation resources, and more, visit FIPSE's World Wide Web site at http://www.ed.gov/FIPSE.

Agenda for Improvement

Since its founding in 1972, FIPSE's dual mission has been to improve the quality and the accessibility of education beyond the high school level. This year, in keeping with its past, FIPSE eagerly invites creative ideas to ensure that as many students as possible enter and successfully complete postsecondary programs of high quality.

The central challenge, common to postsecondary institutions of all sizes and types, is to provide cost-effective learning opportunities for a larger and more diverse student population. This Agenda highlights some of the important issues accompanying this challenge, and we specifically encourage proposals that address these issues. But we recognize that the Agenda does not identify all the important problems and opportunities facing the postsecondary community. FIPSE welcomes proposals addressing important issues of access and quality not discussed in the Agenda for Improvement; the Agenda is intended to stimulate but not limit the thinking of potential applicants.

The Importance of Innovation

FIPSE grants are intended to provide the seed capital for experiments in educational reform, and the knowledge gained through those experiments should be intended to benefit postsecondary students throughout the country. Are the problems or opportunities you wish to address common to other institutions serving similar student populations? If so, can you design an educational reform project that demonstrates to others an effective new way of responding to those problems? FIPSE's goal is to support implementation of innovative reform ideas, to evaluate how well they work, and to share the lessons learned with the larger postsecondary education community.

As a potential applicant, one of the first things you should do is to investigate how others are responding to similar problems or opportunities. How does your idea compare to common or traditional educational practice? More importantly, how does it compare to the experiments of other leading-edge educational reformers? Your project should be designed to make a unique contribution to the professional community. It does not

THE REQUEST FOR PROPOSAL

STAGE ONE: PRELIMINARY PROPOSAL

nization and content, revolutionizing teaching techniques, new adaptations, transform their learning, improves upon current practice, test new approaches to improvement and reform, promising new strategies, build on, alternatives to existing strategies, improves upon previous efforts, effective reform strategies, improve upon present practice.

The RFP guidelines use the term "innovation," including its derivatives, in its syntactic structure both in noun (e.g., proven *innovation*) and adjective forms (e.g., *innovative* reform). The verb form—"to innovate"—is a relatively awkward structure to use. (Synonym verb forms include: to construct, to create, to design, to develop, and to establish.) Similarly, the term "reform," and its various derivatives, is used both as a noun (e.g., a model of *reform*) and an adjective (e.g., innovative *reform* ideas). Curiously, there is no instance in the RFP guidelines where the word "reform" is used as a verb. Successful proposal writers know that verbs are more powerful than nouns and adjectives (e.g., The purpose of this project is *to reform* archaic dental education curricula). When writing this proposal, the Proposal Development Committee will repeat this hot button in all its forms throughout the narrative.

Hot Button: *National Impact*

The RFP guidelines communicate the importance of advancing a proposal with a national impact in many different ways, both directly and indirectly. The sponsor confirms explicitly its value for projects with a national impact in the "Guide to Proposal Development" section of the guidelines: "FIPSE is a federal program and therefore takes a national perspective in its grantmaking." In addition, as the following language indicates, this hot button appears thirty-eight times throughout the guidelines, primarily as noun phrases:

national perspective, national consequences, national contexts, throughout the nation, in the nation, nationally, nationwide, benefit postsecondary students throughout the country, campuses across the country, institutions around the country, disseminating what is learned to other institutions, effectively disseminated to others, share lessons learned with the larger postsecondary education community, common to other institutions, common issues and problems, facing the postsecondary community, postsecondary community as a whole, contribution to the professional community, promise as a model, model program, models, replicability, models for others in postsecondary

education, wide application, potential for implementation in a variety of settings.

Rather than taking a scatter-shot approach to funding projects nationwide, the sponsor prefers to support projects that can become models for others in postsecondary education who face similar challenges. FIPSE values projects that have the potential to make a national impact because it allows them to make the most of their limited resources.

Hot Button: *Evaluation and Assessment*

The terms "evaluation" and "assessment" occur more than two dozen times in the RFP guidelines. Sample entries include the following:

assessing their results, details of your evaluation design, evaluate effectively, evaluate how well they work, evaluate the results, evaluation information, evaluation plans, evaluation resources, overall assessment, rigorous assessment, systematically evaluate the effectiveness of those resources, the extent to which the evaluation will provide guidance about effective strategies, the quality of the project's evaluation, well evaluated, achieved its aims, solid evaluation plan, document the activities and results of your project, evaluate whether you have achieved your goals, successfully evaluated projects.

This hot button of evaluation and assessment uses several different syntactic structures: (1) nouns: "rigorous assessment"; (2) adjectives: "evaluation design"; and (3) verbs: "evaluate effectively." The analysis of syntactic structures is important for it affords the Proposal Development Committee greater options for emphasizing hot button concepts.

In essence, the sponsor values systematic program evaluation and assessment as a means to ensure accountability. FIPSE wants to make sure that its project funds are having the desired impact. To help potential applicants address this hot button concern, the sponsor encourages, "For information on past and current projects, successfully evaluated projects from previous years, information, evaluation resources, and more, visit FIPSE's World Wide Web site."

Distinctive Feature: *Cost-Effectiveness*

While evaluation and assessment is a hot button noted in the RFP guidelines, a related concept—cost-effectiveness—appears as a distinctive feature. Overall, the term "cost-effectiveness" occurs only three times in the RFP, yet in the section on "Curricular and Pedagogical Reform," this distinctive feature is inex-

necessarily have to be a revolutionary or paradigm-shifting reform model, but it should be a significant next step.

Curricular and Pedagogical Reform

FIPSE will continue to support innovative reforms of undergraduate, graduate, and professional curricula. We seek applicants proposing lasting transformations not only of what students learn but also how they learn. Proposed model programs should include a rigorous assessment of their impact on student learning. And they must be cost-effective and sustainable, for both the applicant institution and for others seeking similar solutions.

Core Requirements and General Education: One area of the undergraduate curriculum that requires continuing attention is the core or general education curriculum, typically comprising about one-third of bachelor degree course work. At their best, such curricula can translate lofty institutional mission statements into concrete programs for student academic development. But a proliferation of course offerings and lack of requirements, in the absence of clear educational goals, threatens to reduce general education to a freshman and sophomore year elective program. Conversations with students on many campuses suggest that students have little idea what general education is intended to accomplish, and hence no real basis for choosing a portfolio of general education courses. FIPSE welcomes proposals to make the goals of general education clear, and to guide and link course choices so that general education and serve its true purpose.

The Sciences: In recent years educators in mathematics, the sciences, humanities, and many professional fields have implemented a number of learner-centered reforms in both content and pedagogy, particularly at the introductory levels of their disciplines. Transformation in the social sciences has been slower, but is no less necessary. FIPSE encourages faculty in all disciplines to examine opportunities for rethinking curricular organization and content, as well as revolutionizing teaching techniques, at every level. Is it possible, for example, that the traditional organization of learning into "courses" will no longer be appropriate for learner-centered instruction in the coming century?

Education for Careers: It is increasingly important that curricula in all disciplines include preparation of students in the workplace. Because the United States is the only industrialized nation that does not have a formal apprenticeship system for helping young people make the initial transition from school to work, postsecondary institutions must join with employers and others in the development of other models for integrating work and learning, at all levels of education. Some may choose to explore innovations that build on existing models of cooperative education, tech-prep, or clinical programs. Others might try new adaptations of apprenticeship or internship models to be designed and managed cooperatively with employers. Such programs ensure that students acquire the academic skills necessary for success now and in the future. In order to accomplish this objective, it may be necessary to define general academic competencies appropriate to particular degree, and to expect students to master these in addition to meeting the occupational skills standards currently under development nationwide.

Technology and the Curriculum: Finally, we note the enormous potential of technology to advance curricular reform in these areas and many more. FIPSE will continue to support efforts to develop cost-effective technology-mediated materials that promise to improve teaching and learning in and across the various disciplines. But applicants should note that many valuable materials, already developed and tested on campuses across the country, receive only isolated use because they have not been effectively disseminated to others. Applicants are therefore encouraged to conceive from the beginning of their projects better ways to share materials and expand pilot testing to other institutions. We particularly encourage proposals from faculty, disciplinary associations, and other professional communities to explore collaborative development of technological resources that have potential for wide application, to systematically evaluate the effectiveness of those resources in improving instructional quality, and to disseminate them to other interested practitioners through electronic media and other means.

tricably linked to two hot buttons—national impact and evaluation and assessment: "Proposed model programs should include a rigorous assessment of their impact on student learning. And they must be cost-effective and sustainable, for both the applicant institution and for others seeking similar solutions." That is to say, the sponsor is sensitive to the effectiveness and the cost-effectiveness of proposed projects from a national perspective. Quite simply, given the finite availability of financial resources, the sponsor wants assurance that its funds will be utilized wisely.

Distinctive Feature: Student Diversity

The distinctive feature of student diversity occurs only once in the RFP guidelines. This low frequency of occurrence caused the Proposal Development Committee to debate whether to even classify it as a distinctive feature. Ultimately, we concluded that this concept of student diversity deserved a highlighted mention in our proposal for two reasons. First, in the singular instance of this distinctive feature, it is linked both to the distinctive feature of cost-effectiveness and to the hot button of national impact. In particular, the "Agenda for Improvement" section of the RFP guidelines indicates: "The central challenge, common to postsecondary institutions of all sizes and types, is to provide cost-effective learning opportunities for a larger and more diverse student population."

Second, a review of funding histories at the FIPSE Web site revealed that many graduate and professional education projects had a diversity element to them. For instance: Pennsylvania State University received funding for "Human Diversity Training for Medical Students"; Western Washington University was funded for a "Law and Diversity Program"; and the University of Iowa was awarded grant support for "Recruiting Minority Students into Science, Engineering, and Mathematics Graduate Programs." Together, these factors suggest that the concept of student diversity might carry more weight with reviewers than the RFP guidelines seem to indicate.

Step Three: Probability—Will We Be Competitive?

Step three goes to the heart of establishing our credibility as an applicant:

- Do we have a credible *project idea* that will be competitive?
- Do we have a credible *project director* and staff that will be competitive in carrying out the project?

- Do we have sufficient credibility as an *organization* to compete for this RFP?

In essence, step three is a matter of matching our strengths and weaknesses relative to the values of the sponsor. This will involve "defuzzifying" the ambiguities, inconsistencies, discrepancies, and omissions in the RFP guidelines. Strategic thinking helps to define institutional uniqueness, while preproposal contact allows an opportunity to build credibility with the sponsor. Both strategic thinking and preproposal contact are discussed below. This third level of analysis answers the question, "Will we be competitive?"

Strategic Thinking. The Proposal Development Committee generated the following list of strategic thinking questions that arose from a critical review of each major section of the RFP guidelines. These questions needed to be considered internally to assess our competitiveness before engaging in preproposal contacts with the sponsor.

Introduction

- Can we compete in a national program competition?
- Are our odds of getting funded good enough to merit submitting a proposal?
- How can we make our preliminary proposal stand out from the competition?
- Have we read the authorizing legislation to see if there are other key words, concepts, and ideas that should be incorporated into our preliminary proposal?
- What else can we learn from the FIPSE Web site?

Importance of Innovation

- Does our project represent an effective new way of responding to a problem common to postsecondary institutions?
- Has this approach been tried before at other institutions? With what results?
- How does our approach differ from and improve upon existing educational practices?
- Does our project have the potential to make a significant impact throughout the country?
- Will the postsecondary community embrace our reform ideas?

Curricular and Pedagogical Reform

- Will our project produce a lasting transformation in *what* and *how* students learn?

Guide to Proposal Development

This discussion is intended to help you conceive and write a stronger proposal by alerting you to the ways in which it will be read and judged. We recognize that some of the considerations raised here may not pertain to your particular project, and the following remarks are not intended to oblige you to organize your proposal around direct responses to all of them.

Before You Prepare an Application

Because of FIPSE's broad eligibility criteria and expansive programmatic interests, the Comprehensive Program receives a large number of preliminary proposals each year. The preliminary proposal process is designed to be inclusive, to encourage submission of meritorious ideas. Only a brief narrative is required, covered by a title page and a budget sheet. But the task of composing the preliminary proposal is not an easy one, and its quality will determine whether an applicant is invited to prepare a final proposal. Of those proposals invited into the final round of competition (15–20%), FIPSE is able to fund one in every three or four. Although the Comprehensive Program is certainly competitive, applicants new to federal grantsmanship should not be discouraged. Almost half of FIPSE's current project directors have never before directed a federal grant, and only one in ten has previously been in charge of a FIPSE project. About one-quarter of each year's awards go to applicants who did not receive a grant on their first attempt, but who used the external reviews and conversations with FIPSE staff to prepare an improved proposal in a subsequent year.

FIPSE is a federal program and therefore takes a national perspective in its grantmaking. Both the importance of a project and the innovation represented by its proposed solution are therefore considered in relation to the needs of the postsecondary community as a whole. Applicants are advised to describe the problem or opportunity they wish to address in both its local and national contexts. Is it common to a number of other postsecondary institutions besides your own? Does it affect a substantial number of students at those institutions? If it affects a relatively small number, is the problem so serious that it jeopardizes their ability to succeed in postsecondary education, or the opportunity so great that it can transform their learning?

Model programs addressing many common issues of postsecondary reform already exist. Some have been developed with the support of FIPSE or other funding agencies; many others were implemented without any outside grant support. Applicants are encouraged to begin their search for solutions by examining what others have done to address the issue or problem of concern, and to adapt appropriate current models wherever possible. It is when your research indicates that there are no appropriate models, or that current models can be substantially improved, that you should consider an application to FIPSE. We will welcome your ideas.

FIPSE's World Wide Web site (http://www.ed.gov/FIPSE) contains information resources that would be useful to a prospective applicant in developing a proposal. One of these is *Lessons Learned*, an occasional FIPSE publication, containing descriptions and results of many well evaluated FIPSE projects. The website also has descriptions of all currently funded projects, evaluation information and suggestions, material on other competitions, and funding advice from FIPSE program officers.

Prospective applicants should note that, although we do not review draft proposals, FIPSE program officers are happy to discuss project ideas by telephone or in person, particularly in the summer and fall before the preliminary proposal stage begins. Call the FIPSE office to set up an appointment.

The Review Process

In order to evaluate effectively a broad range of proposals, the Comprehensive Program's review process consists of two stages—the first involving the preliminary proposal (a five-page, double-spaced narrative and a summary budget), and the second involving the final proposal (a twenty-five-page, double-spaced narrative, a budget, and a budget narrative).

- Does our project address more than one of FIPSE's highlighted issues of educational reform: in general education, the sciences, education for careers, and technology and the curriculum?
- Do students understand the relationship between our institutional mission and their academic program?
- Are our proposed reforms learner-centered?
- Does our approach allow for meaningful interactions between students, faculty, potential employers, and the community?
- How will incorporating technology into educational reforms improve the quality of teaching and learning experiences?

Before You Prepare an Application

- Has anyone at the university received FIPSE funding before?
- Do we know individuals outside of the university who have received FIPSE funding? Would they be willing to share their experiences with us?
- Do other dental schools share similar concerns about the quality of their educational programs? How many other dental schools? Which ones?
- How many dental education students are affected?
- Are any dental education reform models available for us to adapt to our specific situation?
- What are the key "lessons learned" other educators have discovered as they implemented their educational reforms? Is there a secret to success?

The Review Process

- Have individuals at the university served as external reviewers for the FIPSE "Comprehensive Program"? What "insider information" might we glean from them?
- Do we know individuals outside of the university who have served as FIPSE reviewers? Would they be willing to share their experiences with us?
- What is the relationship between the recommendations of external reviewers and the selections by FIPSE staff regarding which applicants should be invited to submit final proposals?
- Given such limited space in the preliminary proposal, are some elements more important than others? Which ones?
- Are the page limits strictly enforced?
- Are FIPSE program officers as willing to discuss by telephone the merits of our project as the RFP guidelines seem to indicate?

Selection Criteria

- How can the selection criteria be weighted equally when some criteria contain many more questions to be answered than others?
- Does the reviewer's evaluation form assign specific numerical point values to each selection criteria?
- Is there any specific information *not* requested in the selection criteria that we should be sure to include anyway?

1) Need for the Project

- How many dental schools exist in the United States?
- What is the size of the faculty at these dental schools?
- How many dental school graduates have been produced annually over the past five years?
- Have graduate student enrollment trends been increasing, decreasing, or relatively constant over the past five years?
- What are the current problems with existing dental school curricula?
- Are our problems similar to those found in other dental schools?
- How serious are these curricular problems, locally and nationally?
- What is the magnitude of the need nationwide for curricular reform among dental schools?
- How do these nationwide needs in dentistry compare to other healthcare fields, e.g., medicine, nursing, physical therapy, speech pathology, and so forth?
- What are the consequences to dental educators and to patients regarding the lack of an updated curriculum?
- How many dental schools are involved in curriculum reform in a major way?
- What and when were the last major curricular reforms in dentistry?
- To what extent have reforms attempted by others been successful?
- Are the curricular problems among dental schools sufficiently common to warrant a national reform?
- What are the implications of these problems on the delivery of quality dental care to patients?
- How crucial are curricular reforms to long-term dental school viability?
- Are other dental schools likely to profit from our experiences with curricular reform?

Preliminary Proposals: Preliminary proposals are first examined by a group of external reviewers, identified each year from among faculty, administrators, or other professionals across the country, and chosen for their understanding of a broad range of issues in postsecondary education. A new group of readers is selected each year. Staff then carefully consider both the proposal and the reader reviews, and recommend which applicants should be invited to submit final proposals.

Your preliminary proposal should give external reviewers and staff a concrete understanding of the problem you are addressing and the solutions you propose, including a brief description of how you will evaluate the results. As noted above, it should be clear how your project strategy differs from and improves upon current practice at your institution and elsewhere in the nation.

Applicants should note that, at the preliminary proposal stage, external reviewers may or may not be experts on the particular topics of your grant application. It is therefore important to write the proposal narrative for an audience of generalists, using clear, direct language and avoiding jargon, cliches, and acronyms wherever possible. Given the volume of submissions, the preliminary proposal narrative must be limited to five double-spaced pages, or approximately 1,250 words. We recommend that no appendices or letters of recommendation be submitted at this stage.

Final Proposals: If you are invited to submit a final proposal, a FIPSE program officer will discuss with you by telephone both the external reviewers' and the staff's reactions to your preliminary application, and will remain available to answer questions and offer suggestions to assist you in strengthening the final proposal.

Final proposals are also read by at least two outside reviewers, including specialists in your subject. Additional experts may review proposals when technical questions arise, and FIPSE's National Board may discuss them. FIPSE staff then carefully read and discuss the proposals and the external reviews. Project directors of the most competitive applications are telephoned to clarify information about their projects. Staff may also contact others who know the applicant's work and plans, or who will be affected by the project.

Again at the final proposal stage, it is important to present your ideas in clear language that will help readers to understand precisely what you intend to do and how you will do it. Your final proposal narrative should not exceed 25 double-spaced pages, or approximately 6,250 words.

To ensure that all applicants enjoy the same opportunity to present their ideas, please conform to the page limitations noted above, use minimum 1-inch margins, and avoid font sizes smaller than 11 points.

Selection Criteria

Our intent in this section is to help applicants understand how the selection criteria are applied during the preliminary and final review stages. FIPSE does not separate proposals rigidly by types of activities, sectors of postsecondary education or other fixed categories, nor does it assign specific amounts of its budget to the priority areas described in the Agenda for Improvement. Instead, in our desire to identify the most significant issues and feasible plans, we compare each proposal to all others, using the criteria described below.

Each selection criterion is presented in bold type, and followed by a discussion of how it applies to the competition. The external readers and staff reviewers of your proposal use these criteria to guide their reviews at both stages of the Comprehensive Program competition, so it is in your interest to be familiar with them. The final decision on an application is based on an overall assessment of the extent to which it satisfactorily addresses all the selection criteria, which are weighted equally.

Preliminary proposals will be considered according to the following criteria, weighted equally:
1) The need for the project, as determined by the following factors:

a) the magnitude or severity of the problem addressed by the project; and

b) the magnitude of the need for the services to be provided or the activities to be carried out by the project.

2) Significance of the Project

- Does our proposed project have the potential for a national impact?
- To what extent does our proposed approach build on existing curricular reform strategies?
- To what extent does our approach to curricular reform offer a promising alternative to existing practices?
- Long-term, will our project outcomes truly make a difference?
- Will our project result in useful materials and techniques?
- How will learners be the principal beneficiaries of our project?
- How will student learning be assessed?
- How will improvements in teaching be assessed?
- What are the tangible consequences of enhanced teaching and learning?
- If successful locally, will other dental programs be able to replicate our experience?
- What are the specific components of our project that will be replicable?
- Are there other institutions with whom we should be collaborating?
- Are there other institutions with whom we will be competing for this type of an award?
- What are the costs associated with replicating this project in a variety of other settings?
- Is our education reform project significant enough to the postsecondary community to attract FIPSE interest?

3) Quality of Project Design

- Will we be addressing the central causes of existing barriers to curricular reform?
- What pilot data do we have to demonstrate that this project is realistic and will make a significant difference in the way we approach dental education?
- What specific strategies will be most effective to accomplish quality curriculum reform?
- Can we provide a balanced mix of basic science and clinical practice learning experiences?
- Do we have the collective capability to address the central causes of current curriculum weaknesses?
- Is an adequate infrastructure in place to systematically implement curricular reform?
- Are project strategies based on a combination of the latest research and practical experience?
- Will the curricular reforms be equally effective whether they are implemented all at once or in discrete phases?

- To what extent are the project goals, objectives, and outcomes clear, specific, and measurable?
- Does the design lend itself to rigorous formative and summative evaluations?
- Have we clearly described *who* will do *what, when, where, why* and with *what anticipated results*?
- Which active and passive dissemination strategies will be most effective for sharing the results of this project?
- How can we make our preliminary proposal distinctively different from the competition?

4) Quality of Project Evaluation

- Do we have specific evaluation approaches for each project objective?
- How will we evaluate the project processes, products, and outcomes?
- Do suitable evaluation tools already exist or will new ones need to be developed?
- What are the specific sources of documentation available to provide evaluation data?
- To what extent are our evaluation protocols thorough and feasible?
- Will we have solid quantitative and qualitative evidence of project success, both from formative and summative perspectives?
- Should the evaluation be conducted internally, externally, or both?
- Who will be responsible for project evaluation?
- Do internal evaluators have the expertise, experience, capability, and resources to objectively assess the program and its activities?
- To what extent will the evaluation protocol provide guidance about project replication at other institutions throughout the nation?
- How will we disseminate the results of our project evaluation?

Mailing Address for Preliminary and Final Proposals

- If we are selected to submit a final proposal, will we be able to do so during FIPSE's scheduled timeframe?
- Is the sponsor's projected timetable consistent with our strategic plan for program development?

Submission Procedures for Preliminary Proposals

- Is there any advantage to submitting proposals via express mail or hand delivery?

You should describe the nature and magnitude of the problem or opportunity you wish to address, in both its local setting and a national context. The Agenda for Improvement in this booklet identifies some areas of needed reform, but you may choose to focus on a topic not specifically mentioned in these guidelines, or you may choose to address more than one topic in a single project.

How central is the problem you have identified to your institution's vitality or the effectiveness of your educational services? Does the same problem affect other institutions around the country? Have attempts to remedy the situation been made by you or by others in the past, and with what results? What will be the local and national consequences of a successful completion of your project? Are other institutions or organizations likely to benefit or learn from your experience in ways that would enable them to improve their own programs and services?

Note that FIPSE does not support basic research; rather, its focus is on implementation projects designed to test new approaches to improvement and reform.

2) The significance of the project, as determined by the following factors:

a) the potential contribution of the proposed project to increased knowledge or understanding of educational problems, issues, or effective strategies;

b) the extent to which the proposed project involves the development or demonstration of promising new strategies that build on, or are alternatives to, existing strategies;

c) the importance or magnitude of the results or outcomes likely to be attained by the proposed project, especially improvements in teaching and student achievement; and

d) the potential replicability of the proposed project, including its potential for implementation in a variety of settings.

Reviewers will appreciate any evidence you can include to illustrate how your project differs from and improves upon previous efforts. Describe the potential contribution of your project to increasing the postsecondary community's knowledge about effective reform strategies, and the likely utility of the products (such as information, materials, processes, or techniques) that will result from it. It is the applicant's responsibility to set a context within which reviewers can assess the project's importance to postsecondary education reform.

Directly or indirectly, learners should be the principal beneficiaries of your project. This means, for example, that faculty development proposals should articulate the relationship between what the faculty will experience and what their students will learn. Our focus on the learner also means that FIPSE is especially interested in evaluation plans that assess projects in terms of their consequences for student learning.

FIPSE seeks to make the most of its limited funds by supporting projects that can become models for others in postsecondary education. Applicants should discuss the potential replicability of the proposed project, and its potential for implementation elsewhere. Before a project can become a model, however, its proponents must be able to prove that it has achieved its aims in its original setting. That is why a solid evaluation plan, one that focuses as much as possible on precisely how the project has helped students to become better educated, is an essential component of FIPSE projects.

Keeping in mind that, if your project activities are heavily dependent on external funding, it will be very difficult for other institutions to adapt them on their own, and this may reduce the potential impact of your project.

3) The quality of the project's design, as determined by the extent to which the design of the proposed project is appropriate to, and will successfully address, the needs of the target population or other identified needs.

- Would there be any benefit to the program officer to submit additional copies of our preliminary proposal beyond the original and two complete copies?
- Have we checked with our State's single point of contact for the best way to comply with Executive Order 12372 (intergovernmental review of federal programs)?

Preproposal Contact. Because sponsors vary in their receptivity to preproposal contact, we were encouraged by the statement in the RFP guidelines that "FIPSE program officers are happy to discuss project ideas by telephone or in person." When we called the FIPSE program officer, Dr. Robert Jones, our opening conversation went like this.

> Hello, Dr. Jones. I'm Tony Iacopino, Associate Dean for Dental Education at Marquette University. While we've studied the current FIPSE guidelines carefully, we still have some unanswered questions that we'd like to raise to ensure that our proposal would be of value to you. If I've caught you at a good time, I'd like to ask a few questions not addressed in the guidelines.

This opening statement piqued Dr. Jones' interest. Next, we briefly described our project and then asked the following types of PREP (Position-Rationale-Expectation-Priority) questions.

> Briefly, our proposal requests $400,000 over three years to institute a major curriculum reform in our dental school. We will propose to integrate more closely basic science and clinical practice instruction, while, at the same time, implement new approaches to instructional technology that result in a replicable curriculum for other dental schools nationwide. With that backdrop of our project, I'd welcome your answers to a few questions.

Position: The Baseline Situation

- What can you tell us about the review process, the reviewers, and their level of expertise in dental education?
- Under what conditions are proposals reviewed?
- How much time will reviewers have to read the proposals?
- Will awards be made on the basis of any special criteria, e.g., geography, size of target population, or topic area?
- Is there a specific reviewer's evaluation form that we can see?
- Do you anticipate any modifications to the

timetable of when proposals will be reviewed and when awardees will be announced?
- For budget development purposes, should we estimate an October 1, 2001 start date?
- What is the typical level of indirect costs requested by successful applicants?
- Do you have a preferred level of cost sharing?
- The FIPSE Web site has an article written by a program officer, entitled "Funding Your Best Ideas: a 12 Step Program" and another article by a former program officer, entitled "How To Get a FIPSE Grant." Are there other publications that you recommend that we read?

Rationale: Problems Existing Today

- Why has curricular reform become a funding priority?
- As you view the broad field of education, what are the major barriers to curriculum reform?
- What do you see as the biggest sources of dissatisfaction with current approaches to dental education?
- Generally speaking, what are the disadvantages of the way these problems are being handled now?
- Do you see a movement toward inquiry-based problem solving and hands-on approaches?
- Overall, is curriculum reform getting better or worse?

Expectation: Basic Implications for Addressing Problems

- Does our project fall within your current priorities for "Curricular and Pedagogical Reform"?
- Does FIPSE have preference for curricular reform at the undergraduate level more so than at the graduate and professional levels?
- Do you expect your average award to change from the $75,000 annual average last year?
- Winning proposals are expected to have a national impact. How much of an impact are we talking about? What do you mean by having potential for "wide application"?
- Is there a preferred means for incorporating technology into the curriculum, e.g., self-directed modules on CD-ROM, interactive Web sites, Web casts, Web chats, e-mail discussion groups, video conferences, interactive television, virtual reality simulators?
- Conducting a "rigorous assessment" of the project can mean examining a variety of humanistic, economic, and functional status outcome indicators;

Your strategies should be carefully designed to address the central causes of the problem you are addressing, based on your own research and experience, and based on previous experiments by others. Scatter-shot approaches to vaguely-defined problems make poor prospects for funding.

4) The quality of the project's evaluation, as determined by the extent to which the evaluation will provide guidance about effective strategies suitable for replication or testing in other settings.

Evaluation should be an important part of your project planning, and your preliminary proposal should include a brief description of how you intend to document the activities and results of your project. (In the final proposal we ask for a specific section on evaluation in which you state your objectives clearly and present the details of your evaluation design.)

Submitting Your Proposal

The Comprehensive Program has a two-stage submission and review process. To be eligible to submit a final proposal and to qualify for funding consideration, all applicants must submit a preliminary proposal on or before January 26, 2001.

FIPSE will review the preliminary proposals and, by the end of March 2001, will mail notifications to applicants invited to submit final proposal. The list of applicants invited to the final stage of competition will be posted on the FIPSE website (http://www.ed.gov/FIPSE). Final proposals must be submitted on or before April 27, 2001.

The announced closing dates and procedures for guaranteeing timely submissions will be strictly observed.

Applicants should also note that the closing date applies to both the date the application is mailed and the hand delivery date. A mailed application meets the requirements if it is mailed on or before the pertinent closing date and the required proof of mailing is provided. Proof of mailing may consist of one of the following: (a) a legible dated U.S. Postal Service postmark; (b) a legible receipt with the date of mailing stamped by the U.S. Postal Service; (c) a dated shipping label, invoice, or receipt from a commercial carrier, or (d) any other proof of mailing acceptable to the Secretary of Education.

If an application is sent through the U.S. Postal Service, the Secretary will *not* accept either of the following as proof of mailing: (1) a private metered postmark, or (2) a mail receipt that is not dated by the U.S. Postal Service.

Please use first class or express mail. (Overnight delivery is encouraged.) All applicants will receive acknowledgement notices upon receipt of preliminary and final proposals from the Application Control Center. If you do not receive an acknowledgement notice within six weeks of the closing date, please contact FIPSE using the address or phone number in the introduction to these guidelines.

Please wait the full six weeks before contacting us for an acknowledgement.

Mailing Address for Preliminary and Final Proposals
FIPSE Comprehensive Program
ATTN: 84.116A
U.S. Department of Education

Application Control Center
Room 3633, ROB-3
Washington, DC 20202-4725

Submission Procedures for Preliminary Proposals
Mailed Proposals: Proposals sent by mail must be mailed no later than January 26, 2001. First class mail should be used. Use the address above.

THE REQUEST FOR PROPOSAL

STAGE ONE: PRELIMINARY PROPOSAL

are there any specific outcome indicators that you prefer to see evaluated?

- The FIPSE guidelines indicate that model programs must be "cost-effective"; are you distinguishing between cost-effective analyses, cost-benefit analyses, and cost-minimization analyses?
- Do you have a preference for projects that are evaluated internally versus externally?
- When you say that model programs must be "sustainable," do you mean that activities must be institutionalized?
- Are there other strategies for sustainability that typically appear in proposals for curricular and pedagogical reform?
- What are the preferred means of disseminating project results?
- What are the most common mistakes made in proposals over the past few years?
- What would you like to see addressed in a proposal that other applicants may have overlooked?

Priority: Approaches for an Improved Situation

- What do you see as essential to the future of dental education that isn't happening now?
- What's needed to close the gap?
- Would our approach produce what is needed?
- Are there other long-term benefits of this approach that we should highlight in our proposal?
- What outcomes do you expect from grantees?

In sum, this iterative, three-step RFP Analysis Process allows us to gather the details necessary to develop a persuasive Stage One "preliminary proposal." Next we examine how we arrive at the Persuasion Intersection by connecting our project idea to the values of the sponsor.

Hand Delivered Proposals: Preliminary proposals will be accepted daily between the hours of 8:00 a.m. and 4:30 p.m., Washington, D.C. time except Saturdays, Sundays, or Federal holidays, at the Application Control Center, General Services Administration Building, 7th & D Streets, S.W., Room 3633, Washington D.C. Preapplications will not be accepted after 4:30 p.m. on January 26, 2001.

Number of Copies: All applicants must submit (1) signed original and two (2) complete copies of the preliminary proposal. Each copy must be covered with a Title Page, ED 40-514 (included with these guidelines) or a reasonable facsimile. Applicants are also requested to submit three (3) additional copies of the Title Page itself.

Content: Preliminary proposals should be written clearly and concisely, and should include the following:

1. Title Page: Use Form ED 40-514 or a suitable facsimile to cover each copy of the proposal. At the preliminary stage, you need not complete items 1 and 2. Be sure your proposal abstract (item 8) is clear and concrete, as it will be used at several points in the review. See the Title Page Instructions for additional information.

2. Narrative: It should consist of no more than five double-spaced, numbered pages, or approximately 1,250 words and in font size no smaller than 11 point. Please review the selection criteria in the Guide to Proposal Development above. Although no standard outline is required, you should:
--Briefly describe the problem you intend to address and the objectives of your project.
--State what you propose to do about it.
--Explain how your strategy would improve upon present practice, locally and nationally.
--Describe how you plan to evaluate whether you have achieved your goals.

3. Budget Summary: No detailed breakdowns or justifications are required at the preliminary stage, but you should carefully estimate major expenditures, as indicated on the budget page. Proposals that request equipment funds, student financial assistance monies, or high indirect costs are rarely competitive. FIPSE cannot support construction costs, nor can it purchase facilities.

4. Appendices: We generally recommend that no appendices be included with preliminary proposals; however, it is occasionally essential to include a small amount (no more than one or two pages) of information about the institution, problem, or strategy as an appendix. Unless this appendix is short, it will not be included in the review process. Please do not submit resumes or letters of support at this stage.

Upon receiving your preliminary proposal, the Application Control Center will mail you an acknowledgement that will include the reference number (PR/Award Number) that has been assigned to your application. It will begin with "P116", followed by a six-digit number. Always mention the complete PR/Award number in your communications with FIPSE.

Intergovernmental Review of Federal Programs (Executive Order 12372): This competition is subject to the requirements of Executive Order 12372, Intergovernmental Review of Federal Programs, and the regulations in 34 CFR 79. The objective of the order is to foster a Federal and State intergovernmental coordination and review of proposed Federal financial assistance. Applicants are directed to the appropriate State single point of contact to comply with the State's procedures under this Executive Order. A list of these contacts is available at http://www.sheeo.org/about-sheeo/agencies.htm.

THE REQUEST FOR PROPOSAL

STAGE ONE: PRELIMINARY PROPOSAL

DEVELOPING THE TITLE PAGE APPLICATION FORM

The Fund for the Improvement of Postsecondary Education (FIPSE) requires a completed Title Page application form (ED 40-514) to be submitted with the preliminary proposal and budget summary. This application form is the first read and the last written section of our complete grant application. It helps establish our credibility in a condensed format. In eleven line items, we present information about our organization, project director, project, budget, and compliance with federal assurances. These elements are described in more detail below.

Elements of the Title Page Application Form

FIPSE uses the same Title Page application form (ED 40-514) for both preliminary and final proposals. We indicate to reviewers that this is a Stage One application by putting a checkmark next to the appropriate proposal classification.

Item 1: Application Number. We intentionally leave this item blank. When our proposal arrives at the U.S. Department of Education Application Control Center, it will be assigned an application number. This number allows FIPSE to track each of the 1,200–1,600 preliminary proposals received annually.

Item 2: D-U-N-S Number. The Data Universal Numbering System (D-U-N-S) number is a unique nine-digit identification number assigned to organizations by the commercial company, Dun & Bradstreet. FIPSE uses this D-U-N-S Number to validate address and point of contact information for applicant institutions. D-U-N-S Numbers are available free of charge by calling Dun & Bradstreet's dedicated toll-free request line at 866-705-5711 or by visiting http://www.dnb.com/us.

The application form also requests our Employer Identification Number (EIN). This nine-digit number is assigned by the Internal Revenue Service and is used to identify taxpayers that are required to file various business tax returns. To learn more about obtaining an EIN, visit http://www.irs.gov.

Item 3: Project Director. The Project Director serves as the key point of contact between FIPSE and our institution, and is the individual ultimately responsible for all programmatic aspects of this initiative. FIPSE staff can reach the project director via mail, telephone, fax, and e-mail to discuss programmatic issues and share proposal status notifications.

Of note, our project director has a double doctor-ate: both a dental degree (D.D.S.) and a research degree (Ph.D.). This demonstrates to FIPSE staff and external reviewers that our project director is well credentialed; this level of expertise becomes an asset in the preliminary proposal when we discuss the importance of integrating basic science and clinical education into the new dental curriculum. In short, the dual doctorate is an important credibility statement for this proposal.

Item 4: Institutional Information. FIPSE gathers information about the types of institutions that are applying for and receiving federal grant funding. These details allow FIPSE to assess its funding policies and practices on an ongoing basis and to demonstrate its accountability to Congress.

Item 5: Federal Funds Requested. In this line item we enter the amount of federal funds requested from the sponsor in each year and the total amount requested over the three-year project period. FIPSE staff and external reviewers can quickly determine that our request falls within the sponsor's typical award range of $150,000 to $600,000 over three years.

Item 6: Duration of Project. Following the RFP guidelines, we enter the starting date for the project as October 1, 2001. This means that our three-year project is estimated to end on September 30, 2004, a total of 36 months. Not so coincidentally, the October to September project period corresponds to the federal government's fiscal year.

Item 7: Proposal Title. Our proposal title is short and descriptive, "Dental Education Reform: the MU-SoD Foundational Curriculum." In seven words, we customize a title which communicates that this proposal addresses the sponsor's invitational priority of "Curricular and Pedagogical Reform."

Item 8: Brief Abstract of Proposal. The Title Page application form calls for a brief summary of our project. In four sentences (126 words) we describe the problem being addressed, the proposed project activities, and their intended outcomes. Each sentence corresponds to one of the four major sections in the proposal narrative. In hindsight we could have strengthened the abstract without adding appreciably to its length by including the same boldface headings used in the preliminary proposal: "Magnitude of the Problem," "Significance of this Project," "Project Design," and "Project Evaluation." The abstract must be concise because we are limited to the space provided on the form.

Item 9: Legal Applicant. FIPSE awards grants to institutions, not individuals. Hence, the legal appli-

THE COMPREHENSIVE PROGRAM
FUND FOR THE IMPROVEMENT OF POSTSECONDARY EDUCATION

TITLE PAGE

Check One: __x__ Preliminary Proposal _____ Final Proposal

This application should be sent to: No. 84.116A U. S. Department of Education Application Control Center Rom 3633, ROB-3 Washington, DC 20202-4725	1. Application Number: 2. D-U-N-S Number: 93851-3892 Employer Identification No.: 39-0806251
3. Project Director (Name and MailingAddress) Joseph Best, D.D.S., Ph.D. Marquette University P.O. Box 1881 Milwaukee, WI 53201-1881 Telephone: 414-288-7155 Fax: 414-288-7870 Email: joseph.best@marquette.edu	4. Institutional Information Highest Degree Awarded: _____Two-year _____Four-Year _____Graduate __x__Doctorate _____Non-degree granting Type: _____Public __x__Private
5. Federal Funds Requested: 1st Year: $172,439 2nd Year (if applicable): $138,632 3rd Year (if applicable): $93,456 Total Amount: $404,527	6. Duration of Project Starting Date: 10/01/2001 Ending Date: 09/30/2004 Total No. of Months: 36

7. Proposal Title: Dental Education Reform: the MUSoD Foundational Curriculum

THE TITLE PAGE APPLICATION FORM

STAGE ONE: PRELIMINARY PROPOSAL

cant and fiscal agent for this project is Marquette University. We include a complete mailing address.

Item 10: Population Directly Benefiting from This Project. This line item provides the sponsor with an initial indication of the project's potential impact: It will touch the lives of 320 dental students annually. FIPSE staff and external reviewers can also use this information to conduct a simple cost-benefit analysis. Consider: total project costs ($404,527) divided by the total population directly benefiting from this project over three years (960 people) equals an investment of $421 per person, or approximately $140 per person per year.

Item 11: Certification by Authorizing Official. We enter the name, title, and telephone number of the official who has the authority to accept federal funding and commit the institution to executing the proposed project.

8. Brief Abstract of Proposal *(DO NOT LEAVE THIS BLANK)*

Dental education in the United States has long been criticized for its reliance on passive lecture-style teaching and over emphasis developing technical rather than intellectual expertise. As a result of the failure of dental schools to address these criticisms, dental graduates have a tendency to approach patient care with a "patch-up" mentality rather than seeing oral health as an integral part of total health. To address these problems, Marquette University School of Dentistry is proposing to implement an innovative new dental curriculum. The goals of this implementation will be to reduce passive lecture-style teaching by 33%, introduce intensive problem-based learning sessions that emphasize evidence-based decision making and to thoroughly integrate basic science with clinical education throughout the four-year curriculum to create critical-thinking doctors rather than technicians.

9. Legal Applicant	10. Population Directly Benefiting from the Project
Marquette University School of Dentistry P.O. Box 1881 Milwaukee, WI 53201-1881	320 dental students/dental patients at Marquette University School of Dentistry Congressional District of the Applicant Institution: 5th

11. Certification by Authorizing Official

The applicant certifies to the best of his/her knowledge and belief that the data in this application is true and correct, that the filing of this applicant has been duly authorized by the governing body of the applicant, and that the applicant will comply with the attached assurances if assistance is approved.

Name_____ Title_____ Phone _____

THE TITLE PAGE APPLICATION FORM

STAGE ONE: PRELIMINARY PROPOSAL

DEVELOPING THE PRELIMINARY PROPOSAL

Analyzing the Request for Proposal (RFP) guidelines was the first step in developing a preliminary proposal. We realized immediately that FIPSE's "Comprehensive Program" was a good match for our organization. And because we had institutional support for pursuing this grant opportunity, our Proposal Development Committee was quickly able to move down the Roads to the Persuasion Intersection. That is to say, we examined the RFP for evaluation criteria, hot buttons, and distinctive features, and we subsequently engaged in strategic thinking and preproposal contact to fine-tune our project to closely match the priorities of the sponsor.

Elements of the Preliminary Proposal

Title. In addition to identifying the project title and the acronym for the applicant organization, the boldface heading at the top of the page flags that this proposal addresses the sponsor's invitational priority of "Curricular and Pedagogical Reform." Because FIPSE has multiple priorities annually, this heading serves as an early alert to reviewers to help them establish the proper mindset of what to be looking for as they read our narrative.

Magnitude of the Problem. Of the four major sections within the "Selection Criteria"—project need, significance, design, and evaluation—the first two are the most important in the preliminary proposal. The RFP guidelines indicate that all sections are "weighted equally," yet this does not mean that they will have an equal effect on reviewers. Approximately two-thirds of our narrative is dedicated to these first two sections because they justify *why* the project is needed and the *impact* it will have among the larger postsecondary community. Said differently, at this stage of the application process, preliminary proposals must convince FIPSE reviewers that a significant and widespread pedagogical problem exists. If reviewers agree that the issue in question represents a national priority, then they will invite select applicants to submit a full proposal that elaborates on the proposed solution—the project design and evaluation.

In a scant 146 words, this section on "Magnitude of the Problem" describes the severity of the problem in both its national and local context. The first two sentences identify that, across the nation, there is a growing gap between traditional dental educa-tion programs and dental profession practices. The third sentence states the consequences of this problem; namely, dental schools in the U.S. are so heavily technique-driven that little room exists for development of students as critical-thinking clinicians. The final three sentences describe how this nationwide problem manifests itself at the local level and address the sponsor hot buttons of (1) innovation and reform and (2) national impact; e.g., *radical curricular reform* will improve dental education at Marquette University and will provide a *model for reform nationwide*.

Of note, in an earlier draft of this section, we had included additional information to document the severity of the problem, e.g., the number of dental schools in the United States, the number of faculty and students involved in dental education, the occurrence of the last major curricular reforms in dental education, and a comparison of curricular reforms in dental education to other health care fields. Although these details strengthened our needs statement argument, unfortunately limitations on the overall proposal length prevented them from being included here.

Significance of This Project. As a whole, the section on "Significance of This Project" tells the sponsor *why* the project is needed, *what* we are going to do, and *who* will participate in project efforts. We also address repeatedly all three hot buttons—innovation and reform, national impact, and evaluation and assessment—and touch on both distinctive features—cost-effectiveness and student diversity. As a result, this section of the proposal is, by far, the longest, with more than 1,040 words (58 percent of the total). More significantly, these elements provide structure, coherence, and unity to the entire narrative and, at the same time, help connect our project to the values of the sponsor.

The opening paragraph in this section indicates that the planned changes to the dental curriculum are motivated by an independent assessment and call for "sweeping reform" from a prestigious scientific organization, the Institute of Medicine (IOM). Our planned reforms emphasize six major themes that are responsive to IOM criticisms of the current approaches to dental education in the United States. In essence, these themes provide the intellectual framework for our "Foundational Curriculum," a blueprint for a new type of dental education. Note the use of key words and phrases that address all three sponsor hot buttons: *assessment, in the United States, sweeping reform, aggressive strategic plan,* and *blueprint*.

This project, "Dental Education Reform: the MUSoD Foundational Curriculum," is responsive to the FIPSE invitational priority of curricular and pedagogical reform.

I.   Magnitude of the Problem: Dental Education at a Crossroads

Dental education in the United States has traditionally been characterized by discipline-based lecture-style teaching. As the dental profession has evolved, with new techniques and expanded scope of practice, curricula in U.S. dental schools have failed to keep pace. The result of this failure is that U.S. dental schools are heavily technique-driven, with little room for development of students as critical-thinking clinicians. Marquette University School of Dentistry (MUSoD) is no exception to this problem and has now chosen to radically change its curriculum. This proposal will support implementation of a new curriculum at Marquette. This project will not only improve dental education at MUSoD, but will serve as a model for dental education reform nationwide.

II.   Significance of This Project: Need for Real Change in Dental Education

In 1995, the Institute of Medicine (I.O.M.) conducted an independent assessment of the state of dental education in the United States and published their findings in a report entitled, "Dental Education at the Crossroads: Challenges and Change."[1] This report identified major flaws in U.S. dental education and was a condemnation of the "traditional" dental curriculum. In an attempt to address the criticisms levied against U.S. dental schools by the I.O.M. report, most dental schools made only cosmetic changes in the late 1990's.[2] But unlike these modest changes, the I.O.M. report recommended sweeping reform in the way dentists are trained in the U.S. MUSoD has now committed to definitively addressing the need for change in dental education. In 1999 MUSoD set out an aggressive strategic plan that called for the school to design a new curriculum without regard for what was done in the past. To accomplish this goal, the school developed the "Foundational Curriculum," which was a blueprint for a new type of dental education. This curriculum emphasized several themes based on the I.O.M. criticisms:

1. **Integration:** with basic and clinical sciences being taught in collaboration at all levels of the curriculum with an emphasis on evidence-based dentistry.
2. **Efficiency:** with reduction of passive lecture style teaching by 33%.
3. **Comprehensive:** with patient care models that emphasize oral health as an integral part of total health.
4. **Patient-Based:** with learning sessions call General Dental Rounds where students and faculty use evidence-based decision making strategies to critically review patient treatment.
5. **Productive:** with training milestones aimed at efficiently developing skilled and productive clinicians.
6. **Community Outreach:** with an emphasis on creating a graduate that understands the professional responsibility to provide care to the underserved.

Why Marquette? MUSoD Serving as a Model for Dental Education Nationally:

Many leaders in the dental community have sounded a clarion call for change in dental education.[2,3] Unfortunately, most dental schools are so deeply entrenched in traditional educational approaches that they find it difficult to pursue real change. Interestingly, MUSoD is now in the unique position of having a faculty and administration that are both committed to significant change. This setting has allowed initial planning stages to progress

1

MUSoD Serving as a Model of Dental Education Nationally

This brief paragraph suggests that the Marquette University School of Dentistry (MUSoD) "Foundational Curriculum" will be a success because of its broad-based support from faculty, administration, and the university as a whole. That is, an effective model for curricular reform requires inclusive "buy-in" and participation—it cannot be forced from the top down or the bottom up. Not only do university faculty and administrators agree in principle that curricular reforms are necessary, but they are also ready to take action.

Creating New Didactic Tracks

Four paragraphs are dedicated to explaining how the "Foundational Curriculum" addresses the IOM's six themes of integration, efficiency, comprehensive, patient-based, productive, and community outreach. Together, these paragraphs illustrate that the curriculum revisions we propose to make are major reforms and do not represent "tinkering" or "cosmetic" changes. Each paragraph ends by articulating the benefit of the project activity to dental students; this reflects our understanding of the values of the sponsor.

The first paragraph, "Creating New Didactic Tracks," represents the core of this curriculum reform project. The opening four sentences of this paragraph describe the compound problems with the current curricular approach; namely, there are too many separate dental courses and these courses are taught using the least effective teaching style—passive lecture. The next four sentences provide an example of how the "Foundational Curriculum" takes a whole new approach to dental education by organizing material into ten "tracks," integrated content sequences with multidisciplinary teaching. The last sentence articulates the humanistic benefit of this innovative (i.e., hot button) approach, "[it] will help students better understand and retain clinically relevant information."

General Dental Rounds

The second paragraph, "General Dental Rounds," reinforces the sponsor's hot button of innovation and reform. In particular, this approach to conducting problem-based learning sessions is well-established in medical education and now will be systematically applied to dental education. The first and second sentences identify that the strength of general dental rounds lies in the fact that teaching scenarios are based on real life patient examples. The third and fifth sentences articulate the benefit to dental education students: They develop their critical-thinking skills in a practical and meaningful way.

Clinical Milestones

The paragraph on "Clinical Milestones" justifies our methodology, once again, in terms of the sponsor's hot button of innovation and reform. In the first two sentences, we draw on current research literature to document the trend in medical education that basic science and clinical training are being integrated throughout the four-year curriculum; at the same time, we are directly suggesting that dental education should also be following this trend. The next seven sentences provide a concrete example of how this integration could be achieved, using "milestones" as evidence of clinical competence. Note the strong language used to emphasize the innovativeness of this approach, "This is a *dramatic departure* from the traditional dental curriculum." We end the paragraph by articulating the practical benefits of this specific curricular reform, "the goal of these changes is to have students progressively obtain more clinical responsibility and to integrate science and patient care."

Community-Based Clinics with Teledentistry Support

The fourth paragraph focuses on "Community-Based Clinics with Teledentistry Support." The first sentence defines the current problem situation; namely significant portions of the population do not have access to dental care. The second and third sentences explain our approach to solving this problem: Dental education students can meet community needs through distance technologies. At the same time, these sentences hint at the distinctive feature of cost-effectiveness. Teledentistry is less expensive than trying to hire, place, and support dentists in all of the individually targeted community sites. It is a means to increasing access to oral health care and to reducing the costs of care through shared human and technological resources.

The final sentence of this paragraph explains the benefits of teledentistry in terms of another sponsor distinctive feature—student diversity. "These clinical experiences will enrich our graduates' understanding of *other cultures* and the tremendous need for care in *disenfranchised* portions of the community." More broadly, by addressing these two distinctive features back-to-back, we are communicating to the sponsor that measuring the cost-effectiveness of distance learning systems means considering human costs and

relatively smoothly. The faculty, administration and university as a whole have embraced the Foundational Curriculum and are now poised to act upon it.

How does the Foundational Curriculum specifically address these themes?
Creating New Didactic Tracks: The didactic course load at MUSoD has been problematic. The current curriculum has an astonishing 81 separate courses. These courses poorly integrate basic and clinical science, are overwhelmingly redundant, and rely heavily on passive lecture-style teaching. The result has been a "load and purge" style of education. By contrast, the Foundational Curriculum has only ten courses called "tracks," which are essentially content sequences that allow for more efficient and integrated multidisciplinary teaching. For example, the curriculum proposes that there is a "Biomedical Systems" track that covers material from anatomy, histology, physiology, and pathology courses. In this way, a unit that covers the respiratory system will start with normal anatomy, histology, and physiology of the lung and then proceed to discuss respiratory pathophysiology. Ultimately, the respiratory unit will be tied together with practical exercises in the management of dental patients with respiratory disease. This approach provides integration of basic and clinical science, and will help students better understand and retain clinically relevant information.
General Dental Rounds: General Dental Rounds (GDR) will be intense problem-based learning (PBL) sessions in which students will present their own patients in front of small groups of students and faculty. Students will be asked to understand their patient's medical history and justify treatment decisions based on evidence in the literature rather than simply relying on "what the faculty told me to do." This exercise will require active critical-thinking on the part of students and faculty alike. The positive role of PBL is well documented in medical education,[4] but PBL is not widely or effectively used in dental education today.[5] The strength of the GDR concept at MUSoD is that it is real for the student since the cases they present are their own patients.
Clinical Milestones: Classically, in both medical and dental education, the first two years of school are dedicated to the basic sciences followed by clinical training in the final two years. Many medical schools are now moving away from this long accepted method of training and are now integrating the basic science and clinical training throughout the four-year curriculum.[6] The clinical milestones are a tool to promote better integration in the MUSoD curriculum. First-year dental students will immediately enter the clinic and work as dental assistants for their third and fourth-year colleagues, while third and fourth-year students will spend more time on exercises designed to reinforce basic science applications in clinical practice. This will allow first-year students to see the clinical relevance of the science they are learning while allowing more time for seniors to reinforce the link between basic and clinical science. Students will also work through a set of "milestones" to achieve competence in various aspects of clinical care. Students will achieve milestones by working through specific didactic and preclinical exercises and once an assessment is passed, the student will be given "privileges" to provide that level of care. For example, first-year students will be privileged to provide dental prophylaxis (cleaning) by the end of the first semester of training. This is a dramatic departure from the traditional dental curriculum with students not actively treating patients until their third year. The goal of these changes is to have students progressively obtain more clinical responsibility and to integrate science and patient care.
Community-Based Clinics with Teledentistry Support: Nationally, there are significant portions of the population that do not have access to regular dental care. The Foundational Curriculum calls for more student time to be dedicated to providing care to underserved populations. Because these patients are often located in areas distant from the school, the new curriculum calls for the use of distance-learning techniques to facilitate student

2

educational value as well as capital and operating costs. We elaborate on this point further in the next section, "Project Design."

Project Design. The remaining two major sections of the proposal—project design and evaluation—make up the final one-third of our narrative. The "Project Design" section tells the sponsor *how* we will implement curricular reforms. At this stage of the application process, we intentionally keep the description brief and succinct—a mere 282 words. We provide FIPSE reviewers with just enough information to pique their interest, without overwhelming them in details, so that we will be invited to submit a final proposal.

The first two sentences of the paragraph explain the context for our funding request: the "Foundational Curriculum" provides the framework for our dental education reforms but financial support is still necessary to actually turn theory into practice. The third sentence identifies *who will benefit* from this project, namely, dental education students. In hindsight, we could have made this sentence stronger by indicating how many students would benefit, e.g., 300 students annually.

The remaining seven sentences of this paragraph overview how funding will be used to facilitate program implementation. Notice that one sentence is dedicated to each of the four components described in the previous section—creating new didactic tracks, general dental rounds, clinical milestones, and community-based clinics with teledentistry support. These sentences foreshadow that the majority of funding will support personnel costs for faculty and consultants, and a nominal amount will be used for travel, equipment, and supplies. Following the RFP guidelines for the preliminary proposal, we do not provide a detailed line item budget; rather, we simply include the required Title Page and Budget Summary forms.

This paragraph also touches on the sponsor's distinctive feature of cost-effectiveness. In particular, the sixth sentence describes the development of a CD-ROM for self-directed, independent learning. Once the master disk is completed, CD-ROMs are inexpensive to produce and can be used repeatedly by dental students. Similarly, the last sentence of the paragraph hints that teledentistry, through its shared use of human and technological resources, is a cost-effective means to providing oral health care to the wider community. Equally important, these implementation strategies represent a relatively low-cost way of inculturating students to the idea of using technology both in their everyday dental practice and as a means for lifelong learning.

Preliminary Results

The purpose of this "Preliminary Results" paragraph is to establish the viability of our implementation design. Quite simply, one track of the "Foundational Curriculum" and the general dental rounds have been successfully piloted and evaluated (i.e., hot button), and faculty support exists for continuing the proposed curricular reforms. At the same time, this short paragraph also serves as an effective transition to the next section of the proposal, which addresses in more detail the sponsor's hot button of evaluation and assessment.

Project Evaluation. The "Project Evaluation" section answers *how* project effectiveness will be determined and results systematically shared with other postsecondary education programs. And we do all of this in just over one page of space, 332 words. Clearly this entire section is a hot button for evaluation and assessment, yet we also address the hot buttons of national impact and of innovation and reform. Strategic repetition of key phrases such as the following demonstrate our sensitivity to the sponsor's subjective and objective needs: *outcomes, quality assurance, progress and outcome measures, evaluated, national level, already sparked interest from other dental schools, national dental education meetings and published in peer-reviewed dental education journals*, and *breaks dramatically with the status quo.*

In a bulleted list format, this paragraph defines the scope of the evaluation, identifies key sources of data, and defines the standards that will be used in judging the results of the evaluation. To illustrate that the evaluation process will be comprehensive, we selected carefully a sample of the specific types of outcomes tools that will be used to measure project performance. Reviewers can quickly see that the project evaluation: (1) will be conducted internally by MUSoD faculty and externally by the National Dental Board; (2) will occur *during* and *beyond* the granting period; and (3) will examine changes in students' dental knowledge, attitudes, and behaviors. The second bulleted item even touches on the distinctive feature of student diversity: post graduation surveys will be used to measure "issues related to caring for *underserved populations.*"

Replication and Documentation

The concluding paragraph ties the whole proposal together and appeals, one last time, to all three sponsor hot buttons. The first two sentences reconfirm that the problems in dental education exist nationwide (i.e., a hot button) and that our solution—the "Foundational Curriculm"—will introduce significant innovative re-

communication with faculty at the main campus. These clinical experiences will enrich our graduates' understanding of other cultures and the tremendous need for care in disenfranchised portions of the community.

III.   Project Design: Implementation of the Foundational Curriculum

Although the Foundational Curriculum document has outlined the basic framework and themes of the new curriculum, the task of implementing these changes has yet to begin. This proposal is to support the immense task of actually implementing the transformational changes set out in the Foundational Curriculum document. The primary target population of this project is dental students. Implementation will be organized by establishing task forces to address the refinement of each individual didactic track. Funding will provide salary support for individual faculty that are responsible for leading these task forces. Support will also be used for the development of CD-ROM self-directed teaching modules to allow students the flexibility that this form of independent learning provides. Funding will also support the development of the General Dental Rounds concept through faculty training in how to properly direct PBL teaching environments. Multidisciplinary clinical teaching groups will also be supported to develop the details of each clinical milestone. Once designed, the clinical milestones will be implemented into clinical operations starting with the first available incoming dental class. Community health clinic operations will be supported by supplying equipment for distance learning and supporting faculty with expertise in dental informatics.

Preliminary Results: One track of the Foundational Curriculum has now been piloted. Infectious Disease and Host Defense is a track that integrates basic science concepts related to microbiology and the clinical implications of infection. This track is highly integrated with basic science and clinical faculty teaching multidisciplinary units that help students understand the fundamental pathophysiology of infectious diseases like caries and periodontal disease. The General Dental Rounds have also been successfully piloted and now awaits faculty development for full implementation.

IV.   Project Evaluation

The success of this project will be measured using the following outcomes tools:

- Monitoring performance of MUSoD students on National Dental Board exams part I and part II.
- Tracking MUSoD dental student behavior after graduation by using post graduation surveys to measure scope of practice issues, comfort level with management of medically complicated patients, issues related to caring for underserved populations, and evaluating our graduates' continued exposure to the current literature in clinical dentistry.
- Administering exit examinations to evaluate students' understanding of comprehensive care issues and application of basic science principles to clinical problem solving.
- Tracking student clinical experiences to assess whether these educational reforms lead to improved student productivity.

Replication and Documentation: The Foundational Curriculum breaks dramatically with the status quo in dental education. The problems at MUSoD are clearly not unique, and elements of the Foundational Curriculum have broad application in dental education at the national level. The news of what is being done at Marquette has already sparked interest from other dental schools struggling with the same issues. Faculty involved in the curriculum development have recently been asked to present their progress at an American Association of Dental Education symposium on curricular reform. It is intended that the

3

forms (i.e., a hot button). The next three sentences provide a concrete example of how this MUSoD initiative has already, and will continue to, generate interest at the national level from other dental schools and leading associations such as the American Association of Dental Education.

The final five sentences identify *who* will be responsible for the various evaluation activities (i.e., a hot button) and the frequency of progress reports. And the last sentence of the paragraph demonstrates our confidence that the "Foundational Curriculum" will pass its ultimate test—inspection by the American Dental Association Committee on Dental Accreditation, the governing body responsible for granting MUSoD its accreditation status.

Proposal Design

A well-designed proposal makes even complex information look accessible and simplifies the reviewers' jobs. The following design features highlight the structure, hierarchy, and order of the proposal, helping reviewers find the information that they need.

Headings. Boldface headings reveal to reviewers, at a glance, the organization of our proposal. Headings reflect key words taken from the "Selection Criteria" section of the RFP guidelines. Effective use of white space sets off headings and enhances readability.

Lists. Bulleted and numbered lists visually break up long blocks of text and help to get the message to the reader with a sense of immediacy without being wordy. For instance, the numbered list in the "Significance of this Project" section emphasizes six core elements of our project framework, and the bulleted list in the "Project Evaluation" section quickly identifies a sampling of key outcomes evaluation tools.

Margins. Following the requirements in the RFP guidelines, we used standard one-inch margins. A proposal with ragged right margins is easier to read than one that is fully justified because the proportional spacing of justified type slows down readability.

Page Numbers. We place page numbers at the bottom center of the proposal.

Type Style. The proposal is written in Times Roman, the same type style that the sponsor used in its RFP guidelines. Using 11 point type size allows us to include a few additional lines of information without compromising the readability of the proposal.

White Space. As mandated in the RFP guidelines, the proposal is double spaced. To make the proposal appear inviting and user-friendly, we include an additional line of white space as a visual separator between the major sections.

outcome of this curriculum implementation be presented at national dental education meetings and published in peer-reviewed dental education journals. The Foundational Curriculum will also be monitored as part of the quality assurance (QA) activities of the MUSoD Curriculum Committee. This committee contains representatives from the administration, basic science and clinical faculty, as well as students from each class. Monthly QA reports on implementation progress and outcome measures will be submitted to the committee and administration. Annual reports of the implementation progress will be submitted to the Dean and University for the first 5 years of the curriculum. And finally, the entire curriculum will be evaluated by the American Dental Association Committee on Dental Accreditation when the school is scheduled for renewal in 2005.

References:
1. Institute of Medicine, Committee on the Future of Dental Education, "Dental Education at the Crossroads: Challenges and Change", M.J. Field ed., Nat Acad Press, Washington, D.C. (1995).
2. Nash, DA "And the Band Played On…" J Dent Ed 62: 964-974 (1998).
3. Ismail AI. Dental education at the crossroads: the crisis within. J Dent Ed 63: 327-330 (1999).
4. Margetson DB. The relation between understanding and practice in problem-based medical education. Med Educ 33: 359-364 (1999).
5. Behar-Horenstein LS, Dolan TA, Courts FJ, Mitchell GS. Cultivating critical thinking in the clinical learning environment. J Dent Ed 64: 610-615 (2000).
6. Schmidt H. Integrating the teaching of basic sciences, clinical sciences, and biopsychosocial issues. Acad Med 73: 24-31 (1998).

4

DEVELOPING THE BUDGET

Developing a realistic budget is as important to getting funded as writing a compelling proposal narrative. The budget explains *how much* a project will cost, yet it is also a credibility statement. Reviewers compare the proposal narrative and budget request to ensure that all costs relate directly to the project's goals, objectives, and activities. A budget that is too low calls into question our ability to effectively plan and implement the proposed project. A budget that is too high raises doubts about our true motivations and commitment to the project.

Elements of the Budget

At this first stage of the application process, FIPSE requires only a brief Budget Summary form to be submitted with the preliminary proposal. Interestingly, the sponsor does not request or encourage the inclusion of a budget narrative; the RFP guidelines specifically state, "No detailed breakdowns or justifications are required at the preliminary stage." The Budget Summary form categorizes project costs into seven line items:

1. Salaries and wages
2. Employee benefits
3. Travel
4. Equipment
5. Materials and supplies
6. Consultants and contracts
7. Other

Within these seven categories, the budget can include just about every reasonable expense that is directly applicable to the project. Two expense items prohibited under the RFP guidelines include the acquisition of property and the construction of facilities. In addition, equipment purchases are rarely supported. The following are examples of possible budget elements.

- Accounting
- Advertising
- Animals
- Audiovisual instruction
- Auditing
- Legal services
- Maintenance
- Periodicals
- Postage
- Publication
- Binding
- Books
- Computer time
- Consultants
- Dues
- Equipment
- Fringe benefits
- Indirect costs
- Instruments
- Insurance
- Recruitment
- Rent
- Repairs
- Salaries and wages
- Security
- Subcontracts
- Supplies
- Telephone
- Travel
- Tuition

The Budget Summary form is simple and relatively straightforward, but it is also rather restrictive. It does not allow us to show the basis of our calculations. For instance, we would have liked to include details such as:

- Program faculty (20% effort × $100,000 salary × 1 year) = $20,000
- Employee benefit (rate of 29% of full-time salaries)
- Travel to FIPSE annual meeting ($1,600/person × 2 persons) = $3,200
- Materials for project dissemination ($500/presentation × 2 presentations) = $1,000
- Consultant honoraria and travel ($1,500/day × 3 days) = $4,500
- Other printing/copying of curriculum "track" materials = $4,000

As for including indirect costs in the budget, officially FIPSE does not specify a particular rate. The RFP guidelines simply state that "high indirect costs are rarely competitive." Preproposal contact with FIPSE staff revealed that most grantees request no more than 8 percent of total direct costs, the rate used for U.S. Department of Education training programs. Thus, we too used this unofficial or "recommended" rate of 8 percent.

During this preproposal contact FIPSE staff also recommended that we include some cost sharing as evidence of our institutional commitment to the project. The sponsor was pleased that internal funds were used to pilot one track of the "Foundational Curriculum" and the general dental rounds and wanted to see a continued level of financial support. Given that MUSoD had already committed itself to being a national leader in dental education, it was relatively easy to identify significant amounts of cost sharing for this curricular reform initiative.

Budget Summary*

A. Budget Items Requested from FIPSE
Direct Costs:

	Year 1	Year 2	Year 3
1. Salaries & Wages (professional & clerical employees) $	90,826	77,801	63,204
2. Employee Benefits	26,339	22,562	18,329
3. Travel (employees only)	5,000	5,000	5,000
4. Equipment (purchase)	0	0	0
5. Materials and Supplies	10,000	10,000	0
6. Consultants and Contracts (including any travel)	19,500	8,000	0
7. Other (equipment rental, printing, etc.)	8,000	5,000	0

Total Direct Costs (add 1–7 above): 159,665 | 128,363 | 86,533

Indirect Costs: 8% MTDC: 12,773 | 10,269 | 6,923

Total Requested from FIPSE: 172,439 | 138,632 | 93,456 $

(These figures should appear on the title page)

B. Project Costs Not Requested from FIPSE
(institutional and other support):

	Year 1	Year 2	Year 3
1. Salaries & Wages (professional & clerical employees) $	220,204	159,705	121,144
2. Employee Benefits	63,859	46,315	35,132
3. Travel (employees only)	0	0	0
4. Equipment (purchase)	0	0	0
5. Materials and Supplies	0	0	0
6. Consultants and Contracts (including any travel)	0	0	0
7. Other (equipment rental, printing, etc.)	0	0	0

Total Direct Costs (add 1–7 above): 284,063 | 206,020 | 156,276

Indirect Costs: 0 | 0 | 0

Total Institutional and Other Support: 284,063 | 206,020 | 156,276 $

*Budget items, including institutional support figures, must be detailed in the budget narrative of the final proposal.

THE BUDGET SUMMARY

STAGE ONE: PRELIMINARY PROPOSAL

ANALYZING THE INVITATION TO SUBMIT A FINAL PROPOSAL AND REVIEWER COMMENTS

Our preliminary proposal to the "Comprehensive Program" of the Fund for the Improvement of Postsecondary Education (FIPSE) received a favorable review, and we were invited to submit a final proposal. Along with the invitational letter, FIPSE provided valuable feedback about the strengths and weaknesses of our preliminary proposal in the form of *verbatim* written comments from two external reviewers. By analyzing the invitation to submit a final proposal and reviewer comments, we can gain a better understanding of the sponsor's needs, values, and hot buttons as we prepare our full proposal.

The invitational letter and reviewer comments are key documents that will help us identify areas of improvement and enhance our overall project design. In particular, our Proposal Development Committee begins an iterative analysis process by comparing the written feedback from FIPSE staff and external reviewers against the RFP guidelines and our preliminary proposal. For instance, we look for evidence of hot buttons, distinctive features, and other narrative elements that should have been addressed or expanded upon in the proposal. The aim of this analysis is to identify strengths upon which to build and weaknesses to overcome.

Next, we try to determine why any proposal weaknesses occurred.

- Did we misinterpret some aspect of the RFP guidelines?
- Did we underestimate the value of any preproposal contact information?
- Are any elements of our project design in conflict with the sponsor's expectations?
- Were reviewers instructed to look for elements in preliminary proposals that were not requested in the RFP guidelines?
- Was there a hidden agenda to the RFP guidelines?

Finally, we formulate ways to fix any identified weaknesses. Some weaknesses may be easy to overcome, given the benefit of additional space (twenty-five double spaced pages) in the final proposal. Other weaknesses may require minor programmatic restructuring, e.g., engaging the services of an independent evaluator. Ultimately, the intent of this analytic process is to help us draft a final proposal that will persuade the sponsor to award funding to our project.

Invitation to Submit a Final Proposal

This invitation to submit a final proposal is the "good news" letter one always hopes to receive. Our preliminary proposal ranked in the top 17 percent of a very hefty nationwide competition. While the "Congratulations, you made the short list" message is welcome, the more useful components of the letter indicate the hot buttons and distinctive features that should appear in the final proposal. Of note, once we received this invitational letter we had approximately one month to develop and submit the final proposal.

FIPSE offered seven specific tips to help make our final proposal as competitive as possible.

1. Reviewer Comments. As described in the RFP guidelines, preliminary proposals are first examined by a group of external reviewers and then are examined by FIPSE staff to determine which applicants should be invited to submit final proposals. Comments from the two external reviewers will offer insights into the perceptual reactions generated by our preliminary proposal.

Equally important, because FIPSE staff play a crucial role in the funding decisions for full proposals, we will take advantage of their invitation to engage in preproposal contact: "you should be sure to get telephone feedback from our staff." Preproposal communication affords an additional opportunity to strengthen the quality of our final proposal before it is officially submitted. In other words, we follow the practices of successful grantseekers by gathering and triangulating information from multiple sources to maximize the likelihood of funding success.

2. *The Comprehensive Program* Booklet. FIPSE's *The Comprehensive Program* booklet contains the RFP guidelines for developing the final proposal. Using our three-step RFP Analysis Process we will examine the guidelines for evaluation criteria, hot buttons and distinctive features, and subsequently engage in strategic thinking and preproposal contact to fine-tune our project to closely match the priorities of the sponsor.

3. Final Proposal Review Process. This third tip is a reminder from the RFP guidelines that during the review process for the final proposal at least two external reviewers and FIPSE staff will critique our narrative. Whereas for the preliminary proposal the external reviewers may or may not be experts in our particular topic area, for the final proposal, the external reviewers will include subject specialists. Additional experts may review proposals when technical questions arise. Further, the role of the FIPSE staff

United States Department of Education
Office of Postsecondary Education
Fund for the Improvement of Postsecondary Education

March 16, 2001

Dear Colleague:

Your preliminary proposal to FIPSE's FY 2001 Comprehensive Program (application no. P116A011247) has been reviewed by both field readers and staff. I am pleased to inform you that, on the strength of these reviews, we would like you to elaborate your ideas into a full proposal. This invitation is being extended to some 260 of 1532 preliminary applicants and, accordingly, reflects our genuine enthusiasm for your proposed project. I therefore invite you to submit a full version of your proposal to the Application Control Center by April 27, 2001.

Please bear in mind the following in order to make your final proposal as competitive as possible:

1. We are enclosing copies of the external readers' reviews to help you prepare your full proposal. You should certainly take into consideration any reservations or questions these readers express, but remember that the opinions of FIPSE staff carry considerable weight in the review process. Hence, you should also be sure to get telephone feedback from our staff at this time. Staff can often draw attention to issues that need to be addressed in a full proposal that outside reviewers may have overlooked in their enthusiasm for the strengths of the preapplication.

   If you have not already heard from a FIPSE program officer, please call our office at (202) 502-7500 as soon as possible. When you indicate your application number (identified above), a member of our support staff will identify the program officer assigned to your application. If this program officer is unavailable when you call, please leave as many telephone numbers as are necessary to ensure that he/she can reach you promptly.

2. Consider carefully the section entitled "Guide to Proposal Development" in our *Comprehensive Program—Information and Application Materials* booklet. It specifically addresses the writing of final, as distinct from preliminary, proposals. Note also that the last two pages of the booklet contain certifications that must be signed by an authorized representative of your organization and submitted with your proposal. Finally, note that when the authorizing official signs item #11 on the Title Page, your institution is committed to complying with the "Assurances" printed on the back of the Budget Page in the booklet.

3. Keep in mind that reviewers of your full proposal will not have seen your preapplication. Thus, the full proposal should include a clear argument for the innovation of your project, both in its own setting and from a national perspective. What makes your project distinctive compared to the work of other educational reformers who are addressing similar issues?

4. Be sure to develop a solid evaluation plan for your project and describe it in your final proposal. If you have not already done so, you should engage an independent evaluator with good social science/education research skills to conduct this phase of the project. If you are a grantee, this evaluation will become the core of the "Final Report" that must be submitted according to federal regulations soon after the completion of a funded project.

   Although you will want to assess your project formatively for the sake of monitoring your progress, the Final Report should assess the summative impact of your project—not only for the benefit of FIPSE, but also for the benefit of other secondary educators seeking to learn from your experiences. A useful final evaluation may be impossible to accomplish unless the project has been conceived from the outset with evaluation in mind. Please visit the FIPSE website (http://www.ed.gov/FIPSE) to review our notes on evaluation and a bibliography that you may find

THE INVITATION TO SUBMIT A FINAL PROPOSAL AND REVIEWER COMMENTS

STAGE ONE: PRELIMINARY PROPOSAL

takes an increasing importance at this stage of the application process.

The implications of this review process are twofold. First, because different pairs of external reviewers read our preliminary and final proposals, it is important to repeat key components of our project description in both narratives, particularly elements relating to sponsor hot buttons (innovation and reform, national impact, and evaluation and assessment). Second, we must consider carefully the context for reviewers' comments of the preliminary proposal because reviewers of the final proposal may or may not share the same criticisms, objections, excitement or enthusiasm.

4. Evaluation Plan. The sponsor clearly values systematic program evaluation and assessment as a means of ensuring both fiscal and programmatic accountability. The RFP guidelines foreshadow the importance of a solid evaluation plan: "In the final proposal we ask for a specific section on evaluation in which you state your objectives clearly and present the details of your evaluation design." In like fashion, this invitation to submit a final proposal emphasizes that the proposal must address formative and summative evaluation procedures, preferably under the guidance of an outside consultant. Applicants are encouraged to visit the FIPSE Web site to examine a variety of resources that will facilitate planning a comprehensive evaluation design.

This hot button for evaluation and assessment takes on added significance when it is coupled with the hot button for national impact: "Although you will want to assess your project formatively for the sake of monitoring your progress, the Final Report should assess the summative impact of your project—not only for the benefit of FIPSE, but also for the benefit of other secondary educators seeking to learn from your experiences."

5. Charting Goals/Objectives and Evaluation/Assessment. This fifth tip is based on a change in the federal regulations authorizing support for the FIPSE program. Congress mandated that applicants include in their proposals a two-column chart that lists the major goals and objectives of the project and a description of how attainment of them will be evaluated. This mandate is a direct effort by Congress to ensure a level of accountability in projects that are selected for funding.

While this request for a two-column chart is straightforward and reasonable, it appears only once in the sponsor's application materials, buried within the invitation to submit a final proposal. More broadly, this tip demonstrates the importance of using an iterative analysis process for proposal development. Applicants who follow the RFP guidelines explicitly but forget to include the chart may have their grant applications disqualified on a technicality.

6. Project Budget. For the preliminary proposal, only a simple budget summary was required, an estimate of major expenditures. For the final proposal, a detailed breakout is required, with line item expenditures and a comprehensive budget narrative justifying expenses for each year of the project. Once again, the sponsor encourages applicants to engage in preproposal contact with the program officer; this time as a means to facilitate development of the final budget.

7. Project Director Commitment. The last tip in this invitational letter introduces a *new* distinctive feature to be addressed in the final proposal: project director commitment. This distinctive feature represents a secondary concern of the sponsor that will influence the design of certain aspects of the project. In particular, the project director must have a significant role and personal investment in this initiative. The entire paragraph seems to be written from the lessons of experience, as if, on more than one occasion, an institution was funded but did not have key personnel who were truly committed to implementing the project in a timely manner.

More concretely, the first and last sentences of this paragraph use a decidedly different tact to convey the same message. The first sentence is encouraging, "Note that FIPSE will expect extensive project involvement on the part of the person designated as project director," while the last sentence is foreboding, "If the project director cannot fulfill these commitments, please do not submit a final proposal." The communication is clear: Our final proposal must demonstrate that we have a project director who will champion this project to success, on time and on budget.

Next we present our interpretation of the comments from both external reviewers.

#1 Reviewer Comments

Need for the Project. The weakest section of the proposal, relatively speaking, concerned the "Need for the Project," which received second tier ratings in contrast to most of the other sections that received top tier ratings. Although we integrated information about the severity of the problem and the magnitude of the need for the project throughout the narrative, perhaps we should have consolidated some of those details into this opening section.

useful in planning your evaluation design.

5. Federal regulations imposed since the FIPSE guidelines were approved and printed compel us to request one additional component to your final proposal; namely, a two-column chart listing the major goals and objectives of the project and, for each, a description of how attainment of that goal or objective will be evaluated. Also, it must be clear from the proposal narrative how your budget request relates to the attainment of these goals and objectives.

6. The FIPSE program officer assigned to your application will offer some specific suggestions for preparing the final project budget. Please pay particular attention to this information. Remember that your full proposal must include justification for activities, detailed yearly budgets, and a budget narrative covering the entire period of the grant.

7. Note that FIPSE will expect extensive project involvement on the part of the person designated as project director. We will expect that person to attend the annual project directors' meeting each fall, to complete annual and final reports, and to initiate regular contact with the FIPSE program officer assigned to monitor the project. It is therefore important that the project director be someone who is committed to significant personal involvement. If the project director cannot fulfill these commitments, please do not submit a final proposal.

Thank you for applying to FIPSE. We look forward to receiving your full proposal.

Sincerely,

Kenneth W. Tolo
Director

Enclosures
1. *The Comprehensive Program—Information and Application Materials* booklet
2. Outside reader reviews

* * *

2001 COMPREHENSIVE PROGRAM
PREAPPLICATION REVIEW FORM

Before completing this form, please read carefully "The Comprehensive Program Information and Application Materials" booklet.

I. Need for the Project

A. What is the <u>magnitude or severity of the problem</u> addressed by the project?
    ☐ High   ☑ Medium   ☐ Low   ☐ Don't Know
B. What is the magnitude of the need for the services or activities of the project?
    ☐ Great Need   ☑ Moderate Need   ☐ Low Need   ☐ Don't Know
Explanatory Notes:

THE INVITATION TO SUBMIT A FINAL PROPOSAL AND REVIEWER COMMENTS

STAGE ONE: PRELIMINARY PROPOSAL

Significance of the Project. Interestingly, the reviewer gave our project a second tier rating of "moderate potential" for increasing knowledge and understanding of educational problems, yet gave a first tier rating of "important" to the results and outcomes of our project. This slight discrepancy between having a "moderate" problem and a "significant" project contribution tells us that we will need to be more explicit in the final proposal about the ways this initiative will increase knowledge in dental education.

The two written comments by the reviewer relate to two sponsor hot buttons. The first one speaks to innovation and reform, "This proposal seeks to adapt curricular reforms from medical school changes into a dental curriculum." And the second addresses national impact, "This program could become a model for Dental Education across the country." More broadly, the fact that the reviewer included hot buttons in the explanatory notes is a strong indicator that we successfully connected our project ideas to the values of the sponsor.

Quality of the Project Design. The final two sections of our proposal—"Project Design" and "Project Evaluation"—made up only one-third of the total number of words in our narrative, yet they received higher marks overall than the first two sections. Nevertheless, there does not seem to be a need to make wholesale changes to the approach we used in developing the preliminary proposal because we will have an opportunity to expand on the details of our project design in the final proposal. This means defining project goals, objectives, outcomes, and dissemination plans.

Quality of the Project Evaluation. While these final sections on "Project Design" and "Project Evaluation" received top tier marks, the reviewer did not include any comments to indicate which specific aspects made them "high quality." Also notably absent in this section is any mention of the hot button for evaluation and assessment. We can use this discrepancy between a high rating and a lack of comments about our project evaluation as an opportunity for preproposal contact with the program officer prior to submitting our final proposal.

Overall Assessment. The overall reaction of this reviewer to our preliminary proposal was quite positive, especially with regard to the national potential for impacting dental education. The reviewer's comment, "This is a very well written proposal that clearly outlines needs and solutions," reflects our ability to balance proposal logics and psychologics in the narrative. We logically and systematically developed pro-

posal components to show the relationship between an identified gap, an improved situation, and resulting benefits to the target population. Appealing to hot buttons demonstrates that we are responsive to the emotional needs of the sponsor by establishing critical levels of trust, understanding, and commitment to project success.

Numerical Rating. The final component of the preapplication review form asks reviewers to translate their qualitative assessments for each proposal section into an overall quantitative score. In today's competitive grants environment, "good" proposals (scoring less than 5) seldom get funded; "excellent" proposals (scoring 6–7) get funded. Obviously, our goal is to earn top tier ratings in all proposal sections so that our numerical rating will be high enough to merit an invitation to submit a final proposal. An initial indication that our proposal would receive a high numerical rating came in the overall assessment when the reviewer commented, "This appears to be an *excellent* idea and a logical progression of change in professional clinical education."

#2 Reviewer Comments

Need for the Project. The reviewer awarded second tier ratings consistently across all four sections of the proposal narrative. More telling, however, are the reviewer's explanatory notes. First, the reviewer demonstrates a keen interest in the community outreach aspects of our project. Although we briefly touched on this concept in our proposal vis-à-vis the distinctive feature of student diversity, for this reviewer, our description came off understated. In the final proposal, we will elaborate on how the "Foundational Curriculum" increases the amount of time dental students spend providing care to underserved populations.

Second, the reviewer misinterprets an historical detail: "MUSoD has a program instituted in 1999." In reality the Marquette University School of Dentistry program has been in operation for over 100 years, having been founded in 1894. It was in 1999 when MUSoD set out an aggressive strategic plan to design a new dental education curriculum. We can easily clarify this detail in the final proposal.

Significance of the Project. Again, the reviewer demonstrates an interest in the broader community impacts of this project, "This proposed program is a good means of reaching the community." And yet, the reviewer wonders, "What is being proposed, how would this be different from the 'Foundational Curriculum'?" Perhaps the lack of clarity between the cur-

II. Significance of the Project

A. How great is the potential contribution of the project in <u>increased knowledge or understanding</u> of educational problems, issues, or effective strategies?
   ☐ Great Potential   ☑ Moderate Potential ☐ Low Potential   ☐ Don't Know

B. In what ways does the proposed project involve the development or demonstration of promising <u>new strategies</u> that build upon, or are alternatives to, existing strategies? (write your answer)

This proposal seeks to adapt curricular reforms from medical school changes into a dental curriculum. PBL and early clinical exposure are becoming widespread in professional schools.

C. How important would be the likely <u>results or outcomes</u> of the project, especially with respect to improvements in teaching and student achievement?
   ☑ Important   ☐ Somewhat Important   ☐ Less Important   ☐ Don't Know

D. What is the <u>potential replicability</u> of the project, including its potential for implementation in a variety of settings?
   ☑ Replicable   ☐ Somewhat Replicable ☐ Less Replicable   ☐ Don't Know

Explanatory Notes:

This program could become a model for Dental Education across the country.

III. Quality of the Project Design

Please rate the quality of the <u>project design</u> as determined by the extent to which it is appropriate to, and will successfully address, the targeted needs:
   ☑ High Quality   ☐ Moderate Quality   ☐ Low Quality   ☐ Don't Know
Explanatory Notes:

IV. Quality of the Project Evaluation

Please rate the quality of the project evaluation as determined by the extent to which it will provide guidance about effective strategies suitable for replication or testing in other settings:

   ☑ High Quality   ☐ Moderate Quality   ☐ Low Quality   ☐ Don't Know
Explanatory Notes:

OVERALL ASSESSMENT: Based on the review criteria – Need for the Project, Significance of the Project, Quality of the Project Design, and Quality of the Project Evaluation – please critically analyze the project idea, judging its potential quality as an innovative educational reform model useful in a variety of settings. Describe in detail the reasons for your judgement. Identify specific features of the proposal that contribute to your opinion. Mention any issues that should be addressed in an expanded final proposal, should the applicant be invited to submit one.

This is a very well written proposal that clearly outlines needs and solutions. This new curriculum relies on many innovations currently being utilized in an increasing number of medical and other professional schools. When operational, the "Foundational Curriculum" could well be a model program for other Dental Schools. This appeals to be an excellent idea and a logical progression of change in professional clinical education.

THE INVITATION TO SUBMIT A FINAL PROPOSAL AND REVIEWER COMMENTS

STAGE ONE: PRELIMINARY PROPOSAL

ricular reform activities MUSoD has already piloted and what we propose to do next led the reviewer to rate the results and outcomes of this project as only "somewhat important."

In the final proposal we will need to specify that the "Foundational Curriculum" provides the educational framework for reorganizing dental education content into ten "tracks." MUSoD has already successfully piloted one track and the general dental rounds; the purpose of this request is to secure funding to develop and implement three additional tracks and to support them with integrated systems such as general dental rounds and clinical milestones.

Quality of the Project Design. In this section, the reviewer is still uncertain about the relationship between the pilot phase and the full implementation phase of the "Foundational Curriculum." The reviewer comments, "I am not sure how this proposed program will be different from the 'Foundational Curriculum' program that the university is presently implementing." Quite simply, the proposed project is not "different"; rather, we propose to systematically develop, implement, and support three additional dental education tracks. At the conclusion of this project, MUSoD will have completed four out of the ten total tracks.

In hindsight, it might have been possible to reduce some of this confusion if, when we were writing the "Project Design" section of the preliminary proposal, we had included a list of the titles of the ten new tracks and an estimated timeline for their development and implementation. At a glance, the reviewer would see that only one track had been completed so far and would better understand MUSoD's vision for instituting this major curricular reform over the long-term. In the final proposal, we will include a detailed description of project goals and objectives for creating these three new didactic tracks.

Quality of the Project Evaluation. Curiously, the reviewer's comments in this section do not actually relate directly to project evaluation: "Potential for success. Since MUSoD is a well-established institution with outstanding faculty, the proposed project can have an impact on the community. There is a need for dental health." Credibility exists at three levels—organizational, individual, and project. The reviewer's comment confirms our credibility at the institution and faculty levels, and at the same time, it implicitly bestows a level of trustworthiness to our project and evaluation plan. Because this entire section is a hot button, quite frankly, we expected reviewer comments to more closely reflect the sponsor's concern for evaluation and assessment.

Also of note, for the third and final time, the reviewer acknowledges the broader importance this project may have in the community. Thus, as we prepare our final proposal, we must keep in mind that our target population includes not only the dental education students and faculty at MUSoD (and potentially at dental schools nationwide), but also the multicultural residents in the communities that we serve.

Overall Assessment. This reviewer did not embrace our preliminary proposal with the same degree of enthusiasm as did the first reviewer. However, the questions and reservations posed do not suggest that our proposal is inherently flawed. Rather, the objections are more mechanical and methodological in nature, and are, at least in part, a product of the space limitations imposed by a five-page, double spaced requirement. These "errors" were not significant enough to preclude us from being invited to submit a final proposal, but they are points we will need to clarify and elaborate on in the final proposal.

The reviewer identifies three questions that need to be specifically addressed in the final version of the proposal: "If the dental courses (81) can be implemented as tracks, how will such a change, change the nature of basic sciences that are being taught in a traditional manner? How many individual faculty members will be involved? How many dental students will benefit?"

The first question reveals an insightful understanding that changing the fundamental approach to dental education may have ripple effects within the discipline. Dental education has traditionally been characterized by discipline-based lecture-style teaching with an emphasis on technical expertise. In the final proposal, we will elaborate on the evidence-based integrated approach of the "Foundational Curriculum" as a means of producing well-rounded, critical-thinking clinicians who have the skills to provide new levels of comprehensive patient care.

The second and third questions both focus on the humanistic impact of this project. This means describing in the final proposal how many and which faculty, students, and community members will be involved in the project, and indicating what roles they will play. Significant participation by all groups in the planning phase will improve the likelihood of success in the implementation phase.

Numerical Rating. Although the preliminary proposal received second tier ratings in all four sections and the reviewer posed a number of questions about the implementation plan for the "Foundational

NUMERICAL RATING: Based on the review criteria, please rate the quality of the project as an innovative educational reform model. The numerical score should correspond to your earlier comments. (Please circle only one number!)

1------------2------------3------------4------------5------(**6**)------7
Little potential   Great potential

* * *

2001 COMPREHENSIVE PROGRAM
PREAPPLICATION REVIEW FORM

Before completing this form, please read carefully "The Comprehensive Program Information and Application Materials" booklet.

I. Need for the Project

A. What is the <u>magnitude or severity of the problem</u> addressed by the project?
    ☐ High   ☑ Medium   ☐ Low   ☐ Don't Know
B. What is the magnitude of the need for the services or activities of the project?
    ☐ Great Need   ☑ Moderate Need   ☐ Low Need   ☐ Don't Know
Explanatory Notes:

There is always and there always will be, need to implement community health. MUSoD has a program instituted in 1999. No mention of how this community outreach program has worked out for the needy?

II. Significance of the Project

A. How great is the potential contribution of the project in <u>increased knowledge or understanding</u> of educational problems, issues, or effective strategies?
    ☐ Great Potential   ☑ Moderate Potential ☐ Low Potential   ☐ Don't Know
B. In what ways does the proposed project involve the development or demonstration of promising <u>new strategies</u> that build upon, or are alternatives to, existing strategies? (write your answer)
What is being proposed, how would this be different from "Foundational Curriculum"?

C. How important would be the likely <u>results or outcomes</u> of the project, especially with respect to improvements in teaching and student achievement?
    ☐ Important   ☑ Somewhat Important ☐ Less Important   ☐ Don't Know
D. What is the <u>potential replicability</u> of the project, including its potential for implementation in a variety of settings?
    ☐ Replicable   ☑ Somewhat Replicable ☐ Less Replicable   ☐ Don't Know
Explanatory Notes:

This proposed program is a good means of reaching the community.

THE INVITATION TO SUBMIT A FINAL PROPOSAL AND REVIEWER COMMENTS

STAGE ONE: PRELIMINARY PROPOSAL

Curriculum," our numerical rating was still high enough to merit an invitation to submit a final proposal. In particular, it appears that the innovativeness of our dental reforms and the impact they will have on the community helped to move our overall rating beyond "good" to "excellent."

III. Quality of the Project Design

Please rate the quality of the <u>project design</u> as determined by the extent to which it is appropriate to, and will successfully address, the targeted needs:

☐ High Quality   ☑ Moderate Quality   ☐ Low Quality   ☐ Don't Know

Explanatory Notes:

I am not sure how this proposed program will be different from the "Foundational Curriculum" program that the university is presently implementing.

IV. Quality of the Project Evaluation

Please rate the quality of the project evaluation as determined by the extent to which it will

provide guidance about effective strategies suitable for replication or testing in other settings:

☐ High Quality   ☑ Moderate Quality   ☐ Low Quality   ☐ Don't Know

Explanatory Notes:

Potential for success. Since MUSoD is a well-established institution with outstanding faculty, the proposed project can have an impact on the community. There is a need for dental health.

OVERALL ASSESSMENT: Based on the review criteria – Need for the Project, Significance of the Project, Quality of the Project Design, and Quality of the Project Evaluation – please critically analyze the project idea, judging its potential quality as an innovative educational reform model useful in a variety of settings. Describe in detail the reasons for your judgement. Identify specific features of the proposal that contribute to your opinion. Mention any issues that should be addressed in an expanded final proposal, should the applicant be invited to submit one.

If the dental courses (81) can be implemented as tracks, how will such a change, change the nature of basic sciences that are being taught in a traditional manner? How many individual faculty members will be involved? How many dental students will benefit? Is not clear from the application.

NUMERICAL RATING: Based on the review criteria, please rate the quality of the project as an innovative educational reform model. The numerical score should correspond to your earlier comments. (Please circle only one number!)

1------------2------------3------------4------------5---- **6** ----7
Little potential   Great potential

ANALYZING THE REQUEST FOR PROPOSAL

Staff and external reviewers at the Fund for the Improvement of Postsecondary Education (FIPSE) were suitably impressed with our preliminary proposal, and as a result, invited us to submit a full proposal. In this second section of the chapter, we again follow our three-step Request for Proposal (RFP) Analysis Process to determine how much work will need to go into developing a competitive grant application. Our analysis of the invitation to submit a final proposal and reviewer comments revealed several specific areas in need of improvement. And now, in iterative fashion, we read through the RFP guidelines for FIPSE's "Comprehensive Program" and contemplate a series of questions about *relevance*, *feasibility*, and *probability* for funding success.

Step One: Relevance—Do We Want to Do This?

Prior to submitting our preliminary proposal, we determined that FIPSE's "Comprehensive Program" was indeed relevant to the needs and interests of the Marquette University School of Dentistry (MUSoD). Hence, this time in step one of our RFP Analysis Process we did not need to assess levels of individual and administrative interest for pursuing this funding opportunity. Rather, as a way to generate enthusiasm for our initial success, the Associate Dean for Research and Graduate Studies sent out a one-page memorandum to the Proposal Development Committee and other key participants that summarized the main points of the invitation to submit a final proposal and the RFP guidelines.

RFP Guidelines. Great news! FIPSE invited us to submit a full proposal to their "Comprehensive Program." Their invitational letter and RFP guidelines indicated that:

- 260 of 1,532 applicants (17%) were selected to submit a final proposal.
- 130 of 260 applicants (50%) will be awarded funding.
- Projects should be designed to begin between October 1, 2001 and January 1, 2002.
- A full 25-page double spaced proposal is due April 27, 2001.

Because of the relatively tight turnaround time, let's meet this week Thursday over the noon hour to discuss timeframes and responsibilities for developing the final proposal. Lunch will be provided. Again, congratulations on advancing to this stage of a highly competitive grant process.

Step Two: Feasibility—Can We Do This?

In step two of the RFP Analysis Process, we examined the RFP guidelines for evaluation criteria, hot buttons, and distinctive features. We also considered written feedback from FIPSE staff and external reviewers for primary and secondary, logical and psychological concerns that will influence the design and implementation of our project. The expanded guidelines in this second stage of the application process require us to describe our project design and evaluation plan in considerable detail. The Proposal Development Committee will invest a significant amount of time and effort into planning and writing the final proposal, yet based on the initial enthusiasm FIPSE demonstrated for our project, we remain confident that we can do this.

Evaluation Criteria. FIPSE's "Comprehensive Program" will use the following stated evaluation criteria in their selection process. Final proposals should include:

- A completed Title Page application form (ED 40-514)
- A one-page abstract
- A twenty-five-page, double spaced narrative should describe:
  Need for the project
  Significance of the project
  Quality of project design
  Quality of project evaluation
  Quality of management plan
  Quality of project personnel
  Adequacy of resources for the project
- A budget summary and detailed budget
- A moderate number of appendixes, including:
  Brief two-page summaries for "key project personnel"
  Letters of support and commitment from appropriate officials and partners
  A description of proposed steps to ensure equitable access and participation in the program
- Assurances and certifications
- Restrictions on the use of funds include:
  Requests for equipment funds, student financial assistance monies, and high indirect costs are rarely competitive

The Fund for the Improvement of Postsecondary Education
The Comprehensive Program
Fiscal Year 2001

Deadline for Submission: April 27, 2001

Program Information and Application Materials

Introduction

The Comprehensive Program is the central grant competition of the Fund for the Improvement of Postsecondary Education (FIPSE). The competition is designed to support innovative reform projects that hold promise as models for the resolution of important issues and problems in postsecondary education.

Awards: FIPSE estimates that 130 new awards will be made in FY 2001. Grants may provide one, two, or three years of funding. Since Comprehensive Program grants may support improvement projects of varying scope and complexity, there is no minimum or maximum grant award. FIPSE expects to award grants ranging from $150,000 to $600,000 or more over a typical three-year period. Grant budgets will be considered in the context of the proposed project's significance and promise as a model for the reform of American postsecondary education. Fiscal year 2001 projects may begin as early as October 1, 2001 and no later than January 1, 2002. These figures are only estimates and do not bind the Department of Education to a specific number of grants, or to the amount of any grant, unless that amount is otherwise specified by statute or regulations.

Eligibility: The improvement of postsecondary education requires the participation and cooperation of many types of institutions, organizations, and agencies. FIPSE supports a wide range of non-profit providers of educational services. Proposals may be submitted by two- and four-year colleges and universities, both public and private, accredited or non-accredited; graduate and professional schools; community organizations; libraries; museums; trade and technical schools; unions; consortia; student groups; state and local government agencies; non-profit corporations; and associations. Proposals may be submitted by newly formed as well as established organizations, but not by individuals or for-profit schools or organizations. Other organizations may be eligible; the list here is not exhaustive.

Authority: The Education Amendments Act of 1972 authorized the Secretary of Health, Education, and Welfare to improve postsecondary educational opportunities by providing assistance to educational institutions and agencies for a broad range of reforms and innovations. The specific authority is now contained in Title VII, Part B of the Higher Education Act as amended in 1998 (Public Law 105-244). Regulations are contained in the Code of Federal Regulations, Title 34 Part 75. In addition, the Education Department General Administrative Regulations (EDGAR) in 34 CFR Parts 74, 77, 79, 80, 81, 82, and 85 apply.

Application Notice: The official Application Notice is published in the *Federal Register*. The information in the Agenda for Improvement and the rest of this application package is intended to aid in preparing applications for this competition. Nothing in this application package supersedes the priorities listed in the Federal Register.

FIPSE Address: (For information only; do not use this address for mailing applications.)
FIPSE
8th Floor
1990 K Street, NW
Washington, DC 20006-8544

Telephone: (202) 502-7500
Email: fipse@ed.gov

THE REQUEST FOR PROPOSAL

STAGE TWO: FINAL PROPOSAL

Construction costs and funds to purchase facilities are not allowed

- Use 11 point font or larger
- Submit one original and four copies of the complete grant application, plus three copies of the Title Page application form
- Due date: April 27, 2001

At this second stage, final proposals will be critiqued by FIPSE staff and two different external reviewers, with all narrative elements being weighted equally. The external reviewers will be specialists in the subject matter area, and as necessary, additional experts may be called in to review proposals when technical questions arise. In select cases, FIPSE staff may contact project directors to clarify details about their proposals.

Hot Buttons and Distinctive Features. A nuanced reading of three key documents—the RFP guidelines, the invitation to submit a final proposal, and reviewer comments—revealed three hot buttons and two distinctive features. In particular, the three hot buttons identified during development of the preliminary proposal are once again repeated throughout the application materials:

- innovation and reform;
- national impact;
- evaluation and assessment.

These hot buttons are primary concerns of the sponsor that gain force over other evaluation criteria because they appear repeatedly throughout the application materials. The first incidence of these hot buttons occurs in the opening paragraph of the "Introduction" section of the RFP guidelines: "The competition is designed to support *innovative reform* projects that hold promise as *models* for the *resolution of important issues and problems* in postsecondary education."

Distinctive features represent secondary concerns of the sponsor that influence the design of certain aspects of projects. Distinctive features are not repeated throughout the application materials like hot buttons, yet they are real concerns for the sponsor; failing to acknowledge them may be viewed as a project weakness. More concretely, at this second stage of the application process, distinctive features include:

- project director commitment;
- student diversity.

Note that one distinctive feature changed from the preliminary proposal to final proposal. The issue of "cost-effectiveness" takes on a different role in the final proposal. The sponsor still cares about the cost-effectiveness of projects: "FIPSE is especially interested in projects designed to be cost-effective"; however, this concept is assimilated into a larger discussion of the adequacy of resources for the proposed project. Namely, in the "Selection Criteria" section, the sponsor ends by asking a series of broader questions about financial management and commitment, e.g., *Have sufficient funds been allocated to support project activities? Are costs reasonable and appropriate? Have the applicant and partner institutions made significant financial contributions to the project and commitments to its sustainability?*

This change in status posed an interesting challenge for the Proposal Development Committee. Cost-effectiveness is no longer a distinctive feature because it takes on more prominence in the final proposal as part of a budget justification argument. Yet at the same time, cost-effectiveness has not been elevated to the status of a hot button since it is not repeated throughout the RFP guidelines. Because we hinted at cost-effectiveness in the preliminary proposal, we felt some obligation to continue to do so in the final proposal. In the end, so as not to distract from hot buttons and distinctive features, we used *implicit* statements at strategic locations in the narrative to address this former distinctive feature; we used *explicit* statements in the final section of the proposal to answer the sponsor's questions about the adequacy of resources for the project.

Hot Button: Innovation and Reform

The sponsor has an unmistakable value for supporting innovation and reform in postsecondary education. An entire section of the RFP guidelines is dedicated to the "Importance of Innovation." The opening sentence of this section clearly states, "FIPSE grants are intended to provide the seed capital for experiments in educational reform." More broadly, at least 18 different words and phrases are used throughout the RFP guidelines to emphasize the importance of innovation and reform, including:

> Innovative reform, innovative, reforms and innovations, reform, creative ideas, experiments in educational reform, an effective new way of responding, revolutionary or paradigm-shifting reform, new approaches to improvement and reform, promising new strategies, improves upon previous efforts, reform strategies, postsecondary education reform, improves existing practice.

FIPSE World Wide Web Site: For information on past and current projects, successfully evaluated projects from previous years, information, evaluation resources, and more, visit FIPSE's World Wide Web site at http://www.ed.gov/FIPSE.

Agenda for Improvement

Since its founding in 1972, FIPSE's dual mission has been to improve the quality and the accessibility of education beyond the high school level. This year, in keeping with its past, FIPSE eagerly invites creative ideas to ensure that as many students as possible enter and successfully complete postsecondary programs of high quality.

The central challenge, common to postsecondary institutions of all sizes and types, is to provide cost-effective learning opportunities for a larger and more diverse student population. This Agenda highlights some of the important issues accompanying this challenge, and we specifically encourage proposals that address these issues. But we recognize that the Agenda does not identify all the important problems and opportunities facing the postsecondary community. FIPSE welcomes proposal addressing important issues of access and quality not discussed in the Agenda for Improvement; the Agenda is intended to stimulate but not limit the thinking of potential applicants.

The Importance of Innovation

FIPSE grants are intended to provide the seed capital for experiments in educational reform, and the knowledge gained through those experiments should be intended to benefit postsecondary students throughout the country. Are the problems or opportunities you wish to address common to other institutions serving similar student populations? If so, can you design an educational reform project that demonstrates to others an effective new way of responding to those problems? FIPSE's goal is to support implementation of innovative reform ideas, to evaluate how well they work, and to share the lessons learned with the larger postsecondary education community.

As a potential applicant, one of the first things you should do is to investigate how others are responding to similar problems or opportunities. How does your idea compare to common or traditional educational practice? More importantly, how does it compare to the experiments of other leading-edge educational reformers? Your project should be designed to make a unique contribution to the professional community. It does not necessarily have to be a revolutionary or paradigm-shifting reform model, but it should be a significant next step.

Guide to Proposal Development

This discussion is intended to help you conceive and write a stronger proposal by alerting you to the ways in which it will be read and judged. We recognize that some of the considerations raised here may not pertain to your particular project, and the following remarks are not intended to oblige you to organize your proposal around direct responses to all of them.

The Review Process

Final Proposals: When you are invited to submit a final proposal, a FIPSE program officer will discuss with you by telephone both the external reviewers' and the staff's reactions to your preliminary application,

THE REQUEST FOR PROPOSAL

STAGE TWO: FINAL PROPOSAL

The RFP guidelines again use the terms "innovation" and "reform" in their syntactic structures as both noun phrases (e.g., reforms and innovations) and adjective phrases (e.g., reform strategies). These terms do not appear at all in their respective verb forms, "to innovate" and "to reform." This analysis of syntactic structures is important because it helps us identify myriad ways to emphasize hot buttons throughout the full proposal.

Hot Button: National Impact

The RFP guidelines confirm and justify the sponsor's preference for projects with a national impact: "FIPSE seeks to make the most of its limited funds by supporting projects that can become models for others in postsecondary education." By supporting innovative educational reforms that address problems common to many institutions, the sponsor can leverage its philanthropy to have a significant national impact. Hot button phrases are repeated more than two dozen times throughout the RFP guidelines and include:

> models, promise as a model, postsecondary community, throughout the country, common to other institutions, larger postsecondary community, contribution to the professional community, national, national context, other institutions around the country, national consequences, other institutions or organizations likely to benefit, replicability, implementation in a variety of settings, models for others in postsecondary education, potential for implementation elsewhere, other institutions to adapt them on their own, improve upon methods used elsewhere, wider impact.

In its syntactic structure, this hot button appears primarily as a noun phrase (e.g., promise as a model; throughout the country) and in a few instances as an adjective phrase (e.g., national consequences). The noun phrases used in the RFP guidelines tend to be broad and abstract, e.g., "implementation in a variety of settings." This begs the questions of "Which settings?" and "How many settings?" The final proposal should address this hot button in both broad and concrete terms.

Hot Button: Evaluation and Assessment

The invitational letter affirms that evaluation and assessment will be a significant element in our final proposal: "Be sure to develop a solid evaluation plan for your project and describe it in your final proposal." Two dozen words and phrases appear more than forty-

five times in the RFP guidelines, emphasizing the importance of evaluation and assessment. The guidelines explain the sponsor's rationale for this hot button in terms of another hot button, national impact: "Before a project can become a model, however, its proponents must be able to prove that it has achieved its aims in its original setting. That is why a solid evaluation plan, one that focuses as much as possible on precisely how the project has helped students become better educated, is an essential component of FIPSE projects." Examples of hot button words and phrases include the following:

> Resolution of important issues and problems, successfully evaluated projects, evaluation resources, evaluate how well they work, assessment, effectiveness, what results, results or outcomes, achieved its aims, solid evaluation plan, project evaluation, methods of evaluation, outcomes of the proposed project, performance measures, intended outcomes, formative evaluation, summative evaluation, project's effects, final evaluation report, quantitative and qualitative evidence, project has succeeded or failed, short-term indicators, evaluation design, immediate and long-range outcomes.

Syntactically, this hot button of evaluation and assessment takes the form of noun phrases (e.g., formative and summative evaluation), adjective phrases (e.g., evaluation plan), and verb phrases (e.g., assess projects). While all three forms will appear in the final proposal, we will use more noun and verb phrases because they tend to be stronger, be more specific, and express action.

Distinctive Feature: Project Director Commitment

The invitational letter introduces a new distinctive feature to be addressed in the final proposal: project director commitment. The sponsor wants assurance that we have an individual who is committed personally and professionally to leading this project to fruition. More specifically, the Director of FIPSE's "Comprehensive Program" states:

> Note that FIPSE will expect extensive project involvement on the part of the person designated as project director. We will expect that person to attend the annual project directors' meeting each fall, to complete annual and final reports, and to initiate regular contact with the FIPSE program officer assigned to monitor the project. It is therefore important that the proj-

and will remain available to answer questions and offer suggestions to assist you in strengthening the final proposal.

Final proposals are also read by at least two outside reviewers, including specialists in your subject. Additional experts may review proposals when technical questions arise, and FIPSE's National Board may discuss them. FIPSE staff then carefully read and discuss the proposals and the external reviews. Project directors of the most competitive applications are telephoned to clarify information about their projects. Staff may also contact others who know the applicant's work and plans, or who will be affected by the project.

Again at the final proposal stage, it is important to present your ideas in clear language that will help readers to understand precisely what you intend to do and how you will do it. Your final proposal narrative should not exceed 25 double-spaced pages, or approximately 6,250 words.

To ensure that all applicants enjoy the same opportunity to present their ideas, please conform to the page limitations noted above, use minimum 1-inch margins, and avoid font sizes smaller than 11 points.

Selection Criteria

Our intent in this section is to help applicants understand how the selection criteria are applied during the final review stage. FIPSE does not separate proposals rigidly by types of activities, sectors of postsecondary education or other fixed categories, nor does it assign specific amounts of its budget to the priority areas described in the Agenda for Improvement. Instead, in our desire to identify the most significant issues and feasible plans, we compare each proposal to all others, using the criteria described below.

Each selection criterion is presented in bold type, and followed by a discussion of how it applies to the competition. The external readers and staff reviewers of your proposal use these criteria to guide their reviews at both stages of the Comprehensive Program competition, so it is in your interest to be familiar with them. The final decision on an application is based on an overall assessment of the extent to which it satisfactorily addresses all the selection criteria, which are weighted equally.

Final proposals will be considered according to the following criteria and their factors, all weighted equally.

1) The need for the project, as determined by the following factors:

a) the magnitude or severity of the problem addressed by the project; and

b) the magnitude of the need for the services to be provided or the activities to be carried out by the project.

You should describe the nature and magnitude of the problem or opportunity you wish to address, in both its local setting and a national context. The Agenda for Improvement in this booklet identifies some areas of needed reform, but you may choose to focus on a topic not specifically mentioned in these guidelines, or you may choose to address more than one topic in a single project.

How central is the problem you have identified to your institution's vitality or the effectiveness of your educational services? Does the same problem affect other institutions around the country? Have attempts to remedy the situation been made by you or by others in the past, and with what results? What will be the local and national consequences of a successful completion of your project? Are other institutions or organizations likely to benefit or learn from your experience in ways that would enable them to improve their own programs and services?

ect director be someone who is committed to significant personal involvement. If the project director cannot fulfill these commitments, please do not submit a final proposal.

This distinctive feature does not appear as directly in the RFP guidelines. Rather, it takes on a broader form: "describe your institution's capacity and commitment to the project." We could interpret project director commitment to be an aspect of our institutional commitment. However, the emphatic nature of this distinctive feature occurring in the invitational letter commands that we address it directly in the final proposal.

Distinctive Feature: Student Diversity

The distinctive feature of student diversity occurs twice in the RFP guidelines, once directly and once more subtly. First, it appears in the same location in the guidelines for the final proposal (within the "Agenda for Improvement" section) as it did for the guidelines for the preliminary proposal. Second, it emerges in the section on "Submitting Your Proposal," near the end of the RFP guidelines: "Sectional 427 of the General Education Provisions Act (GEPA) requires each applicant to include in its application a description of proposed steps to ensure equitable access to, and participation in, its Federally assisted program."

In practical terms, this distinctive feature means providing explicit assurance to the sponsor that MU-SoD will comply with federal regulations for encouraging equitable access and participation in the program. And as was noted in the reviewer comments, our target population includes not only the dental education students and faculty, but also the multicultural residents in the communities in which we serve. In the final proposal, we must describe how we will have inclusive participation from all of these major stakeholders.

Step Three: Probability—Will We Be Competitive?

Step three of the RFP Analysis Process requires us to participate in an exercise in strategic thinking prior to engaging in preproposal contact with the sponsor. We must systematically assess our organizational strengths and weaknesses in relation to the values of the sponsor and then pose questions raised by ambiguities, inconsistencies, discrepancies, and omissions in the RFP guidelines. This third level of analysis will improve our competitiveness, and chances for success, by enhancing our credibility with the sponsor.

Strategic Thinking. The Proposal Development Committee generated the following list of strategic thinking questions that arose from a critical review of each section of the RFP guidelines. These questions needed to be addressed internally to assess our competitiveness before engaging in preproposal contacts with the sponsor.

Introduction

- Can we compete in a national program competition?
- Are our odds of getting funded good enough to merit submitting a final proposal?
- How can we make our final proposal stand out from the competition?
- Have we read the authorizing legislation to see if there are other key words, concepts, and ideas that should be incorporated into our final proposal?
- What else can we learn from the FIPSE Web site?

Importance of Innovation

- Does our project represent an effective new way of responding to a problem common to postsecondary institutions?
- Has this approach been tried before at other institutions? With what results?
- How does our approach differ from and improve upon existing educational practices?
- Does our project have the potential to make a significant impact throughout the country?
- Will the postsecondary community embrace our reform ideas?

The Review Process

- Have individuals at the university served as external reviewers for the FIPSE "Comprehensive Program"? What "insider information" might we glean from them?
- Do we know individuals outside of the university who have served as FIPSE reviewers? Would they be willing to share their experiences with us?
- What is the relationship between the recommendations of external reviewers and FIPSE staff to the funding decisions made by FIPSE's National Board?
- Are some elements of the final proposal more important than others? Which ones?
- Are FIPSE program officers as willing to discuss by

Note that FIPSE does not support basic research; rather, its focus is on implementation projects designed to test new approaches to improvement and reform.

2) The significance of the project, as determined by the following factors:

a) the potential contribution of the proposed project to increased knowledge or understanding of educational problems, issues, or effective strategies;

b) the extent to which the proposed project involves the development or demonstration of promising new strategies that build on, or are alternatives to, existing strategies;

c) the importance or magnitude of the results or outcomes likely to be attained by the proposed project, especially improvements in teaching and student achievement; and

d) the potential replicability of the proposed project, including its potential for implementation in a variety of settings.

Reviewers will appreciate any evidence you can include to illustrate how your project differs from and improves upon previous efforts. Describe the potential contribution of your project to increasing the postsecondary community's knowledge about effective reform strategies, and the likely utility of the products (such as information, materials, processes, or techniques) that will result from it. It is the applicant's responsibility to set a context within which reviewers can assess the project's importance to postsecondary education reform.

Directly or indirectly, learners should be the principal beneficiaries of your project. This means, for example, that faculty development proposals should articulate the relationship between what the faculty will experience and what their students will learn. Our focus on the learner also means that FIPSE is especially interested in evaluation plans that assess projects in terms of their consequences for student learning.

FIPSE seeks to make the most of its limited funds by supporting projects that can become models for others in postsecondary education. Applicants should discuss the potential replicability of the proposed project, and its potential for implementation elsewhere. Before a project can become a model, however, its proponents must be able to prove that it has achieved its aims in its original setting. That is why a solid evaluation plan, one that focuses as much as possible on precisely how the project has helped students to become better educated, is an essential component of FIPSE projects.

Keeping in mind that, if your project activities are heavily dependent on external funding, it will be very difficult for other institutions to adapt them on their own, and this may reduce the potential impact of your project.

3) The quality of the project's design, as determined by the following factors:

a) the extent to which the goals, objectives, and outcomes to be achieved by the proposed project are clearly specified and measurable; and

b) the extent to which the design for implementing and evaluating the proposed project will result in information to guide possible replication of project activities or strategies, including information about the effectiveness of the approach or strategies employed by the project.

Your narrative should offer reviewers a clear description of who will do what, when, where, why, and with what anticipated results. The project's goals and objectives should be clearly identified and measurable.

telephone the merits of our project as the RFP guidelines seem to indicate?

Selection Criteria

- How can the selection criteria be weighted equally when some criteria contain many more questions to be answered than others?
- Is there any specific information *not* requested in the selection criteria that we should be sure to include in our final proposal?

1) Need for the Project

- How many dental schools exist in the United States?
- What is the size of the faculty at these dental schools?
- How many dental school graduates have been produced annually over the past five years?
- Have graduate student enrollment trends been increasing, decreasing, or relatively constant over the past five years?
- What are the current problems with existing dental school curricula?
- Are our problems similar to those found in other dental schools?
- How serious are these curricular problems, locally and nationally?
- What is the magnitude of the need nationwide for curricular reform among dental schools?
- How do these nationwide needs in dentistry compare to other healthcare fields, e.g., medicine, nursing, physical therapy, speech pathology, and so forth?
- What are the consequences to dental educators and to patients regarding the lack of an updated curriculum?
- How many dental schools are involved in curriculum reform in a major way?
- What were the last major curricular reforms in dentistry? When did they occur?
- To what extent have reforms attempted by others been successful?
- Are the curricular problems among dental schools sufficiently common to warrant a national reform?
- What are the implications of these problems on the delivery of quality dental care to patients?
- How crucial are curricular reforms to long-term dental school viability?
- Are other dental schools likely to profit from our experiences with curricular reform?

2) Significance of the Project

- Does our proposed project have the potential for a national impact?
- To what extent does our proposed approach build on existing curricular reform strategies?
- To what extent does our approach to curricular reform offer a promising alternative to existing practices?
- Long-term, will our project outcomes truly make a difference?
- Will our project result in useful materials and techniques?
- How will learners be the principal beneficiaries of our project?
- How will student learning be assessed?
- How will improvements in teaching be assessed?
- What are the tangible consequences of enhanced teaching and learning?
- If successful locally, will other dental programs be able to replicate our experience?
- What are the specific components of our project that will be replicable?
- Are there other institutions with whom we should be collaborating?
- Are there other institutions with whom we will be competing for this type of an award?
- What are the costs associated with replicating this project in a variety of other settings?
- Is our education reform project significant enough to the postsecondary community to attract FIPSE interest?

3) Quality of Project Design

- Will we be addressing the central causes of existing barriers to curricular reform?
- What pilot data do we have to demonstrate that this project is realistic and will make a significant difference in the way we approach dental education?
- What specific strategies will be most effective to accomplish quality curriculum reform?
- Can we provide a balanced mix of basic science and clinical practice learning experiences?
- Do we have the collective capability to address the central causes of current curriculum weaknesses?
- Is an adequate infrastructure in place to systematically implement curricular reform?
- Are project strategies based on a combination of the latest research and practical experience?
- Will the curricular reforms be equally effective

All proposed projects should include plans for disseminating their findings. There are many ways of informing others of a project's results, and of helping others make use of your experience. In reviewing plans for dissemination or adaptation, we ask whether the methods proposed are appropriate for the project in question and whether they improve upon methods used elsewhere.

4) The quality of the project evaluation, as determined by the following factors:

a) the extent to which the methods of evaluation are thorough, feasible, and appropriate to the goals, objectives, and outcomes of the proposed project; and

b) the extent to which the methods of evaluation include the use of objective performance measures that are clearly related to the intended outcomes of the project and will produce quantitative and qualitative data to the extent possible.

Formative evaluation can help you manage your project more effectively, and a strong summative evaluation, especially if it documents the project's effects on the learner, can turn a successful project into a national model for improvement in postsecondary education. As you develop your evaluation plan, place yourself in the position of the recipient of your final evaluation report. What would count as solid quantitative and qualitative evidence that your project had succeeded or failed? It may be difficult, within the term of the grant, to assess the accomplishment of long-range objectives, but you should be able to identify some short-term indicators. Bear in mind that the goals of local institutionalization and wider impact may well elude you unless you can provide solid evidence that your project is achieving its aims. Developing such evidence should not be put off until the last stages of a project. It must be a consideration from the design stage onward.

FIPSE provides a short bibliography of books and articles on program evaluation to assist you with evaluation design. These references clarify formative and summative evaluation. They address evidence, measurement, and sampling questions, and discuss the immediate and long-range outcomes you can expect, based on your project objectives. This bibliography is available on FIPSE's website, or by telephone or mail request to the FIPSE office.

5) The quality of the management plan, as determined by the plan's adequacy to achieve the objectives of the proposed project on time and within budget, including clearly defined responsibilities, timelines, and milestones for accomplishing project tasks.

6) The quality of project personnel, as determined by the following factors:

a) the qualifications, including training and experience, of key project personnel; and

b) the extent to which the applicant encourages applications for employment from persons who are members of groups that have traditionally been underrepresented based on race, color, national origin, gender, age, or disability.

The qualifications of key personnel, including the project director and any consultants or subcontractors, should be briefly outlines in an appendix to the final proposal. Please note that a standard curriculum vitae is usually not appropriate for this purpose. What is needed is a brief (two pages maximum) narrative summary of each individual's background, with a special focus on those experiences related to the topic of your application.

7) The adequacy of resources for the proposed project, as determined by the following factors:

a) the extent to which the budget is adequate to support the proposed project;

whether they are implemented all at once or in discrete phases?

- To what extent are the project goals, objectives, and outcomes clear, specific, and measurable?
- Does the design lend itself to rigorous formative and summative evaluations?
- Have we clearly described *who* will do *what, when, where, why,* and with *what anticipated results?*
- Which active and passive dissemination strategies will be most effective for sharing the results of this project?
- What will make our proposal distinctively different from the competition?

4) *Quality of Project Evaluation*

- What conceptual model will guide the evaluation approach?
- Do we have specific evaluation approaches for each project objective?
- How will we evaluate the project processes, products, and outcomes?
- Do suitable evaluation tools already exist or will new ones need to be developed?
- What are the specific sources of documentation available to provide evaluation data?
- To what extent are our evaluation protocols thorough and feasible?
- Will we have solid quantitative and qualitative evidence of project success, both from formative and summative perspectives?
- How will evaluation feedback be used?
- Should the evaluation be conducted internally and externally, or externally only?
- Who will be responsible for project evaluation?
- Have we identified evaluators with the expertise, experience, and capability to objectively assess the program and its activities?
- To what extent will the evaluation protocol provide guidance about project replication at other institutions throughout the nation?
- How will we disseminate the results of our project evaluation?
- Who will be responsible for promoting community awareness of the initiative?

5) *Quality of the Management Plan*

- Is the methodological approach of sufficient quality to ensure that the project objectives will be met on time and on budget?
- Does the proposal include timelines and milestones for accomplishing project tasks?

- Does the project management plan clearly indicate the locus of responsibility for each project task?
- Have appropriate collaborators and consultants been identified and endorsed the project?
- Are the interrelationships among project tasks apparent?

6) *Quality of Project Personnel*

- Are key project personnel adequately trained and experienced to ensure project success?
- Will key project personnel include persons from underrepresented groups?
- Do resumes of key personnel emphasize pertinent project expertise and conform to the two page limitation?
- Do the key project personnel have a demonstrated track record of success in handling similar projects?

7) *Adequacy of Resources for Proposed Project*

- Is the budget adequate to support the proposed project?
- Are the costs reasonable relative to the objectives, design, and project significance?
- Have external collaborators signed a memorandum of agreement that specifies the specific contributions each will make to the total project?
- Are the facilities, equipment, supplies and other resources adequate to ensure project success?
- What cash and in-kind resources can we contribute to this project?
- Does our institutional commitment include direct cost sharing and a low indirect cost rate?
- Do we have sample letters of support and commitment from senior administrators authorizing and endorsing this project?
- Does a plan exist to cover future funding once the federal grant expires?
- Can we absorb future funding responsibilities within general operating budgets once grant funds end?
- Is there another profitable service or activity that could be expanded to cover the costs of running this new project?

Mailing Address for Final Proposals

- If we are selected to submit a final proposal, will we be able to do so during their scheduled timeframe?
- Is the sponsor's projected timetable consistent with our strategic plan for program development?

b) the extent to which costs are reasonable in relation to the objectives, design, and potential significance of the proposed project;

c) the demonstrated commitment of each partner in the proposed project to the implementation and success of the project;

d) the adequacy of support, including facilities, equipment, supplies, and other resources from the applicant organization; and

e) the potential for continued support of the project after Federal funding ends, including the demonstrated commitment of appropriate entities to such support.

It should be clear that you have carefully allocated appropriate resources and personnel for the tasks and activities described in your proposal. There is no point in jeopardizing the success of the project through insufficient allocation of funds; nor is it helpful to over-estimate its costs to the host institution of to FIPSE. A detailed budget and justification attached to your final proposal should itemize the support you request from FIPSE and the support you expect to obtain from sources other than FIPSE.

FIPSE cannot purchase facilities and it rarely supports equipment purchases. These costs should be included in your institutional contribution.

FIPSE is especially interested in projects designed to be cost-effective, to increase the likelihood that successful efforts may be continued beyond the period of a FIPSE grant, and to be replicated by others. But cost-effectiveness must not imply insufficient resources to accomplish the project's goals and objectives. Costs should be allocated, and will be judged, in comparison to the scope of the project and the requirements for achieving its objectives.

It is important to provide evidence that the plans you propose have the support of those who will authorize them, those who will carry them out, and those who will be affected by them. Final proposals should include, in an appendix, letters of commitment and support from senior administrators of the host institution, any partners in the project, and, if desired, national experts on the issues addressed in the proposal. Applicants are advised that the quality of letters of support is important, not their quantity.

The applicant institution and any partners should support the project both philosophically and financially. Because FIPSE applicants are often seeking support that will develop or strengthen their own programs or capacities, we expect the host institution and its partners to make a significant commitment to the project in the form of direct cost sharing and low indirect cost rates. FIPSE does not specify a particular percentage of cost-sharing or an indirect rate, however, because the rate proposed is taken as an indication of institutional commitment, and this may vary from institution to institution and from project to project. Some of our applicants request no indirect costs at all. As a reference point, FIPSE staff generally use the U.S. Department of Education training rate of eight percent (8%) of total direct costs as a basis for judgements about reasonable indirect costs.

FIPSES grants are generally used to support the start-up of new programs or activities that are intended to continue after a grant ends. When this is the case, your proposal should have a clear and convincing plan for long-term continuation of the project that includes explicit commitments from those who will be responsible for sustaining the activity. When long-term institutionalization of the project is the goal, it is often desirable to plan for an increasing share of institutional support with declining FIPSE support during the life of the grant.

Because issues of costs are often critical for institutionalization, proposals requiring grant dollars for student financial aid or equipment are rarely competitive. Instead we expect that projects requiring such funds will acquire the money from other sources. Grants cannot be used for the purchase of real property or for construction.

STAGE TWO: FINAL PROPOSAL

Submission Procedures for Final Proposals

- Is there any advantage to submitting proposals via express mail or hand delivery?
- Would there be any benefit to the program officer to submit additional copies of our final proposal beyond the original and four complete copies?
- Have we checked with our state's single point of contact for the best way to comply with Executive Order 12372 (intergovernmental review of federal programs)?

Preproposal Contact. The invitation to submit a final proposal and the RFP guidelines both emphasize the importance of engaging in preproposal contacts with program officers. The RFP states, "When you are invited to submit a final proposal, a FIPSE program officer will discuss with you by telephone both the external reviewers' and the staff's reactions to your preliminary application, and will remain available to answer questions and offer suggestions to assist you in strengthening the final proposal." When we called the FIPSE program officer, Dr. Robert Jones, our opening conversation went like this.

> Hello, Dr. Jones. I'm Tony Iacopino, Associate Dean for Dental Education at Marquette University. Thank you for sending a copy of the reviewer comments along with the invitation to submit a full proposal. They have been very helpful. If I've caught you at a good time, I'd like to ask you a few questions about the reviewer comments and a few issues not specifically addressed in the RFP guidelines.

This opening statement piqued Dr. Jones' interest. Next, we briefly described our project and then asked the following types of PREP questions. Notice that at this second stage of the application process we ask fewer introductory "Position" and "Rationale" questions in favor of more higher order "Expectation" and "Priority" questions.

> Briefly, our proposal requests $400,000 over three years to institute a major curriculum reform in our dental school. We will propose to integrate more closely basic science and clinical practice instruction, while, at the same time, implement new approaches to instructional technology that result in a replicable curriculum for other dental schools nationwide. With that backdrop of our project, I'd welcome your answers to a few questions.

Position: The Baseline Situation

- From a review of the FIPSE Web site, it appears that few dental education projects have been funded recently. Is this a conscious decision on the part of FIPSE, or is there some other explanation, e.g., none has applied?
- Given that few dental projects have been funded by FIPSE in the past, what can you tell us about reviewers' level of expertise in dental education?

Rationale: Problems Existing Today

- Why has curricular reform become a funding priority?
- What are the biggest hurdles applicants face in reaching their grant objectives?

Expectation: Basic Implications for Addressing Problems

- Does our project fall within your current priorities for "Curricular and Pedagogical Reform"?
- What's the desired local impact you'd like to see, while maintaining a balance across project breadth, depth, and financial resources available?
- Winning proposals are also expected to have a national impact. How much of an impact are we talking about? What do you mean by having potential for "wide application"?
- Is there a preferred means for incorporating technology into the curriculum, e.g., self-directed modules on CD-ROM, interactive Web sites, Web casts, Web chats, e-mail discussion groups, video conferences, interactive television, virtual reality simulators?
- The RFP guidelines indicate that model programs must be sustainable. Does that mean activities must be institutionalized, or are there other strategies for supporting project continuation that typically appear in proposals for curricular and pedagogical reform?
- What are the most common mistakes in proposals you receive?
- What would you like to see addressed in a proposal that other applicants may have overlooked?

Priority: Approaches for an Improved Situation

- What do you see as essential to the future of dental education that isn't happening now?
- What would be the key features of an ideal solution?

Submitting Your Proposal

The announced closing dates and procedures for guaranteeing timely submissions will be strictly observed. Final proposals must be submitted on or before April 27, 2001.

Applicants should also note that the closing date applies to both the date the application is mailed and the hand delivery date. A mailed application meets the requirements if it is mailed on or before the pertinent closing date and the required proof of mailing is provided. Proof of mailing may consist of one of the following: (a) a legible dated U.S. Postal Service postmark; (b) a legible receipt with the date of mailing stamped by the U.S. Postal Service; (c) a dated shipping label, invoice, or receipt from a commercial carrier, or (d) any other proof of mailing acceptable to the Secretary of Education.

If an application is sent through the U.S. Postal Service, the Secretary will *not* accept either of the following as proof of mailing: (1) a private metered postmark, or (2) a mail receipt that is not dated by the U.S. Postal Service.

Please use first class or express mail. (Overnight delivery is encouraged.) All applicants will receive acknowledgement notices upon receipt of final proposals from the Application Control Center. If you do not receive an acknowledgement notice within six weeks of the closing date, please contact FIPSE using the address or phone number in the introduction to these guidelines. Please wait the full six weeks before contacting us for an acknowledgement.

Mailing Address for Final Proposals
FIPSE Comprehensive Program
ATTN: 84.116A
U.S. Department of Education
Application Control Center
Room 3633, ROB-3
Washington, DC 20202-4725

Submission Procedures for Final Proposals
Mailed Proposals: Proposals sent by mail must be mailed no later than April 27, 2001.

Hand Delivered Proposals: Hand delivered proposals will be accepted daily between the hours of 8:00 a.m. and 4:30 p.m., Washington, D.C. time except Saturdays, Sundays, or Federal holidays, at the Application Control Center, General Services Administration Building, 7th & D Streets, S.W., Room 3633, Washington D.C. Proposals will not be accepted after 4:30 p.m. on April 27, 2001.

Number of Copies: All applicants must submit (1) signed original and two (2) complete copies of the final proposal, although four (4) copies are requested. Each copy must be covered with a Title Page, ED 40-514, or a reasonable facsimile. Applicants are also requested to submit three (3) additional copies of the Title Page itself.

Content: Proposals should be written clearly and concisely, and should include the following:

1. Title Page: Use Form ED 40-514 or a suitable facsimile to cover each proposal copy. Please include a brief abstract of your project in the space provided. Additional instructions are found in the Title Page Instructions.

2. Abstract: Attach a one-page double-spaced abstract following the Title Page (this is in addition to the abstract requested on the Title Page itself). The abstract should identify the problem or opportunity being

THE REQUEST FOR PROPOSAL

STAGE TWO: FINAL PROPOSAL

- What outcomes do you expect from grantees?
- Conducting a "rigorous assessment" of the project can mean examining a variety of humanistic, economic, and functional status outcome indicators; are there any specific outcome indicators that you prefer to see evaluated?
- What are the preferred strategies for disseminating project results on a national basis?

In short, this three-step RFP Analysis Process systematically examines questions about *relevance, feasibility*, and *probability* for funding success in order to move us along the Roads to the Persuasion Intersection. Next we examine how we arrive at the Persuasion Intersection by connecting our project idea to the values of the sponsor.

addressed, the proposed project activities, and their intended outcomes. It should also include a concise summary of what is innovative about the project.

3. Proposal Narrative: Please review the selection criteria described in these guidelines. While FIPSE does not prescribe a standard outline for all applicants, in no more than 25 double-spaced, numbered pages, or approximately 6,250 words and in font size no smaller than 11 point, you should: (1) identify the issue or problem you are addressing and the project's objectives; (2) describe the proposed strategies and how they improve existing practice; (3) describe your institution's capacity and commitment to the project; and (4) discuss your plans for evaluation and dissemination. If someone other than the named project director was the principal writer of the proposal, please include his or her name, title and affiliation at the end of the narrative.

4. Budget Summary and Detailed Budget. Use the one-page budget summary included with these guidelines or a suitable facsimile to present a complete budget. In addition, provide a detailed budget using the same line items used in the budget summary and a separate narrative budget justification. Provide a detailed line-item budget for each year of the project. The narrative should explain: (1) the basis for estimating the costs of professional personnel salaries and waged, including annual salary or hourly wage rate and percentage of staff time; employee benefits per person, including rates and percentage of staff time; employee benefits per person, including rates and percentage of staff time; employee travel per person/per trip; consultants and subcontracts, including non-employee travel; materials and supplies; other costs, including printing and equipment rental; indirect costs; (2) how the major cost items relate to the proposed activities; and (3) the costs of evaluation. Your detailed budget should also include a detailed breakdown of institutional and other support for the project.

5. Appendices: (a) "Key Project Personnel": Please provide a brief summary (two pages) of the background and experience of key project staff as they relate to the specific project activities you are proposing. Letters of support and commitment from appropriate officials at the sponsoring institution and project partners are also welcomed. Do not attach any other appendices or information unless they are directly relevant to your project. Appendices must be attached to all copies of the final proposal to be included in the review. (b) "Equitable Access and Participation": Sectional 427 of the General Education Provisions Act (GEPA) requires each applicant to include in its application a description of proposed steps to ensure equitable access to, and participation in, its Federally assisted program. Each application should include this description in a clearly identified appendix. The statue, which allows applicants discretion in developing the required description, highlights six types of barriers that can impede equitable access or participation: gender, race, national origin, color, disability, or age. You may use local circumstance to determine the extent to which these or other barriers prevent equitable participation by students, faculty, or other relevant audiences. Your description should be a succinct description of how you plan to address any barriers.

6. Assurances and Certifications: Please sign and include the certifications. When your institutional representative signs the Title Page, the applicant is certifying that it will comply with the assurances contained in these guidelines.

Intergovernmental Review of Federal Programs (Executive Order 12372): This competition is subject to the requirements of Executive Order 12372, Intergovernmental Review of Federal Programs, and the regulations in 34 CFR 79. The objective of the order is to foster a Federal and State intergovernmental coordination and review of proposed Federal financial assistance. Applicants are directed to the appropriate State single point of contact to comply with the State's procedures under this Executive Order. A list of these contacts is available at http://www.sheeo.org/about-sheeo/agencies.htm.

THE REQUEST FOR PROPOSAL

STAGE TWO: FINAL PROPOSAL

DEVELOPING THE TITLE PAGE APPLICATION FORM

The Title Page application form is the first page of our complete grant application. It provides the sponsor with summary information about our organization, project director, project, budget, and compliance with federal assurances. The eleven line item elements on the application form (ED 40-514) serve to establish three types of credibility—organizational, individual, and project.

Elements of the Title Page

The Fund for the Improvement of Postsecondary Education (FIPSE) uses the same Title Page application form for both preliminary and final proposals. We indicate to reviewers that this is a Stage Two application by putting a checkmark next to the appropriate proposal classification.

Item 1: Application Number. The invitation to submit a final proposal provides us with the application number assigned to our project by the U.S. Department of Education Application Control Center. This number allows the sponsor to track each of the 260 applicants invited to submit full proposals.

Item 2: D-U-N-S Number. In addition to supplying our Employer Identification Number (EIN), we provide our Data Universal Numbering System (D-U-N-S) Number. These two identification numbers, assigned to us by the Internal Revenue Service and Dun & Bradstreet, respectively, allow FIPSE to validate our institution's contact information and legal and tax status.

Item 3: Project Director. Marquette University School of Dentistry (MUSoD) proposes to implement a dental reform initiative that will integrate basic science and clinical education into a new "Foundational Curriculum." This ambitious undertaking requires a proven leader with a unique combination of expertise. Our Project Director, Dr. Joseph Best, has both a dental degree (D.D.S.) and a research degree (Ph.D.). This dual degree establishes instantly the credibility of the project director. We provide all relevant contact information: mailing address, telephone number, fax number, and email address.

Item 4: Institutional Information. In this line item we identify Marquette University as a private, doctoral granting institution. FIPSE gathers this information from grant applicants and awardees as a means of assessing its funding practices and demonstrating its accountability to Congress.

Item 5: Federal Funds Requested. The RFP guidelines recommend, "When long-term institutionalization of the project is the goal, it is often desirable to plan for an increasing share of institutional support with declining FIPSE support during the life of the grant." Accordingly, the amount of federal funds requested from the sponsor decreases each year of the three-year project period. FIPSE staff and external reviewers will also recognize that our total request amount is comfortably within the sponsor's typical award range of $150,000 to $600,000 over three years.

Item 6: Duration of Project. In accordance with the RFP guidelines, we establish October 1, 2001, as the project start date. Sponsor-funded curricular reforms will take place over a total of thirty-six months, with the project concluding on September 30, 2004.

Item 7: Proposal Title. The project title is descriptive without being cutesy or a tricky acronym. Equally important, in just a few words we communicate that this proposal addresses the sponsor's invitational priority of "Curricular and Pedagogical Reform." The proposal title serves as an early alert to external reviewers, helping them establish the proper mindset of what to be looking for as they read our narrative.

Item 8: Brief Abstract of Proposal. The instructions on the application form for this line item explicitly state, "do not leave this blank." This may seem like common sense, but in reality, it's a reaction to the fact that the sponsor really wants *two* abstracts: a "short" version (one paragraph) on the Title Page application form and a "long" version (one page) that comes before the proposal narrative. We dedicate four sentences to describing the significance of our project, highlighting innovative project design elements, and stating the major benefits that will occur. This brief abstract (123 words) was written *after* the final proposal was completed, and in fact, the sentences are taken verbatim from the proposal narrative.

Item 9: Legal Applicant. The legal applicant and fiscal agent for this project is Marquette University. (Grants awards are made to institutions, not individuals.) As requested, we provide a complete mailing address.

Item 10: Population Directly Benefiting from This Project. Conservatively estimated, our curricular reform initiative will impact 320 dental students and patients annually. FIPSE staff and external reviewers may use this information to conduct a simple cost-benefit analysis. That is, the total project cost ($404,527) divided by the total population directly

Form No: ED 40-514
OMB No: 1840-514
Form Expires 10/31/2003

THE COMPREHENSIVE PROGRAM
FUND FOR THE IMPROVEMENT OF POSTSECONDARY EDUCATION

TITLE PAGE

Check One: _____ Preliminary Proposal __x__ Final Proposal

This application should be sent to: No. 84.116A U. S. Department of Education Application Control Center Rom 3633, ROB-3 Washington, DC 20202-4725	1. Application Number: P116B011247 2. D-U-N-S Number: 93851-3892 Employer Identification No.: 39-0806251
3. Project Director (Name and MailingAddress) Joseph Best, D.D.S., Ph.D. Marquette University P.O. Box 1881 Milwaukee, WI 53201-1881 Telephone: 414-288-7155 Fax: 414-288-7870 Email: joseph.best@marquette.edu	4. Institutional Information Highest Degree Awarded: _____Two-year _____Four-Year _____Graduate __x__Doctorate _____Non-degree granting Type: _____Public __x__Private
5. Federal Funds Requested: 1st Year: $172,439 2nd Year (if applicable): $138,632 3rd Year (if applicable): $93,456 Total Amount: $404,527	6. Duration of Project Starting Date: 10/01/2001 Ending Date: 09/30/2004 Total No. of Months: 36

7. Proposal Title: Dental Education Reform: the MUSoD Foundational Curriculum

THE TITLE PAGE APPLICATION FORM

STAGE TWO: FINAL PROPOSAL

benefiting from this project over three years (960 people) equals an investment of $421 per person, or approximately $140 per person per year.

Item 11: Certification by Authorizing Official.

We enter the name, title, and telephone number of the official who has the authority to accept federal funding and commit the institution to executing the proposed project.

8. Brief Abstract of Proposal *(DO NOT LEAVE THIS BLANK)*

The Marquette University School of Dentistry (MUSoD) is currently working to radically change its entire curriculum so that it is more responsive to the changing needs of students and the community. This project will implement several novel curriculum elements at MUSoD. These include comprehensive integration/reinforcement of basic science and clinical science content in continuous four-year educational "tracks," use of interdisciplinary case-based teaching approaches in the form of "General Dental Rounds," and application of acquired knowledge/skills/attitudes in community-based settings designed to maximize experiential learning. These elements are designed to create new dental graduates in the form of "oral physicians" who are recognized as much for their comprehensive approach to patient care as for their superior technically-based traditional dental services they are able to provide.

9. Legal Applicant Marquette University School of Dentistry P.O. Box 1881 Milwaukee, WI 53201-1881	10. Population Directly Benefiting from the Project 320 dental students and faculty Congressional District of the Applicant Institution: 5th

11. Certification by Authorizing Official

The applicant certifies to the best of his/her knowledge and belief that the data in this application is true and correct, that the filing of this applicant has been duly authorized by the governing body of the applicant, and that the applicant will comply with the attached assurances if assistance is approved.

Name_____ Title_____ Phone _____

DEVELOPING THE PROJECT ABSTRACT

The project abstract offers a concise summary of our entire proposal. In 333 words, we identify the problem being addressed, the proposed project activities and their intended outcomes. Further, we introduce all three hot buttons that will be addressed repeatedly throughout the final proposal: innovation and reform, national impact, and evaluation and assessment. The project abstract was written *after* the final proposal was completed, thus ensuring consistency of style and tone. In fact, 90 percent of the sentences are taken *verbatim* from the proposal narrative.

Elements of the Project Summary

Title. Identical to the preliminary proposal, the boldface heading at the top center of the page identifies the project title and the acronym for the applicant organization, "Dental Education Reform: The MUSoD Foundational Curriculum." The title is descriptive and succinct without being cutesy. Moreover, the words "education reform" suggest that our project addresses the sponsor's invitational priority of "Curricular and Pedagogical Reform."

Paragraph #1. The first paragraph justifies *why* our project is necessary. It identifies and describes the magnitude of the problem in dental education in its national context. In particular, the first two sentences confirm that dental schools across the United States have failed to adapt their curricula to meet the changing oral health needs of the nation. This provides reviewers with a "big picture" perspective of the status of dental education and foreshadows that our proposed project can have a national impact, a sponsor hot button. The third and fourth sentences state the consequences of an inadequate and outmoded dental curriculum; namely, dental schools are so heavily technique-driven that dental graduates are inadequately prepared to be critical-thinking professionals in their dental practices.

Paragraph #2. The second paragraph identifies the applicant organization and defines the significance of the project in terms of *what* we will accomplish and *who will benefit* from targeted activities. In essence, we describe the local context for addressing this nationwide problem: "The Marquette University School of Dentistry (MUSoD) is currently working to radically change its entire curriculum so that it is more responsive to the changing needs of students and the community." Also note that the first time we name our organization, we spell out its title in full, followed in parentheses by the acronym that we will use subsequently.

The second and third sentences in this paragraph provide specific examples of the innovative curricular reforms that we plan to implement. Redesigning the curriculum into educational "tracks," implementing case-based learning sessions called "general dental rounds," and maximizing experiential learning in community-based settings all appeal to the sponsor's hot button for innovation and reform. The fourth and fifth sentences describe two major outcomes of this initiative. Our approach will create students who are prepared as "oral physicians" rather than trained as "craftsman-clinicians" and, more importantly, will serve as a model for curricular reform in dental education nationwide—a sponsor hot button.

Paragraph #3. The third paragraph emphasizes the larger significance of our curriculum reforms in terms of their potential replicability. "Replication" is a conceptual synonym for the hot button of national impact. The opening sentence provides a concrete reason why this project could be readily implemented in a variety of postseceondary settings: Reforms are divided into manageable segments that can be gradually phased into existing dental curricula. The second sentence furnishes examples of key constituent components. For instance, in addition to developing the curriculum, this project has goals and objectives relating to enhancing faculty teaching effectiveness and to developing assessment instruments and approaches—a sponsor hot button. Together, these elements illustrate the innovative and comprehensive nature of this reform initiative.

Dental Education Reform: The MUSoD Foundational Curriculum

Dental education in the United States has traditionally been characterized by discipline-based lecture-style teaching with an emphasis on technical expertise. As the dental profession has evolved and the oral health needs of the nation have changed, curricula in US dental schools have failed to adapt to these changes. The result of stagnant dental curricula is that instruction in US dental schools is now too heavily technique-driven, with insufficient attention paid to development of critical-thinking and problem-solving skills. Additionally, current graduates are not adequately prepared to access technology-based educational/training and informational resources critical to life-long learning and professional growth.

The Marquette University School of Dentistry (MUSoD) is currently working to radically change its entire curriculum so that it is more responsive to the changing needs of students and the community. This project will implement several novel curriculum elements at MUSoD. These include comprehensive integration/reinforcement of basic science and clinical science content in continuous four-year educational "tracks", use of interdisciplinary case-based teaching approaches in the form of "General Dental Rounds", and application of acquired knowledge/skills/attitudes in community-based settings designed to maximize experiential learning. These elements are designed to create new dental graduates in the form of "oral physicians" who are recognized as much for their comprehensive approach to patient care as for the superior technically-based traditional dental services they are able to provide. Development and implementation of these elements will not only improve the quality of dental education at MUSoD, but will also serve as a model for curriculum reform in dental education nationwide.

The proposed curriculum redesign project is highly replicable because it partitions comprehensive reform into manageable areas that can be gradually phased into existing dental curricula anywhere in the world. Additionally, the approach includes an emphasis on faculty preparation/training for delivery of educational materials using newly developed teaching tools, evaluation of student progress/program effectiveness using newly developed assessment instruments, and selection of students for admission based on potential for success in a self-directed learning environment.

THE ABSTRACT

STAGE TWO: FINAL PROPOSAL

DEVELOPING THE FINAL PROPOSAL

The invitation to submit a final proposal came as a direct result of our preliminary proposal. We want to build on that success. The first step in developing the full proposal was to analyze the invitation to submit a final proposal, the reviewer comments, and the Request for Proposal (RFP) guidelines. This analysis revealed evaluation criteria, hot buttons, and distinctive features that influenced the form and structure of the final proposal. Strategic thinking and preproposal contact gave us additional information so that the details of our proposal match the values of the sponsor. These steps increase the persuasiveness of our proposal because we present the right balance of logical, emotional, and relational elements.

Because the final proposal recaps and expands on the preliminary proposal, there will be some overlap in the information presented. In fact, some sentences are repeated verbatim. The invitation to submit a final proposal also reminds us that the external reviewers for Stage Two proposals are unaware of the details of Stage One proposals. Said differently, select redundancy is a proposal strength. It shows the sponsor a level of consistency in project development, and more importantly, ideas gain strength through repetition.

The same three hot buttons that we identified for the preliminary proposal are once again addressed repeatedly throughout the final proposal: innovation and reform, national impact, and evaluation and assessment. Distinctive features in the final proposal are similar, but not identical, to those in the preliminary proposal. Both distinctive features—project director commitment and student diversity—are addressed four times in the full proposal, thus ensuring that reviewers who skim read do not miss them.

Elements of the Final Proposal

Need for the Project. The importance of this "Need for the Project" section cannot be overestimated. It provides the rationale for conducting our project. It explains to the sponsor *why* our project is necessary. Without a convincing statement of need there is no justification for proceeding. We do not assume that reviewers will see the problem as clearly as we do. Accordingly, in this section we indicate both the severity of the current problem and the shortcomings of the present situation to address the need.

In the preliminary proposal, approximately two-thirds of our narrative was dedicated to the opening two sections on project need and significance. This was necessary to convince reviewers that a significant and widespread problem existed. Once we advanced to the second stage of FIPSE's application process, we scaled down the amount of space devoted to these sections to one-fourth of the total narrative. Reducing this proportion in the final proposal allows us to establish sufficiently the context and rationale for our project and, more importantly, still have adequate space in the narrative to elaborate fully on our project design and evaluation.

Invitational Priority

In this particular "Comprehensive Program" funding competition, FIPSE had seven different invitational priorities: (1) Access, retention, and completion; (2) Improving campus climates for learning; (3) Curricular and pedagogical reform; (4) Controlling costs; (5) Faculty development; (6) Improving K–12 teaching and schools; and (7) Dissemination of successful innovations. The purpose of the first sentence in our proposal is to alert reviewers that our project addresses the sponsor's invitational priority of "Curricular and Pedagogical Reform." This single-sentence paragraph provides reviewers with a context for reading the rest of our narrative.

Magnitude of the Problem

The RFP guidelines specify that the magnitude of the problem should be described "in both its local setting and a national context." Accordingly, in this subheading we dedicate one paragraph to "national context" and one paragraph to "local context." In the preliminary proposal, we characterized the "Magnitude of the Problem" in 146 words. In this full proposal, we use 1,238 words. Said differently, although the proportion of the narrative dedicated to the project need and significance has decreased from the preliminary proposal, the overall word count has increased by nearly 1,000 words. This translates into approximately four additional pages of narrative description for these two sections.

The first paragraph describes the magnitude of the problem from a national level. This provides reviewers with the big picture perspective of the fundamental challenge in dental education; namely, dental schools in the United States have failed to adapt their curricula to meet the changing oral health needs of the nation. The first two sentences support this claim with the type of evidence that external reviewers with expertise in the subject matter would expect to see—citations from recent articles published by leading journals in the field.

I.   Need for the Project
        A.   Invitational Priority
This project responds to the FIPSE invitational priority of curricular and pedagogical reform.
        B.   Magnitude of the Problem: The Challenge for Dental Education
National Context: Dental education in the United States has traditionally been characterized by discipline-based lecture-style teaching with an emphasis on technical expertise.[1] As the dental profession has evolved and the oral health needs of the nation have changed, curricula in US dental schools have failed to adapt to these changes.[2] The current standard of care is based on advances in biomaterials, modern biology/molecular medicine, integrated interdisciplinary services, and management of complex patients. Additionally, the technology explosion has produced a wealth of web-based resources that are increasingly available to practitioners and the public. Thus, the current healthcare environment requires problem-solving and self-directed learning skills. The result of stagnant dental curricula is that instruction in US dental schools is now too heavily technique-driven, with insufficient attention paid to development of critical-thinking and problem-solving skills.[3] Additionally, current graduates are not adequately prepared to access technology-based educational/training and informational resources critical to life-long learning and professional growth.

Local Context: The current educational approach at the Marquette University School of Dentistry (MUSoD) shares this problem and MUSoD is currently working to radically change its entire curriculum so that it is more responsive to the changing needs of students and the community. This project will implement several novel curriculum elements at MUSoD. These include comprehensive integration/reinforcement of basic science and clinical science content in continuous four-year educational "tracks", use of interdisciplinary case-based teaching approaches in the form of "General Dental Rounds", and application of acquired knowledge/skills/attitudes in community-based settings designed to maximize experiential learning. These elements are designed to create new dental graduates in the form of "oral physicians" who are recognized as much for their comprehensive approach to patient care as for the superior technically-based traditional dental services they are able to provide. Development and implementation of these elements will not only improve the quality of dental education at MUSoD, but will also serve as a model for curriculum reform in dental education nationwide.

        C.   Magnitude of the Need for Project Activities
National Context: The Institute of Medicine (IOM), a part of the National Academy of Sciences, recently assembled a panel of experts from diverse backgrounds comprising dentists in private-practice, dental/medical evaluators, public health specialists, oral health researchers, and other leaders from higher education to evaluate the effectiveness of US dental education and chart a course for its future. The panel ultimately published its findings in a report entitled "Dental Education at the Crossroads: Challenges and Change."[4] This report identified major flaws in US dental education and was essentially a condemnation of the "traditional" dental curriculum. Several recommendations in the area of curricular and pedagogical reform received particular emphasis and these recommendations were as follows:

*   Achieve better integration of basic and clinical sciences in the dental curriculum.
*   Focus on outcomes and the application of scientific knowledge in clinical decision making.
*   Shift to active learning with an emphasis on critical-thinking and problems-solving skills.
*   Increase the amount of time students spend in experiential learning activities.
*   Complement clinic time with in-depth discussions of diagnosis, treatment planning, and treatment/complex interdisciplinary patient management issues.

The IOM report called for significant changes in the way dentists are trained in the United States. In response to the report, US dental schools made many well-publicized, but largely cosmetic changes to their curricula.[5] However, these modest changes do not approach the sweeping reform in dental education that the IOM recommended. To date, no US dental school has comprehensively addressed the criticisms of the IOM report.[6,7]

Local Context: MUSoD is a dental school that suffers from many of the weaknesses and problems described by the IOM report. Steeped in the traditions and long-held beliefs of classic dental education (emphasizing the student as "craftsman-clinician" rather than an "oral physician"), MUSoD has struggled to meet the challenges of educating a dentist equipped to deal with the present healthcare environment. Like other schools, MUSoD has attempted some curricular changes in response to the IOM report, but the small modifications made to date have not resulted in the outcomes desired by the IOM. Additionally, when critically evaluated, its curriculum has become a large and unwieldy mass that has grown to be primarily dependent on passive lecture-style teaching and that is weighted heavily toward the technical rather than academic aspects of the profession.

        D.   Local and National Consequences of Successful Project Completion
Improvements in the MUSoD curriculum and the manner in which it is delivered as part of this demonstration project will have three immediate local consequences. First, the changes that have been initiated will result in the eventual matriculation of students how are better prepared to serve the increasingly complex oral health needs of the citizenry. In addition to acquiring the technical skills traditionally associated with dentistry, MUSoD graduates will have

1

THE FINAL PROPOSAL

The third, fourth, and fifth sentences contrast traditional dental education programs with current dental profession practices. Dental programs place an emphasis on technical expertise, while professional practice values problem-solving and self-directed learning skills. The last two sentences state the consequences of this ever-growing gap. In the vernacular, "Dental schools are so heavily technique-driven that dental graduates are inadequately prepared to be critical-thinking professionals in their dental practices." We reinforce this claim by citing sources in the literature, i.e., from the *Journal of Dental Education*.

In the second paragraph, we put this national problem in context at the local level. The opening sentence acknowledges that the current approach to dental education at the Marquette University School of Dentistry (MUSoD) is inadequate and outmoded. More significantly, however, we are doing something about it: radically changing our entire curriculum to be more responsive to the changing needs of students and the community. The second and third sentences in this paragraph provide concrete examples of the innovative curricular reforms that we plan to implement. In essence, these sentences foreshadow the specific purpose of this funding request. At the same time, these sentences introduce the hot button of innovation and reform, which will be reiterated throughout the full proposal.

The remaining two sentences summarize the significance of these curricular changes: "These elements are designed to create new dental graduates in the form of 'oral physicians' who are recognized as much for their comprehensive approach to patient care as for the superior technically-based traditional dental services they are able to provide." The phrase "oral physicians" has particular "earworm" value; that is, like a jingle that keeps replaying in one's head, it is a phrase that will stick positively in the minds of reviewers. This phrase conveys a new level of professionalism; oral physicians will be trained to take a more holistic approach to healthcare. Equally important, this approach will serve as a model for curricular reform in dental education nationwide—a sponsor hot button. National impact is the second hot button that will be repeated throughout the narrative.

Magnitude of the Need for Project Activities

Just like in the last subheading, we describe the "Magnitude of the Need for Project Activities" in its national and local context. At the national level, we

indicate that the motivation for our curricular reforms stems from an independent assessment of dental education conducted by a prestigious scientific organization, the Institute of Medicine (IOM). Specifically, in the second and third sentences we cite the IOM report, "Dental Education at the Crossroads: Challenges and Change," as justification of the need for sweeping reform. The fourth sentence and subsequent bulleted list summarize the IOM's recommendations for a new type of dental education. These recommendations also foreshadow the intellectual framework for our "Foundational Curriculum," which will be introduced in the next section, "Significance of the Project."

In essence, the 1995 IOM report provides the baseline yardstick for what *should* be happening in dental education today. The remaining four sentences in this paragraph assert that dental schools across the country are not measuring up to this standard. Three articles published in the *Journal of Dental Education* in 1998, 1999, and 2000, respectively, document that since the IOM report was released, dental schools nationwide have only made cosmetic changes, not comprehensive revisions, to their curricula. In other words, five years after a national needs assessment was conducted, little has been done to address the identified problems.

The second paragraph describes how this national problem manifests itself at the local level. The first sentence acknowledges that the IOM report accurately characterizes the challenges MUSoD was experiencing in its dental education program. Quite simply, we admit that we have a problem. The second, third, and fourth sentences provide concrete examples of program weaknesses. Although we have attempted some changes in response to the IOM report, our curriculum still has too many separate dental courses that are taught through passive lecture—the least effective teaching style—and emphasize technical, rather than academic, aspects of the profession. Note how the second sentence repeats our "earworm" phrase to emphasize the gap between what *is* happening versus what *ought to be* happening in dental education: "emphasizing the student as 'craftsman-clinician' rather than an 'oral physician'."

Together, these two paragraphs touch on all three sponsor hot buttons. For the hot button of innovation and reform, notice the use of key phrases, such as *curricular and pedagogical reform, sweeping reform, curricular changes*. The hot button of national impact shows up once because the IOM report calls for "significant changes in the way dentists are trained *in the United States*." The third hot button of evaluation and

enhanced reasoning abilities that will enable them to provide new levels of comprehensive patient care. Second, faculty development in the use and application of evidence-based medicine and case-based learning techniques is an important part of this project. The establishment of an initial cadre of instructors capable of using these teaching methods will serve as an important mechanism in the eventual adaptation of these important curriculum delivery methods among all MUSoD faculty. Broad-scale presence of faculty with these knowledge and skills is essential to the full implementation of this new, future-directed curriculum. Third, the use of information technology to support independent self-directed learning and participation in institutional educational activities from community-based sites represents another key component of the project. This will facilitate experiential learning in real office/clinic settings and practical application of knowledge, skills, and attitudes acquired in the institutional setting. Additionally, it will help to create a faculty/student comfort level with web-based education/training and informational resources that is required for effective life-long learning and continued professional growth in the present multidisciplinary healthcare setting. Given the problems associated with current dental education described in the IOM report, successful completion of this project will have implications that extend well beyond serving local oral healthcare and educational needs. For example, the modifications MUSoD has initiated are part of a large-scale process that will have profound effects on virtually every aspect of oral health education including the selection of students, curriculum content/delivery, and the assessment of student, faculty, and institutional performance. To some degree, the curriculum that ultimately emerges from these efforts could serve as a model for many other schools of dentistry. These efforts will contribute directly towards the resolution of the conundrum defined in the IOM report.

E. Serving as a Model for Other Institutions

Because of its relatively recent issuance, insufficient time has elapsed since the emergence of the IOM report to allow any new dental educational models to emerge and be fully tested. Consequently, while several institutions around the world and a few in the US have initiated some forms of curriculum revision efforts,[3,7] as implied earlier, at this writing there are no extant models available for emulation. Thus, the pioneering efforts in curriculum revision described in this project will be closely monitored by other dental schools that would like to gain from the MUSoD experience. This is reflected in the letters of cooperation that have been obtained from dental educators at other institutions attempting curricular reforms who have agreed to serve as consultants on this endeavor (see appendix 2).

II. Significance of the Project
A. Potential Contribution of the Project to Increased Knowledge

Successful pursuit of the three goals and their associated objectives identified for this project will contribute to increased knowledge in dental education in several ways. First, we will obtain first-hand knowledge/experience with the problems, issues, and benefits to be accrued through the development and implementation of a curricular model specifically designed to integrate the principles of evidence-based medicine and critical-thinking into dental education. These efforts will provide a better understanding of how to convey these important principles to dental students. Second, we will obtain increased first-hand knowledge about how to develop/implement faculty development plans directed at enhancing the ability of dental educators to expand their cognitive and teaching capabilities beyond what has been traditionally called for in more conventional dental education. Acquisition of new knowledge in this domain is essential for dental education to progress into the next century as envisioned by the IOM report. Third, we will gain critical knowledge/experience concerning the adaptation of existing assessment instruments and the creation of new instruments for specific evaluation of case-based teaching/learning tools for dental education. Presently, dental education lags far behind other clinical professions in development and implementation of effective evaluation strategies for student progress and programmatic effectiveness related to curricula based on self-directed practically-applied teaching/learning approaches.[7,8,9]

B. Development of Promising New Strategies

Dental schools in the US have undergone an inadequately controlled expansion of the amount of course material comprising the average dental curriculum.[2] Most schools currently have 70–90 separate courses. This is the result of compartmentalization of the curriculum into the various disciplines of basic science and specialties of dentistry. MUSoD currently has 81 separate courses, most of which are primarily based on a passive-learning lecture format. These courses poorly integrate basic/clinical science and are overwhelmingly redundant. This number of courses also has produced a fragmented assessment strategy. Currently, students have 12–15 multiple-choice style examinations in a single exam week. The result of this course/assessment structure has be a "load and purge" style of education that has led to inadequate retention and ability to assimilate subject material. The MUSoD "Foundational Curriculum" offers a strategy for correcting this problem by reorganizing the curriculum into ten "tracks" which are essentially integrated multidisciplinary content sequences that facilitate more efficient teaching and more effective learning. The "tracks" will be developed with an emphasis on team teaching bringing together multiple specialties/sciences to more efficiently and effectively deliver the content and will continuously integrate basic science principles with relevant clinical correlations. Reorganization of health science curricula in this fashion has been successful in medical education,[10,11]

2

assessment is introduced in the form of the IOM report, which *evaluated the effectiveness* of U.S. dental education. It also appears in the national context in terms of the IOM's recommended *outcomes* for dental education. In the local context, this hot button occurs twice: to date, small curricular changes at MUSoD "have not resulted in the *outcomes desired* by the IOM," and "when *critically evaluated*, its curriculum has become a large and unwieldy mass." Strategic repetition of hot buttons increases the competitiveness of our proposal because it demonstrates our sensitivity to the sponsor's subjective and objective needs.

Local and National Consequences of Successful Project Completion

While the previous two subheadings follow directly from the RFP guidelines, the next two subheadings required some artistic interpretation. That is to say, the RFP guidelines formally ask applicants to describe the need for the project in terms of two factors: the "Magnitude of the Problem," and the "Magnitude of the Need for Project Activities." However, the guidelines also pose an informal series of five need-related questions. These questions group into two themes, which became the subheadings for this and the next paragraph: the "Local and National Consequences of Successful Project Completion" and "Serving as a Model for Other Institutions."

Rather than dedicating separate paragraphs to the "national context" and "local context" for successful project completion, due to space limitations we combined them into one long paragraph. Because this paragraph is so long, we also needed to include transitional devices to help guide reviewers through the information. The first sentence provides an overview of the entire paragraph, particularly indicating that improvements in the MUSoD curriculum "will have three immediate local consequences." Subsequent sentences begin with transitional words to show this sequence, e.g., "first," "second," and "third."

The first local consequence appears in the third sentence: "MUSoD graduates will have enhanced reasoning abilities that will enable them to provide new levels of comprehensive patient care." The second local consequence is described in the sixth sentence: "Broad-scale presence of faculty with these knowledge and skills [evidence-based medicine and case-based learning techniques] is essential to the full implementation of this new, future directed curriculum." The third local consequence occurs in the seventh sentence: "the use of information technology to support independent self-directed learning and participation in institutional educational activities from community-based sites represents another key component of the project." This sentence also hints at the distinctive feature of student diversity by describing equitable access and participation in the program by all major stakeholders—students, faculty, administrators, and community members.

In the tenth sentence we transition from the local consequences to the national impact of this project: "successful completion of this project will have implications that extend well beyond serving local oral healthcare and educational needs." The eleventh and twelfth sentences provide examples of the far-reaching benefits of this project. And the last sentence of the paragraph emphasizes the larger significance of this initiative, in essence saying that MUSoD can bridge the gap between dental education and professional practice nationwide: "These efforts will contribute directly towards the resolution of the conundrum defined in the IOM report."

Note how this paragraph, particularly the final four sentences, also appeals to each of the sponsor's three hot buttons. Conceptual synonyms for innovation and reform include: *improvements in the MUSoD curriculum, enhanced reasoning abilities, future-directed curriculum, profound effects on virtually every aspect of oral health education.* Key phrases for national impact include: *extend well beyond serving local oral healthcare and educational needs, large-scale process, model for many other schools of dentistry.* And evaluation and assessment is addressed by the phrase: *assessment of student, faculty, and institutional performance.*

Serving as a Model for Other Institutions

This final paragraph, in essence, summarizes the need for the project and acts as a transition to the next section on "Significance of the Project." The first and second sentences reiterate that although the IOM report identified major shortcomings in dental education programs nationwide, little has been done to improve the situation because no extant models are available for widespread emulation. The third sentence foretells the importance of this project; namely, it will be closely monitored by other dental schools that would like to gain from the MUSoD experience. The fourth sentence emphasizes this claim by referring reviewers to the appendix, which contains letters of support and commitment from dental educators at other institutions who have agreed to serve as project consultants. Note that all three hot buttons are ad-

however, due to the heavy technical training demands of dentistry, it has only been attempted in piecemeal fashion for dental education.[3,6,7] Supporting and integrating all of the didactic tracks will be case-based learning sessions termed "General Dental Rounds". The rounds will consist of small group meetings between students and faculty mentors where students will be required to present cases and defend their diagnosis/treatment decisions based on the best evidence in the literature. This format is actually a combination of the traditional problem-based and case-based teaching that has been shown to be effective in medical education.[12,13] These approaches have yet to be widely or effectively applied in dental education because they are not compatible with the time/resource environments comprising the educational model.[14,15,16] The MUSoD plan is to develop/implement a "modified" case-based approach that incorporates elements/advantages of both problem-based and case-based teaching and is ideally suited to dental education. This strategy will be carefully considered by other dental schools attempting to respond to the IOM report.

C. Importance of Results

Current dentists need to be better equipped in diagnosis/management of complex treatment plans and function more like an "oral physician." Dental school curricula have failed to recognize and respond to this need and still train the skilled technician much like their "trade school" heritage. Unfortunately, this long-established craftsman-like tradition in dental education has led to a "patch-up" mentality in the delivery of dental care in the US with dentists approaching oral healthcare delivery as a repair of disease rather than early diagnosis/prevention of disease. The present oral healthcare environment does not require the craftsman-clinician of the past (expert in fabrication of dental appliances). Instead, the community needs dentists that are far more sophisticated in the areas of diagnosis/evidence-based decision making and conversant in the management of complex medically compromised patients.[1] This curriculum reform project is designed to produce the critical-thinking doctors that represent the future of dentistry. The revisions will serve to transform dental education at MUSoD and the newly created curriculum elements could easily be implemented at other dental schools nationwide.

D. Potential Replicability

The proposed curriculum redesign project is highly replicable because it partitions comprehensive reform into manageable areas that can be gradually phased into existing dental curricula anywhere in the world. The methodologies used to coalesce related content information from existing courses into "track" sequences are readily understandable to dental faculty and provide an efficient approach to elimination of redundancy and presentation of material in an integrated multidisciplinary fashion. The concepts of continuous reinforcement and clinical application of acquired knowledge, skills, and attitudes throughout the entire four-year curriculum are not new to dental education. The existence of "artificial" separations between disciplines has simply prevented any educational approach without a specific course structure.[2,7] Additionally, an increasing amount of professional schools, including some dental schools, are now realizing the educational value of community-based experiential learning as an approach to reinforcement through practical application. Thus, the dental education community is universally prepared to embrace a model such at the MUSoD "Foundational Curriculum".

III. Project Design

A. Target Population

The primary target population of this project is dental students (MUSoD maintains a total student population of 300 comprising all four class years, 75 students per class). Secondary target populations include dental faculty (MUSoD employs 40 full-time faculty and 160 part-time faculty), dental practitioners (the State of Wisconsin maintains approximately 3,000 active clinicians), and dental patients (in the State of Wisconsin, dental services are provided to approximately 2,000,000 patients each year). The new curriculum will change the way dental education is delivered to students and will require dental faculty to "retool" in order to appropriately utilize new teaching methodologies/strategies and assessment instruments. Since many of the new curriculum approaches are also applicable to continuing education paradigms, the new curriculum will have a significant impact on practitioners and the patients they serve.

B. Research and Experience

Thus far, significant progress has been made during the initial planning phases of this project. One content sequence component (Oral Biology) of an educational "track" (Disease and Host Defense) within the "Foundational Curriculum" has been piloted. This component integrates basic science concepts related to microbiology and the clinical implications of infection. The content sequence is highly integrated with basic science and clinical faculty teaching multidisciplinary units that help students understand the fundamental pathophysiology of infectious diseases like caries and periodontal disease. The "General Dental Rounds" has also been successfully piloted and can be fully implemented once a sufficiently large cadre of faculty are trained in the use and delivery of this teaching/learning tool. The Oral Biology component and "General Dental Rounds" pilots initiated during the Fall 2000 semester received positive student, faculty, and alumni feedback. Survey and interview data were collected from 75 students, 12 faculty, and the project leader, Dr. Joseph Best. Analysis indicates that students and faculty felt that students acquired

3

dressed in this short paragraph. Key phrases include: *curriculum revision efforts, pioneering efforts in curriculum revision, attempting curricular reforms, dental education models, extant models, other dental schools,* and *be fully tested.*

Significance of the Project. The "Significance of the Project" places our curricular reforms into a larger historical context, describing the need for the project, our approach to the problem, and the anticipated immediate and long-term results. The four subheadings in this section, detailed below, are taken directly from the RFP guidelines. We characterized the "Significance of the Project" in approximately the same amount of space in the final proposal (939 words) as in the preliminary proposal (1,043 words). However, by moving much of the discussion of mechanics of our approach—the details of the "Foundational Curriculum"—into the next section on "Project Design," we were able to elaborate here on the project's importance to the postsecondary community. This, of course, means addressing all three sponsor hot buttons repeatedly throughout this section: innovation and reform, national impact, and evaluation and assessment.

Interestingly, following the RFP guidelines for this section, in a sense, means putting the cart before the horse. In this opening paragraph, the sponsor asks us to describe the potential contribution of the project to increased knowledge in dental education; however, it's not until the second paragraph that we are invited to set forth the promising new strategies that we intend to use in this project. The third and fourth paragraphs call for a description of the importance of the project outcomes and their potential to be replicated in other settings. This format forces reviewers to make inductive leaps as they read proposals—from the project's potential contributions (end products), back to proposed implementation strategies (a process approach) then forward to the significance of results and outcomes (end products). To guide reviewers through this section we use forceful opening sentences and effective transitional devices.

Potential Contribution of the Project to Increased Knowledge

Serving as an overview to the entire subheading, the first sentence indicates that this project will contribute to increased knowledge in dental education in three ways. Project contributions are listed in chronological order: (1) the second sentence focuses on the curricular model as a whole—a hot button for national impact; (2) the fourth sentence centers on enhancing

the abilities of dental educators who will be implementing the model; and (3) the sixth sentence concentrates on developing appropriate assessment instruments to evaluate the model—a hot button for evaluation and assessment. The ordering of these contributions is also deliberate in that it sets the stage for the project goals that will be presented in the upcoming section on "Project Design."

More broadly, most sentences in this paragraph work in pairs, where the first explains the specific contribution and the second describes the implications of this contribution. This dual sentence approach reinforces the immediate local and long-term national impacts of this project. Integrating literature citations from various leading journals, including an article published by two project key personnel, also lends authority to our claims.

Development of Promising New Strategies

In this subheading we present both the national and local context for our proposed curricular reform strategies. The first half of this paragraph focuses on the problems in dental education, and the second half focuses on our proposed solution. More specifically, the opening two sentences establish the national baseline for dental programs; namely, most dental schools have too many separate courses in their curriculums. The third sentence describes the consequence of this uncontrolled expansion of courses: compartmentalization of the curriculum.

The fourth and fifth sentences explain how MU-SoD compares to this national yardstick. With eighty-one separate courses, it's easy to understand that course information is overwhelmingly redundant and poorly integrated. The sixth and seventh sentences describe another failing of the MUSoD curriculum in terms of a sponsor hot button: "this number of courses has produced a fragmented assessment strategy." The eighth sentence summarizes the consequences of these shortcomings; namely, dental education students are not adequately assimilating the subject material.

The ninth and tenth sentences begin to overview our clever solution to this national problem. Appealing to the sponsor's hot button for innovation and reform, we explain that the "Foundational Curriculum" will revolutionize dental education by reorganizing the curriculum into ten "tracks," or multidisciplinary content sequences that effectively integrate basic and clinical sciences. We justify this novel approach in the eleventh sentence by documenting its successful application in a parallel health-related field, i.e., medical

significant scientific and technical knowledge. Additionally, both groups reported satisfaction with the acquisition of clinical dentistry knowledge/skills. Overall, evaluative data confirm many of the impressions of the project team and will help the team focus on issues that need to be addressed to complete the model. Data from the pilot implementation will also provide a point for future reference. Presentations at national and local meetings/symposia for various educational and professional audiences (American Dental Education Association, Wisconsin Dental Association, American Association for Dental Research) have been well received. Additionally, a major manuscript concerning the new MUSoD approach to dental education has been published by Drs. Iacopino and Wells.[7]

C. Goals, Objectives, and Outcomes

The project is an important component of a complete revision of the MUSoD curriculum. The ultimate goal is to create a new curriculum termed the "Foundational Curriculum" providing an educational framework that will enable the school to effectively address the shortcomings identified in the IOM report and thereby to educate clinicians who are capable of comprehensively serving patient oral health needs. Towards this end, three general goals have been identified for this project. These goals focus on curriculum development, enhancement of faculty teaching effectiveness, and development/implementation of assessment approaches for a case-based, practically applied curriculum. Each of these goals is accompanied by several objectives and associated outcomes (see Table 1). Upon their attainment, these goals and their attendant objectives will provide a model that can be used as a national template to broaden the scope of dental curriculum innovation and change.

Table 1: Project Goals, Objectives, and Outcomes		
Goals	**Objectives**	**Outcomes**
Goal 1: Develop three curriculum "tracks" (Biomedical Systems, Disease and Host Response, and Community-Based Education).	1) Combine basic and clinical science content into fully integrated continuous four-year curriculum "tracks". 2) Create clinical learning environments that mimic private practices in community-based settings 3) Develop educational milestones and associated behavioral markers to monitor student progress towards clinical competency. 4) Fully implement "General Dental Rounds". 5) Develop CD-ROM/web-based teaching modules and educational resources.	1) Development/implementation of Biomedical Systems, Disease and Host Response, and Community-Based Education curriculum "tracks". 2) Creation of twenty self-directed learning modules. 3) Demonstrated improvements in student progress through academic sequences. 4) Increased student participation in "active" learning with a corresponding decrease in less effective "static" learning methods. 5) Increased faculty/student satisfaction and comfort with integrative case-based educational approaches and electronic learning media.
Goal 2: Faculty development to support implementation of curriculum "tracks", case-based teaching, evaluation methodologies, and student success.	1) Train faculty in the process of identifying scientific/clinical concepts that must be integrated and reinforced in the curriculum "tracks". 2) Train faculty to direct "General Dental Rounds". 3) Train faculty to produce CD-ROM/web-based learning modules. 4) Train faculty in providing guidance for experiential learning in community-based clinical environments. 5) Train faculty in recruitment/interview skills and methods to enhance student success in integrative case-based and applied educational environments.	1) Creation of a group of faculty capable of developing curriculum "tracks". 2) Creation of a group of faculty capable of leading "General Dental Rounds". 3) Increased generation of self-directed CD-ROM instructional modules and web-based cases for teaching applications. 4) Increased use of teledentistry and videoconferencing at remote sites. 5) Measurable improvement in faculty/student abilities to lead and attitudes towards engaging in orchestrated small-group instruction. 6) A recruitment/interview process that improves overall student success. 7) Improved teaching skills and student performance.

4

education. Further, we cite several journal articles that explain why this approach has not caught on in dental education before now.

The twelfth and thirteenth sentences describe the value-added strategy that will make this curricular reform a success. Namely, case-based learning sessions, called "general dental rounds," will support the integration of principles learned in the didactic tracks. We justify this strategy in the fourteenth sentence by citing its effectiveness in medical education. General dental rounds combine traditional problem-based and case-based teaching. The fifteenth sentence documents from the literature the innovativeness (i.e., a hot button) of this curricular reform approach: "these approaches have yet to be widely or effectively applied in dental education."

The remaining two sentences bring the paragraph full circle, emphasizing how the MUSoD experience will benefit the larger dental education community nationwide. The sixteenth and seventeenth sentences summarize why this modified case-based approach will be of interest to other dental schools attempting to respond to the IOM report. Namely, our model addresses an important behavioral principle: *Organization prevents reorganization.* That is, being organized one way makes it difficult to be organized another way. Because dental programs are organized into courses, it prevents them from being organized into didactic tracks. MUSoD is at a unique point in its evolution where faculty and administration are ready to design a new curriculum without regard for what was done in the past, to adopt a new system of curricular organization. Establishing a viable model for change that produces enhanced learning outcomes will motivate others to want to change as well.

Importance of Results

This paragraph on "Importance of Results" takes a national perspective on improvements in student achievement outcomes. Twice in the proposal we foreshadowed the notion of dental students of the twenty-first century being prepared as "oral physicians" rather than "craftsman-clinicians." Now we elaborate on this concept. The opening sentence states the reality of today's situation, "Current dentists need to be better equipped in diagnosis/management of complex treatment plans and function more like an 'oral physician.'" The second, third, and fourth sentences confirm that institutional inertia has prevented dental schools from responding to the changing oral health needs of the community.

The fifth and sixth sentences define a vision for the future of dentistry. In particular, dentists need to be critical-thinking doctors who are sophisticated in the areas of diagnosis/evidence-based decision making and conversant in the management of complex, medically compromised patients. By changing the fundamental approach to dental education, i.e., the "Foundational Curriculum," we can significantly alter and improve learning outcomes. Of note, the final two sentences of this paragraph systematically address the sponsor hot buttons of innovation and reform and of national impact: this curriculum reform project will transform dental education at MUSoD and has the potential to be implemented at other dental schools nationwide.

Potential Replicability

The final subheading in this section, "Potential Replicability," speaks to the hot button of national impact. Each of the first five sentences in this paragraph specify one reason why this project could be readily implemented in a variety of settings: (1) reforms are divided into manageable segments that can be gradually phased into existing dental curricula; (2) methodologies for developing "track" sequences are readily understandable to dental faculty; (3) concepts of continuous reinforcement and clinical application are familiar in dental education; (4) "track" sequences provide a structure for interdisciplinary teaching; and (5) community-based experiential learning is taking on greater importance in dental education.

These five reasons appeal to multiple audiences—administrators, faculty, students, and the community. They also hint at the distinctive feature of student diversity by demonstrating our commitment to inclusive "buy-in" and participation from all major stakeholders. The last sentence in this paragraph summarizes that, for these collective reasons, the larger dental education community will also embrace the MUSoD "Foundational Curriculum."

Project Design. In the preliminary proposal, the sections on "Project Design" and "Project Evaluation" together made up one-third of the total narrative. In the final proposal, the section on "Project Design" alone makes up more than half of our narrative. With more than 4,209 words (approximately fifteen pages), it is by far the most detailed section in the entire proposal. The "Project Design" tells the sponsor *what* we are going to do to solve the identified problem, *how* we will accomplish our objectives, *when* key project activ-

Goal 3: Develop assessment methods to monitor project progress, student/faculty performance, and student/faculty satisfaction.	1) Develop computer-based simulations designed to provide ongoing self-assessments. 2) Develop/refine use of standardized patients for assessment of comprehensive knowledge, skills, and attitudes. 3) Develop Objective Structured Clinical Examinations (OSCE's) for use in assessing clinical decision making. 4) Develop a portfolio assessment system to evaluate student clinical outcomes. 5) Refine existing teaching surveys to assess faculty performance and the effectiveness of faculty development efforts. 6) Refine existing surveys (Student Exit, Alumni, and Competency Completion) to determine student perceptions of effectiveness and change. 7) Develop faculty/student peer assessment systems.	1) Creation of assessment instruments that can be used for formative and summative evaluations of the new curriculum initiatives. 2) Provide feedback to faculty to improve teaching effectiveness. 3) Provide information/data that can be used by other institutions to replicate these initiatives.

D. Detailed Description of Project Goals/Objectives: Management/Timetable

Goal 1: Creating Three New Didactic "Tracks"

"Track 1" – Biomedical Systems: This "track" will cover material from anatomy, histology, physiology, and pathology courses utilizing a systematic review of biological organ systems. In this way, a unit that covers the respiratory system will start with normal anatomy, histology, and physiology of the lung and then proceed to discuss respiratory pathophysiology. Ultimately, the respiratory unit will be tied together with practical exercises and cases in "General Dental Rounds" concerning the management of dental patients with respiratory disease. The intent is for material related to an organ system to be presented as a module and ultimately the clinical implications for managing patients with problems related to that particular organ system. This approach provides integration of basic/clinical science and will help students better understand/retain clinically relevant information.[17]

"Track 2" – Disease and Host Defense: This "track" will be designed to provide a comprehensive and integrated review of topics related to systemic/oral diseases, host response mechanisms, disease progression, and disease interventions. Emphasis will be place on how various basic science and clinical science content areas relate to each other relative to disease, hot defense, and treatment. The current Oral Biology pilot content sequence designed in the preliminary phase of the "Foundational Curriculum" used they type of integration effectively for the areas of periodontology, microbiology, cariology, and immunology providing a working model for continued development of this "track". Additionally, it provides an example of the types of collaborative efforts required to design "tracks" in general.

"Track 3" – Community-Based Education: This "track" will introduce students to the practice of dentistry in settings that mimic private practice and community clinics. In addition to the scientific and clinical aspects (patient assessment, diagnosis, and treatment planning) and technical aspects (restoration of teeth and fabrication of appliances) of dental practice, there will be exposure to the biopsychosocial aspects of practice. Behavioral sciences, jurisprudence, ethics, practice management, and issues related to public health/community dentistry will be addressed in this applied "track". This full spectrum of student extramural community experiences will have increasing importance as students progress through the four-year educational period participating in increasing amounts of experiential learning.

Establishment of Task Forces to Formulate Each Didactic "Track": Two project faculty members will serve on each of three task forces (one for each didactic "track"). Each task force will meet weekly in project year one to create specific goals, objectives, and outcomes for each track. Content analysis of the IOM report, the 2001 Surgeon General report, accreditation materials, and other relevant curricular guidelines will be utilized to initiate the process. This will produce a description of activities and sequencing of content/educational experiences for each "track". The

5

ities will occur, *who* is responsible for project activities, *who will benefit* from targeted activities, and *what results* will occur.

The RFP guidelines formally call for two specific subheadings in this section: (1) "Goals, Objectives, and Outcomes"; and (2) "Replication of Project Activities." In addition, the guidelines also informally request a project dissemination plan. Following a strict interpretation of the RFP guidelines, however, would mean not being able to tell reviewers all of the details that we felt they needed to know about our project. For instance, because the sponsor values that "learners should be the principal beneficiaries of your project," we included a subheading on the "Target Population." Further, because we had already piloted one content sequence of an educational "track" and the general dental rounds, we included a subheading on our "Research and Experience."

For all practical purposes, providing reviewers with two additional "unsolicited" paragraphs of valuable information was a rather innocent deviation from the RFP guidelines. More significant, however, was our decision to synthesize two subsequent sections, "The Quality of the Management Plan" and "The Quality of Project Personnel," into this one on "Project Design." After much internal debate, the Proposal Development Committee concluded that it would be easier for reviewers to understand our project design if we included details about key personnel, their qualifications, and timelines and milestones here, rather than listing this information in later sections of the proposal.

In our case, following the RFP guidelines exactly would have meant either: (a) repeating much of the information about the project design in the management plan section; or (b) running the risk of confusing reviewers because the details describing which personnel are responsible for which specific activities are located so far apart in the narrative. Neither were encouraging options. Thus, we made a conscious decision to deviate from the guidelines. We attempt to communicate this change to reviewers by strategically including the key words "Management/Timetable" in the fourth subheading.

Target Population

This paragraph specifies *which* and *how many* people will benefit from this dental education reform project. Notice the multiplier effect as we describe our target population in terms of primary and secondary audiences. The first sentence explains that 75 dental education students per class, or a total of 300 students, will be the direct beneficiaries of project activities. In the second sentence we point out that in addition to these students, more than 200 dental faculty, 3,000 dental practitioners, and 2,000,000 dental patients throughout the state of Wisconsin will also benefit from this project. The third and fourth sentences suggest that the curricular reforms may be able to reach an even larger audience of dental practitioners and patients *on an ongoing basis* via continuing education programs. Due to the significant numbers of individuals touched by this project, this paragraph, in effect, is also a subtle way of hinting at a distinctive feature raised in our preliminary proposal: cost-effectiveness.

Research and Experience

The purpose of this paragraph on "Research and Experience" is to establish the viability of our implementation design and the credibility of our faculty to carry it out. It elaborates on the activities, first introduced in our preliminary proposal, that were piloted during the initial planning phases of this project—one track within the "Foundational Curriculum" and the general dental rounds. The seventh sentence names our project leader, Dr. Joseph Best, and the last sentence identifies two other key personnel, Dr. Anthony Iacopino and Dr. Linda Wells. These sentences also pave the way for addressing in subsequent sections the distinctive feature of project director commitment.

In a sense, this paragraph represents a condensed version of the entire proposal. That is, the first six sentences describe project activities, the next five sentences explain how project activities were evaluated and how evaluation results were used, and the final two sentences indicate how project results were disseminated to the larger postsecondary community. Hot buttons are woven throughout the paragraph. Innovation and reform appears in terms of the integration of basic and clinical science into one educational track within the "Foundational Curriculum." National impact emerges in terms of the national symposia and publications where project results have been presented. Evaluation and assessment presents itself in terms of the survey and interview data that was collected from students, faculty, and alumni.

Goals, Objectives, and Outcomes

This subheading on "Goals, Objectives, and Outcomes" describes how we intend to solve, at MUSoD, the problems identified by the IOM report. Goals represent the long-range benefits we hope to accomplish.

institutional curriculum analysis tools (CATS) system will be utilized to organize the foundational knowledge/clinical concepts that are identified. "Tracks" will be developed and then reviewed by a team of three institutional faculty for appropriate inclusion of foundational knowledge and clinical concepts. Two out of three team members will need to agree for acceptance. Also during project year one, faculty members will be trained on how to implement the "tracks" in the teaching program. Six in-services (full-day retreats) will be required of all faculty members during project year one with "booster" sessions being offered in each semester of project year two. The "tracks" will be implemented in project years two and three with semesterly meetings of each task force to assess the effectiveness of the track components. Dr. Best will be responsible for creating the task forces and monitoring their progress. Drs. Taft and Iacopino will coordinate/facilitate the in-services. Drs. Taft and Donate-Bartfield will develop/implement assessment instruments specific for each track in order to review written descriptions of the educational experience.

Establish Clinical Milestone Criteria: Classically, in both medical and dental education, the first two years of school are dedicated to the basic sciences followed by clinical training in the final two years. Many medical schools are now moving away from this long-accepted method of training and are integrating basic science and clinical training throughout the four-year curriculum.[10] As part of the MUSoD "Foundational Curriculum", first-year dental students will immediately enter the clinic and work as dental assistants for their third- and fourth-year colleagues, while third- and fourth-year students will spend more time on exercises designed to reinforce basic science applications in clinical practice. This will allow first-year students to see the clinical relevance of the science they are learning while allowing more time for senior students to reinforce the link between basic and clinical science. Students will work through a set of "milestones" to achieve competence in various aspects of clinical care. Students will achieve milestones by working through specific didactic and pre-clinical exercises and once an "applied" assessment is passed, the student will be given "privileges" to provide that level of care. For example, first-year students will be privileged to provide dental prophylaxis (cleaning) by the end of the first semester of training. This is a dramatic departure from the traditional dental curriculum with students not actively treating patients until their third year. The goal of these changes is to have students progressively obtain more clinical responsibility and to integrate science and clinical patient care.

Develop/Implement Comprehensive "General Dental Rounds": General Dental Rounds will be established as an ongoing teaching/learning tool that integrates all curriculum "tracks". Dr. Best will be responsible for the establishment of rounds in collaboration with the project faculty. "General Dental Rounds" will be assessed by Drs. Taft and Donate-Bartfield throughout the project period. In project year one, faculty members will be trained by external consultants in how to properly direct case-based learning sessions through "General Dental Rounds". In project years two and three, faculty members will be expected to implement case-based rounds for students in the "tracks". The rounds will consist of small group meetings between students and mentor faculty where students will be required to present cases and defend their treatment decisions based on the best evidence in the literature. This type of case-based patient-centered teaching has been shown to be an effective teaching/learning tool in medicine but has yet to be used effectively in dental education.[12,13,15,16,17] Using rounds, MUSoD will create a dental graduate that is a critical-thinking doctor capable of evidence-based decision making. This exercise will require active critical-thinking on the part of students and faculty alike.

Develop CD-ROM/Web-Based Self-Directed Teaching Modules: Drs. Robinson and Iacopino will develop CD-ROM/web-based self-direct teaching modules for each "track" in collaboration with the respective task forces. These will be used by students/faculty to acquire basic knowledge and participate in "General Dental Rounds" both on and off site. These types of teaching modules have been very effective in dental/medical education.[12,13,15,16] The modules will be assessed by Drs. Taft and Donate-Bartfield throughout the project period. Modifications will be made as necessary by Drs. Robinson and Iacopino. The modules will be created in project year one for implementation in project years two and three. The modules will be assessed and refined as needed each semester by Drs. Robinson and Iacopino.

Goal 2: Faculty Development

Currently, faculty members in dental schools have been educated within the same basic fashion. Few have spent any significant time studying the educational process either formally or informally and have formed their "model of education" from interactions with faculty where they were trained.[3,5] For a new model of dental education to emerge at MUSoD, it will be critical that all full-time and part-time faculty participate in an ongoing multi-dimensional development program that focuses on providing them with elements/skill sets that are necessary to deliver the new curriculum. The faculty development program will involve two primary components. The first of these will be oriented at providing programming that will allow the faculty to appreciate the key scientific and clinical concepts that need to be included in the didactic curriculum and that need to be reinforced through inclusion in one-on-one teaching opportunities on the clinic floor. Introduction of the concepts involved in utilizing evidence-based decision making strategies will be included in this component of the faculty development program. This aspect of the program will be coordinated by a team of faculty led by Drs. Taft and Iacopino (Administrative Director of the MUSoD Faculty Development Committee). The team will include DDS/PhD trained individuals and external consultants who are

6

Objectives are the specific, measurable steps that will help us to reach our goals. Outcomes are the humanistic results of our project. Clearly, an intimate relationship exists among project goals, objectives, and outcomes. We illustrate this relationship in Table 1.

The first and second sentences of this paragraph summarize the ultimate goal of this project in terms of two hot buttons: innovation and reform (i.e., "a complete revision of the MUSoD curriculum"), and national impact (i.e., "providing an educational framework"). The third and fourth sentences overview that this project has three synergistic and interrelated goals. These goals provide the conceptual orientation for understanding how we will create a new "Foundational Curriculum." Indeed, the comprehensive nature of this project necessitated that we "chunk" it up into several broad areas: developing the curriculum, enhancing faculty teaching effectiveness, and developing/implementing assessment approaches (i.e., a hot button).

Although these are valuable goals, as we indicate in the fifth sentence, they cannot stand by themselves. They need to be followed by concrete objectives, which will produce associated outcomes. Project objectives are designed to be SIMPLE—specific, immediate, measurable, practical, logical, and evaluable. No single objective can fulfill a single goal; a series of objectives must work in tandem to satisfy a project goal. The final sentence of the paragraph, again, appeals to the hot buttons of innovation and reform and of national impact to describe the broader significance of MUSoD achieving project goals, objectives, and outcomes: "provide a model that can be used as a national template to broaden the scope of dental curriculum innovation and change."

The RFP guidelines want to know "the extent to which the goals, objectives, and outcomes to be achieved by the proposed project are clearly specified and measurable." Accordingly, we provide a table that illustrates the relationship between project goals, objectives, and outcomes. Reviewers can quickly recognize linkages inherent to the project, ones that may otherwise go unnoticed if described in narrative format alone. For instance, reviewers understand in:

- Goal 1 the relationship between curriculum "tracks," educational milestones, and improvements in student progress.
- Goal 2 the association between faculty development training, guidance for experiential learning in community-based clinical environments, and increased use of teledentistry and videoconferencing at remote sites.

- Goal 3 the connection between assessment methods, a portfolio system to evaluate student clinical outcomes, and improved teaching effectiveness.

The added value of Table 1 is that we can demonstrate project activities and results are significant, realistic, and manageable, without burying them in a morass of narrative.

Detailed Description of Project Goals/Objectives

This subheading is the heart of the proposal. It makes up a full one-third of the total narrative (2,776 words). Fourteen paragraphs describe, in expanded detail, the activities associated with the project goals and objectives presented in Table 1. While the length of the description for each goal varies, in each case we follow a similar format. First we indicate *what* major activities will be taking place. Then we draw on recent literature to justify *why* we are using this approach. Next we identify the timeframes *when* activities will occur. And finally we articulate exactly *who* will be responsible for coordinating project activities. Collectively, these paragraphs appeal broadly to the hot button of innovation and reform; the idea of transforming a curriculum with 80 distinct courses into a "Foundational Curriculum" with ten multidisciplinary content sequences is clearly unique to the field of dental education.

Goal 1: Creating Three New Didactic "Tracks." Seven paragraphs are used to explain goal one. The first three paragraphs overview the content of the three new didactic tracks while the fourth paragraph describes the administrative processes by which tracks will be developed and assessed (i.e., a hot button). The third paragraph also relates the didactic track of "community-based education" to the distinctive feature of student diversity: "This full spectrum of student extramural community experiences will have increasing importance as students progress through the four-year educational period participating in increasing amounts of experiential learning."

The fifth paragraph draws on current literature to document the trend in medical education of integrating basic science and clinical training throughout the four-year curriculum; at the same time, we contend that dental education should also follow this trend. We provide a concrete example of how this integration could be achieved, using "milestones" as evidence of clinical competence. The final two sentences of this paragraph are taken verbatim from our prelimi-

currently providers of this form of education at other dental schools (see letters of support in appendix 2). The external consultants will lead two full-day faculty retreats addressing this area each semester of year one and one such retreat in the first semester of year two. It is anticipated that the training will occur by means of self-study modules based on actual clinical dental cases that provide an opportunity for faculty to review the basic and clinical sciences concepts that are crucial to an adequate diagnosis/treatment plan for the patient. These modules will be supplemented with opportunities for faculty to participate in seminars where unique cases are presented and interactive discussions take place concerning the critical scientific concepts present in the cases that will be influential in diagnosis/treatment planning decisions.

The second primary component will consist of several opportunities to develop instructional/teaching skills. These opportunities will be as follows:

- Development of skills necessary to effectively lead small group, case-based seminars involving use of an evidence-based protocol including specifically how to conduct/facilitate an effective "General Dental Rounds" session.
- Utilization of technology in the delivery of "learning modules". This area will include instruction on developing and utilizing power-point presentations, setting up and delivering courses through use of Internet tools/software packages, and utilizing web-based resources in the instructional process including electronic reference searches.
- One-on-one teaching skills to enhance the clinical teaching environment. This unit will be particularly oriented to the development of appropriate questioning strategies designed to prompt students to recognize and solve patient treatment issues leading to effective diagnosis, treatment plan development, and care delivery without significant intervention by the dental faculty member.

Development of these activities will also be accomplished by a team of faculty lead by Dr. Taft (Director of Educational Development and Assessment). This team will include Dr. Robinson (Director of Dental Informatics), Dr. Donate-Bartfield (Clinical Psychology/Dental Education background), and external consultants who currently function in this role at other dental schools (see appendix 2). The activities will consist of self-study modules combined with seminars/workshops conducted by the external consultants during the first semester of years one and two. The development of skills necessary to facilitate the case-based sessions will need to involve many MUSoD faculty. It might be necessary to adopt a "train-the-trainers" approach, where a small core of MUSoD faculty are highly trained in these skills and then conduct the training of other faculty on a continuing basis. This "train-the-trainer" strategy will also be utilized in several of the development areas as the most efficient and acceptable way to maintain and upgrade faculty competence. Additionally, the training will continue to be available to new MUSoD faculty members. Support is requested to advance the efforts of the existing development program and to provide the resources necessary for our initial efforts. Long-term maintenance of this development program including an ongoing development program directed at all new faculty as well as at maintaining the skills of existing faculty will be supported by MUSoD as part of its general operation.

Goal 3: Development of Assessment Methods/Instruments
Proper assessment of students and programming utilizing problem-based and/or case-based formats remains a huge question. The types of assessments used are not always appropriate or consistent with the way students learn in this setting (context of working problems). Additionally, many dental schools that have experimented with these approaches do not utilize them across the entire curriculum.[15,18] They may be used piecemeal in certain courses or parts of courses. Additionally, there has been a rush toward implementation with little regard for evaluation. Thus far, most of the evaluative work has relied on traditional tests of content knowledge to compare the approaches to traditional achievement rather than on measures which assess the specific curricular goals/learning outcomes of the methods. The MUSoD case-based approach will emphasize continuous formative evaluation, particularly with instruments that promote self-directed learning. In addition, since case-based approaches represent diverse ways of learning, evaluation should utilize diverse methods of assessment. Since no single assessment method is adequate, use of multiple distinct instruments is required to obtain a fair judgement about student abilities and program effectiveness. Medical schools have recently started to utilize a wide variety of formative and summative processes to assess knowledge, problem-solving skills, practical skills, and professional attitudes.[2,3,4] Since such a wide range of assessment instruments is already available, MUSoD proposes to concentrate on coming up with the right combination of existing instruments rather than developing new ones. Most of these can probably be adapted to suit the needs of dental education.

A continuous program evaluation process will be used to assure that adequate documentation is available for all aspects of the project. A modified Stufflebeam CIPP model will be used. An important aspect of this model is use of

7

nary proposal: we emphasize the innovativeness (i.e., a hot button) of this approach, "This is a *dramatic departure* from the traditional dental curriculum"; we articulate the practical benefits of these reforms, "the goal of these changes is to have students progressively obtain more clinical responsibility and to integrate science and patient care."

The sixth paragraph justifies our methodology of using general dental rounds to reinforce the learning that takes place in the didactic tracks. Recent literature confirms that conducting problem-based learning sessions is well-established in medical education, and now we intend to systematically apply it to dental education. The final two sentences in this paragraph articulate the humanistic outcomes of this approach: dental education students will develop their critical-thinking skills and will be capable of making evidence-based decisions.

The seventh paragraph describes how a CD-ROM for self-directed, independent learning will be developed for each didactic track. Again, a series of literature citations document the effectiveness of this approach in both dental and medical education. This paragraph is also a subtle way of hinting at the distinctive feature of cost-effectiveness raised in our preliminary proposal. That is, once the master disk is completed, CD-ROMs are inexpensive to produce and can be used repeatedly by dental students.

Goal 2: Faculty Development. Three paragraphs are dedicated to describing goal two: faculty development. The first paragraph describes how faculty will be oriented to the key scientific and clinical concepts that need to be included in the didactic curriculum and reinforced through one-on-one teaching opportunities in clinical settings. The second paragraph provides a bulleted list of instructional/teaching skills that will be imparted to dental education faculty. The third paragraph addresses the logistics of this faculty development program—*who* will be responsible for doing *what* and *when*. And because faculty development is not a one-time event, in the last sentence of this paragraph we lay out our long-term technical and financial plans for reaching current and new faculty. This sentence, in effect, hints at the project's cost-effectiveness: "an ongoing development program directed at all new faculty as well as at maintaining the skills of existing faculty will be supported by MU-SoD as part of its general operation."

Goal 3: Development of Assessment Methods/Instruments. In four paragraphs we elaborate on our approach to goal three: development of assessment methods and instruments. The first paragraph describes the baseline situation about student assessment practices in dental education; namely, they are inadequately and inconsistently applied. In contrast, we will use a variety of formative and summative evaluations (i.e., a hot button) to assess students' knowledge, problem-solving skills, practical skills, and professional attitudes. This approach is consistent with the latest practices in medical education documented in the literature. Moreover, in the final two sentences of this paragraph we confirm that we will not reinvent the wheel; rather, valid and reliable tools used in assessing medical students will be adapted to meet the needs of dental education.

The second paragraph defines the program evaluation as a continuous process of assessment, which will be integrated into a larger evaluation plan for the entire dental school. Assessment data will be collected on an ongoing basis with formal reports being produced annually. The third paragraph expands upon the content of the evaluation reports. We specify that our program evaluation will focus separately on student performance (i.e., goal 1) and faculty performance (i.e., goal 2). We even provide examples of existing assessment tools and protocols that will be adapted to gather baseline and primary data. More broadly, the value of these evaluation reports is that they can be used by other dental schools to replicate project outcomes (i.e., a hot button for national impact).

In a bulleted list format, the fourth paragraph defines the standards that will be used in judging the results of the evaluation. Just like in the preliminary proposal, we describe a sample of the specific types of outcomes tools that will be used to measure project performance. Moreover, because the invitation to submit a final proposal strongly recommended that applicants engage an independent evaluator, we acknowledge in the second bulleted point that we took this suggestion seriously. Our project assessment will: (1) be conducted by a team of faculty in collaboration with an external evaluator; (2) occur *during* and *beyond* the granting period; and (3) examine changes in students' dental knowledge, attitudes, and behaviors. At a glance, reviewers can see the comprehensive nature of our evaluation approach.

Replication of Project Activities

"Replication" is a conceptual synonym for national impact. Hence, this entire subheading is a hot button.

formative assessments. Evaluation of the project will be integrated into the ongoing outcome assessment process utilized at MUSoD. Separate documentation will be maintained to facilitate reporting and to provide appropriate data that can be used by other dental schools to replicate project outcomes. An evaluation team led by Drs. Taft and Donate-Bartfield will manage the evaluation process. To initiate the process, an evaluation plan will developed during year one that identifies timelines, data sources, reporting protocols, and outcome measures. This evaluation plan will involve a continuous process of data collection with interim reports designed to assess progress and yearly reports focused on project outcomes. Input from interested groups such as students, faculty, dental practitioners, and government officials will be used to ensure that assessment strategies provide adequate information for each of these stakeholders.

Progress on the project will be monitored and assessed using a variety of formative evaluation methods that focus separately on student and faculty performance. The effects of curriculum revisions described in association with our first goal on student performance will be measured by student surveys, faculty satisfaction surveys, focus groups designed to allow students/faculty/staff to provide input regarding changes and to make suggestions for modifications, and by input from various advisory groups including the institutional advisory group to the Dean. Results will be reported by the evaluation team to the institutional Administrative Council as all other outcomes data is handled. Formative assessments of faculty performance in association with our second goal will include comparisons of course syllabi and teaching methods as well as use of new assessment strategies by the evaluation team that augment currently existing materials. Students will continue to share their opinions using the battery of course, laboratory, and clinical assessment instruments already in place in the institution. Those instruments will be modified to include appropriate questions where appropriate. The school is currently examining a web-based evaluation process that, if adopted, will provide a seamless environment for gathering this data and summarizing the results for the evaluation team.

Faculty/student progress during the project will be measured using the following outcome tools:
- Monitoring performance of MUSoD students on National Dental Board exams part I. Outcomes obtained in the third year of the project will be compared with MUSoD student performance levels in prior and subsequent years.
- The evaluation team with the assistance of the external evaluator will develop a comprehensive case-oriented exam to be administered at the end of the first year to students who have not experienced the proposed changes. The same instrument will be administered to those students who do undergo these curriculum changes and performance will be compared. A variety of data points exist for all students who enter the school and these will be used as covariates in the analysis of differences between the two groups. A more ideal research design would have the new curriculum introduced to a pilot group matched in characteristics to another group receiving traditional instructional concurrently, however, a variety of ethical/practical problems will not permit that approach. Thus, we will rely on statistical methods to account for any violations in external validity that are created.
- Administering exit examinations to evaluate student understanding of comprehensive care issues and application of basic science principles to clinical problem-solving.
- Tracking MUSoD dental student professional behavior after graduation by using post-graduation surveys to measure scope of practice issues, comfort level with management of medically complicated patients, and continued exposure to current literature in clinical dentistry.
- During the years two and three of this project, student productivity increases should be evident. Current clinical management software will allow tracking and reporting of these changes.

E. Replication of Project Activities

For goal one, the key consideration for project replication involves manpower issues related to curricular redesign. MUSoD maintains one of the smallest dental faculty nationwide. Thus, other dental schools have a larger faculty pool that might participate in such a project independent of external support. The biggest obstacles to implementation/delivery of case-based approaches are cost/manpower issues.[14,15] The MUSoD model for case-based rounds utilizes student facilitators to augment faculty coverage. Faculty will work with selected students in their junior year to train them to lead case-based discussion sessions. This is an important component of student maturation and the culmination ("capstone") of the four-year educational experience. Senior students will be "rewarded" with the prestige and honor of facilitating rounds sessions among their peers. Additionally, it provides capable students with an additional learning experience as well as motivation to consider a faculty/teaching career. For goal two, the main issue to consider is the institutional infrastructure that supports faculty development. Fortunately, current accreditation requirements force all dental schools to maintain a meaningful and active faculty development program with a significant budget.[19] Many schools have an administrative director for faculty development and maintain faculty development committees. Thus, most dental schools should be able to support the programming outlined in this project. For goal three, similarly, accreditation requirements mandate that all dental schools maintain a significant

8

Note the use of words and phrases such as: *replication, nationwide, other dental schools, all dental schools, can be reproduced*. Quite simply, the sponsor views the potential replicability of a project in other postsecondary settings as a means of leveraging its limited funding. The RFP guidelines also indicate, "Before a project can become a model, however, its proponents must be able to prove that it has achieved its aims in its original setting." Thus we also integrate the hot button of evaluation and assessment in this paragraph, using the following key words: *outcomes and assessment, administrative director for outcomes/assessment, faculty assessment teams, evaluation budget, evaluation plan*.

This paragraph on "Replication of Project Activities" systematically pinpoints the elements within each project goal that can be reproduced in other dental schools nationwide. The opening sentence identifies "manpower" as the key issue related to our goal of developing three curriculum tracks. Subsequently, we provide two reasons why manpower will not be a barrier to curricular redesign in other settings: (1) sentences two, three, and four confirm that MUSoD maintains one of the smallest dental faculty nationwide, saying, in the vernacular, "If we can do it, larger dental schools certainly can do it too" and (2) sentences five, six, seven, and eight explain how using student facilitators to lead case-based discussion sessions is an organic way of augmenting faculty manpower. Sentence nine describes another added value of using student facilitators—these learning experiences may motivate dental students to pursue faculty/teaching careers.

In the tenth sentence we identify "institutional infrastructure" as the key issue related to our goal of enhancing faculty teaching effectiveness. The next three sentences justify why most dental schools will easily be able to assimilate new educational processes into their programs. Namely, accreditation standards require dental schools to maintain an active faculty development program with a significant budget. We document this claim by citing appropriate journal references.

A similar argument is used to justify the availability of an "institutional infrastructure" for realizing our goal of developing assessment methods to monitor project progress, performance, and participant satisfaction. The fourteenth and fifteenth sentences, once again, defer to published literature to confirm that most dental schools have an established outcomes and assessment program because it is mandated by the national bodies governing the accreditation of dental education programs. The last sentence summarizes that, for these reasons, MUSoD and other dental schools nationwide already have the human and capital resources in place to reproduce project activities.

Dissemination Plan

The RFP guidelines specify that "all proposed projects should include plans for disseminating their findings." As grants become increasingly competitive, dissemination of project outcomes takes on increasing importance. It's a way for sponsors to get "more bang for their buck" by sharing with others the details of successful projects: their purpose, methods, and results. In this case, FIPSE hopes that when other postsecondary institutions learn about new educational models, they will adopt or adapt these innovative approaches to their own situations. Thus, the sponsor is able to leverage its limited funding to achieve a national impact.

Dissemination offers many advantages, including increasing public awareness of common problems and potential solutions, soliciting additional support, locating more clients, alerting others in the field to new ideas, and adding to the stockpile of knowledge. The first two sentences in this subheading reiterate the successes we have already had sharing the results of our pilot activities with the dental education community. In particular, we used two forms of dissemination that are typical in higher education: conference presentations and journal publications.

The third sentence transitions from what we have already done to what we plan to do to promote our project. Beyond giving presentations at professional meetings and publishing in peer-reviewed journals, the final three sentences of this paragraph describe three additional dissemination strategies: a project Web site, electronic newsletters sent to listservs, and instructional materials. Said differently, we use a variety of different dissemination techniques to reach different audiences—administrators, faculty, practitioners, and consumers.

In hindsight, we could have made this description stronger by including additional details such as the names and locations of professional meetings, the names of targeted journals, the names of specific listservs, and the names of commercial distributors who might produce or market instructional materials. Because some dissemination approaches have costs associated with them, we reflect this fact in the budget and budget narrative.

Note that we also touch on the distinctive feature

outcomes and assessment program.[19] Again, most schools have an administrative director for outcomes/assessment, faculty assessment teams, and a significant evaluation budget. Thus, the expertise and support mechanisms are in place at most dental schools such that the proposed evaluation plan can be reproduced.

F. Dissemination Plan

The MUSoD initiative has already sparked interest from other dental schools struggling with similar issues. As described previously, faculty involved in curriculum development have recently presented progress reports at national/local meetings and symposia and have published a major manuscript concerning pedagogy in dental education. It is intended that the outcome of this curriculum implementation continue to be presented at national/local dental education and professional meetings and published in peer-reviewed dental education/professional journals. The project faculty will also establish/maintain a web site devoted exclusively to consideration of problems/issues associated with the MUSoD curriculum redesign efforts and dental curriculum reform in general. Drs. Iacopino and Robinson will be responsible for this activity throughout the entire project period. Additionally, electronic newsletters will be sent out through several higher education/dental education listservs, project faculty will be actively advertised/promoted to other institutions for workshops/conferences, and project materials will be packaged as print/electronic instructional modules for use at other institutions.

IV. Project Evaluation

A. Replication or Testing in Other Settings

The MUSoD evaluation model should be ideally suited for reproduction and testing in other settings. Dental education is remarkably similar across different dental schools because almost all schools have competency-based curricula.[7,20] Thus, evaluation methods need to address integrated multidisciplinary learning and applied knowledge, skills and attitudes. Many schools have been struggling to adapt or develop assessment instruments that will meet the specific needs of dental education. Thus, these institutions will be eager to utilize the products of this project. The project faculty will make themselves available to other institutions as collaborators, consultants, and/or facilitators. They will be able to provide training and expertise in the use of the MUSoD assessment tools for various applications.

B. Documentation of Project Activities and Results

Process: Evaluation is a multifaceted term. In a general sense, the term "evaluation" means to gather information to judge the effectiveness of the project. However, more precise types of evaluation are warranted for this project. Specifically, formative and summative approaches will be used.

Formative Evaluation: Generating information to improve education effectiveness of the project during the grant period. This evaluation will help determine whether the processes/procedures are working and whether the participants are satisfied with their instruction. This approach represents a good management tool for making "mid-course corrections" providing the project director with immediate feedback to make constructive revisions in training, resource development, and information transfer activities. Formative assessments will be used to determine any changes that need to be made in the overall curriculum restructuring process. For example, the formative process will examine resource availability and reallocations/adjustments will be made if lack of resources appears to be a factor in moving the project forward. Both quantitative and qualitative assessments will be conducted so that all aspects of the environment are considered in the decision matrix. Use of qualitative data analysis allows consideration of anecdotal data that may provide richness to interpretation of quantitative data sets.

Summative Evaluation: Collecting data necessary to judge the ultimate success of the completed project. The goal is to document the extent to which the project measurable objectives were achieved (the project did what it was designed to do). Evaluation feedback will be used for formulating or modifying dental education policies and procedures nationwide. This will improve the likelihood of successfully accomplishing project goals. Final outcomes will be compared whenever possible to data from recent graduates to judge the scope of changes. Where external markers (assessments) are available to be compared to those developed as part of the program such comparisons will be made. Multiple assessments will be utilized if possible. For example, student competency will be assessed using portfolios and faculty reviews. A final report will be issued that provides a comprehensive evaluation of the project (including positive/negative conclusions) and suggests future directions for change.

C. Goals/Objectives and Specific Evaluation/Assessment Instruments

Table 2: Project Evaluation	
Goals/Objectives	**Evaluation/Assessment**
Goal 1: Develop three curriculum "tracks" (Biomedical Systems, Disease and Host Response, and Community-Based Education).	N/A
Objective 1: Combine basic and clinical science content into fully integrated continuous four-year curriculum "tracks".	Student performance on tests that require identification of critical foundational concepts associated with clinical cases will be expected to improve (National Board part

9

of project director commitment by naming the specific individuals who will be responsible for dissemination activities. Because the names of the five key project personnel keep reappearing throughout the narrative, we are able to demonstrate their extensive involvement and commitment to project success.

Project Evaluation. The "Project Evaluation" answers *how* project effectiveness will be assessed. Without a doubt, this entire section is a hot button. Conceptual synonyms for evaluation and assessment are repeated eighty times throughout this section and include key words such as:

> evaluation methods, assessment instruments, assessment tools, results, formative and summative approaches, formative evaluation, summative evaluation, feedback, quantitative and qualitative assessments, judge the ultimate success, objectives were achieved, outcomes, external markers, multiple assessments, student performance, satisfaction surveys, indicators of success, attitudinal measures, evaluation team, effective questioning strategies, peer assessment, improved scores, improved class grade point average, evaluate student and clinical outcomes.

We dedicate nearly 4.5 times more space to this "Project Evaluation" section in the final proposal (1,483 words) compared to the preliminary proposal (332 words). The RFP guidelines ask for two specific subheadings in this section, describing the extent to which the methods of evaluation (1) are thorough, feasible, and appropriate; and (2) include the use of objective performance measures. In addition, we took an artistic liberty with the guidelines in order to include an additional subheading on "Replication or Testing in Other Settings." This new subheading provides reviewers with some extra information that was not specifically requested and, at the same time, appeals to sponsor hot buttons.

Replication or Testing in Other Settings

The motivation for including this unsolicited subheading came from the section on "Need for the Project," which described the severity of the problem in its national and local contexts. The RFP guidelines request a description of the project evaluation in its "local context" but not in its "national context." Our Proposal Development Committee decided it would be beneficial to include this information anyway. This new subheading helps bring the proposal full circle and reinforces our argument that this curriculum reform project will truly have a national impact.

The opening sentence asserts that "The MUSoD evaluation model should be ideally suited for reproduction and testing in other settings." The next three sentences justify this stance; namely, dental education—with all its strengths and weaknesses—is remarkably similar across the country. As documented in the IOM report, many schools face challenges developing appropriate assessment instruments. The final three sentences describe how the MUSoD evaluation model can address this nationwide problem. In essence, once project faculty have designed and refined an effective assessment system, they will be available to share their experience, training, tools, and process with other dental schools in a variety of settings.

Documentation of Project Activities and Results

The "Documentation of Project Activities and Results" subheading follows from the RFP guidelines and demonstrates the appropriateness of the project evaluation. In three paragraphs we define our approach to evaluation and describe two different types of evaluations that will be used to assess the effectiveness of the project *during* and *at the conclusion of* the granting period. Equally significant, we describe how evaluation feedback will be used to ensure that we meet project goals, objectives, and outcomes. That is to say, assessment and evaluation are integral to a process of continuous improvement—a system of checks and balances to pinpoint what is really happening so that we know the project is making a difference, especially in students' academic performance.

The RFP guidelines emphasize that a solid evaluation plan should examine a project's processes as well as outcomes: "Formative evaluation can help you manage your project more effectively, and a strong summative evaluation, especially if it documents the project's effects on the learner, can turn a successful project into a national model for improvement in postsecondary education." Accordingly, the first paragraph overviews that for this project we will be conducting both formative and summative evaluations.

The second paragraph explains our formative approach, and the third paragraph presents our summative approach. Formative evaluations generate information that will improve the effectiveness of the project during the granting period. Summative evaluations examine the end result of an intervention. Both evaluations use a combination of quantitative and qualitative, direct and indirect methods and measures

	II). These tests will be case-based and students will need to demonstrate an ability to analyze the case and generate solutions that include knowledge of the underlying science.
Objective 2: Create clinical learning environments that mimic private practices and clinics in community-based settings.	Success in this area will be identified based on the degree to which students become involved in delivering care in private and public community-oriented settings. The percentage of a student's total clinical experience obtained outside of the school will increase by approximately 25% for this objective to have been satisfactorily met. Document the number of new community-based sites. Student/faculty satisfaction surveys.
Objective 3: Develop educational milestones and associated behavioral markers to monitor student progress towards clinical competency.	Students will be assessed using a variety of clinical and simulated assessment tools (see Goal #3). An educational milestone will be "reached" when the behavioral marker is identified as having been met.
Objective 4: Fully implement "General Dental Rounds".	This objective will be met if a CATS analysis demonstrates a reduction in the number of didactic lecture hours across the first two years. Further decreases in lecture hours will occur over the entire curriculum as this objective is phased in over a three-year period. The decreases will occur as faculty acceptance of this teaching format increases. There should be a 15–25% decrease in lectures during the initial implementation stages.
Objective 5: Develop CD-ROM/web-based teaching modules and educational resources.	A gain of 10 modules per year will be adequate evidence of the attainment of this objective. Further indicators of success will include an increase in the percentage of faculty who receive training in development of these types of materials and the initiation of a variety of independent learning materials.
Goal 2: Faculty development to support implementation of curriculum "tracks", case-based teaching, evaluation methodologies, and student success.	N/A
Objective 1: Train faculty in the process of identifying scientific/clinical concepts that must be integrated and reinforced in the curriculum "tracks".	Identification of the number of full-time and part-time faculty that complete a defined course of instruction and who demonstrate their working knowledge by developing cases, learning modules and appropriate assessment instruments for a unit of instruction. These units will be assessed by a team of faculty and by student performance. Attitudinal measures will also be employed to identify changes in faculty perspectives.
Objective 2: Train faculty to direct "General Dental Rounds".	Each faculty will conduct a rounds session. It will be videotaped and the faculty will self-evaluate their performance as well as receiving evaluation from a faculty evaluation team and from students who participated in the "test" session.
Objective 3: Train faculty to produce CD-ROM/web-based learning modules.	Demonstrate working knowledge by developing cases, learning modules and appropriate assessment instruments for a unit of instruction. The number/percentage of faculty who complete a formal course provided by the Director of Dental Informatics will increase each year. Students will evaluate faculty effectiveness more positively for those modules and the number of cases available for use in test development will increase annually.
Objective 4: Train faculty in providing guidance for	Measurable improvement in faculty abilities to lead and

10

of data collection. By using multiple assessment measures, we can improve the reliability and validity of our results. The last sentence in this subheading confirms that at the conclusion of the project we will issue a comprehensive final evaluation report, a direct acknowledgement of the distinctive feature of project director commitment raised in the invitation to submit a final proposal.

Goals/Objectives and Specific Evaluation/Assessment Instruments

This subheading addresses the RFP guidelines expectation that the methods of evaluation include the use of objective performance measures. Following the mandate in the invitation to submit a final proposal, we present, in a two-column chart, a listing of the major goals and objectives of the project and, for each, a description of how attainment of the objectives will be evaluated. The evaluation draws on quantitative and qualitative data gathered from a variety of internal and external sources. For example, quantitative evidence includes documenting a decrease in the number of didactic lecture hours, and qualitative evidence includes the open-ended responses on student/faculty satisfaction surveys; student performance will be measured internally by class grade point average and externally by the National Board Exam. Our evaluation plan is designed to be comprehensive, yet is replicable in other postsecondary settings. In fact, some of the newly designed assessment instruments (i.e., goal three) may be valuable to dental schools whether or not they adopt the "Foundational Curriculum."

Resources for the Project. This final section of the proposal explains *how much* direct and ancillary funding MUSoD is committing to this project. In the preliminary proposal, "cost-effectiveness" was a distinctive feature. In the final proposal, this concept is assimilated into a larger discussion of the adequacy of resources for the project.

The RFP guidelines formally call for five specific subheadings: (1) "Adequacy of the Budget," (2) "Reasonableness of Costs," (3) "Demonstrated Commitment of each Partner," (4) "Adequacy of Facilities, Equipment, Supplies, and Other Resources," and (5) "Potential for Continued Support." The guidelines also request a detailed budget and budget narrative: "a detailed budget and justification attached to your final proposal should itemize the support you request from FIPSE and the support you expect to obtain from sources other than FIPSE." In practical terms, the first

three subheadings in this section and the budget narrative are asking for the same information.

Rather than repeating the rationale for budget items in both of these sections, we made a conscious decision to again deviate slightly from the guidelines and provide these details only in the budget narrative. This decision was also influenced by the fact that page limitations are not a factor in the budget narrative; we can use as much space as necessary to justify budget expenditures. As a result, our "Resources for the Project" section is relatively short (391 words) and includes only the final two subheadings. Nevertheless, we manage to address all three hot buttons and both distinctive features one last time in the narrative.

Facilities, Equipment, Supplies, and Other Resources

The sponsor's position about applicants sharing in the total cost of the project is unmistakably clear in the RFP guidelines: "The applicant institution and any partners should support the project both philosophically and financially. . . . we [FIPSE] expect the host institution and its partners to make a significant commitment to the project in the form of direct cost sharing and low indirect cost rates." In a sense, the entire narrative up to this section has demonstrated our administrative and programmatic commitments to the project, and now we are beginning to demonstrate our financial commitment. We dedicate four paragraphs to this cause and, of course, the budget and budget narrative will make this case as well.

The first paragraph provides a brief overview of this entire subheading, in essence confirming that our total contributions are so substantial that they are difficult to quantify. The second paragraph identifies sources of extramural grant funding that have been secured from the national and state level to support the teledentistry component of this project. These grants also reflect the innovativeness of our project (i.e., a hot button). That is, with new telecommunications equipment, MUSoD will be able to connect to satellite clinics throughout the state, thus enabling dental students and faculty to participate regardless of their physical location. In a broader sense, the ability of project directors to attract sizable grant dollars from a variety of sources demonstrates their commitment to the success of this initiative—a distinctive feature raised in the invitation to submit a final proposal.

The final two paragraphs provide concrete examples of the significant institutional commitments MUSoD is making to its dental education program. Over

experiential learning in community-based clinical environments.	attitudes towards engaging in orchestrated small-group instruction. Improved one-on-one clinical teaching skills including using effective questioning strategies to elicit problem solutions. Faculty ability to conduct small-group sessions will be identified using appropriate teaching surveys filled out by students. Attitudinal change will be assessed by attitude surveys given to the faculty. Clinical teaching surveys filled out by students will also provide input needed to assess this objective. Peer assessment.
Objective 5: Train faculty in recruitment/interview skills and methods to enhance student success in integrative case-based and applied educational environments.	Faculty members who participate in the admissions process will receive a standardized training session that will facilitate their identification of students who are most likely to succeed in a less structured educational environment. Faculty will be calibrated through exercises developed to give them a chance to judge student overall interest in such things as case-based and self-directed learning. Improved scores on National Board exams. Improved class grade point average.
Goal 3: Develop assessment methods to monitor project progress, student/faculty performance, and student/faculty satisfaction. **Objective 1:** Develop computer-based simulations designed to provide ongoing self-assessments. **Objective 2:** Develop/refine use of standardized patients for assessment of comprehensive knowledge, skills, and attitudes. **Objective 3:** Develop Objective Structured Clinical Examinations (OSCE's) for use in assessing clinical decision making. **Objective 4:** Develop a portfolio assessment system to evaluate student clinical outcomes. **Objective 5:** Refine existing teaching surveys to assess faculty performance and the effectiveness of faculty development efforts. **Objective 6:** Refine existing surveys to determine student perceptions of effectiveness and change. **Objective 7:** Develop faculty/student peer assessment systems.	The success of this goal and its various objectives will be determined as follows: The actual number of new instruments and their utilization in the assessment of students will be tracked on a quarterly basis. Objective will be met if new assessments are introduced over a two-year period and traditional assessments such as multiple-choice tests are reduced in number. Each assessment strategy that is developed will be evaluated using the following standards: 1) Content/face validity determined by examination of the content of the exam as compared to the instructional objectives of the unit of instruction. 2) Reliability of the exam determined either through standard reliability estimates or through an appropriate alternative scoring mechanism for the type of instrument (an external measurement consultant from a regional lab or another dental school will be used in this process). 3) Criterion related/predictive validity will also be assessed by comparing student performance against ratings of student performance in actual clinical settings.

V.   **Resources for the Project**
     A.   **Facilities, Equipment, Supplies, and Other Resources**
There are numerous significant sources of support for this proposal that will be operative during the project period. It is difficult to assign an exact dollar amount to these sources and it is probably more appropriate to discuss these in a narrative setting. In this way, the importance and contribution of these resources to the project can be judged/evaluated on an individual basis.

Teledentistry Grants: Drs. Robinson and Iacopino have secured considerable funding ($267,000) from the State of Wisconsin (Wisconsin Advanced Telecommunications and Universal Service Funds) and the Federal Government (Milwaukee Area Health Education Center) to support the acquisition and use of telecommunications/electronic media to enhance and deliver the new MUSoD curriculum. This equipment will be used to connect the institution to various satellite clinics through the State of Wisconsin providing the ability for all students and faculty to participate in "educational tracks" and "General Dental Rounds" regardless of physical location.

11

the long-term, as described in the third paragraph, we are in the final stages of construction for a $30 million state-of-the-art dental facility. This new building was specifically designed with the physical space and technology infrastructure necessary to support the "Foundational Curriculum" blueprint (i.e., a hot button for national impact). At the same time, we touch on the distinctive feature of student diversity by describing how teledentistry technologies promote access to dental care for the multicultural residents who will be served by community-based sites. The fourth paragraph describes our more immediate financial contributions in terms of cost sharing faculty effort. In this case, the amount of cost sharing for personnel salaries and fringe benefits exceeded the total budget requested during each year of the project. Together, these capital and human resources will contribute directly to the success of this curriculum reform initiative.

Continuation Beyond the Grant Period

This closing paragraph confirms to the sponsor that this project will continue beyond the granting period. In particular, while grant-sponsored activities will occur over a three-year time frame, developing and implementing the entire "Foundational Curriculum" will take at least five years. Said differently, in terms of time invested, our institutional commitment to this project pre- and post-grant award is equal to the duration of the grant. MUSoD invested internal dollars for one year to pilot the project prior to requesting FIPSE funding and will continue to allocate resources for two years after the granting period in order to complete the project. Moreover, the curriculum will continually be evaluated and refined based on outcomes/assessment data (i.e., a hot button). In a sense, this is really a six-year curriculum reform initiative, of which we invite the sponsor to share in roughly 40 percent of the costs during the three critical start-up years.

Proposal Design

A well-designed proposal makes even complex information look accessible and simplifies the reviewers' jobs. The following design features highlight the structure, hierarchy, and order of the proposal, helping reviewers find the information that they need. For the purpose of consistency, we incorporated many of the same proposal design features that we used in the preliminary proposal.

Headings. Boldface headings reveal to reviewers, at a glance, the organization of our proposal. Headings reflect key words taken from the "Selection Criteria" section of the RFP guidelines. Effective use of white space sets off headings and enhances readability.

Lists. Bulleted and numbered lists visually break up long blocks of text and help to get the message to the reader with a sense of immediacy without being wordy. For instance, the numbered list in the "Significance of this Project" section emphasizes six core elements of our project framework, and the bulleted list in the "Project Evaluation" section quickly identifies a sampling of key outcomes evaluation tools.

Margins. Following the requirements in the RFP guidelines, we used standard one-inch margins. A proposal with ragged right margins is easier to read than one that is fully justified because the proportional spacing in justified type slows down readability.

Page Numbers. We place page numbers in the bottom center of the proposal.

Type Style. The proposal is written in Times Roman, the same type style that the sponsor used in its RFP guidelines. Using 11 point type size allowed us to include a few additional lines of information without compromising the readability of the proposal.

White Space. As mandated in the RFP guidelines, the proposal is double spaced. To make the proposal appear inviting and user-friendly, we include an additional line of white space as a visual separator between the major sections.

New Dental Facility: MUSoD has designed and initiated construction of a new dental facility to open in August 2002 (budget year two of the project). The new facility was specifically designed to support the "Foundational Curriculum" blueprint relative to physical space and technology support. This includes conference rooms of various sizes specifically allocated to "General Dental Rounds", computing facilities to support self-directed electronic learning in the "educational tracks", and teledentistry technologies to facilitate participation in institutional educational activities from community-based sites. The total cost for the new facility is approximately $30,000,000. Thus, there is clearly an institutional commitment and support for the new dentistry curriculum and the future of dentistry education as a whole at MUSoD.

Faculty Effort Cost-Share: There is significant faculty effort cost-share from MUSoD (The amount of personnel cost-share significantly exceeds the total budget requested in all project years). Thus, the institution is making a significant contribution of faculty resources to the project during each budget year.

B. Continuation Beyond the Grant Period

The project duration is three years, however, it is estimated that the total curriculum development efforts will not be completed for at least five years. Thus, the institution will continue to allocate resources to the curriculum reform effort long after project completion. Additionally, the curriculum will continue to be evaluated and refined based on outcomes/assessment data on a perpetual basis.

VI.   References

1. Glassman P and Meyerowitz C. Education in dentistry: preparing dental practitioners to meet the oral health needs of America in the 21st Century. J Dent Ed 63:615-625, 1999.

2. Tedesco LA. Issues in dental curriculum development and change. J Dent Ed 59:97-147, 1995.

3. Tedesco LA. Curriculum change during post-IOM dental education. J Dent Ed 60:827-830, 1996.

4. Institute of Medicine, Committee on the Future of Dental Education, "Dental Education at the Crossroads: Challenges and Change". Field MJ Ed, Nat Acad Press; Washington, DC 1995.

5. Nash, DA. "And the Band Played On". J Dent Ed 62:964-974, 1998.

6. Ismail AI. Dental education at the crossroads: the crisis within. J Dent Ed 63:327-330, 1999.

7. Whipp JL, Ferguson DJ, Wells LM and Iacopino AM. Rethinking knowledge and pedagogy in dental education. J Dent Ed 64:860-866, 2000.

8. Nendaz MR and Tekian A. Assessment in problem-based learning medical schools: a literature review. Teach Learn Med 11:232-243, 1999.

9. Shatzer JH. Instructional Methods. Academic Med 73:38-45, 1998.

10. Schmidt H. Integrating the teaching of basic sciences, clinical sciences, and biopsychosocial issues. Acad Med 73:24-31, 1998.

11. Kassenbaum DG, Cutler ER, and Eaglen RH. The influence of accreditation on educational change in US medical schools. Academic Med 72:1127-1133, 1997.

12. Vernon DTA and Blake RL. Does problem-based learning work: a meta-analysis of evaluative research. Academic Med 68:550-563, 1993.

13. Albanese MA and Mitchell S. Problem-based learning: a review of the literature on its outcomes and implementation issues. Academic Med 68:52-81, 1993.

14. Chambers DW. Some issues in problem-based learning. J Dent Ed 59:567-571, 1995.

15. Lim LP and Chen AY. Challenges and relevance of problem-based learning in dental education. Eur J Dent Ed 3:20-26, 1999.

16. Behar-Horenstein LS, Dolan TA, Courts FJ, Mitchell GS. Cultivating critical thinking in the clinical learning environment. J Dent Ed 64:610-615, 2000.

17. Valachovic RW. Making science clinically relevant. J Dent Ed 61:434-436, 1997.

18. Barrows HS. The essentials of problem-based learning. J Dent Ed 62:630-633, 1998.

19. Chambers DW. Dental curriculum and accreditation: means, ends, and the continuum. J Dent Ed 60:816-820, 1996.

20. Chambers DW. Competencies: a new view of becoming a dentist. J Dent Ed 58:342-345, 1994.

12

DEVELOPING THE BUDGET AND BUDGET NARRATIVE

A budget and budget narrative describe *how much* the project will cost. Yet they are more than a simple statement of proposed expenditures. They are an alternate way to express a project's value. The budget and budget narrative demonstrate to the sponsor that sufficient funds have been requested to achieve project goals and objectives in a cost-effective manner.

The budget and budget narrative are frequently developed after the proposal narrative is nearly completed; nevertheless, they should be planned and constructed with the same level of care. Reviewers will scrutinize the budget and budget narrative to judge whether expenses are allowable, allocable, and reasonable. Expenses must be incurred during the proposed granting period and should relate directly to activities described in the proposal narrative or appendixes. Any combination of ambiguities, inconsistencies, discrepancies, and omissions between the proposal narrative and the budget and budget narrative may provide reviewers with enough justification to reduce a funding request or reject the grant application.

Elements of the Budget

The budget should be independent of the proposal narrative, and unless sponsor regulations indicate otherwise, can include every reasonable expense associated with the project. In this case, the RFP guidelines preclude using grant dollars for the purchase of real property or for construction, and state that proposals requesting funds for student financial aid or equipment are rarely competitive.

FIPSE requires applicants to complete a brief Budget Summary form. This form divides the budget into seven line item categories, and for multiyear initiatives, across three twelve-month project periods. At a glance, reviewers can determine exactly how much funding is being requested from the sponsor and how much is being contributed by the applicant in terms of:

1. Salaries and wages
2. Employee benefits
3. Travel
4. Equipment
5. Materials and supplies
6. Consultants and contracts
7. Other

Taking a cue from the RFP guidelines, we demonstrate our financial commitment to this project by cost sharing some items (i.e., salaries and wages, employee benefits) and by decreasing the amount of FIPSE support requested in each year of the grant. First-year funding is higher because of inevitable start-up costs, whereas subsequent funding levels decrease over time. The fact that we contributed significant matching dollars to the project ($1.60:1) is more important than the actual distribution of the cost sharing among the seven line item categories.

The RFP guidelines also call for evidence of institutional financial commitment in terms of a low indirect cost rate, even suggesting, "some of our applicants request no indirect costs at all." Rather than forgoing indirect costs completely, we follow the recommendation of FIPSE staff, which uses the U.S. Department of Education training rate of 8 percent of total direct costs as a basis for determining the reasonableness of indirect costs. The budget narrative explains our institutional contributions in full detail.

Beyond the Budget Summary form, we consult three additional federal documents that provide guidance for developing grant budgets:

- Education Department General Administrative Regulations (EDGAR)—Title 34 Code of Federal Regulations Parts 74–86 and 97–99. (http://www.ed.gov/policy/fund/reg/edgarReg/edgar.html)
- Office of Management and Budget (OMB) Circular A-21, "Cost Principles for Institutions of Higher Education." (http://www.whitehouse.gov/omb/circulars/a021/a021.html)
- Office of Management and Budget (OMB) Circular A-110, "Uniform Administrative Requirements for Grants and Agreements With Institutions of Higher Education, Hospitals, and Other Non-Profit Organizations." (http://www.whitehouse.gov/omb/circulars/a110/a110.html)

Recent amendments (March 2001) to EDGAR give grantees more flexibility in implementing program activities by reducing administrative burdens. That is, project directors are allowed to make certain changes in the management of their programs without securing prior written approval. For instance, they can reallocate up to 10 percent of the total budget among direct cost categories, extend the grant at the end of the project period for up to one additional year, and carry funds over from one budget period to the next.

In practical terms this means that as long as grantees remain true to their goals and objectives, the sponsor will allow modifications to project timeframes and budget allocations; grantees can, within reason,

Budget Summary*

A. Budget Items Requested from FIPSE	Year 1	Year 2	Year 3
Direct Costs:			
1. Salaries & Wages (professional & clerical employees) $	90,826	77,801	63,204
2. Employee Benefits	26,339	22,562	18,329
3. Travel (employees only)	5,000	5,000	5,000
4. Equipment (purchase)	0	0	0
5. Materials and Supplies	10,000	10,000	0
6. Consultants and Contracts (including any travel)	19,500	8,000	0
7. Other (equipment rental, printing, etc.)	8,000	5,000	0
Total Direct Costs (add 1–7 above):	159,665	128,363	86,533
Indirect Costs: 8% MTDC	12,773	10,269	6,923
Total Requested from FIPSE: $	172,439	138,632	93,456

(These figures should appear on the title page)

B. Project Costs Not Requested from FIPSE (institutional and other support):	Year 1	Year 2	Year 3
1. Salaries & Wages (professional & clerical employees) $	220,204	159,705	121,144
2. Employee Benefits	63,859	46,315	35,132
3. Travel (employees only)	0	0	0
4. Equipment (purchase)	0	0	0
5. Materials and Supplies	0	0	0
6. Consultants and Contracts (including any travel)	0	0	0
7. Other (equipment rental, printing, etc.)	0	0	0
Total Direct Costs (add 1–7 above):	284,063	206,020	156,276
Indirect Costs:	0	0	0
Total Institutional and Other Support: $	284,063	206,020	156,276

*Budget items, including institutional support figures, must be detailed in the budget narrative of the final proposal.

THE BUDGET AND BUDGET NARRATIVE

STAGE TWO: FINAL PROPOSAL

adjust their activities to accommodate unanticipated and unexpected circumstances as their projects evolve. It is still good practice, however, to informally notify FIPSE staff of program changes as part of routine communications with the sponsor. This can often be done (and documented) electronically via e-mail and fax.

Elements of the Budget Narrative

The budget narrative must include an explanation for every line item, describing in as much detail as possible:

- the specific item
- the item's relevance to the project
- the basis of cost calculations for the item

This level of detail explains *what* items are needed, *why* they are needed, and *how much* they will cost. Headings in the budget narrative correspond to the line items on the Budget Summary form. This budget narrative justifies both the funds requested from the sponsor and the costs shared by our institution over the duration of the three-year project period.

Personnel. Although not specifically called for in the RFP guidelines, we distinguish between "key personnel" and "other personnel." For the five key personnel we include a detailed description that includes their names, titles, professional degrees, roles in the project, and cross-references to their two-page biosketches in the appendixes. From the biosketches, reviewers can tell that the key personnel are exceptionally well credentialed to successfully carry out this project. For instance, two individuals, Drs. Best and Iacopino, hold dual doctorates, e.g., a dental degree (D.D.S. or D.M.D.) and a research degree (Ph.D.). As experienced clinicians *and* researchers they are uniquely postured to lead this project. Two additional key personnel, Drs. Taft and Donte-Bartfield, are experienced clinical psychologists working at MUSoD and have a demonstrated track record of evaluating complex research and training projects. Their skills will transfer directly to the assessment and evaluation of this curricular reform initiative.

The other personnel are described en masse according to the type of position they will hold for this project, e.g., program administrator, faculty leader, faculty/administrative participant, track/case development. For the most part we were able to name the specific individuals who will serve in these various positions. In a few instances, when a distinct individual is not available, we describe the type of person who will be hired for the position.

For all project personnel, we describe the percent effort and duration of work to be put forth, including delineating the portions to be funded by the sponsor and cost-shared by MUSoD. OMB Circular A-110 provides guidance on the conditions and type of documentation that can serve as evidence of cost sharing. For example, contributions must be verifiable from institutional records, allowable under the applicable cost principles, and necessary and reasonable for accomplishing project objectives. At the same time, these contributions must *not* be offered as cost sharing on any other federally sponsored project or paid for by the federal government under another award. Our proposed cost sharing satisfies all of these conditions.

Cost sharing on faculty salaries and fringe benefits offers an added benefit: we are able to demonstrate our institutional financial commitment to this project *without any additional cash layout.* Consider: The project director will dedicate 25 percent effort to this initiative, 20 percent of which represents cost sharing. This means that instead of receiving his full salary from MUSoD's internal personnel budget, the project director will now receive five percent from the sponsor and the remaining 20 percent from a cost sharing account on the grant. A portion of his salary is merely reallocated; his total income remains the same. The sources of income are changed on the bookkeeping records. Over the course of three years, we cost share in personnel salaries more than the entire amount requested from the sponsor.

Consistent with our approach to developing the preliminary and final proposals, in this budget narrative, we systematically address all three sponsor hot buttons. Phrases used to describe the specific activities performed by project personnel are associated with:

- innovation and reform—*curriculum reform efforts, organization/development of the "Foundational Curriculum," curriculum revision, integration of basic/clinical science into three "tracks," innovative general dental rounds, community-based education, electronic/distance learning, case-based educational tools.*
- national impact—*manager of the dissemination area of the project, blueprint for curricular redesign, experienced/recognized author and national lecturer, attendance of project faculty at national/local meetings and symposia.*
- evaluation and assessment—*demonstrate feasibility and effectiveness, project assessment, assessment methods, design of appropriate assessment tools/instruments for monitoring and reporting project outcomes, data interpretation/analysis, assessment activities, collection and evaluation of assessment data.*

Budget Justification

Personnel:

Key Personnel:

Dr. Joseph Best – Dr. Best will function as the project director dedicating 25% effort to this project (20% cost-share) for all three years. Dr. Best will function under the supervision of Dr. Ordean Oyen, Special Assistant to the Dean, who is responsible for management of all MUSoD curriculum development efforts (see below). Dr. Best has been instrumental in MUSoD curriculum reform efforts for the past two years and co-authored the MUSoD blueprint for curricular redesign entitled the "Foundational Curriculum" (see biosketch in appendix 1). Additionally, he has initiated steps designed to demonstrate feasibility and effectiveness of the proposed educational changes. As part of the overall curriculum revision, Dr. Best is responsible for integration of basic/clinical sciences into three "tracks" of the "Foundational Curriculum" described in the proposal (Biomedical Systems, Disease and Host Defense, and Community-Based Education). He will supervise and work with faculty designated as "leaders" for each of the educational "tracks". A particular concern of Dr. Best will be incorporation of case-based educational tools that cut across all "tracks" in the form of unique and innovative "General Dental Rounds".

Dr. Thomas Taft—Dr. Taft will function as the manager of the faculty development and project assessment areas of the project and will dedicate 25% effort to the project (15% cost-share) for all three years. As Director of Educational Development and Assessment at MUSoD for several years, he has considerable experience in educational approaches, assessment methods, and faculty development (see biosketch in appendix 1). Dr. Taft will be responsible for selection and design of appropriate assessment tools/instruments for monitoring and reporting project outcomes including data interpretation/analysis. Working with the MUSoD Faculty Development Committee, Dr. Taft will also provide guidance in organization of faculty development activities coordinating interactions with external consultants, project faculty, and students.

Dr. Michelle A. Robinson—Dr. Robinson will function as the manager of the informatics/technology area of the project and will dedicate 20% effort to the project (15% cost-share) for all three years. She has extensive experience in data management/technology support as they apply to educational instruction and community-based education (see biosketch in appendix 1). Additionally, she has secured significant external funding on the state/local levels to provide the hardware/software and equipment necessary to support the proposed curriculum, especially at community-based clinics. She will work with Dr. Best to facilitate delivery of electronic educational materials and with Dr. Taft to perform/analyze assessments.

Dr. Anthony M. Iacopino—Dr. Iacopino will function and the project assistant director, provide assistance with all areas of the project, function as the manager of the dissemination area of the project, and will dedicate 25% effort to the project for all three years. He has broad experience in many areas of dental education, electronic/distance learning, curriculum reform, faculty development, and assessment (see biosketch in appendix 1). He is an experienced/recognized author and national lecturer. Additionally, he has participated in the organization/development of the "Foundational Curriculum" blueprint with Dr. Best, worked with Dr. Taft on various faculty development/assessment activities, and maintains collaboration on the external grants of Dr. Robinson. Dr. Iacopino will assume primary responsibility for management of the project budget, project updates/progress reports, presentation/abstract/manuscript preparation, organization of materials and media for dissemination of project results/progress, and attendance of project faculty at national/local meetings and symposia.

Dr. Ordean Oyen—Dr. Oyen, Special assistant to the Dean, is currently responsible for overseeing all curriculum development activities at MUSoD (see biosketch in appendix 1). Dr. Oyen will function as the manager of the curriculum development areas of the project dedicating 50% effort to the project in year one (all cost-share) and 25% effort in year two (all cost-share). Dr. Oyen will ensure that the proposed project maintains congruence with the overall MUSoD curriculum development efforts. This is important as the proposed project only covers development of three out of ten four-year educational "tracks" outlined in the "Foundational Curriculum" blueprint for MUSoD. All seven "tracks" necessarily influence/impact each other, thus to comprise an effective and complete dental curriculum, it will be essential to have an individual maintain the global institutional view. Dr. Oyen will assist Dr. Best in development of three educational "tracks"

In addition, we appeal to the distinctive feature of project director commitment. The project director, Dr. Best, demonstrates a significant professional investment in this initiative by dedicating 25 percent effort to it in each year of the granting period. Further, the total percent effort of the five key personnel illustrates their extensive project involvement. Cumulatively, their committed efforts represent a full-time equivalency of 1.45 FTE in Year 1, 1.20 FTE in Year 2, and .95 FTE in Year 3. In other words, the equivalent of one director-level dental faculty member will be working on curricular reform efforts every day, full time for three consecutive years.

Employee Benefits. Often called "fringe benefits" in grant budgets—but not with FIPSE—the budget narrative explains the components of the employee benefits package and the benefit rate. At MUSoD, different benefit rates apply depending on whether project personnel are full- or part-time and whether they are contracted on an academic or calendar year. Benefits include health, life, dental, and disability insurance; retirement contribution; tuition remission; and social security and worker compensation payroll taxes.

Travel. To determine the components to be included in this line item, we reference OMB Circular A-21, which defines travel costs as "the expenses for transportation, lodging, subsistence, and related items incurred by employees who are in travel status on official business of the institution." Accordingly, travel expenditures for project personnel outline the destination, purpose, and the basis of cost calculations. Following a tip raised in the invitation to submit a full proposal, we budget for two personnel to attend FIPSE's annual project directors' meeting in the fall. Budget figures include airfare, lodging, meals, and ground transportation.

In addition, we request funding for one faculty member to attend a national meeting relevant to this initiative. We note that additional project personnel will utilize their personal/institutional travel budgets to cover the costs of attending pertinent local/national meetings. While this is an example of cost sharing, because it was difficult to pinpoint exactly how many faculty would be attending which meetings, we did not quantify this amount on the Budget Summary form.

Materials and Supplies. While the majority of our budget request will support personnel costs, some materials and supplies are necessary for producing electronic educational resources and for disseminating project results. In hindsight, we could have made our budget narrative stronger by providing a more detailed breakdown of the costs associated with educational technology (CD-ROMs, videotapes, Web development tools/software) and dissemination strategies (posters, presentations, publications).

Sponsors often vary in their categorization of technology: for some it means "equipment," while for others it means "supplies." The RFP guidelines state clearly that proposals requesting equipment are rarely competitive, so we would prefer our technology needs to be considered as supplies. According to OMB Circulars A-21 and A-110, "equipment" means an article of nonexpendable, tangible personal property having a useful life of more than one year and an acquisition cost that equals or exceeds the lesser of the capitalization level established by the organization for financial statement purposes, or $5,000. Since the costs of our electronic educational resources fall well below this capitalization threshold, it is appropriate to include them as supplies.

Two of the most common dissemination strategies in postsecondary education include publishing articles in peer-reviewed journals and sharing project results at professional conferences. In addition to these strategies, we will package educational materials developed as print and electronic instructional modules for use at other dental schools. These publications and materials represent important pieces of intellectual property. The federal government allows grantees to copyright any work that is developed in conjunction with or as the result of a funding award.

OMB Circular A-110 also states that the federal awarding agency "reserves a royalty-free, nonexclusive and irrevocable right to reproduce, publish, or otherwise use the work for federal purposes, and to authorize others to do so." Meaning, the sponsor can use and redistribute, free of charge, any educational materials that we might develop. Understanding this reality, we volunteer to host a Web site and distribute CD-ROMs that contain copies of our progress reports and training modules. This proactive dissemination strategy allows us to share our results with other dental schools and yet maintain distinct ownership and control of our intellectual property.

Consultants and Contracts. Consultants are individuals who are brought into grant projects to add expertise in specific areas of professional activity. When these individuals are employed by and represent other organizations, contractual agreements are used to describe the collaborative arrangements between multiple organizations. Consultants often have great intuitive knowledge of problems and issues and can

described in the proposal while simultaneously working with faculty responsible for developing the remaining seven tracks. This will ensure optimal articulation/effectiveness.

Other Personnel:
Program Administrator—A program administrator will be assigned to 100% effort (25% cost-share) on the project for all three years. This position will be recruited should the applicant be funded and will be responsible for overall clerical support/assistance and administrative duties associated with the project. This includes word processing, generation of educational print materials, administration of mailings, maintenance of records/files, updating web pages, assisting with travel arrangements for project faculty/external consultants, organization/scheduling of meetings, monitoring of phone/fax machine, and serving as an initial point of contact for all matters related to the project.

Faculty Leaders—There will be five leaders (Drs. Anthony Ziebart, Linda Wells, Gerald Bradley, Kenneth Hinkelman, and Andrew Dentino) designated to work with Dr. Best to develop the three educational "tracks" and "General Dental Rounds". These faculty will dedicate 20% effort in year one (all cost-share), 10% effort in year two (all cost-share), and 10% effort in year three (all cost-share). These faculty will function primarily as "content experts" providing the educational materials for lectures, electronic media, and modified case-based approaches. Additionally, one faculty member (Dr. Evelyn Donate-Bartfield) will function as a faculty leader in the areas of faculty development and project/student assessment. Dr. Donate-Bartfield will work closely with Dr. Taft and will oversee the actual implementation of project assessment and faculty development efforts dedicating 20% effort to the project for all three years (all cost-share). Dr. Donate-Bartfield will oversee the actual collection and evaluation of assessment data related to the project. Additionally, Dr. Donate-Bartfield will work closely with Dr. Taft in the organization of faculty development related to the adaptation of evidence-based and case-based learning.

Faculty/Administrative Participants—There will be two faculty participants (Drs. Richard Abrams and Darryl Pendleton) and one administrative participant (Dr. Timothy Creamer, Associate Dean for Clinical Affairs) designated to work with Dr. Best to address organizational/implementation issues associated with the three educational "tracks" and "General Dental Rounds". These faculty will dedicate 10% effort in year one (all cost-share) and 10% effort in year two (all cost-share). Working with Dr. Best, they will function primarily in an organizational role providing assistance with conversion and reformulation of student schedules/activities. This is important as the new educational approaches will affect clinic operations/student schedules both within the institution and at the various community-based satellite areas.

Track/Case Development—An amount of $25,000 is requested for budget year one and $10,000 is requested for budget year two for personnel expenses related to educational "track" and "General Dental Rounds" development. Project faculty leaders who maintain 10-month appointments and agree to assume major responsibilities for the content development of educational "tracks" or cases to be used in "General Dental Rounds" will be provided with a "summer" salary. This will take the form of $5,000 for track development and $1,000 for case development. Thus, in year one, funds are requested to provide for three tracks ($15,000) and ten cases ($10,000). In year two, funds are requested to provide for an additional ten cases ($10,000).

Employee Benefits:
Marquette University fringe benefit rates are 29% of full-time ten-month or twelve-month salaries, 16% of summer salary for ten-month employees, and 14% of part-time salaries. The full package includes health, life, dental, and disability insurance; TIAA-CREF; tuition remission; and social security/worker compensation payroll taxes.

Travel:
An amount of $5,000 is requested for each of the three budget years to cover costs of travel for project personnel. This includes national/local meetings and symposia (American Dental Education Association, American Association for Dental Research, American Dental Association, Wisconsin Dental Association) as well as specific FIPSE meetings mandated by the funding agency (US Department of Education). We anticipate sending two project personnel to the FIPSE meeting each year at a cost of $1,600 each ($3,200). The remaining $1,800 will be used to sponsor one member of the project team to attend one national meeting each year. It is anticipated that many project personnel will attend some or all of the meetings listed above. Thus, costs of travel will exceed the amount requested. Personnel will utilize personal/institutional travel budgets to

communicate that information in an immediately usable form. They can act as strong advocates for planned and systematic change.

In particular, our project requires the assistance of two categories of consultants: curricular reform experts and faculty development facilitators. In each case we define the specific tasks and deliverables for which consultants will be responsible, the frequency and duration of their service, and their total compensation (i.e., preparation work, travel, and honoraria). We refer to OMB Circular A-21 to ensure the allowability of these costs for professional consulting services.

Other. "Other" encompasses the remaining direct cost items associated with the project that are not covered in the line items above. In this case, "other" includes printing, copying, and phone charges. These items are often treated as indirect costs. However, for the purpose of this curricular reform project we include them as direct cost items because we will exceed their "typical" usage. As much as possible, we itemize expenditures according to their contributions to fulfilling project goals and objectives, e.g., preparing materials for the three curriculum "tracks" and developing the faculty development workshops.

Indirect Costs. Although Marquette University has a federally approved indirect cost rate of 45 percent of modified total direct costs, as recommended in the RFP guidelines, we request only 8 percent, the standard rate for educational training projects. This indirect costs line item is intended to cover grant-related expenses that are not easily identified but are necessary to conduct the grant, i.e., physical plant operation and maintenance, utility costs, use allowances on equipment, payroll and accounting, legal counsel, library materials, and general project administration.

attend these meetings since there is overlap in purpose within broad areas of dental education/training, research, and dissemination of project progress/results.

Materials and Supplies:
An amount of $10,000 is requested for budget years one and two and to cover expenses associated with production of educational materials (CD-ROMs, videotapes, web development tools/software), materials related to project dissemination (posters/presentations, publications), and office supplies.

Consultants and Contracts:
Curriculum Consultants:
An amount of $15,000 is requested in budget year one and $5,000 is requested in budget year two for expenses associated with obtaining expertise from external curriculum consultants. These funds will provide for preparation work, travel, and honoraria for each of three consultants to make two trips to MUSoD in year one ($2,500 each trip) and two consultants to return in year two ($5,000). The consultants have been identified as nationally/internationally recognized leaders in dental education and curricular reform. They represent institutions that have previously implemented partial curricular revisions utilizing "problem-based/case-based" approaches or integrating basic/clinical sciences. Their experiences with faculty development/acceptance, implementation, and problem-solving will be invaluable to the proposed comprehensive curriculum redesign project.

Faculty Development Consultants:
An amount of $4,500 is requested for budget year one and $3,000 is requested for budget year two for expenses associated with obtaining expertise from external faculty development consultants. These consultants will provide education/training for all MUSoD faculty relative to targeted student recruitment, integrative case-based teaching methods, and student/program assessment by acting as speakers and/or facilitators for three full-day faculty retreats in year one and two full-day faculty retreats in year two. The retreats will provide comprehensive education/training as well as "train-the-trainer" approaches to enable project faculty to continue additional institutional programming as needed during the project period and in the future. For each retreat, the consultant will receive honoraria and travel expenses ($1,500 each).

Other:
Printing/Copying/Phone Charges:
An amount of $8,000 is requested for budget year one and $5,000 is requested for budget year two for expenses related to printing, photocopying, and phone charges for the project. In year one, $3,000 will be used in preparing manuals/workbooks associated with the three faculty development retreats ($1,000 each). In year two, $2,000 will be used in a similar manner for the two scheduled retreats. For year one, $4,000 will be required to cover costs associated with printing/copying materials for each of the three curriculum "tracks", teaching cases, and student manuals. Additionally, in year one, $1,000 is requested for phone charges related to faculty consultations with the external curriculum and faculty development consultants. For year two, $2,000 will be required to cover costs associated with printing/copying materials for teaching cases and student manuals. Additionally, in year two, $1,000 is requested for phone charges related to faculty consultations with external curriculum/faculty development consultants.

Indirect Costs:
The Marquette University federally approved indirect cost rate is 45% of Modified Total Direct Cost (MTDC). MTDC represents total direct costs excluding capital expenditures, student tuition, and that portion of any sub-award exceeding $25,000. This rate was established with the US Department of Health and Human Services (DHHS) on January 14, 1998. In accordance with US Department of Education guidelines, an 8% indirect cost rate is being used for this proposal.

RECEIVING THE GRANT AWARD NOTIFICATION

Nearly a year after the Request for Proposal (RFP) for the "Comprehensive Program" was first issued, the U.S. Department of Education, Fund for Improvement of Postsecondary Education (FIPSE) notified us that our curricular reform project was selected for grant funding. In particular, nearly two months passed from the submission of our preliminary proposal to the arrival of the invitation to submit a final proposal, and an additional five months passed after we submitted our final proposal until we received the grant award notification. The award notice is a tangible confirmation of our ability to match up our needs with the sponsor's priorities. Our proposal is persuasive because it presents a seamless argument that stands the test of reason, addresses psychological concerns, and connects project ideas to the values of the sponsor.

Figure 4 summarizes the key elements that we brought together to reach the Persuasion Intersection.

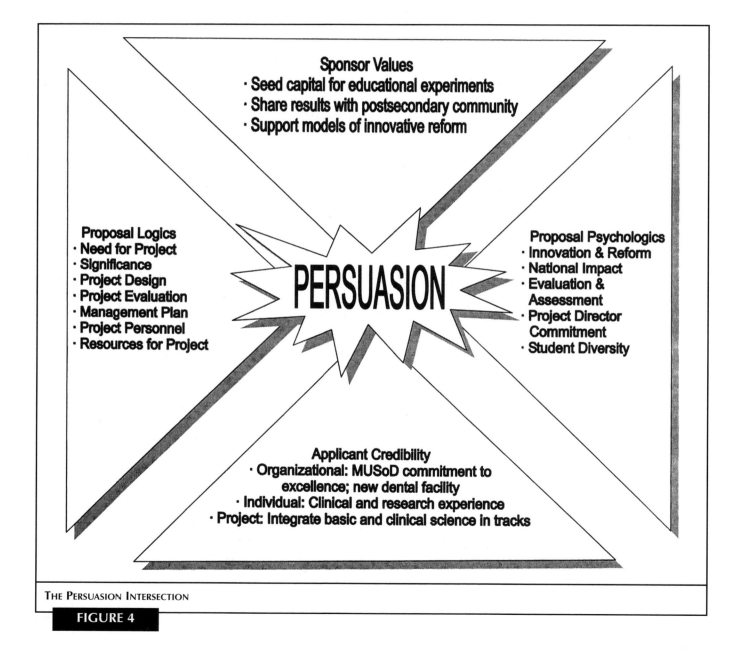

THE PERSUASION INTERSECTION

FIGURE 4

US Department of Education
Washington, D.C. 20202

GRANT AWARD NOTIFICATION

1 **RECIPIENT NAME** Marquette University School of Dentistry P.O. Box 1881 Milwaukee, WI 53201-1881	5 **AWARD INFORMATION** PR/AWARD NUMBER: P116B011247 ACTION NUMBER: 01 ACTION TYPE: New AWARD TYPE: Discretionary
2 **PROJECT TITLE** Dental Education Reform: the MUSoD Foundational Curriculum	6 **AWARD PERIODS** BUDGET PERIOD: 10/01/2001–09/30/2002 PERFORMANCE PERIOD: 10/01/2001– 09/30/2004 FUTURE BUDGET PERIODS: 10/01/2002–09/30/2003: $138,632 10/01/2003–09/30/2004: $93,456
3 **PROJECT STAFF** RECIPIENT PROJECT DIRECTOR Joseph Best (414) 288-7155 EDUCATION PROGRAM CONTACT Frank Frankfort (202) 502-7500 EDUCATION PAYMENT CONTACT GAPS PAYEE HOTLINE (888) 336-8930	7 **AUTHORIZED FUNDING** THIS ACTION: $172,439 BUDGET PERIOD: $404,527 PERFORMANCE PERIOD: $404,527
4 **KEY PERSONNEL** NAME, TITLE, LEVEL OF EFFORT Joseph Best, Project Director 25% Anthony Iacopino, Co-Director 25% Thomas Taft, Co-Director 25% Michelle Robinson, Co-Director 25% Ordean Oyen, Co-Director 25%	8 **ADMINISTRATIVE INFORMATION** DUNS/SSN: 93851-3892 REGULATIONS: CFR Title 34 Part 75, EDGAR AS APPLICABLE ATTACHMENTS: N/A

9 **LEGISLATIVE AND FISCAL DATA**

AUTHORITY: PL 105-244 Title VII, Part B of the Higher Education Act as amended in 1998
PROGRAM TITLE: FIPSE Comprehensive Program
CFDA/SUBPROGRAM NO: 84.116A

Version 1
ED-GAPS001 (01/98)

THE GRANT AWARD NOTIFICATION

STAGE TWO: FINAL PROPOSAL

CHAPTER 6
The Emory T. Clark Family Charitable Foundation

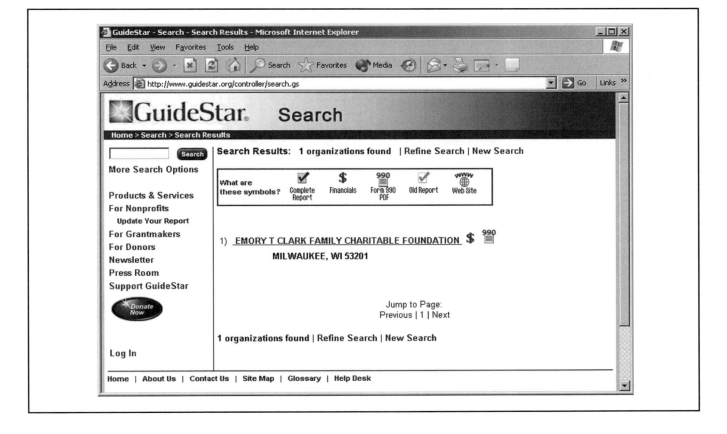

The Emory T. Clark Family Charitable Foundation was incorporated as a private foundation in the state of Wisconsin in 1982. Fifty years earlier, Emory T. Clark, entrepreneur and founder of the Clark Oil and Refining Corporation, opened the first Clark gas station in Milwaukee, Wisconsin. By 1979 business had expanded to 1,814 gas stations in ten midwestern states with total sales in excess of $1 billion. In 1981 Mr. Clark sold his share of the company and assigned a portion of the proceeds to the creation of the Emory T. Clark Family Charitable Foundation. Today the family foundation has assets worth nearly $10 million (2002 figure) and concentrates its resources on activities in education, health and human services, and the arts and culture.

In this chapter we will take an in-depth look at a successful application to the Emory T. Clark Family Charitable Foundation. With its dual interest in education and health and human services, this foundation was identified as a potential sponsor that might support a special project that aims to enhance the teaching skills of educators in grades K–12 who serve children with disabilities. The Foundation uses a single stage application process that requires submission of a three-page full proposal. The elements of this chapter include the following.

Stage One: Full Proposal

- The Request for Proposal
- The Cover Letter
- The Grant Request Application Form
- The Abstract
- The Full Proposal
- The Budget and Budget Narrative
- The Grant Award Notification

In contrast with previous chapters where sponsors issued detailed Request for Proposal (RFP) guidelines, the Emory T. Clark Family Charitable Foundation publishes application guidelines that are brief and written in the broadest sense. Accordingly, this chapter presents a strategy for gaining additional financial and funding information from foundations that do not provide details about their giving patterns and do not have Web sites; namely, we examine their tax returns online at http://www.guidestar.org.

The design of this chapter is consistent with earlier ones. The right-hand (odd numbered) pages present the actual RFP, complete grant application, and grant award notification. The left-hand (even numbered) pages interpret and explain subtle nuances of the RFP, cover letter, application form, abstract, full proposal, budget and budget narrative, and award notification. Thus, you can read this chapter in three ways:

- Read only the odd numbered pages to see the finished written products.
- Read only the even numbered pages to understand the planning process.
- Read the pages sequentially to detail the planning and writing process step by step.

This application models a process of proposal planning and writing that integrates a mix of logical and psychological elements to connect our credibility to the values of the sponsor.

ANALYZING THE REQUEST FOR PROPOSAL

A Request for Proposal (RFP) is an invitation to submit a grant application. Sponsors may issue RFP guidelines that range from broad and flexible to specific and rigid. Whatever the case, analyzing the RFP means asking a series of questions to determine whether or not our organization can develop a proposal that will persuade sponsors that we can be a change agent to solve a problem important to them. To effectively analyze the RFP, we read it in multiple passes, attempting to answer questions about *relevance*, *feasibility*, and *probability*.

Step One: Relevance—Do We Want to Do This?

For nearly a decade, the St. Norbert College teacher education program has offered master's level and certification programs in adaptive education. Teachers who are trained in adaptive education can help children with physical and cognitive disabilities participate fully in the classroom and express themselves to the world through the use of assistive technologies. For example, hands-free voice recognition systems aid children who do not have control over their upper extremities, e.g., paralysis due to a cervical spinal cord injury. As an institution of higher education, the challenge we face is that technologies are changing faster than teaching pedagogy. To overcome this gap we needed to identify a sponsor who shared our concern for educational initiatives and for improving the quality of life for children with disabilities.

The *Foundation Directory* has been a basic prospect research tool for many years. The current 24th edition (2002) is divided into two parts. Part 1 provides information on the 10,000 largest grantmaking foundations, and Part 2 lists the next largest 10,000 grantmaking foundations. These 20,000 largest grantmaking foundations represent less than one-third of the total number of existing foundations in the United States, yet they control more than 90 percent of all foundation assets and make more than 90 percent of all foundation grants. Collectively, they donate more than $21 billion annually. Each entry in the *Foundation Directory* identifies the foundation's name, contact information address, a statement of purpose, financial data, giving limitations, and brief application information.

In step one, we searched the *Foundation Directory*

and identified the Emory T. Clark Family Charitable Foundation as a possible funding source. Next we obtained a copy and skimmed through their RFP guidelines. From these two sources we developed a one-page summary of the main points and distributed it to key personnel to assess their interest in pursuing this grant possibility further. In thrity seconds or less, our colleagues, supervisors, and administrators can read the following memorandum and answer the question, "Do we want to do this?"

RFP Guidelines. The Emory T. Clark Family Charitable Foundation makes grants to nonprofit organizations that help people in their collective community efforts to improve themselves and the quality of life in all its aspects. Some key points in their broad application guidelines include:

- Approximately $475,000 is distributed annually.
- 20–25 awards are made annually.
- Giving is primarily for education, health and human services, the arts and culture.
- A three-page full proposal is due by July 15.
- Funding decisions are made by December 1.

This appears to be a good match for us. Let's meet next week Tuesday at 1:00 p.m. in my office to discuss further the possibility of developing an application.

Step Two: Feasibility—Can We Do This?

After securing organizational support to pursue this funding opportunity, in step two we examined the RFP guidelines for evaluation criteria, hot buttons, and distinctive features. This second level of analysis begins to answer the question, "Can we do this?"

Evaluation Criteria. The Emory T. Clark Family Charitable Foundation will use the following stated evaluation criteria in their selection process. Proposals for special projects should include:

- A completed Grant Request Application Form
- A one-page abstract that summarizes the proposed project
- A three-page project narrative that:
    Introduces the organization and identifies its experience and qualifications
    States the problem, including the size and characteristics of the population to be served
    Describes project objectives
    Indicates project methods, including a timeline of activities

EMORY T. CLARK FAMILY CHARITABLE FOUNDATION

"Contributing to improve the quality of life."

TRUSTEES:
Ruth Clark La Badie
Majorie J. Takton
Gerald E. Connolly
First Wisconsin Trust Company

EXECUTIVE DIRECTOR:
William J. La Badie

Philosophy . . . "to help people in their collective community efforts to improve themselves and the quality of life in all of its aspects."

Policy . . . "to make this help possible through meaningful grant to a wide variety of qualified organizations."

The Emory T. Clark Family Charitable Foundation was created by Emory T. Clark because of his great desire to help people in their collective community efforts to improve themselves and the quality of life in all of its aspects through education, health care facilities and programs, civic, art and cultural organizations, and other worthy endeavors.

These will include efforts to improve the cultural environment in which we live and work, and to contribute to the continued strength and changing community needs of a free society. By assisting such services, we contribute to the communities' growth and their citizens' quality of life.

Other long-term benefits include prospects of more jobs, better community health and education, and a wider variety of recreational and cultural opportunities available to more citizens.

The Foundation makes this help possible through meaningful grants to a wide variety of qualified organizations. It supports causes which will have the greatest impact, in the opinion of the trustees, on the community served and its residents. The Foundation contributes to causes with the same care and attention with which it invests its funds.

The Foundation will not make grants to individuals, political organizations or candidates, veteran organizations, religious organizations, fund raising benefits or advertisements.

THE REQUEST FOR PROPOSAL

STAGE ONE: FULL PROPOSAL

Describes an evaluation plan

Identifies future and other necessary funding to support the project.

- A two-page budget that presents line item detail of project expenses and income sources
- Attachments:

  A complete list of the organization's officers

  The organization's actual income and expense statements for the past fiscal year

  The organization's projected income and expense budget for the current fiscal year

  The organization's most recent audited financial statement

  Copies of the IRS federal tax exemption determination letter
- Submit one copy of the proposal
- Due date: July 15, 2002

Hot Buttons and Distinctive Features. As we read the RFP guidelines, two hot buttons stand out immediately: *improving quality of life* and *collective community efforts*. These hot buttons, repeated throughout the RFP, gain force over other criteria and influence the design, shape, and direction of the proposed project. One distinctive feature raised in the RFP guidelines is *financial planning*. Responding to this distinctive feature will not guarantee funding success; however, failing to acknowledge it may be viewed as a project weakness. In other words, to increase the competitiveness of our proposal, hot buttons and distinctive features—logical and psychological needs—must be addressed strategically in the narrative.

Hot Button: Improving Quality of Life

The Emory T. Clark Family Charitable Foundation's first hot button concern is stated in the form of their motto on front cover page of the RFP guidelines: "Contributing to improve the quality of life." Nine key words and phrases appear a dozen times throughout the RFP guidelines emphasizing the sponsor's hot button concern for improving quality of life, including: *quality of life, improve themselves, long-term benefits, greatest impact, outcomes, who will be better off, progress and ultimate success, significance, past program accomplishments.*

Hot Button: Collective Community Efforts

The sponsor's focus on collective community efforts is also emphasized up front in the RFP guidelines in their philosophy statement: "to help people in their collective community efforts to improve themselves." Five key words and phrases are repeated nearly a

dozen times, stressing the importance of project efforts being cooperative community initiatives. Broad descriptive words for this hot button include: *collective community efforts, client and community support, community, collaboration, complement existing community services.*

Distinctive Feature: Financial Planning

A distinctive feature noted in the RFP guidelines is the sponsor's expectation that applicants have a financial plan for the viability of their proposed projects. In particular, on the Grant Request Instructions page, the "Future and Other Necessary Funding" section states, "Describe the financial plan for current support of the project." This directive is immediately followed by four additional questions regarding the funding resources necessary to complete and sustain the proposed project. This rapid-fire use of interrogative sentences makes *financial planning* stand out as a distinctive feature. The other elements of the project narrative, in contrast, use mainly imperative sentences to make a request or command, e.g., "Describe the significance. . . . Describe the scope. . . . Document the size and characteristics. . . . Indicate the level of collaboration . . ." Quite simply, the sponsor wants assurance that its funds will be utilized wisely.

Step Three: Probability—Will We Be Competitive?

In step three, we ask probing questions about our organizational strengths and weaknesses in relation to the values of the sponsor. This strategic thinking helps us define our institutional uniqueness. Typically, strategic thinking questions lay the basis for preproposal contacts with the sponsor. However, prospect research revealed that the family foundation does not have a professional staff to answer preproposal contact questions. Indeed, the vast majority of all foundations do not have any paid staff. Even among the larger foundations—those giving away more than $100,000 annually—only 15 percent have any paid employees. As a result, tax records serve as the only source of information on activities of many foundations. Collectively, this third level of analysis answers the question, "Will we be competitive?"

Strategic Thinking. As we read each criterion in the project narrative section of the RFP guidelines, we generated the following list of strategic thinking questions that needed to be addressed internally to assess our level of competitiveness.

How to submit a Grant Request

ALL REQUESTS MUST BE MADE IN WRITING

1. All requests for grants must be accompanied by a Grant Request Form.

2. Follow the instructions that you received on the Grant Request Form.

3. Observe the deadline notice that was stated on the cover letter you received on your Grant Request Form.

4. Do not send more information than requested on the instructions.

Address all Proposals to:
William J. La Badie, Director
Emory T. Clark Family Charitable Foundation
125 North Executive Drive, Suite #363
Brookfield, Wisconsin 53005

✳   ✳   ✳

GRANT REQUEST INSTRUCTIONS
EMORY T. CLARK FAMILY CHARITABLE FOUNDATION

PROPOSAL OUTLINE FOR SPECIAL PROJECTS

SPECIAL PROJECT OUTLINES: Applicants seeking funds for special projects other than capital should use this outline referring to each point that is relevant to the proposed project, present their case clearly and concisely, and adhering to the recommended space limitations. The format is intended as a guide, providing direction; not every item will be relevant to every application.

A.   PROJECT ABSTRACT (Do not exceed one page).

   Briefly summarize the proposed project. Identify the problem or need to be addressed, the project's objectives and the proposed strategy for achieving them. Indicate the total estimated project cost, the amount requested from the Foundation and identify other principal sources of support.

B.   PROJECT NARRATIVE (Do not exceed three pages).

   Introduction: Describe the organization's capacity to undertake the proposed project. Indicate its previous achievement experience and qualifications. Document past

Introduction

- How can we make our proposal stand out from the competition?
- What are our capabilities to successfully implement this project?
- Do we have data to document the effectiveness of current activities?
- What levels of community support exist for this project?
- What is the relationship between this project and our organizational mission?

Problem Statement

- Do we have recent needs assessment data to document how many children are affected by physical and cognitive disabilities in our community and statewide?
- What is the race/ethnicity, age, and gender status, and geographic disbursement of targeted children with disabilities?
- How many teachers locally and statewide serve children with disabilities?
- How many teachers are adequately trained to do so?
- What level of collaboration exists with other agencies serving similar populations?
- How does the proposed project expand or complement existing community services?

Program Objectives

- How many children with disabilities can we realistically serve?
- How many teachers can we realistically serve?
- What outcomes do we plan to achieve?
- Are these outcomes realistic?

Methods

- Why is this the best approach to meeting the needs of teachers and their students?
- What previous experience and qualifications do we have to serve this population of teachers and children with disabilities?
- What steps do we need to take to complete our objectives?
- What does the project timeline look like?

Evaluation Plan

- Should evaluations be conducted internally, externally, or both?
- Do internal evaluators have the expertise, experience, capability, and resources to objectively assess the program and its activities?
- What types of evaluation indicators are most appropriate to measure the progress and ultimate success of this project?

Future and Other Necessary Funding

- What cash and in-kind resources can we contribute to this project?
- Are additional funds necessary to complete the project?
- What resources are currently serving or could be tapped to serve the community?
- What strategies do we have for sustaining program efforts?
- Do we have examples of other programs that have been sustained beyond an initial granting period?
- Will we be able to meet the sponsor's requirements for submitting an annual progress and financial report?

About Emory T. Clark Family Charitable Foundation

- Do we know any of the trustees or directors identified at the family foundation?
- Do we know any individuals at other organizations who have received funding from this family foundation?
- Are our odds of getting funded good enough to merit submitting a proposal?

Preproposal Contact. Because the Emory T. Clark Family Charitable Foundation does not have a Web site and does not have a professional staff to answer preproposal contact questions, we reviewed their tax records to gain additional financial and funding information. By law, foundations are required to submit IRS 990-AR (Annual Reports) or 990-PF (Private Foundation) returns. The 990s are the private foundation equivalents of individuals' 1040 income tax records; the 990s are inching their way onto the Internet, thus inviting a new era of public scrutiny. One of the leading Web sites is GuideStar, a charity group working with the IRS to post over 850,000 nonprofit tax records online at http://www.guidestar.org.

As we review foundation tax records, we pay particular attention to seven key pieces of information.

1. *Line I: Fair market value of all assets at end of year.* We multiply this value by five percent to determine the minimum amount of money the foundation must disperse by law during the reporting year.

program accomplishments and show evidence of client and community support. Address the relationship between the proposed project and the organization's mission.

Problem Statement of Needs Assessment: Describe the significance of the proposed project to the community. Define the scope and significance of the problem or need to be addressed by the project. Document the size and characteristics of the population to be served. Indicate the level of collaboration with other agencies serving similar populations. Indicate how the proposed project would expand or complement existing community services.

Program Objectives: Describe the outcomes of the project in measurable terms. Who will be better off, and how, at the end of the grant period.

Methods: Indicate the sequence of activities needed to accomplish the program objectives. Describe staff qualifications and responsibilities, and staff and volunteer training, and client selection procedures or policies. Include a project timeline. Is this the best approach to achieve program objectives? Why?

Evaluation Plan: Describe how the applicant plans to measure the progress and ultimate success of the proposed project.

Future and Other Necessary Funding: Describe the financial plan for current support of the project. What is the rationale for the amount requested from the Emory T. Clark Family Charitable Foundation? If other funding is necessary to complete the project budget, where will it come from? If the project will be continued, how will it be supported in the future?

C.   PROJECT BUDGET (Do not exceed two pages).

Present a line item budget including project expenses and income sources, delineating how funds requested from the Emory T. Clark Foundation would be spent.

CAPITAL REQUEST OUTLINE

The following outline must be used in preparing grant proposals for CAPITAL requests. Please adhere to the recommended space limitations.

A.   AGENCY DESCRIPTION (Do not exceed one page).

Briefly describe the organization and purposes. Indicate the principal geographic area of service and the population served. Include numerical estimates for the last year.

B.   PROPOSED PROJECT (Do not exceed two pages).

THE REQUEST FOR PROPOSAL

STAGE ONE: FULL PROPOSAL

2. *Part I, Line 24: Total operating and administrative expenses.* It costs money to do business. This value tells us how much the foundation had to spend in order to disperse its grant dollars, i.e., its indirect costs. Divide this value by the total expenses and disbursements in order to calculate the foundation's indirect cost rate.

3. *Part I, Line 25: Contributions, gifts, grants paid.* This value tells us exactly how much money the foundation distributed.

4. *Part I, Line 26: Total expenses and disbursements.* This value is the sum of the foundation's operating and administrative expenses and its contributions, gifts, and grants paid. This value should be equal to or greater than five percent of its fair market assets.

5. *Part VIII, Line 1: List all officers, directors, trustees, foundation managers, and their compensation.* We circulate this list of key personnel within our organization to identify possible linkages or networks.

6. *Part XV, Line 2: Information regarding contribution, grant, gift, loan, scholarship, etc., programs.* This section tells us how to apply. It provides the name, address, and telephone number of the person to whom applications should be addressed; the form in which applications should be submitted and information and materials they should include; any submission deadlines; and any restrictions or limitations on awards.

7. *Part XV, Line 3: Grants and contributions paid during the year or approved for future payment.* We study this list to determine whether any organizations similar to ours have received foundation dollars. Further, we look for patterns in foundation giving amounts. We compare and contrast patterns in an overall grant profile and by categories of interest. Common patterns include measures of clustering (the mean, median, and mode) and a measure of dispersion (the range). Each is described below.

- The **mean**, or average, is the sum of the individual grant award amounts divided by the total number of awards made.
- The **median** is the middle number in an ordered list of grant award amounts arranged from smallest to largest. In the case when there are two "middle numbers," use the mean (average) of those two numbers.
- The **mode** is simply the most frequently occurring grant amount(s) in the list of total awards.
- The **range** shows the spread of grant awards and is calculated as the difference between the highest award amount and the lowest award amount.

"Since your average award last year was $xx,xxx, do you expect that to change?" is a common preproposal contact question asked of sponsors. Because the Emory T. Clark Family Charitable Foundation does not have a professional staff to answer questions, we conduct a detailed analysis of their tax records over the past three years. As the following table indicates, although the greatest number of awards are made to health and human service agencies, the mean (average) award amount to an educational institution was $6,000 greater than the mean award to a health and human service agency. In addition, by category, the mean and median award amounts to educational institutions exceeded the mean and median awards to health and human service agencies and were greater than the overall mean and median awards. Also of note, educational institutions consistently received the largest single award amounts.

	2001	2000	1999
A. Grant Profile: Overall			
Total giving	$445,150 (100%)	$514,000 (100%)	$477,737 (100%)
Number of awards	23 (100%)	20 (100%)	20 (100%)
Giving range	$48,350	$40,000	$55,237
	High: $50,000	High: $50,000	High: $60,237
	Low: $1,650	Low: $10,000	Low: $5,000
Mean award amount	$19,354	$25,700	$23,886
Median award amount	$20,000	$20,000	$20,000
Mode award amount	$25,000	$20,000	$50,000

Describe the project including the anticipated significance both for the organization and the community. Explain the impact of the proposed project on the organization's operating budget. Cite other project alternatives that were considered and reasons for rejecting them. Indicate the status of any of the required regulatory approval, as appropriate.

C.   PROJECT BUDGET (<u>Do not exceed two pages</u>).

Present a line item budget including project expenses and income sources, delineating how funds requested from the Emory T. Clark Family Charitable Foundation would be spent.

Submit the following attachments with the completed proposal:

1. A complete list of the organization's officers.
2. The organization's actual income and expense statements for the past fiscal year. Identify the agency's principal sources of support.
3. The organization's projected income and expense budget for the current fiscal year. Identify the projected revenue sources.
4. The organization's most recent audited financial statement.
5. Copies of the IRS federal tax exemption determination letter.

$* \quad * \quad *$

Emory T. Clark Family Charitable Foundation
125 North Executive Drive
Suite 363
Brookfield, Wisconsin 53005
(262) 821-8610

Grant Request Form

COMPLETE THE FOLLOWING AND DESCRIBE THE PROJECT USING EITHER THE SPECIAL PROJECT OUTLINE OR THE CAPITAL REQUEST OUTLINE ON PAGE TWO.

Date Submitted _____

Organization Name _____

Address _____

Chairperson of the Governing Body _____

Contact Person _____ Title _____ Telephone _____

Amount Requested _____

	2001	2000	1999
B. Grant Profile by Category: Education			
Total giving	$190,000 (42.7%)	$247,000 (48.1%)	$225,237 (47.1%)
Number of awards	8 (34.8%)	9 (45.0%)	7 (35.0%)
Giving range	$45,000	$40,000	$50,237
	High: $50,000	High: $50,000	High: $60,237
	Low: $5,000	Low: $10,000	Low: $10,000
Mean award amount	$23,750	$27,444	$32,177
Median award amount	$25,000	$25,000	$25,000
Mode award amount	$25,000	$25,000; $50,000	$10,000; $50,000
Observations	Largest single award	3 of 5 largest awards; 2 of 4 smallest awards	Largest single award; 3 of 5 largest awards
C. Grant Profile by Category: Health/Human Service			
Total giving	$240,150 (53.9%)	$267,000 (51.9%)	$207,500 (43.4%)
Number of awards	14 (60.9%)	11 (55.0%)	9 (45.0%)
Giving range	$33,350	$40,000	$45,000
	High: $35,000	High: $50,000	High: 50,000
	Low: $1,650	Low: $10,000	Low: $5,000
Mean award amount	$17,154	$24,273	$23,056
Median award amount	$17,500	$20,000	$20,000
Mode award amount	$15,000; $20,000; $25,000	$20,000	$5,000; $20,000; $25,000; $50,000
Observations	Second largest award; 2 smallest awards	2 of 5 largest awards; 2 of 4 smallest awards	2 of 5 largest awards; 3 of 4 smallest awards
D. Grant Profile by Category: Arts/Culture			
Total giving	$15,000 (3.4%)	$0 (0.0%)	$45,000 (9.4%)
Number of awards	1 (4.3%)	0 (0.0%)	4 (20.0%)
Giving range	$0	$0	$10,000
	High: $15,000	High: $0	High: $15,000
	Low: $15,000	Low: $0	Low: $5,000
Mean award amount	$15,000	$0	$11,250
Median award amount	$15,000	$0	$12,500
Mode award amount	$15,000	$0	$15,000
Observations	Only 5 awards are smaller	No awards	1 of 4 smallest awards

Using this iterative, three-step RFP Analysis Process, we move along the Roads to the Persuasion Intersection, gathering the details necessary to develop a persuasive full proposal. Next we examine how we arrive at the Persuasion Intersection in the complete grant application; our project idea appeals to the values of the sponsor through a strategic blend of logical and psychological elements.

Duration of Project _____

Total Project Budget _____

When are Funds Needed? _____

Type of Grant Requested: Capital Request ☐   Special Project Request ☐

AGENCY INFORMATION

Date Established _____ Number of Full-Time Employees _____

General description of organization and purposes with an indication of population served (including numerical estimates for the last year) and principal geographic area of service:

What are the dates of the organization's fiscal year? _____

Total operating expenses for the past fiscal year? _____ For the current year? _____

Has the governing body approved a policy which states that the organization does not discriminate as to age, race, religion, sex, national origin, or handicapped? Yes ☐ No ☐

Does the organization have FEDERAL tax exempt status? _____ Tax ID Number _____

Attach a copy of the organization's Federal tax exemption determination letter.

Internal Revenue Code Sections covering exemption are Section 501(c)(3) and Section 509(a)

Has this request been authorized by the organization's governing body? Yes ☐ No ☐

When?

The undersigned, an authorized officer of the organization, does hereby certify that the information set forth in this grant application is true and correct, that the Federal tax exemption determination letter attached hereto has not been revoked and the present operation of the organization and its current sources of support are not inconsistent with the organization's continuing tax exempt classification as set forth in such determination letter.

Signature _____ Title _____

DEVELOPING THE COVER LETTER

To ensure consistency in the presentation of our main ideas, we begin developing the cover letter *after* the full proposal is completed. That is to say, while the cover letter is the first section of our grant application to be read, it is the last one to be written. In one page (250 words) we:

- overview the proposal;
- provide an understanding of the project's significance;
- highlight organizational uniqueness, qualifications, and capabilities to conduct the project;
- reflect the project's consistency with sponsor values, funding priorities, evaluation criteria and hot buttons;
- name the project director who can be contacted for more information.

Elements of the Cover Letter

Paragraph #1. This first paragraph is an overview of the entire application packet. It names the applicant organization, relates to the sponsor eligibility criteria for supporting special projects in education, requests a specific dollar amount, and states the outcome of the project. In generic form, the paragraph takes the form: [self-identification] is pleased to submit a proposal to [sponsor] requesting [budget amount] to [project benefit]. Note that the project benefit is expressed in terms of sponsor-oriented values rather than self-oriented needs.

Paragraph #2. The second paragraph begins to establish our organizational uniqueness and credibility—the only institution of higher education in the state with graduate and certificate programs in Adaptive Education. This paragraph also foreshadows our approach to one of the sponsor's hot buttons: improving quality of life. Namely, program activities help children with disabilities to develop their academic abilities, an appreciation for the arts, and independent living skills.

Paragraph #3. In the third paragraph we state the purpose of this project and appeal to both sponsor hot buttons: (1) collective community efforts, and (2) improving quality of life. The first sentence characterizes project objectives, describing *what* the project will do; namely, revising and updating Adaptive Education certificate programming. The second sentence describes our long-term collaborative relationship with an alternative school that specializes in serving children with disabilities. The last sentence of the paragraph humanizes the significance of achieving project objectives: Enhancing training experiences for teachers will improve the quality of life and learning opportunities for students with disabilities.

Paragraph #4. The last paragraph provides telephone and e-mail contact information for the project director and ends on a positive note that nudges the sponsor toward a favorable funding decision.

Signature Line. The highest ranking organizational official signs the cover letter to show that this application has full institutional support.

July 8, 2002

William J. LaBadie
Executive Director
Emory T. Clark Family Charitable Foundation
125 North Executive Drive, Suite 363
Brookfield, WI 53005

Dear Mr. LaBadie:

St. Norbert College is pleased to submit a proposal to the Emory T. Clark Family Charitable Foundation requesting $25,000 in funds to support a special project, "Preparing Teachers for Students with Disabilities." This project will enhance the teaching skills of educators who work with children with cognitive and physical disabilities.

Our Center for Adaptive Education and Assistive Technology (CAEAT) fosters unique interactions between teachers and children ages 3 to 21 with special needs. CAEAT is a valuable training ground for undergraduate education students, graduate students, and current practicing teachers to work with children with disabilities to develop their academic abilities, an appreciation for the arts, and independent living skills. In fact, St. Norbert is the only school in the state with graduate and certificate programs in Adaptive Education.

To better prepare teachers to serve students with disabilities, with your support we propose to revise and update Adaptive Education certificate programming. CAEAT has a long-term close working partnership with Syble Hopp School, an alternative school for children with cognitive and physical impairments, which provides numerous opportunities for teachers to interact with students with disabilities. In short, enhanced training experiences for teachers will translate into improved quality of life and learning opportunities for students with disabilities.

Thank you for your consideration of this proposal. Please contact Barbara Natelle, Director of CAEAT to answer questions or provide further information—phone: (920) 403-3901; email: barb.natelle@snc.edu. We look forward to working with you on this important initiative.

Sincerely,

William J. Hynes
President

THE COVER LETTER

STAGE ONE: FULL PROPOSAL

DEVELOPING THE GRANT REQUEST APPLICATION FORM

The Emory T. Clark Family Charitable Foundation requires a completed "Grant Request Form" to be submitted with the proposal. This application form helps establish our credibility in a condensed format. In twenty line item elements, we present information about our organization, institutional officials, project director, project, and budget. Each element is described below.

Elements of the Grant Request Application Form

Item 1: Date Submitted. A search of the *Foundation Directory* revealed that the deadline for submitting proposals is July 15. Accordingly, we mail our proposal in advance of this due date.

Item 2: Organization Name. Grant awards are made to institutions, not individuals. Thus, St. Norbert College is the legal applicant for this project.

Item 3: Address. As required, we provide a complete mailing address.

Item 4: Chairperson of Governing Body. We enter the name of the official who provides leadership and administrative oversight to the institution.

Item 5: Contact Person. The Project Director serves as the key point of contact between the Emory T. Clark Family Charitable Foundation and our institution and is the individual ultimately responsible for all programmatic aspects of this initiative. Although not specifically requested, we provide a telephone number.

Item 6: Amount Requested. In this line item we enter the amount of project funding requested from the sponsor. At a glance, reviewers can determine that our request is within the sponsor's typical award range of $10,000 to $50,000 for a one-year grant.

Item 7: Duration of Project. The sponsor's typical award period is twelve months. Thus, we designed the project to take place during the span of the calendar year.

Item 8: Total Project Budget. A detailed analysis of the sponsor's tax records over a three-year period revealed that a reasonable budget request from an educational institution is $25,000.

Item 9: When are Funds Needed? The *Foundation Directory* reveals that final notifications of grant awards will occur by December 1. Since this date is close to the end of fall semester, right before final exams, we decided it would be more appropriate to begin the project on January 1.

Item 10: Type of Grant Requested. The Emory T. Clark Family Charitable Foundation supports two types of requests, capital and special projects. We check the appropriate box.

Item 11: Date Established and Number of Full-Time Employees. These details about our date of establishment and number of full-time employees help establish our organizational credibility. With more than a century's worth of experience, the sponsor can trust that we are committed to providing quality educational opportunities to students.

Item 12: General Description of Organization. The application form limits our description to one succinct paragraph, five sentences totaling 143 words. The sentences are taken verbatim from the full proposal. The first sentence identifies *who* we are. The second establishes our credibility to implement this project. The third describes *what* we do in terms of the hot button of improving quality of life. The fourth addresses the hot button of collaborative community efforts. And the fifth sentence describes the major *outcome* of this special project and reflects sponsor-oriented values.

Item 13: Dates of Organization's Fiscal Year. This line item element is the first of three questions that work in tandem to establish our fiscal credibility, demonstrating to the sponsor that we will be good stewards of their funding.

Item 14: Total Operating Expenses for Past Year. Listing our total operating expenses for the past year provides the sponsor with baseline information about our financial health and viability.

Item 15: Total Operating Expenses for Current Year. Listing our total operating expenses for the current year allows the sponsor to compare our financial status against the baseline.

Item 16: Policy of Nondiscrimination. This line item element is another way for the sponsor to validate our credibility; we are an organization that believes in fair and ethical treatment for all individuals. Our policy of nondiscrimination is consistent with the federal Civil Rights Act of 1964.

Item 17: Tax-Exempt Status. Under federal law, most grant awards made by private foundations are to tax-exempt nonprofit organizations. St. Norbert College is such an organization under Section 501(c)(3) of the Internal Revenue Code.

Item 18: Tax ID Number. The application form requests our tax identification number. This nine-digit number is assigned by the Internal Revenue Service and is used to identify taxpayers that are required to file various business tax returns.

Emory T. Clark Family Charitable Foundation
125 North Executive Drive
Suite 363
Brookfield, Wisconsin 53005
(262) 821-8610

Grant Request Form

COMPLETE THE FOLLOWING AND DESCRIBE THE PROJECT USING EITHER THE SPECIAL PROJECT OUTLINE OR THE CAPITAL REQUEST OUTLINE ON PAGE TWO.

Date Submitted _July 10, 2002_

Organization Name _St. Norbert College_

Address _100 Grant Street, De Pere, WI 54115_

Chairperson of the Governing Body _Thomas M. Olejniczak, Esq._

Contact Person _Barbara Natelle, Director – (920) 403-3901_

Amount Requested _$25,000_

Duration of Project _January 1, 2003 to December 31, 2003_

Total Project Budget _$25,000_

When are Funds Needed? _January 1, 2003_

Type of Grant Requested: Capital Request ☐   Special Project Request ☒

AGENCY INFORMATION

Date Established _October 10, 1898_   **Number of Full-Time Employees** _530_

General description of organization and purposes with an indication of population served (including numerical estimates for the last year) and principal geographic area of service:

St. Norbert College, a regionally renowned private liberal arts college, has an enrollment of 2,100 undergraduate and graduate students. Widely regarded as the premier teacher training school in the state, the College offers unique learning experiences for educators of children with disabilities through the Center for Adaptive Education and Assistive Technology (CAEAT). CAEAT programs foster interactions between teachers and children ages 3 to 21 with disabilities in activities designed to develop academic abilities, an appreciation for the arts, and independent living skills. A long-term partnership with Syble Hopp School, an alternative school for nearly 150 children with cognitive and physical impairments, provides numerous opportunities for teachers-in-training to interact with assistive technologies and students with disabilities before they enter their

THE GRANT REQUEST APPLICATION FORM

STAGE ONE: FULL PROPOSAL

Item 19: Request Authorized by Governing Body. This line item element ensures that there is timely communication of fundraising activities across the institution.

Item 20: Institutional Authorization. We enter the name and title of the official who has the authority to accept grant funding and commit the institution to executing the proposed project.

professional fields. The outcome of this project is to enhance the teaching skills of the 130 practicing teachers annually who take coursework through CAEAT.

What are the dates of the organization's fiscal year?   June 1–May 31

Total operating expenses for the past fiscal year? $47 million

Total operating expenses for the current year? $56 million

Has the governing body approved a policy which states that the organization does not discriminate as to age, race, religion, sex, national origin, or handicapped? Yes ☒ No ☐

Does the organization have FEDERAL tax exempt status? Yes

Tax ID Number   39-1399196

Attach a copy of the organization's Federal tax exemption determination letter.

Internal Revenue Code Sections covering exemption are Section 501(c)(3) and Section 509(a) Yes

Has this request been authorized by the organization's governing body?

Yes ☒   No ☐ **When?** July 8, 2002

The undersigned, an authorized officer of the organization, does hereby certify that the information set forth in this grant application is true and correct, that the Federal tax exemption determination letter attached hereto has not been revoked and the present operation of the organization and its current sources of support are not inconsistent with the organization's continuing tax exempt classification as set forth in such determination letter.

Signature   William J. Hynes   **Title**   President

DEVELOPING THE PROJECT ABSTRACT

The project abstract serves as a condensed summary of our entire proposal. In one page (approximately 400 words) we provide a brief overview of the problem situation, our proposed solution, and the total project cost. To ensure consistency of presentation and tone, the project abstract was written *after* the proposal was completed. In fact, the vast majority of sentences in the abstract are taken verbatim from the narrative.

Elements of the Project Abstract

Paragraph #1. This first paragraph identifies the applicant organization, describes our organizational uniqueness, and establishes the credibility of our program. It lets the sponsor know *who* is responsible for implementing the proposed project. Note that the first time we identify our Center for Adaptive Education and Assistive Technology, we spell out its name in full, followed by the acronym in parentheses (CAEAT); subsequently we use the acronym only. The last sentence of this paragraph hints at *who will benefit* from project activities, e.g., teachers and children ages 3 to 21 with cognitive and physical disabilities.

Paragraph #2. The "Problem" statement justifies *why* our project is needed. The first sentence defines the problem: a shortage of well-trained teaching professionals. The second sentence quantifies the *magnitude* of this problem, particularly relating to teachers working with children who have special needs. In the third sentence we further illustrate the *severity* of the problem by listing the vast range of children's special needs that must be accommodated. The final sentence of the paragraph pulls double duty, indicating the *frequency* of the problem and articulating the *shortcomings of the status quo* to address the problem. These shortcomings also facilitate the transition to the next section, foreshadowing our approach to solving the problem.

Paragraph #3. This "Objectives" paragraph tells the sponsor exactly *what* we are going to do to overcome the shortage of teaching professionals trained in adaptive education. Although the sponsor did not ask for a project goal, we included one as a way of setting our objectives into context. In the final two sentences, we articulate the humanistic results—the outcomes—of achieving these goals and objectives; enhancing teachers' skills with assistive technologies will promote student learning and development, a sponsor hot button relating to improving quality of life for children with disabilities.

Paragraph #4. The "Strategy" describes our project methodology—*how* the project will be implemented. The first sentence identifies *who* is responsible for leading project efforts. The second sentence describes the qualifications of project consultants. And the third sentence justifies the use of consultants in terms of a sponsor hot button—collective community efforts; namely, consultants serve as the vital link between higher education and the realities of daily participation in school settings.

Notice that this "Strategy" section is the shortest of the three major sections in the project abstract: roughly two-thirds of the length of the "Problem" section and half of the length of the "Objectives" section. That's because in this summary format we want the sponsor to understand the purpose and significance of our project without getting bogged down in the details of it. The sponsor can read the specifics of our methodology in the full proposal.

Paragraph #5. This final paragraph on "Budget Request" overviews *how much* the project will cost. Yet at the same time we humanize these costs by articulating the benefit of the project to the target populations of teachers and children with disabilities. Finally, all three sentences of this paragraph touch on the sponsor distinctive feature of financial planning. The first sentence indicates that this project is "cost-effective." The second sentence suggests that the project will continue beyond the granting period because program enhancements will be "institutionalized." And the third sentence reassures the sponsor that this is a one-time project request; they will not have to provide ongoing financial support: "no additional funding will be necessary to complete or sustain this project."

Project Abstract: "Preparing Teachers for Students with Disabilities"

St. Norbert College, widely regarded as the premier teacher training school in the state, offers unique learning experiences for educators of children with disabilities through the Center for Adaptive Education and Assistive Technology (CAEAT). CAEAT programs foster interactions between teachers and children ages 3 to 21 with cognitive and physical disabilities.

Problem: Lack of Training for Teachers who Serve Students with Disabilities

Our nation is faced with a wide range of challenges in our primary and secondary educational system and none is greater than the shortage of well-trained teaching professionals. Only 20% of teachers feel comfortable teaching children with special needs. Special needs students have long-term, chronic physical, developmental, behavioral, and emotional conditions that limit activities and require higher than usual amounts of service. Over the last decade, teachers have left special education at nearly twice the rate that they have left regular education positions because of lack of training, limited professional resources, and too few special education certification programs.

Objectives: Quality Training Experiences for Teachers of Disabled Students

CAEAT is a valuable training ground for teachers, and offers certificate programs in Adaptive Education. The goal of this project is to better prepare teachers for students with disabilities.

- *Objective 1: Revise and Update the Adaptive Education Certification Program.* This 12 credit add-on program will be restructured to better address the needs of educators.

- *Objective 2: Enhance Training on Assistive Technologies.* To be prepared in the classroom, teachers need access to and training on assistive technologies for children with disabilities.

The key project outcome is to enhance the teaching skills of the 130 practicing teachers annually who take coursework through the CAEAT. Teachers who have adaptive education training and experience with assistive technologies will be able to promote student learning and development.

Strategy: Identify and Implement Best Practices for Teaching and Learning

During the granting year, Barbara Natelle, CAEAT Director, will coordinate with special education and curriculum development consultants to revise and update Adaptive Education certification programming. Consultants will be specialists in results-based, research-driven knowledge about teaching and learning. They will also serve as the vital link between higher education and the realities of daily participation in school settings.

Budget Request: $25,000

This project represents a cost-effective approach to systematically preparing current and future teachers in adaptive education and assistive technologies that will enable them to better serve children with disabilities. Curriculum enhancements will be institutionalized into regular course offerings. No additional funding will be necessary to complete or sustain this project.

THE ABSTRACT

STAGE ONE: FULL PROPOSAL

DEVELOPING THE FULL PROPOSAL

Analyzing the Request for Proposal (RFP) guidelines was the first step in developing a full proposal. We quickly determined that the program was a good match for our organization. And once we secured institutional support to pursue this grant opportunity, we examined the RFP for evaluation criteria, hot buttons, and distinctive features. Together, these elements dictated the form and structure of our application. Strategic thinking and preproposal contact supplied us with additional information to fill in the details of the proposal, fine-tuning it to closely match the sponsor's priorities. This iterative analysis process moved us down the Roads to the Persuasion Intersection.

Elements of the Full Proposal

Title. The boldface heading at the top of the page identifies the project title. The title is descriptive and hints at the sponsor's hot button concern for improving quality of life; namely, students with disabilities will be better off.

Overview. The opening paragraph is a one-sentence summary of the entire proposal. This sentence has five crucial elements, including

- *Self-Identification:* We name our organization as the applicant.
- *Organizational Uniqueness:* We state a brief "claim to fame."
- *Sponsor Expectation:* We explain what we want the sponsor to do, e.g., invest in us.
- *Budget Request:* We ask for a specific amount of money.
- *Project Benefit:* We state the major project outcome in terms of a sponsor-oriented benefit.

This 39-word paragraph is crafted carefully to facilitate skim reading. That is, even if reviewers do not read any further than the first sentence of the proposal, they will still know what the whole project is about. At the same time, it establishes the notion that we share common values with the sponsor: to improve educational opportunities for disadvantaged youth.

Introduction. The "Introduction" section lets the sponsor know *who* is responsible for and *who* is participating in the project. In three paragraphs we establish the credibility of our organization, program, and collaborative partners. We describe our capacity to implement the proposed project and relate it to our overall educational mission. This section also touches on both sponsor hot buttons: improving quality of life and collective community efforts.

In the first paragraph, the first two sentences define our mission, our reason for being. This lays the groundwork for the second paragraph, where we tie the proposed project to our mission. We draw on a widely recognized national publication, *U.S. News & World Report*, in the third sentence of the paragraph as testimony of our long-standing reputation for quality.

The second paragraph makes a transition from describing the credibility of our organization, e.g., "the premier teacher training school in the state," to the capabilities of the program, e.g., "offers unique learning experiences for educators of children with disabilities through the Center for Adaptive Education and Assistive Technology (CAEAT)." Because the name of the Center is rather long, we write out the complete term the first time and follow it with the acronym form in parentheses. Acronyms are convenient because they allow us to abbreviate multiword terms into a single understandable term. We define the purpose of the Center in the second sentence, making an explicit connection to the sponsor hot button for improving quality of life: "activities are designed to develop academic abilities, an appreciation for the arts, and independent living skills." The last sentence and subsequent bulleted list affirm that this program is consistent with our educational mission.

The final paragraph in this section addresses the sponsor hot button of collective community efforts. That is, we have a long-term working partnership with a local school that specializes in serving children with disabilities. The last sentence of this paragraph also serves as a transition to the next section of the proposal, foreshadowing the need for this project: "opportunities for teachers-in-training to interact with assistive technologies and students with disabilities *before* they enter their professional fields."

Problem Statement. The statement of the problem is the single most important proposal component that influences funding success. It justifies to the sponsor *why* this project is needed. Accordingly, we document the growing gap between the number of children who have special education needs and the number of teachers prepared to serve them. The consequence of this problem situation: "Many school districts do not have enough qualified staff to provide the special education services required by law."

The importance of the "Problem Statement" cannot be overestimated. It provides the rationale for conducting our project. And so, in three paragraphs we indicate the extent of the current problem, its fre-

Preparing Teachers for Students with Disabilities

St. Norbert College, a regionally renowned private liberal arts college, invites your investment of $25,000 in a special project, "Preparing Teachers for Students with Disabilities," designed to enhance the teaching skills of educators who work with children with disabilities.

Introduction: St. Norbert College *Center for Adaptive Education and Assistive Technology*

St. Norbert College provides a superior education that is personally, intellectually and spiritually challenging. Respected for academic quality, St. Norbert is recognized for sustaining an environment that encourages students to develop their full potential in understanding and serving their world. For the past 12 years, St. Norbert College has ranked among the top 10 best comprehensive colleges in the Midwest in *U.S. News & World Report's* guide to "America's Best Colleges" —including a #2 ranking for academic reputation and #3 overall ranking in 2002.

St. Norbert College, widely regarded as the premier teacher training school in the state, offers unique learning experiences for educators of children with disabilities through the Center for Adaptive Education and Assistive Technology (CAEAT). CAEAT programs foster interactions between teachers and children ages 3 to 21 with cognitive and physical disabilities in activities designed to develop academic abilities, an appreciation for the arts, and independent living skills. CAEAT offers four basic types of programming consistent with our educational mission:

- certification programs for graduate students in four Adaptive Education areas: art, music, regular education, and assistive technology
- a master's degree in Adaptive Education designed for inservice teachers
- enrichment and summer day camp experiences for children and youth with disabilities
- laboratory-based assistive technology demonstrations, training and experiences for teachers, therapists, education students, students, and children with disabilities

A combination of theoretical and practical training ensures that teachers are adequately prepared to engage children with disabilities in their classrooms. A long-term close working partnership with Syble Hopp School, an alternative school for approximately 150 children with cognitive and physical impairments, provides numerous opportunities for teachers-in-training to interact with assistive technologies and students with disabilities before they enter their professional fields.

Problem Statement: Lack of Training for Teachers who Serve Students with Disabilities

Our nation is faced with a wide range of challenges in our primary and secondary educational system and none is greater than the shortage of well-trained teaching professionals. The shortage of teachers prepared and qualified to serve children with disabilities is even more pronounced. The National Center for Education Statistics reports (1999) that nationwide only 20% of teachers feel comfortable teaching children with special needs. In Wisconsin, special education teachers are so hard to find that they represent nearly half of the emergency certificates issued annually—1,137 in 2000—by the Department of Public Instruction to those who fall short of full licensure.

Equally alarming, the number of students classified as needing special education has more than doubled in the last 26 years, and now represents 14.5% of the state's public school population. Children with special needs have long-term, chronic physical, developmental, behavioral, and emotional conditions that limit

St. Norbert College   1

quency and severity, and the shortcomings of the present situation. The first paragraph focuses on the problem from the point of view of teachers. In particular, the first sentence of the paragraph establishes the baseline situation nationwide: There is a shortage of well-trained teaching professionals. The second and third sentences document that this shortage is even greater for teachers prepared and qualified to serve children with disabilities. The fourth sentence describes the impact of this teacher shortage at the state level. Said differently, rather than relying exclusively on national data to justify the project need, we use local data to illustrate how we compare to the national trend.

In the second paragraph, we focus on the problem from the point of view of children with disabilities. We use state level data to document the *frequency* of the problem, e.g., more than 127,000 children were in need of special education services last year, and the *severity* of the problem, e.g., the number of students needing special education services has more than doubled in the last twenty-six years. In other words, a greater number of students are requiring higher than usual amounts of service, but very few educators are qualified to deliver those services.

The third paragraph adds one more emphatic complication to the problem situation, "Over the last decade, teachers have left special education at nearly *twice* the rate that they have left regular education positions." That is to say, if we don't do anything about it, the problem situation will go from bad to worse. The final sentence of this paragraph explains why special education teachers are leaving the field, and more importantly, it serves as a transition that foreshadows and justifies our approach to solving this problem—teachers want access to special education certification programs, resources, and training.

Program Objectives. "Program Objectives" tell the sponsor exactly *what* we are going to do to solve the identified problem. Although the sponsor did not ask for a project goal, we included one as a way of setting our objectives into context. The goal represents the big picture vision of what we wish to accomplish, namely, as the project title suggests, "to better prepare teachers for students with disabilities." In order to accomplish this goal, we must satisfy two specific, measurable objectives: (1) revise and update the adaptive education certificate program, and (2) enhance training on assistive technologies.

The last paragraph in this section describes *who will benefit* from this project. The immediate beneficiaries are the practicing teachers who take coursework through our adaptive education program. The ulti-

mate beneficiaries are children with physical and cognitive disabilities who have classes with these teachers. The final sentence reinforces this sponsor hot button: "quality training experiences for teachers translates into *improved quality of life* and learning opportunities for hundreds of students with disabilities."

Methods. Whereas program objectives tell the sponsor exactly *what* we plan to do, the "Methods" section describes *how* we plan to accomplish those objectives. More precisely, this section: (1) justifies our methodological approach; (2) describes roles and responsibilities of key personnel; and (3) relates project activities to sponsor hot buttons and distinctive features.

The first sentence of the first paragraph establishes common ground: "teachers and researchers agree on the benefits of using assistive technologies with students with disabilities." Notice that we do *not* provide an in-depth literature review of which researchers have determined which technologies have produced which benefits for children with disabilities. This is intentional for two reasons. First, we want to convey that we are familiar with the best practices in the field without overwhelming the sponsor with details. Second, we respect the sponsor-imposed limitations on proposal length, which do not allow for such an analysis. The last sentence in this paragraph identifies *who* will be responsible for leading this project.

The second paragraph is dedicated to explaining our approach to fulfilling objective 1, and the third paragraph elaborates on how objective 2 will be accomplished. At the same time, these paragraphs also appeal to the sponsor's two hot buttons—improving quality of life and collective community efforts. The final sentence of the second paragraph touches on a distinctive feature of the sponsor: financial planning.

Although we do not cite the research that forms the basis of our methods, the third paragraph provides three bulleted point examples of how assistive technologies benefit students with specific disabilities. Said differently, we do not simply provide a list of equipment that we intend to purchase with grant funds. We move toward the Persuasion Intersection by demonstrating the relationship between our organizational needs, e.g., for curriculum revision and technology acquisition, and sponsor values, e.g., for improving quality of life. Assistive technologies are not an end in themselves; rather, they are a means whereby children with disabilities are able to express themselves to the world for the first time.

Evaluation Plan. The "Evaluation Plan," similar to the "Methods" section, answers *how*—how project

activities and require higher than usual amounts of service. In 2001, the Wisconsin Department of Public Instruction designated 127,035 children ages 3 to 21 in need of special education services; 50% of students were categorized as learning disabled.

Many school districts do not have enough qualified staff to provide the special education services required by law. Over the last decade, teachers have left special education at nearly twice the rate that they have left regular education positions. They cite three main reasons why: too few special education certification programs, lack of training, and limited professional resources.

Program Objectives: Quality Training Experiences for Teachers of Disabled Students

CAEAT provides a valuable training ground for undergraduate education students, graduate students, and current practicing teachers to work with children with disabilities. Building on this foundation, we can begin to overcome the shortage of teachers certified to serve children with special needs. The **goal** of this project is to better prepare teachers for students with disabilities.

- *Objective 1: Revise and Update the Adaptive Education Certification Program.* This 12 credit add-on program for graduate students will be restructured to better address the professional and technological needs of educators working with children with disabilities.

- *Objective 2: Enhance Training on Assistive Technologies.* To be prepared in the classroom, teachers and therapists need access to and training on assistive technologies for children with disabilities such as alternative keyboards, voice recognition systems, and screen readers.

The outcome of this project is to enhance the teaching skills of the 130 practicing teachers annually who take coursework through CAEAT. St. Norbert College teaching graduates are highly sought after because their education and training prepare them for immediate success in the classroom. Equally important, quality training experiences for teachers translates into improved quality of life and learning opportunities for hundreds of students with disabilities.

Methods: Identify and Implement Best Practices for Teaching and Learning

Teachers and researchers agree on the benefits of using assistive technologies with students with disabilities. For example, technology that incorporates visual and collaborative teaching practices has helped promote learning among all students, but especially those with mild learning disorders. The key to unlocking these benefits lies in the abilities of teachers, therapists and other educators—their familiarity with assistive technologies and comfort level working with children with disabilities. CAEAT, under the experienced direction of Barbara Natelle, provides teachers with the adaptive education training they need to be effective in the classroom.

During the granting year, Ms. Natelle will coordinate with special education and curriculum development consultants to revise and update CAEAT certification programming. Consultants will be specialists in results-based, research-driven knowledge about teaching and learning. They will also serve as the vital link between higher education and the realities of daily participation in school settings. Meaning, rather than training teachers on specialized software that may be prohibitively expensive for school districts, we will investigate approaches to customized adaptations of standard word processing and presentation software already available. This represents a cost-effective and utilitarian approach to increasing student achievement.

St. Norbert College   2

effectiveness will be determined. The first paragraph defines and explains the value of the two types of evaluations that will be used: Process evaluations provide immediate feedback, which facilitates practical revisions in project design, and outcome evaluations document the extent to which project objectives were achieved.

The heart of the "Evaluation Plan" lays in the bulleted list. This list describes the specific evaluation indicators that have been selected for measurement. Evaluation indicators encompass both quantitative and qualitative measures of humanistic and performance outcomes. For instance, faculty members will examine the number of students and quality of their participation in program activities, and students will complete surveys in which they will self-report changes in their knowledge and attitudes about incorporating assistive technology into teaching practices. By gathering multiple types of evaluation feedback from multiple perspectives and systematically applying their results, we will improve our overall chances for project success.

Future Funding. This entire section on "Future Funding" relates to a sponsor distinctive feature: financial planning. In reality, sponsors are not looking for an absolute guarantee of future project funding; rather, they want to know that their funds will be utilized wisely. For this project, once curricular enhancements are implemented, they will be institutionalized and offered as part of regular course catalog listings. The second sentence of this paragraph provides the sponsor with assurance that our sustainability plan does *not* include coming back year after year for additional support: "No additional funding will be necessary to complete this project." The paragraph ends on a positive note and touches on sponsor hot buttons and distinctive feature. The final sentence summarizes that this project represents a *cost-effective* approach to training teachers and *improving the quality of life* and learning experiences for children with disabilities.

Proposal Design

A well-designed proposal makes even complex information look accessible and simplifies the reviewers'

jobs. The following design features highlight the structure, hierarchy, and order of the proposal, helping reviewers find the information that they need.

Bulleted Lists. Bulleted lists visually break up long blocks of text and help get the message to the reader with a sense of immediacy without being wordy. For instance, in the "Methods" section, the bulleted list of assistive devices quickly draws attention to the diverse ways technologies can improve the quality of life for children with physical and cognitive disabilities.

Headings. Headings act like a table of contents placed directly in the proposal text; at a glance they reveal the organization of our proposal to reviewers. Boldface headings reflect key words taken from the RFP guidelines for developing the "Project Narrative" and are customized to reflect our specific project, e.g., "Introduction: St. Norbert College Center for Adaptive Education and Assistive Technology." Effective use of white space sets off headings and enhances readability.

Margins. A proposal with ragged right margins is easier to read than one that is fully justified because the proportional spacing in justified type slows down readability. We used standard one-inch margins all around.

Page Numbers. Page numbers are placed in the bottom center of the proposal, and in the bottom left-hand corner of the page we included the name of our organization.

Type Style. The text of the proposal is written in Times Roman, a serif typeface, and headings are in Arial Narrow, a sans serif typeface. This contrast in type styles makes headings stand out from the body of the text. For ease of readability, we used 12 point type size.

White Space. In a page full of print, a block of unprinted lines, or white space, stands out immediately, making the proposal appear inviting and user-friendly. By design, most paragraphs are less than six lines long, preceded and followed by a line of white space.

Ms. Natelle and the consultants will also oversee the training of teachers and students in the latest assistive technologies. Assistive devices allow children with disabilities to access activities in which they otherwise would not be able to participate. For example,

- Full-featured keyboards have multi-colored keys 4 times bigger than the traditional keyboard, and are designed to aid children with physical and learning disabilities.
- Hands-free voice recognition systems aid children who do not have control over their upper extremities, e.g., paralysis due to cervical spinal cord injury.
- Screen readers articulate information displayed on magnified computer monitors—text, menu selections, and error messages—for children who are blind and visually impaired.

In many cases, it is through these technologies that children with disabilities are able to express themselves to the world for the first time. Teachers who have adaptive education training and experience with assistive technologies will be able to encourage student learning.

Evaluation Plan: Process and Outcome Measures of Success

Evaluation is an essential component for achieving project success. Process evaluations provide us with immediate feedback to make practical revisions in project design, implementation, and resource utilization. Outcome evaluations involve collecting data to document the extent to which project objectives were achieved. Methodologically, we will:

- Gather ongoing program development information from diverse stakeholders—faculty, pre-service and in-service teachers, and students with disabilities.
- Systematically review and update pedagogy to meet best practice standards.
- Examine the number of attendees and quality of participation in program activities.
- Survey participants to assess the change in knowledge and attitudes toward incorporating assistive technology into teaching practices.

Evaluation feedback will be used to generate information to improve our services, better allocate resources, strengthen program performance, and measure the overall worth of the project.

Future Funding: Institutionalizing Curriculum Enhancements

Once enhancements to the Adaptive Education certificate program are implemented, CAEAT will institutionalize the changes and continue to offer courses as part of its regular catalog listings. No additional funding will be necessary to complete this project. In essence, this "Preparing Teachers for Students with Disabilities" project represents a cost-effective approach to systematically training current and future generations of teachers in adaptive education and assistive technologies that will enable them to better serve children with disabilities.

St. Norbert College   3

STAGE ONE: FULL PROPOSAL

DEVELOPING THE BUDGET AND BUDGET NARRATIVE

A detailed budget and budget narrative describe *how much* the project will cost and allow the sponsor to examine the relationship between a proposed project approach and associated cost items. Reviewers will scrutinize the budget and budget narrative to see whether expenses are realistic, necessary and sufficient, allowable, and accurately calculated.

The budget and budget narrative should demonstrate to reviewers that sufficient funds are requested to achieve project goals and objectives in a cost-effective manner. Line item costs need to be clearly identified and explained, and more importantly, must be compatible with the sponsor's vision, priorities, and budgeting practices. Expenses listed in the budget must be incurred during the proposed project period and should relate directly to activities described in the proposal narrative or appendixes.

Elements of the Budget

The budget should be independent of the proposal narrative. Thus we begin with a short three-sentence paragraph that describes the goal of our project, requests a specific amount of grant funding, and relates to a sponsor hot button (improving quality of life) and distinctive feature (financial planning). Because some sponsors expect projects to continue even after grant funding expires, we indicate that programmatic changes will be "institutionalized" and that "no additional funds will be necessary to complete this project."

A detailed analysis of the tax records of the Emory T. Clark Family Charitable Foundation over the past three years helped us to determine the size of our funding request. By examining the family foundation's overall grant profile, we see that the median award amount is the same in all three years ($20,000), while the mean award amount changes in relation to the total giving. That is, in 2000 when total giving was higher ($514,000), the average award was higher ($25,700); in 2001 when total giving was lower ($445,150), the average award was lower ($19,354). In this context, it might appear that we should target our grant request for approximately $20,000.

However, when we examine the grant profile by category (education, health and human services, art and culture), a new pattern emerges. In particular, we see that the median award amount in education is

$25,000 for all three years. In 2001 when total giving to education was its lowest, the mean award amount was $23,750, and in 2000 when total giving to education was its highest, the mean award amount was $27,444. Further, in all three years, the largest single grant award by category was in the area of education. With this more complete financial picture, we targeted our grant request for approximately $25,000. This amount is $5,000 higher than if we had relied on the overall grant profile alone.

Unless sponsor regulations indicate otherwise, the budget can include every reasonable expense associated with the project. In this case, we presented our budget in tabular format, divided into four line item categories: consultants, equipment, travel, and materials and supplies. Within these line item categories, we illustrate the basis of budget calculations, e.g., consultant fees of $125/hr * 150 hr = $18,750.

Two budget expenses are noticeably absent from our request: personnel costs and indirect costs. While these are legitimate expenses, the reality of our situation argued against including them. Namely, we estimated that the project director would spend less than 5 percent of her time coordinating with special education and curriculum development consultants as they revised and updated certification programming. As a result, we decided that the funding that could have been requested for salary and fringe benefits would be better spent in other budget categories.

This decision, at the same time, influenced our reasoning to forgo requesting indirect costs. Because our federally negotiated indirect cost rate is based on salaries and wages, absorbing personnel costs also means that we must absorb indirect costs. (In contrast, if our federal indirect cost rate was based on modified total direct costs, we might have requested approximately 12 percent of total direct costs for project administration, the same rate that the sponsor incurred in their last three fiscal years, according to their tax records.) Together, these in-kind contributions of personnel costs and indirect costs also demonstrate to the sponsor our institutional financial plan and commitment to this project—a distinctive feature raised in the RFP guidelines.

Elements of the Budget Narrative

The budget narrative must include an explanation for every line item that describes in as much detail as possible: the specific item, the item's relevance to the project, and the basis of cost calculations for the item. This level of detail explains *what* items are needed,

Budget Request: "Preparing Teachers for Students with Disabilities"

With the demonstrated concern that you have shown for improving quality of life and educational opportunities, we request a grant of $25,000 to better prepare teachers for students with disabilities. Once enhancements to the Adaptive Education certificate program are implemented, St. Norbert College will institutionalize the changes and continue to offer courses as part of regular catalog listings. No additional funds will be necessary to complete this project.

Description	Budget Request
Consultants • Special education and curriculum development specialists will update Adaptive Education certificate programming ($125/hr * 150 hr)	• 18,750
Equipment • (2) IntelliKeys USB /Overlaymaker/ClickIt is a programmable keyboard for students with physical disabilities • (2) Headmaster plus remote adaptor is an alternative mouse device for students with physical disabilities • (2) JAWS Professional for screen reading assists the visually impaired and students who cannot read written symbols	• 1,010 • 1,990 • 2,390
Travel • Local travel (185 mi/month * 9 month * $.365/mi)	• 610
Materials and supplies • Basic office supplies	• 250
TOTAL	$25,000

why they are needed, *how much* they will cost. In three short paragraphs, the budget narrative also addresses the sponsor's hot buttons and distinctive feature. This allows us to demonstrate that we are sensitive to the logical and psychological concerns of the sponsor, even if reviewers read the budget and budget narrative before (or instead of!) the full proposal.

In the first paragraph we focus on "people" costs, defining the roles that consultants will play in the project. The second paragraph describes the costs associated with "things"—the equipment that is necessary for use by teachers and students. This paragraph also appeals to the sponsor hot button of collective community efforts: "a long-term close working partnership with Syble Hopp School." And finally, the third paragraph articulates the humanistic impact that this project will have on the lives of program participants. We end the budget narrative with a sentence that strategically reinforces the sponsor's hot button of improving quality of life and the distinctive feature of financial planning: "In making this investment you will be supporting a *cost-effective approach* to systematically training current and future generations of teachers in adaptive education and assistive technologies that will enable them *to better serve students with cognitive and physical disabilities*."

Budget Narrative

Barbara Natelle, Director of the Center for Adaptive Education and Assistive Technology, will coordinate with special education and curriculum development consultants to revise and update Adaptive Education certification programming. Consultants will be specialists in results-based, research-driven knowledge about teaching and learning. They will spend approximately 150 hours updating and restructuring course materials at a total cost of $18,750.

A long-term close working partnership with Syble Hopp School, an alternative school for approximately 150 children with cognitive and physical impairments, provides numerous opportunities for teachers to interact with students with disabilities and assistive technologies. Teachers will be trained on assistive technologies such as oversized keyboards, alternative mouse input devices, and screen readers. Equipment costs total $5,390.

This "Preparing Teachers for Students with Disabilities" project will touch the lives of over 130 teachers, undergraduate and graduate students annually. In making this investment you will be supporting a cost-effective approach to systematically training current and future generations of teachers in adaptive education and assistive technologies that will enable them to better serve students with cognitive and physical disabilities.

RECEIVING THE GRANT AWARD NOTIFICATION

Five months after our proposal was submitted, we received a letter from the Emory T. Clark Family Charitable Foundation notifying us that our project was awarded grant funding. In fact, a check for the full amount was enclosed along with the award letter. The grant award notice is strong evidence that our proposal was able to convey to the sponsor that funding us will help them achieve their mission. We were able to balance successfully the relationship between sponsor values and our organizational capabilities and between proposal logics and proposal psychologics. In short, our proposal was persuasive because it reflected the values of the sponsor.

Figure 5 summarizes the key elements that we brought together to reach the Persuasion Intersection.

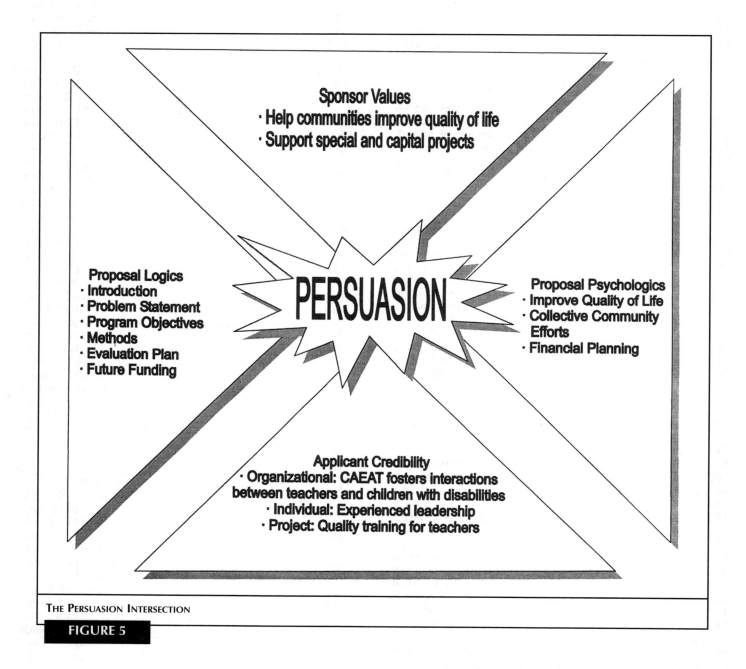

THE PERSUASION INTERSECTION

FIGURE 5

Emory T. Clark Family Charitable Foundation

125 North Executive Drive, Suite 363

Brookfield, Wisconsin 53005

December 13, 2002

Ms. Barb Natelle, Director

Center for Adaptive Education and Assistive Technology

St. Norbert College

100 Grant Street

De Pere, Wisconsin 54115

Dear Ms. Natelle:

The trustees of the Emory T. Clark Family Charitable Foundation are pleased to advise you that they have approved a contribution to St. Norbert College in the amount of $25,000 in support of your special project "Preparing Teachers for Students with Disabilities." A check in that amount is enclosed. The Foundation has adopted a policy of approving contributions annually and not making commitments extending beyond the current year.

Please forward the confirmation required by the IRS concerning goods and services and any other correspondence directly to Ms. Linda Hansen at the Foundation's office.

Sincerely,

Gerald E. Connolly

Trustee

THE GRANT AWARD NOTIFICATION

STAGE ONE: FULL PROPOSAL

Index

About the Authors

JEREMY T. MINER, M.A., is director of sponsored programs at St. Norbert College, DePere, Wisconsin. In addition to developing and administering proposals for the college, he has served as a reviewer for federal grant programs and has helped private foundations streamline their grant application guidelines. Miner is a member of the National Council of University Research Administrators. Along with Lynn Miner, he co-authored *Proposal Planning & Writing,* 3rd edition (Greenwood Press). As a partner in Miner and Associates, Inc., a grant consulting firm in Milwaukee, Wisconsin, he provides proposal writing, computerized grantseeking, and workshop services for academic, health care, and nonprofit organizations nationwide.

LYNN E. MINER, Ph.D., is a principal in Miner and Associates, Inc., a leading nationwide grants consulting group that specializes in training successful grantseekers. He has been an active grantseeker in academic, health care, and other nonprofit environments for the past three decades. He has been affiliated with public and private universities and hospitals as a professor and research administrator. He spent twenty-five years at Marquette University where he served as executive director of research and sponsored programs as well as deanships in the Graduate School and the College of Engineering. He has served on the board of directors for several private foundations and has helped public and private agencies establish guidelines for awarding grants. Miner regularly reviews proposals for several federal government agencies. Along with Jeremy Miner, he co-edits *Grantseeker Tips,* a free biweekly electronic newsletter on successful grantseeking, available through http://www.MinerAndAssociates.com.